The
Unofficial History
of the People Who Built
the Great Financial Empire

Peter Z. Grossman

CROWN PUBLISHERS, INC., New York

For Polly

Published by Crown Publishers, Inc., 225 Park Avenue South, New York, New York, 10003 and represented in Canada by the Canadian MANDA Group

CROWN is a trademark of Crown Publishers, Inc.

AMERICAN EXPRESS Box Logo® is a registered service mark of American Express and is reprinted with permission.
American Express Card®, Gold Card® and Platinum Card® are registered service marks of American Express and are copyright © AMEX.

Manufactured in the United States of America

Library of Congress Cataloging-in-Publication Data

Grossman, Peter Z., 1948–
   American Express.

   1. American Express Company—History.   I. Title.
HE5903.A55G76   1987   380.5′2   86–19925

ISBN 0-517-56238-3

Book designed by Lesley Blakeney

10 9 8 7 6 5 4 3 2 1

First Edition

CONTENTS

PREFACE

Why the story of American Express?

Two reasons.

First, American Express has made a tremendous impact on our lives. We do not simply know its name; millions of us have relied on its services. Over the years, we have bought American Express Travelers Cheques before starting out on our vacations. Overseas, when we have wanted our mail or a meeting place, we have chosen the American Express office on the Rue Scribe in Paris, or the company's offices in London, Rome, Athens, Bombay, Tokyo, or hundreds of other cities around the world. We have known the company for its familiar charge card, its symbols, its logo, and its ubiquitous ad campaigns. And in recent years, American Express has become a stockbroker, financial planner, insurer, and banker through its celebrated acquisitions of such companies as Shearson Loeb Rhoades, Lehman Brothers

Kuhn Loeb, and Investors Diversified Services (IDS). It is one of the richest and largest financial organizations in the world.

And so a book to tell the company's story.

But this book also tells a different kind of story. It is not just the history of a company but of a business. American Express is an object lesson in corporate success and endurance. In the course of more than a century, it has changed drastically, faced war, scandal, and depression; yet it has remained an American business institution. How and why has it succeeded? How and why did it change and evolve? How did executives make the decisions that allowed the company to endure? In recent years, much has been written on how to achieve business success. But often these management theories never answer the question of how businesses actually have succeeded—not just in a moment of time, but over decades. This book examines the success of one of the best known American corporations, and the decision making that led to it.

This is not a company project; the material has not been edited or even reviewed by American Express officials prior to publication. They have had no control over its point of view or its content. All of the opinions and analyses are those of the author.

That said, it must be acknowledged that this book could not have been written without the cooperation of the American Express Company. In order to examine decision making at the company, I have depended on access to company records. The company's archives are extensive and provided the basic information concerning most of the major decisions at American Express from 1850 to 1970.

For access to the archives, I owe thanks to the former president of American Express, Sanford I. Weill, as well as executive VP Harry L. Freeman. But I especially want to thank the company's archivist, Stephen R. Krysko, for his cooperation, assistance, and support through the many months I spent working in his office. I want to thank, as well, director of general services Karl W. Grimmelmann, whose department includes the archives, and his staff for their indulgence at having an outsider in their midst for weeks on end.

I also received the invaluable support and assistance of senior VP Walter G. Montgomery, director of corporate communications, and his staff, particularly Gayla Sangallo and Patti Shea. I owe thanks, too, to First VP Paul D. Feldman of the American Express Bank and Mary McDermott of Shearson Lehman Brothers. I also wish to thank those officials who consented to be interviewed for the book: James D. Robinson III, chairman and chief executive officer of American Express; Messrs. Weill and Freeman; president Louis V. Gerstner, Jr.; executive VPs Howard L. Clark, Jr., and Gary A. Beller; former executive VP George W. Waters; Peter A. Cohen, chairman and chief executive officer of Shearson Lehman Brothers; and Robert F. Smith, chairman and chief executive officer of the American Express Bank.

I also had the opportunity to interview several former officials, many of whom asked that their contributions not be acknowledged by name. But I wish to express my special appreciation to Norman F. Page, who began his career at American Express in 1927 and retired thirty-eight years later as a senior VP and company secretary.

I feel it important to note that several people declined to be interviewed for this book. It was especially regrettable that former chairman Howard L. Clark did not consent to an interview. However, an extensive record of his early years in office does exist in the company archives, and in 1975, he commissioned a book which presumably reflected his view of the events during his years at American Express.

I also wish to thank the following: Allene G. Hatch, Adelheid K. Dalliba, Carman Russell of the University of Florida Library, Mark A. Mastromarino of the Baker Library at the Harvard University Graduate School of Business Administration, Marie Delany of the Wells College Library, Sally Brazil of the archives of the Chase Manhattan Bank, Bruce Weindruch and Alden Hathaway of FDG in Washington, D.C., James Welter, director of internal corporate communications at Fireman's Fund, the Buffalo and Erie County Historical Society, Harold P. Anderson of the Wells Fargo Bank, the New York Historical Society, Jean Strouse, Fred Marks, Larry Chiger, Charles Silverstein,

Rita Marie Cimini, Margaret Unser Schutz, Felicia Eth, and my editor Lisa Healy.

Finally, I want to acknowledge the assistance of my wife, Polly Spiegel; this book owes a great deal to her astute eye and discerning ear.

THE
FOURTH
LEG

1

It was perhaps the most embarrassing time in the history of the American Express Company.

After years of talking about major acquisitions, the company made not one but two offers within sixteen months, and both had failed. In the first, Amexco, as the company is often called, tried to buy a life insurance company and was simply outbid. The second offer, on the other hand, produced a fiasco. Twice in early 1979, Amexco bid for the publishing giant, McGraw-Hill, and twice it was rebuffed. But far worse, McGraw-Hill counterattacked with a negative publicity campaign of such vehemence that American Express sued for libel. The takeover was shaping up as one of the bloodiest in Wall Street history, when abruptly, to the dismay of the investment community, American Express backed out.

In the bars and restaurants in Manhattan's financial district where brokers and bankers meet, there was head shaking and snickering about American Express for weeks afterward. Here was a company with tremendous resources—over $10 billion in assets, $1.5 billion of which were in cash, revenues of over $4 billion a year, and profits of $300 million—yet it seemed Amexco could not spend its money. The press likened the takeover efforts of the two young executives who headed Amexco—James D. Robinson III and Roger H. Morley—to a Laurel and Hardy routine and wondered if they were long for the corporate world.

Though they had botched this effort, Robinson and Morley's decision to try for McGraw-Hill was neither comic nor absurd. A big acquisition had seemed a necessity not only to them, but to people both inside and outside the company.

The company's immediate future appeared in doubt. For all its wealth, Amexco faced new problems and competitive pressures in all three of its businesses: insurance, banking, and its "crown jewel," Travel-Related Services, the division which included its well-known travelers cheque and charge card. Amexco's young leaders also had an added burden: what some people called "The Record." They did not just have to keep the company growing; that would have been difficult enough. They had to keep it growing *continuously*, to maintain a record of twenty-nine straight years of rising income. Their predecessor, Howard L. Clark, had been conscientious guardian of the Record during his seventeen years as CEO. Never mind that he had managed to keep it intact for two or three years with what some observers considered mere bookkeeping maneuvers. The fact that he had resorted to such methods showed how important the Record had become to him in particular. Though Clark had increased revenues fortyfold and profits thirtyfold, he seemed very concerned about the *appearance* of nonstop growth. In the process, he turned maintenance of the Record into a policy that took on the urgency of a mission for his successors. As Morley admitted, "Sooner or later our record will break. Jim and I want to read about it—after we retire."

Yet observers wondered whether the company's business problems were inherently insolvable, and if the two men—Robinson was CEO, but the men called themselves a team—were personally up to the task of preserving the Record. They had ability and brains and the right training: engineering degrees and Harvard MBAs. And they had served ably in a succession of high-level jobs both at Amexco and at other companies. They seemed an effective combination, too: the restless, chain-smoking Morley had a reputation as an "accounting whiz" and a corporate planner and thinker. The self-possessed, meticulous Robinson was regarded as a top manager.

But the financial world remained skeptical. Robinson's appearance alone caused misgivings. He looked impossibly young, almost, one journalist said, "cherubic," and was dubbed by Wall Streeters with the diminutive and condescending title of Jimmy Three Sticks (for the III after his name). But more important, did he, at forty-one, and Morley, at forty-six, have enough experience, enough savvy to run a huge business institution and maintain its famous Record? Despite Clark's outspoken support ("Hell, I was only forty-four when I took over," he noted), observers doubted the two men could do the job.

Wall Street, however, believed there was a way for Robinson and Morley to preserve the Record and at the same time give themselves instant stature: they could acquire a major new business. To accomplish both goals, the acquisition would have to cost in the hundreds of millions of dollars. But the bigger the better for Robinson and Morley. Though the two men never admitted that they had a personal motive, a large acquisition would make them look like big deal-makers, would, as one Amexco executive saw it, make their "corporate manhood." Nearly everyone, in fact, Amexco executives and business analysts alike, thought the idea of an acquisition a good one. Even Clark had talked of the desirability of a fourth business, what he and Robinson called the "fourth leg" of the American Express Company.

An acquisition seemed both a popular idea and a relatively simple matter for a company as rich as American Express, and Robinson and Morley made the decision to acquire the fourth leg as soon as they took office. But while that decision was straightforward, the process of implementing it proved anything but. The two young executives started with a detailed systematic planning process that broke down very quickly. Instead of a smooth road to a big acquisition, Robinson and Morley stumbled along a circuitous, uncertain path. They would often lose their footing and change direction and heart. From one relatively simple decision, the two men would launch themselves and their company on an odyssey of corporate decision making that would destroy Morley's career, make Robinson's, and culminate months after the debacle of McGraw-Hill with the celebrated acquisition of the brokerage house of Shearson Loeb Rhoades—an acquisition that appeared a daring masterstroke, but which, in reality, came as the result of miscalculations, opportunity, and just plain luck, an acquisition no one at Amexco would have dreamed of or wanted when the process began in 1977.

In April 1977, CEO Howard L. Clark retired at the unusually young age of sixty-one. He remained chairman of the executive committee of the board of directors, but his role was advisory. He handed over power and responsibility for the company's problems to Robinson and Morley.

They faced the potential for business reversals throughout the organization. In each of the three divisions—the Fireman's Fund Insurance Company, American Express International Bank Corp. (AEIBC), and the Travel-Related Services Group (TRS)—earnings growth appeared uncertain at best. Most problematic was Fireman's Fund, which Clark had acquired in his one big deal in 1968. The seventh largest property and casualty insurer in the nation, Fireman's Fund, like all property and casualty (P&C) insurers, produced enormous earnings in some years and poor or no earnings in others. The problem stemmed from the "underwriting cycle." Over time, because of competition, insurance premiums were forced down to unprofitable levels, leading to an industry washout: losses followed by a period of higher, profitable premiums. Amexco experienced a washout in the mid-1970s. When the cycle hit bottom, pretax operating earnings at Fireman's Fund slipped almost 50 percent for two straight years. In 1974 and 1975,

Amexco managed to keep the Record intact partly by boosting income through maneuvers at Fireman's Fund that, while legal, raised questions of propriety on Wall Street and sparked an SEC investigation. Robinson, however, believed he knew how to overcome the P&C cycle. He said he would demand from Fireman's Fund a "rigorous budget-planning process," and he ordered the insurance subsidiary not to write unprofitable policies. It sounded sensible enough, but few analysts believed he could change a long-standing pattern of the industry.

The outlook was not much better at the bank. The AEIBC pursued what appeared to many a dubious strategy: to compete among the world's largest commercial banking organizations. The AEIBC had no U.S. presence and was not subject to U.S. banking laws. It was strictly an international bank with a network of offices in thirty-one countries, and it engaged in all aspects of international banking: investment-related merchant banking, trade finance, correspondent banking, and commercial branch banking. But compared to giants like Citicorp and the Deutsche Bank, it was a relatively small operation. The head of the AEIBC, Richard Bliss, intended to change that. From the time he took over AEIBC in 1972, he began aggressively building assets, from around $1.8 billion to $4 billion, mainly through loans to less developed countries. He pursued all clients so tenaciously, in fact, that competitors charged he was giving services away. But despite his policies (or because of them), the bank did not perform well; in 1977 its return on assets came to a below-average 0.6 percent, and though profits rose, they went up with the help of a cut in loan-loss reserves. Since that left the bank more vulnerable to loan defaults, it was not an ideal way to boost income in the long run. Bliss remained as aggressive as ever, but even within the company, his policies had begun to raise eyebrows. When AEIBC opened its *third* office in Bangladesh, one of the world's poorest countries, an official said dryly, "That's really taking the long view."

The third leg, Travel-Related Services (TRS), provided more secure and steady income. In 1976, it brought in more than half of the $207 million Amexco earned. The money came almost entirely from two products: its travelers cheque and charge card. Amexco sold about $13 billion in cheques and though the company attached a service charge to each sale, it made its money from what is known as "the float." The company sold its cheques at face value and held the money until the cheques were cashed, on average six to eight weeks later. During that time, Amexco could invest the money and pocket the interest. But the real earning power of the float derived from the fact that the company maintained an *average* balance of $1.5 billion of cheques outstanding, which it invested in medium- and long-term, tax-free bonds. These investments generated a huge amount of tax-free income, tens of millions of dollars each year.

The American Express Card* actually made a greater net profit. Amexco had put eight million of its plastic cards into circulation, and the $20 membership fee for its basic card ($25 for the Gold Card, which carried a line of credit) brought in more than $160 million a year in fees alone. Total annual charge volume topped $10 billion, out of which Amexco took an average discount of 3.75 percent or $375 million. Analysts estimated net profits on the card at $70 million. With the help of an aggressive advertising campaign, that figure had been growing rapidly for more than a decade.

Both the card and the cheque had added ever-increasing amounts of income to Amexco's treasury for years, but could the growth continue?

---

*American Express is quite insistent that its card be called a charge card, not a credit card. The company has a point: the basic American Express Card is different from a bank credit card. The latter carries a line of credit while Amexco's card does not. But few people, including journalists, are willing to make this semantic distinction and persist in calling the American Express Card a credit card. (According to the dictionary definition of credit, that label is not incorrect since Amexco's card does extend credit of a sort.) To the extent that there is any confusion about the nature of the American Express Card, the company can be held responsible for it. For the first decade of its existence, the card was called the "American Express Credit Card"—the words "credit card" were initially printed on the card's face—even though it was the same sort of charge instrument that it is today. As a result, in telling the story of the card's creation in Chapter 9, this book will refer to the "credit card" since that was what company officials called it at that time.

Many inside and outside the company thought it could not. They considered the two products "mature" with no appreciable growth ahead of them. This appraisal seemed reasonable; after all, rapid growth could not continue indefinitely, and now both the cheque and card faced more competitive pressures than ever before. From the 1930s through the 1950s, Amexco had dominated the traveler's check business. By the 1960s, while its cheque volume increased, Amexco began losing market share, mainly to Citicorp and Bank of America. Now it had to contend with new competitors. The bank credit-card operations, Master Charge and Visa, announced that they were going into the traveler's check business as well. Amexco still held 50 percent of the market—down from over 60 percent a decade earlier—but it seemed unlikely that its share would hold at that level. While the company was fighting back with a vigorous ad campaign featuring former TV cop Karl Malden, observers wondered just how much good it would do. Some research suggested that consumers had no brand loyalty to traveler's checks, that they bought whatever bankers gave them. And if the banks gave out Visa or Master Charge checks, Amexco might well see the end of growth in its travelers cheque business.

The card, too, seemed headed for hard times. Even insiders thought that eight million cardholders might be close to the ultimate limit. The company had positioned the card as a prestige product, and how many more "prestige" clients existed? At the same time, the bankcards Visa (which had just been renamed from the less sexy Bankamericard) and Master Charge were attacking Amexco's card, as well as its check business. Master Charge and Visa both began a drive for more corporate customers and would soon trot out their own prestigous gold-colored cards. Said D. W. Hock, president of Visa, "We're taking dead aim at American Express's markets."*

Robinson hoped that rapid growth in both businesses could con-

---

*In 1978, Amexco received another challenge to its card business. Citicorp, the banking giant, bought a competitor, the nearly moribund Carte Blanche card, and announced a $39 million advertising campaign to revive it.

tinue, publicly expressed his belief that Amexco would triumph over the competition, and sought a person inventive in developing new marketing ideas to run the entire travel-related division to prove him right. He chose Louis V. Gerstner, Jr., a thirty-five-year-old Harvard MBA who had worked at Mc Kinsey & Co. as a consultant. Gerstner agreed with Robinson's optimistic appraisal. He took over the card in 1978 (and later, all of TRS) and pronounced himself eager for the challenge. But it would take more than enthusiasm to fulfill his mandate, and the odds seemed long against him succeeding in any great way.

Robinson thought that he had the answers for the company's problems, but Wall Street was skeptical; Amexco's stock was out of favor. Even Robinson wondered if he could solve all of the problems. "Who the hell knows?" he would say later. Indeed, there seemed only one way for Robinson and Morley to carry on Clark's policy and preserve the Record—to develop a new income stream, the fourth leg.

Robinson and Morley made up their minds to add a fourth business, but they never resolved a basic issue first. At the heart of any consideration of expansion lay the question of the company's definition: what was American Express and what did it want to become? Should it be, for example, "the company for people who travel"? The company had cultivated that as a public image and, in the 1960s, had made that its ad slogan. Or did it want to become in the public mind a financial services company? The company needed to define itself for development planning to proceed coherently.

Yet since the 1960s, officials had resisted defining the company. Howard Clark never did it, according to his successor, because he liked to remain "inscrutable." But his inscrutability had a price: no one inside Amexco knew exactly what the company was, what it was supposed to become, or what new business might fit into it. And Robinson and Morley appeared no more willing to define American Express than Clark had been.

Amexco's young leaders had two options in creating a fourth leg: to start a business or buy one. The last big business Amexco had started was the card, and paradoxically, that posed one of the biggest psychological barriers to undertaking another start-up operation. Those executives who could remember the birth of the card recalled problems that cost millions and took years to straighten out. Amexco needed a business to smooth out the bumps and make up for the falloff in growth elsewhere. The sooner the fourth leg produced income, the better.

So the only real alternative was to buy a new business. But what to acquire? It was a question Amexco officials had puzzled over for years. In the 1960s, before Robinson had joined the company, in-house planners had conducted numerous acquisition studies, and top executives had discussed takeover possibilities continuously. But in all that time, no in-house study had led to a single major purchase. Most of the company's acquisitions, including Fireman's Fund, had been brought to Amexco's door.

Robinson and Morley did not want to create a conglomerate of disparate businesses. They intended to buy a company that "fit" with the rest of Amexco. But what was that? Their criteria excluded manufacturing: "No manufacturing, no inventory." Beyond that, however, they seemed to leave almost any "service" company on the list of possibles. Travel, entertainment, insurance, banking, information, data processing—the list of categories was long, the universe of potential targets even larger, and the basis by which one would be chosen over another, unclear.

Nevertheless, Robinson and Morley wasted little time in seeking an acquisition. They approached the task rigorously and systematically; that was how they did most things. They liked to study and analyze huge amounts of detailed information before making decisions, and they applied themselves in the same way to the question of an acquisition. They began to immerse themselves in the kind of data that would give them an exact idea of the value and potential of acquisition targets.

Not long after they came into office, they investigated their first possibility. An investment banker brought them a proposal—the Book-of-the-Month Club. Robinson expressed interest in the deal. But

Morley, who performed much of the analytic work and handled preliminary negotiations, decided that the price was too high. Also, the Book-of-the-Month Club did not offer large enough earnings potential to be a true fourth leg.

In search of something bigger, Robinson and Morley looked into what seemed the most obvious fit: life insurance. Through Fireman's Fund, Amexco had knowledge and experience in the insurance business. But a life insurance company offered greater stability and predictability of earnings than a P&C operation, and so could compensate for the P&C underwriting cycle.

Amexco asked its investment bankers to study life insurance companies, but the bankers, surprisingly, recommended that Amexco look elsewhere. They explained that though earnings from life insurance companies appeared attractive on paper, because of accounting rules, the earnings did not represent cash that the parent company could use. The investment bankers warned that a life insurance company might not even generate enough cash to pay for the debt Amexco would incur to buy it. A life insurance company would, however, allow Amexco to report increased earnings, and Morley and Robinson decided to acquire one anyway. That decision suggested just how important maintenance of the Record had become; Robinson and Morley opted for an acquisition that would add to the appearance of growth even if it actually drained the company's resources.

In September, Morley and Robinson made their first genuine offer, $230 million for Philadelphia Life Insurance Company. Wall Street considered it a fair price for a good company, but Amexco faced one obstacle: Tenneco owned 24 percent of Philadelphia and had made an offer of $171 million for the rest. Tenneco had led Robinson and Morley to believe, however, that it would sell its stake at the right price. This price seemed right, yet two weeks later, Tenneco executives changed their minds and made a higher bid instead. Since Tenneco owned almost a quarter of the stock already, it had control of the situation, and Amexco was out of a deal.

Robinson and Morley soon chose another takeover target—Walt

Disney. Robinson later explained his thinking: "We have the over twenty-fives, they have the under twenty-fives," or, as one analyst put it, "[To feed] people American Express from babyhood." Robinson, Morley, and Howard Clark flew out to California, but as Robinson recalled, "Three pinstripe suits showing up at Burbank was more than the rumor mill could handle." The discussions never progressed. Reportedly, Disney's sixty-three-year-old chairman Donn B. Tatum had no intention of working for Amexco's youthful and inexperienced CEO. Amexco and Disney ended negotiations without even mentioning a price.

Nine months. Three possibilities. No acquisition. No fourth leg. Robinson and Morley put a good face on it; they told the press that they were not going to push a deal and might even stop looking for one. "We have no need to acquire," sniffed Morley, and Robinson added, "This might be a good time to stay home."

The media and the financial community, however, portrayed Amexco's failure to acquire as the result of a lack of daring and savvy on the part of Robinson and Morley. Some on Wall Street and reportedly within the company muttered that the two young executives were being put off too easily. If they intended to acquire, they could not let something as trivial as the Hollywood rumor mill dissuade them. They had to grit their teeth and put their money on the table. To two young men barely established in the financial world, all the talk of failure must have smarted.

Despite what they indicated publicly, Robinson and Morley had not abandoned the hunt for an acquisition. In fact, they announced the creation of a new planning department called the Office of Strategic Program Development (OSPD), and to run it, they picked executive VP George Waters, who in the 1960s had built the credit-card operation into a great success story. Amexco's two leaders established the office to "act as a catalyst, and to develop and evaluate opportunities for new and important sources of earnings." However, the OSPD was more a symbol of the acquisition effort than a real addition to it. Planning offices at Amexco had a peculiar history; they never identified, much less planned, any takeovers. Even to some company executives it seemed that Amexco kept a planning office because a modern corporation was supposed to have one, not because it actually functioned.

Robinson and Morley appeared to be more serious. They created a new office with a new name, an experienced director, and a new mandate. But in fact, this planning office did no more than any of the others. While Waters and his staff brainstormed, Amexco's two leaders independently identified the next target, and they did not even tell Waters what they had in mind: the publishing giant, McGraw-Hill.

In choosing McGraw-Hill, the two leaders applied their usual rigorous attention to detail and intense study. They carefully calculated and plotted their moves. But their thinking was flawed. It appeared that Morley and Robinson had not fully considered some very basic issues involved in a takeover and even that they had missed some special vulnerabilities of their own company that made an acquisition potentially very dangerous. As a result, they headed carefully and blindly into one of the ugliest takeover fights in Wall Street history.

Robinson had a particular interest in data processing, communications, and information services, and from the time he and Morley began planning acquisitions, he had kept an eye on the information business. Although McGraw-Hill made most of its money from trade books, textbooks, sixty trade magazines, *Business Week*, and four television stations, Robinson regarded it as an information company. A significant portion of McGraw-Hill's earnings—about a quarter—came from computer services, Standard & Poor's financial services (which had begun electronic data services), and the F. W. Dodge construction data base services. Robinson and Morley identified a fit with Amexco's own data and information services.* Because of its need to process

---

*The view that a fit existed between the companies was not shared by everyone. Most observers still regarded McGraw-Hill as a publishing house and considered Amexco's takeover plan to be, as one Wall Street analyst called it, "straight diversification." Amexco did publish a magazine, *Travel & Leisure*, but the company viewed *T&L* as a travel-related activity, not a publishing venture.

literally millions of transactions a year, Amexco had developed a highly sophisticated data and communications network; in 1977 alone, it spent $130 million on electronic data and communications systems.

Robinson and Morley liked McGraw-Hill for other reasons, too. Its earnings had risen steadily from 1971 and now topped $63 million. The publisher came with a sound balance sheet and $93 million in cash. And Robinson and Morley knew McGraw-Hill better than any other communications company; since January 1977, Morley had sat on the McGraw-Hill board.

Morley and Robinson had initiated a study of information companies, but the takeover of McGraw-Hill began when they heard from investment bankers that members of the McGraw family (which owned over 20 percent of the shares) wanted to sell out. As Morley already knew, there was unrest at McGraw-Hill. In 1977, company chairman Harold McGraw, Jr., who owned 825,000 shares (3.3 percent), ousted his cousin Donald, who owned 622,000, from any active role in the company. The next year, cousin John (609,000 shares) resigned as an officer. He remained on the board, but relations with Harold were cool to say the least. "Let me put it this way," John said about his cousin. "We haven't had Thanksgiving dinner at grandmother's house in a number of years."

In June 1978, prior to launching a takeover, Robinson called Harold and suggested a friendly merger. They had what by all accounts was a courteous chat, but beyond that, reports of the conversation differed greatly. McGraw claimed later that he asked for assurances that if he said no, that would be the end of it. He said Robinson agreed, then McGraw thought about the idea and said no. Robinson denied that he had promised McGraw anything of the kind, and he recalled that McGraw had said he might ask Amexco to step in as a "white knight" in the event of a bid from someone else. McGraw, Robinson maintained, went on to express his "deep respect and admiration" of Amexco. From Robinson's point of view, that hardly seemed an irrevocable rejection.

Whatever Robinson actually did or did not say, he had failed in one respect: he did not read Harold McGraw clearly and was unable to gauge what the publishing executive really felt. More importantly, Roger Morley also misjudged McGraw even though he sat on the company's board. His failure was especially crucial. Amexco expected Morley to provide a reading of McGraw's intentions. If McGraw was going to block a takeover attempt, Amexco needed to know it.

That fall, Robinson and Morley began putting together a takeover bid. Few people at American Express Plaza, the company's headquarters at the southern tip of Manhattan, knew of the plan. But Robinson and Morley had engaged the services of leading investment bankers from the firm of Blythe Eastman Dillon (including Howard Clark, Jr., the former CEO's son), as well as one of Wall Street's stars, Felix Rohatyn of Lazard Frères. Several members of the Amexco board became involved in the takeover through an ad hoc advisory committee. This committee, the company lawyers, and the investment bankers approved each part of the takeover strategy. Once Robinson and Morley decided to go ahead with it, they all agreed Amexco would pursue McGraw-Hill, even if it meant fighting a hostile takeover. There would be no backing off this time.

The Amexco team readied the plan for action in early 1979. Robinson and Morley put the offer in a letter to Harold McGraw. "Our proposal is to acquire McGraw-Hill for cash at a price equivalent to $34 per share or a total of approximately $830 million. [The stock was selling for $25.75 at the time of offer.] Alternatively, we would be willing to discuss entering into an agreement whereby 49 percent of McGraw-Hill's shares of common stock would be acquired for cash and the balance for suitable American Express securities." The cash offer, a "bear hug" in merger and acquisition parlance, would force McGraw to take the offer to his board. The alternative arrangement demonstrated Amexco's willingness to make a deal. On balance, the proposal showed flexibility and in all likelihood should have led to a negotiated agreement.

Still, Robinson wondered what kind of reception the offer would receive, and he appeared to have some misgivings about Harold

McGraw's attitude. The two Amexco leaders decided to deliver the letter in person to McGraw in his Sixth Avenue office. On the evening of January 8, Robinson and Morley entered the office hoping for a friendly meeting but "ready to dodge an ashtray or two." They expected a brief conversation, but they stayed forty-five minutes because "Harold wanted to talk." Robinson and Morley did a lot of the talking, however, about how McGraw-Hill could grow as a subsidiary of American Express.

McGraw remembered the talk differently—in fact, on different occasions he remembered it in various ways. He told the press that he thought it was a social call, but after he learned the true purpose, he (a) lapsed into a state of shock and could not speak; (b) wondered aloud if Morley had not been guilty of a conflict of interest; and (c) told the two young executives that if they persisted with the offer they were in for "the toughest fight of your lives." He said the conversation ended after twenty testy minutes.

Almost certainly, he invented his fighting words after the fact. Robinson did not emerge from the meeting thinking he had heard a declaration of war. Afterward, he phoned Rohatyn, who recalled that Robinson seemed "ecstatic," certain McGraw would not stand in the way of a deal. Robinson also called George Waters to tell him about the deal and at that time, too, the young CEO seemed confident of the outcome.

But Robinson again had misread McGraw. That McGraw did not reject the offer outright suggested that either he *was* in shock, or he just wanted more time to think about it. He huddled with his aides immediately after the meeting with Robinson and Morley. His executives expressed their dismay; within a few hours, so did McGraw.

Amexco announced the offer the next day, and McGraw, his opposition. Wall Street analysts figured initially that McGraw-Hill objected mainly to the price, and they believed Amexco would have to raise its bid. Some arbitrageurs began buying McGraw-Hill stock, although one unnamed professional trader told the *Wall Street Journal* that he was wary because American Express did not have "any acquisition track record." However, the buyers seemed to be making the right move. American Express sources revealed to the press that the company intended to raise the ante and fight until it won. Market analysts guessed that Amexco would succeed at the cost of a billion dollars, perhaps a bit more, but they felt the company could easily afford it. One stock market professional said, "What's another $100 million to a company like American Express?"

Harold McGraw, however, did not want to sell, period. He planned to use any and every tactic to block Amexco and intended to fight Amexco in the market, the courts, and the press. He first hired investment bankers at Morgan Stanley to advise the company on financial tactics; he assembled a public relations group to attack Amexco and its offer; and he sought the best legal help, going to Martin Lipton of Wachtel, Lipton, Rosen & Katz. Lipton at first refused to take the case, but McGraw sat obstinately in the waiting room of the noted attorney's office until Lipton agreed to join the defense team.

McGraw quickly demonstrated how badly Robinson and Morley had miscalculated. The problem was not that Amexco had done something wrong, but rather that it had two intrinsic weaknesses. It operated in highly regulated businesses, insurance and banking, and so could be attacked on the regulatory front. And it made most of its money from two products—the card and the travelers cheque—which depended for sales in large measure on the *image* of integrity.

Over the next week, Lipton and his staff, working long hours with no advance preparation, launched several different legal assaults. They asked the Federal Communications Commission to delay the merger until it could hold full hearings on whether Amexco should own licenses to operate McGraw-Hill's TV stations. They petitioned the New York State attorney general to investigate violations of state antitrust laws, and they also filed a complaint in New York State Supreme Court specifically charging that Morley, by using insider information, had in fact violated those laws. Lipton tried to galvanize antimerger feelings in Washington as well, and he succeeded in persuading Congressman Henry Reuss of the House Banking Committee to begin an investigation of conglomerate mergers that impact "the public interest." The congressman left no doubt which merger (or rather proposed merger) he had in mind.

McGraw-Hill also hammered away at Amexco's image. For American Express, image was almost as important as reality. The card and cheque depended on public confidence, and on the company's willingness and ability to stand behind them and meet its financial obligations. Both products could be destroyed if customers lost faith in Amexco's integrity; and, because of the importance of the cheque and the card, Amexco could be destroyed along with them. Company officials had recognized this for decades. Yet for some reason, Robinson, Morley, and everyone else involved in the takeover seemingly failed to see how vulnerable they were. Ironically, Robinson and Morley had been right before when they had not pushed deals that appeared unfriendly. Now by mounting a hostile takeover, they placed their company in danger.

McGraw-Hill's most devastating attack came when it published in the nation's leading newspapers a "reply" to Amexco's "unconscionable action." The charges bordered on the ridiculous in some cases, but they all struck at the company's integrity. McGraw-Hill, for instance, questioned the *morality* of the travelers cheque because Amexco did not pay any interest on the funds. Amexco never had pretended it did, but McGraw-Hill tried to make the business sound at least dishonorable.

Other charges raised more valid questions. The letter asked whether McGraw-Hill's *Business Week* should be owned by a company likely to be the subject of its articles. More importantly, it wondered about the propriety of Amexco controlling Standard & Poors. S&P rated the billions in tax-free bonds which American Express owned. In theory, Amexco could abuse its position. If it learned beforehand that a rating change was in the offing, it could adjust its portfolio to its own profit at the expense of the market.

The letter cleverly moved from the possibility of unethical conduct by Amexco to what McGraw-Hill saw as actual misconduct—the be-

17

havior of Roger H. Morley. The letter accused Morley, who had resigned from the McGraw-Hill board on January 11, with a "breach of trust," said his actions were "conspiratorial," and promised to pursue legal action because he had failed to meet his responsibilities as a director of McGraw-Hill. A few people wondered later if, by bringing an offer that would benefit shareholders, Morley had not discharged those responsibilities better than McGraw, but that was a minority view. McGraw-Hill portrayed him as a conspirator (later it called him a "Trojan Horse"), and nothing Morley or Amexco subsequently said could dispel the image McGraw-Hill painted.

The publishing house tweaked Robinson in the letter as well, noting the "impulsive, precipitous and immature actions taken by younger members of management." In the days after the letter was published, McGraw-Hill more pointedly charged that Robinson and Morley had launched their bid "to restore their own egos" after three failed acquisition attempts. The campaign, Robinson admitted, hurt personally.

For days after the letter appeared, McGraw-Hill continued on the offensive. The publisher revived the question of whether Amexco had violated U.S. laws by cooperating with the Arab boycott of Israel. In the 1950s, Amexco had indeed closed its office in Tel Aviv in a move that appeared the result of Arab pressure. But it hardly seemed fair to raise this issue in 1979. The incident had occurred at a time when Robinson was an undergraduate at Georgia Tech, and the company had long since reestablished a presence in Israel.

Others joined in the assault on American Express. The Authors Guild asked the government to block the merger which it saw as a threat to the First Amendment. Media figure Fred W. Friendly, writing in the *Wall Street Journal*, expressed his concern about the concentration of media control in the hands of corporate giants. Lewis Young, editor of *Business Week*, wondered, for public consumption, whether executives at American Express might "taboo certain subjects," and he sat down and compiled an unsolicited list of white knights to rescue the parent company.

The scope and fury of the attacks shocked everyone at American

Express; executives referred to Harold McGraw's "shotgun strategy" and "scorched earth policy." But the charges struck at Amexco's integrity, and the company had to respond. Robinson made public a broad offer to insulate *Business Week* and the television stations from editorial interference. Then Amexco sued McGraw-Hill for libel. Wall Street and the media relished the counterattack and saw the fight now as a test of wills between the young Amexco executives and Harold McGraw. The financial community still bet that Amexco's money would win out.

But Robinson and Morley did not see it that way. Because of the tactics McGraw-Hill had adopted, a protracted battle could irreparably damage not only American Express, but also McGraw-Hill. Amexco's leaders expressed the fear that the publisher's actions threatened to devastate the morale of McGraw-Hill employees, leaving only a shell of a company to a victorious Amexco. As a result, Robinson and Morley changed tactics. They made a new offer, $40 a share, and gave McGraw-Hill thirty days to take it or leave it. If the publisher accepted, Robinson and Morley demanded an end to the propaganda war; they stated that if McGraw-Hill turned down the offer, Amexco would give up and walk away.

The new offer surprised the financial press and infuriated Wall Street. Investment professionals had expected Robinson and Morley to fight it out and thought of $40 a share as being at only the low end of the range of acceptability. Those who had bought heavily in the low $30s envisioned heavy losses for themselves; as they saw it, they were going to lose money because Robinson and Morley did not have the guts to persevere, and they raged at Amexco from one end of Wall Street to the other.

Whether or not Amexco had offered enough, its new tactic made some sense in principle. It took Amexco, and all of the questions about its motives and behavior, out of the spotlight and shone it instead on McGraw-Hill and the McGraw family. The press had delighted in what it portrayed as a clan soap opera, and the new offer predictably engendered some good copy. Donald, who had appeared ready to settle for $34, took the opportunity to provide a few choice comments about Harold. Cousin John, who voted against $34, felt Amexco was "getting awfully close" at $40 and apparently contemplated defying Harold. And American Express tried to win the support of other family members; company representatives even followed cousin William (100,000 shares) to his dentist, looking for an opportunity to talk to him. But William sided with Harold, who did not plan to sell at even $100 a share, at least according to Donald.

Amexco hoped it could get the support of a few McGraw-Hill directors, which would amount to a no-confidence vote against Harold and lead to an American Express triumph. But Harold survived a two-hour grilling by directors, who in the end rejected the new offer unanimously. The investment bankers and legal team dispelled all doubts. They told the board that the offer was inadequate, and that so many legal and regulatory hurdles remained that even a friendly merger might hurt McGraw-Hill. A significant minority of stockholders promptly sued the board, but finally shareholders, too, ratified the decision to reject Amexco's offer. *

Robinson and Morley had lost their most concerted attempt at the fourth leg. "I blew it," Robinson admitted to one reporter. But while Robinson took the blame, Roger Morley took the fall. It was said that by the appearance of wrongdoing (not legal, but ethical), and by his gross misreading of Harold McGraw, he had destroyed his career. The following October, he announced his resignation to become a CEO somewhere else. But no offers awaited him, and he was soon living quietly in Europe, by and large a forgotten man of the corporate world.

The financial community speculated that Robinson too would be replaced, or that he would step down voluntarily. But even though he had led the company into and through a traumatic period, he had not

---

*Morley and Robinson proved correct in their analysis of the prospects for McGraw-Hill. Its earnings increased every quarter through 1985—a record, which, ironically, became an end in itself to executives at the publishing house.

lost his taste for the job, nor had he lost the support of the board. He had made a mistake, but the board had approved it beforehand and so shared some of the responsibility. Although the company was embarrassed, it was still making money; the Record was still intact. The directors expressed their confidence in the man they had chosen only a couple of years before.

They had chosen him because he had demonstrated that he was a model young business leader. In fact, until this episode, it seemed he had never made a mistake. With the help of the right background and connections, he had traveled smoothly to the top of corporate America. The son and grandson of Atlanta bankers, Robinson began training early for the highest echelons of the business world. After Georgia Tech and Harvard (MBA '61), he became an assistant to Thomas Gates, chairman of Morgan Guaranty Trust, where according to Gates himself, Robinson was seen as potential CEO material. In 1968, after his father died, Robinson contemplated returning to Atlanta, but was dissuaded by an offer to become a partner at the investment banking firm of White Weld & Co. Two years later, on the recommendation of Eugene Black—a Robinson family friend and an Amexco board member—Robinson, thirty-four, joined American Express as head of AEIBC, with the understanding that he might one day succeed Howard Clark.

From the outset, he won the respect of fellow executives at American Express. He saw his background not as a crutch, his colleagues felt, but as something to live up to. They praised him for his hard work—twelve- to fourteen-hour days became his routine—his seriousness of purpose, and his self-confidence. One colleague said, "He knows exactly what he wants." He was also articulate (he never flubbed a line), publicly always under control, and courtly, with a gentlemanly hint of a southern accent. At times, he projected a cool, aristocratic aloofness, but he was also capable of a winning quip or two.

Not everyone admired his style of management, however. He sometimes swamped his subordinates with demands for endless forecasting, budgeting, analysis. The bureaucratic controls he and Morley instituted in 1977 frustrated some older employees who preferred Howard Clark's more personal style. (One AEIBC executive complained that Robinson demanded budget reports the size of telephone books.) But for all his bureaucratic demands, Robinson also tried to encourage creative thinking. He listened to new ideas, and he surrounded himself with people who were imaginative and aggressive.

Whatever employees thought of his management style, it seemed to work. Before 1977, Robinson succeeded in every task assigned him. After a stint at the bank, Robinson ran TRS for a few years and proved to the board that he was capable of becoming CEO. But now in the aftermath of McGraw-Hill, he had to prove himself all over again. He came out of the disaster with greater resolve to do the job, to push for earnings growth, and to acquire Amexco's fourth leg.

As he began to consider takeover candidates once more, a friend from outside the company advised him to think in an entirely different direction. Before the final resolution of the McGraw-Hill battle, he had breakfast one day with an associate from his investment banking days, Salim B. "Sandy" Lewis. Lewis explained to Robinson his vision of the future of the financial world. He believed that soon financial businesses would be dominated by huge companies able to offer a wide range of services from stockbrokerage to insurance to real estate. Amexco was in a position to play a major role in this new environment, Lewis felt, but it needed a brokerage arm. He suggested Amexco acquire Shearson Loeb Rhoades, the second-largest publicly traded brokerage firm in the country.

Robinson considered Lewis a "brilliant, driven" person and heard him out. But at the time, Robinson was not interested in pursuing the idea. The thought of buying a brokerage company was not a new one at American Express. The idea had been discussed and tested, and Amexco's experience in the securities business had not been happy. In the 1960s and early 1970s, Amexco had picked up two small investment banking and institutional brokerage houses as well as a 25 percent stake in the larger investment banking firm of Donaldson Lufkin & Jenrette (DLJ). But these ventures came at a time of trouble and change for the securities industry, which forced dozens of firms to merge or liquidate and severely crimped profits even at the best houses. By the mid 1970s, so far from wanting a bigger stake in the business, Amexco wanted out. It unloaded its holdings in DLJ at a loss and wound down its other brokerage activities. In subsequent years, other brokerage houses had proposed ties with Amexco, but the company had rejected them.

Indeed, around the same time he met with Lewis, Robinson received the most extraordinary proposal Amexco ever heard from a brokerage firm. Donald Regan, chairman of Merrill Lynch & Co., offered to merge his company into Amexco. The offer was surprising, on the surface at least, because Merrill Lynch was clearly the dominant firm in the securities business. But like Lewis, Regan saw that in the future a company such as his would have to offer diversified financial services, not just brokerage service. In fact, Regan had already taken his company into insurance and real estate and had created an account called the "Cash Management Account" (CMA for short), which resembled a bank checking account. As a result, Regan regarded his principal competition not on Wall Street but among all financial institutions. While Merrill Lynch's resources topped the rest of Wall Street, they came nowhere near those of a Citicorp or an Aetna Insurance. In that light, the overture to Amexco made sense. A Merrill Lynch–American Express combination had the diversity of services and, even more importantly, weight of capital to compete with anyone in the world.

The deal Regan proposed had two big pluses for Robinson: it would be friendly and large scale. But it also had a lot of negatives. Morley, who was still with the company, thought the price too high. Lawyers warned of possible bad press and antitrust actions if Amexco snapped up the dominant firm in the industry. Reportedly, Amexco officials also felt that merging with the giant brokerage firm would produce what they called a "management headache." On balance, Robinson concluded that the deal was a bad one and rejected the offer.

After the talks broke off, Robinson showed no immediate interest in pursuing other brokerage houses and still focused on communications, information, and publishing. Indeed, the blood pressure of executives had barely settled down from the McGraw-Hill debacle when Robinson began discussing an approach to Prentice-Hall or to A. C. Nielsen Co. But neither idea went anywhere, and both companies were subsequently taken over by others.

Yet toward the end of the year, just after Morley's departure, Amexco made two significant deals. In November, Robinson reached a friendly agreement to buy a 50 percent stake in a partnership with Warner Communications to develop cable TV systems and cable programming. Amexco officials especially liked Warner's pioneering, interactive cable system called Qube. Robinson and TRS head Louis Gerstner hoped that Qube would allow for home electronic retailing, banking, and text operations, which they saw as major opportunities for the future. The stake cost Amexco $175 million.

A couple of months later, Amexco finally acquired a company outright: First Data Resources (FDR), a leading processor of bank credit-card transactions. More than anything else the deal represented a notable change in the style of Amexco's acquisition efforts. Previously, Robinson and Morley had pursued companies by crunching numbers and digesting reports. This time, the deal began with personal contact. Through planning director George Waters, Robinson met with the head of First Data to see if they could work together. They held several meetings before any analysis or even discussion of a merger began. Only after both sides expressed interest in a combination did Amexco even look at First Data's balance sheet. But then discussions moved swiftly toward a friendly conclusion. By January 1980, Amexco had acquired a new subsidiary for $50 million.

Although both companies had the potential for considerable profit, neither was strong enough at the time to constitute the fourth leg. And so, even as the discussions with Warner and FDR proceeded, Robinson once again began a new planning effort. He and Waters called on the company's Washington lobbyist, Harry L. Freeman, to play a major role in that effort. Freeman did not have any specific experience as a corporate planner and hired a tutor to teach him planning methodologies. But the choice had a special logic for American Express; takeovers of McGraw-Hill or Merrill Lynch presented the possibility of government opposition. Freeman knew Washington and had a sense of what the company could do from a legislative and regulatory standpoint. His experience could help the company avoid serious mistakes.

One of Freeman's first assignments was to study the financial-services industry and recommend possible new business opportunities. Even though Amexco had rejected Merrill Lynch's offer, as well as proposals from other brokerage firms,* the company always considered expanding its financial services. In the OSPD's brainstorming sessions, planners typically focused on both communications and financial services. The study began as an analysis of the financial services industry as a whole, but as the deals with Warner and First Data began to take shape, Freeman focused his attention more specifically on electronic systems for finance. His idea was to build on the two deals. As the cover of his report indicated graphically with a little triangle, financial services came together with telecommunications (Warner-Amex) and data processing (FDR). Freeman suggested Amexco look closely at involvement with such emerging technologies as automated-teller machines and home computer-terminal systems.

Although Freeman's report focused on the developing technology of finance, he also noted the "obvious synergistic benefits" of financial services themselves, particularly in the brokerage business. He did not recommend purchase of a brokerage house or any other company, but he pointed to, among other opportunities in brokerage services, the potential of selling P&C insurance or international banking services to corporate brokerage clients.

Amexco's planners, Robinson, and the senior aides he now consulted on acquisition decisions, a group referred to as the Executive Office of the Chairman (EOC), continued to discuss involvement in

---

*Oppenheimer & Company, for one, approached Amexco about a joint takeover of Bache Halsey Stuart Shields, but the idea was not pursued.

the technology of financial services. They also never completely abandoned the idea of making an acquisition of a major publishing or information company. But, partly because they could not find a significant acquisition in those areas, both planners and senior officials began to consider whether the synergistic benefits Freeman had identified presented a real opportunity for the company.

They decided the opportunity was substantial. The main question for Amexco was, would people buy financial assets through American Express? To most executives, the answer clearly was yes. After all, how did most people think of Amexco? Probably they thought first of the card, a financial instrument, and cardholders, studies showed, held something like 70 percent of the financial assets of the country. Amexco officials envisioned selling investment products through the card and vice versa.

Robinson and his advisors discussed three possible targets: Merrill Lynch, Shearson Loeb Rhoades, and E. F. Hutton, numbers one, two, and three in terms of capital on Wall Street. In Freeman's 1979 report, he seemed to favor Hutton above the others. But in later years, Robinson claimed that the first choice was always Shearson. Shearson had a large customer and capital base and the reputation for being the best-run firm on the Street. It had the highest pretax profit margins and return on equity of publicly traded brokerage houses, as well as a reputation for being fast moving and innovative.

But before Robinson acted, he needed some questions answered. Did Shearson want to be taken over? Robinson had of course learned caution after McGraw-Hill, but he knew that a hostile takeover of a brokerage firm in particular made no business sense whatsoever. The brokerage business depended on personal contact. As Wall Street liked to say, at brokerage houses, the assets—the employees—walked out the door every evening. If they felt disgruntled or dissatisfied and did not come back, they could take all the firm's earning capacity with them.

And even if Amexco could convince Shearson to join a friendly takeover, what would the rest of the world say? Though a takeover of only the second-ranking brokerage house might not have antitrust complications, it could generate negative publicity. Amexco could not go by precedent; no one had ever acquired a publicly traded brokerage house before. After McGraw-Hill, few Amexco officials wanted to be ground breakers.

The deal posed other barriers for American Express. Though a brokerage house seemed a natural fit, some officials opposed the idea. They noted the company's unsuccessful ventures in the brokerage business. They worried, too, about the reaction of the banks. Bankers had objected to Merrill's CMA account, which they saw as an invasion of their territory, and Shearson planned to create accounts similar to the CMA. The last thing Amexco wanted was to anger the banks, whose goodwill the company needed to sell its travelers cheques. No brokerage house was worth jeopardizing that multibillion-dollar business.

Also, and in many ways most importantly, the acquisition of Shearson would represent a major change in company policy; from the standpoint of the Record, a brokerage company made a poor fourth leg. Like P&C insurance, brokerage earnings followed a cyclical path, rising and falling with the market. If Robinson bought a brokerage company, he would in effect be abandoning the plan for continuous earnings growth. The cyclical nature of the business almost guaranteed that the Record would fall one day.

While Amexco officials pondered the questions, Sandy Lewis again pressed Robinson to acquire Shearson. In the summer of 1980, he met both Robinson and Amexco's new number two, vice chairman (later president) Alva O. Way. Over breakfast, he made his pitch again, and he came away feeling no more encouraged than he had in 1979. But as Robinson himself had noted, Lewis was a driven man who now refused to give up on the idea that this merger would take place. So in August, Lewis decided to approach the other side of the equation: Sanford I. "Sandy" Weill, the forty-six-year-old CEO of Shearson.

Weill had made himself one of Wall Street's most notable figures. Born into a middle-class, Jewish family in Brooklyn, he had started his career in the brokerage business in 1955 as a messenger for Bear

Stearns & Co. Five years later, he and three partners, with a modest amount of capital, formed a new firm Carter Berlind Potoma & Weill— later renamed Carter Berlind & Weill, and then Cogan Berlind Weill & Levitt (CBWL), as the partnership evolved over time. The firm specialized in institutional business and thrived during the bull market of the 1960s, but when circumstances forced CBWL to create its own back-office order-processing operation in the late 1960s, it needed a greater volume of business to justify the expense. Weill and his partners saw only one obvious way to generate volume. As Weill said, "We had to build up the retail side."

That decision, however, coincided with a falling stock market and what was called the Paper Crisis on Wall Street. The need to process increasing amounts of information suddenly overwhelmed the antiquated bookkeeping systems of many Wall Street firms. The crisis led to ill will and financial losses for some companies but provided an opportunity for CBWL. Beginning in 1970 with the acquisition of the venerable Hayden Stone & Company, Cogan and Weill, and later Weill alone, continued to pick up the pieces of damaged or destroyed old firms, making eight acquisitions in less than a decade of such Wall Street fixtures as H. Hentz & Co.; Shearson, Hamill & Co.; Faulkner Dawkins & Sullivan; and Loeb Rhoades Hornblower.* With each acquisition of a crippled company, Weill seemed to be performing more of a public service than a sound business deal. Yet unlike American Express, Weill knew precisely what "fit," what business he was in, and what he needed. Each of these mergers added positive elements to the company he already had.

He also had unparalleled ability among Wall Street managers to consolidate operations and run them efficiently. He managed people well; employees knew very quickly where they stood after a merger,

---

*Weill and his partners took advantage of a second crisis in the securities business in the mid-1970s. The end of fixed commission rates in 1975 forced many old firms to merge or liquidate, providing Weill with some of the important pieces of his company.

avoiding the morale problems that damaged countless other mergers. By 1980, Weill's deal-making and management skill had created the company known as Shearson Loeb Rhoades, the second-largest retail brokerage house with 3,500 account executives, 265 offices, and $273.9 million in capital.

Weill's personality was the opposite of James Robinson's. An outsider—Weill lost a merger with Kuhn Loeb allegedly because he was not a member of the old Wall Street club—Weill had an unpolished, informal personal quality and management style. His door was always open to *any* employee—and he usually could be found in his office in his shirt-sleeves puffing on a long Te Amo cigar. While Robinson was the picture of self-assurance, Weill publicly admitted doubts about himself and his decisions. While Robinson exuded control, Weill aired his emotions, and he sometimes lost his temper at insiders and outsiders alike.

As CEO, he encouraged farsighted entrepreneurial thinking among all his managers. "Rather than sending down directives and having them come back with budgets," he once said, "we try to get [managers] to think strategically and think through how they're going to help the company as a whole accomplish its financial purpose." At the same time, he squeezed operations for every ounce of efficiency he could get with an obsessive attention to operating details. The combination of entrepreneurship and tight operational control—termed the Shearson ethic—created not just a successful company but also a cadre of successful managers with high morale, who believed that their ideas were valued and could be realized through the system. The ethic did exactly what Weill hoped; it encouraged innovation and gave Shearson the reputation as the most dynamic firm on Wall Street.

When he heard Lewis's pitch, Weill said he might consider a merger if he were named president of Amexco. Weill could see the changes that were coming to Wall Street as well. But though he suggested he might go along, he was not in fact ready to make any commitment, especially to American Express. In 1975, Weill had come to Amexco and asked Howard Clark if he wanted to buy a stake in Shearson. Clark referred him to Morley, who promised to call back in a few weeks; Morley called back, but four years later, after he had resigned from Amexco. Not only had that experience left Weill cautious, he also had less reason to entertain a deal now. In 1975, Wall Street was suffering through dark days, and Shearson remained a relatively small and vulnerable firm. Since then, he had come an incredible distance on his own and had bigger plans; he intended to more than double revenues by 1985 to $1 billion, and he expected to do it his way. Before he would consider a tie with Amexco in 1980, he had to be convinced it would work and would benefit his company. He admired Amexco. He liked its reputation, its wealth, liked the potential tie-in between Amexco's and Shearson's products, and Weill even appreciated the fact that Amexco was in close physical proximity to Shearson and all of Wall Street. But he wanted to be certain that the two companies could work together and feared Shearson could suffocate in Amexco's vast bureaucracy.

Lewis, with his usual persistence, arranged for a luncheon meeting with himself, Robinson, and Weill at American Express Plaza. Though Lewis had raised the idea of a merger to both men, though Amexco was studying the idea of a brokerage acquisition, there was little merger talk at the table that day. Lewis apparently brought up the matter of his fee if something did develop, but for the most part, substantive talk centered on the possibility of a joint project between Shearson and American Express. Shearson wanted to develop a plan like Merrill's CMA account, and he and Robinson discussed a tie-in to the American Express Card. They agreed to pursue this further, but they said nothing about merging.

Meanwhile Robinson and the EOC continued planning in several directions at once, and they began active pursuit of other targets. Between September 1980 and March 1981, Amexco spent $100 million for six companies—two insurers, a British publishing house, *Food & Wine* magazine, another bankcard processor, and a toll-free, telephone-order operation. But at the same time, in the planning councils of the EOC, Robinson focused more and more on brokerage.

Whatever Amexco thought of a brokerage acquisition, it was becoming clear that brokers themselves very much favored it. More companies called offering themselves. Dean Witter Reynolds, the number five company, came looking for a partner; Robinson thought about it, but decided no. Bache made inquiries, no again. Amexco's planning office also was seeing brighter and brighter possibilities in brokerage. Freeman's group pointed out that the new Reagan administration in Washington intended to loosen regulatory strings on business and encourage investment. He and many outside observers believed this could lead to a rebirth of investment in financial assets—stocks, bonds, and so on. But the advice did not lead to any immediate decision; Robinson still had not committed himself.

As he dawdled over his decision, though, the financial world underwent a dramatic and sudden change. On March 20, 1981, Prudential Insurance, one of the giants of the financial world, purchased Bache Halsey Stuart Shields for $385 million, a pittance for the $60 *billion* Prudential. Bache had been the sixth-largest publicly traded brokerage house, but now it had the backing of a company whose resources dwarfed those of Merrill Lynch. And together, Prudential and Bache could offer an enormous range of financial products— stocks, bonds, mutual funds, insurance—a financial supermarket on a grand scale. Overnight, it appeared Lewis's prediction was coming to pass.

At 6:45 the morning after the Prudential-Bache deal, Lewis called Robinson. Prudential's move had cleared up some of Robinson's questions. Amexco no longer would have the responsibility of being first, and it was evident from the outset that the takeover would not bring bad press or the ire of the regulators down on Prudential's head. Robinson could be bolder now. "Well, it's a whole new ball game," Amexco's CEO acknowledged. He told Lewis he was ready to negotiate a deal for Shearson. But the deal also depended on Weill. He read about the Prudential acquisition in a hotel room in Hong Kong, and when Lewis tracked him down, Weill told him, "I think I'd like to talk about it now."

31

Negotiations began soon after Weill returned to the U.S. They were short and intense. For the emotional Weill, selling his company was not easy, and his top aides, too, expressed misgivings. But the deal moved forward nonetheless. Weill asked his men: how would they feel if Amexco merged with E. F. Hutton, which was a real prospect if these talks fell through? In the new world, companies like Amexco and Prudential would dominate; the Shearsons could either join the giants or fall to the back of the pack.

Some American Express officials also dissented. Executives and members of the board of directors ran through all of the old objections. Even Howard Clark expressed reservations with the deal. But Robinson had decided to do it. In a real sense, he was implementing his own policy for the first time instead of Clark's. By choosing to buy a cyclical company, he risked the loss of the Record; in picking a brokerage house, he defined American Express as a financial-services company. His decision went counter to some of the original premises behind an acquisition, but he assumed the risk and the consequences of making it. As he had needed to do following McGraw-Hill, he was proving his leadership, and in choosing to team up with as high-powered a figure as Sanford Weill, Robinson was demonstrating that his self-confidence remained intact, as well. Board members swallowed their reservations and approved a merger unanimously.

The negotiations over price, Weill recalled, concluded in a matter of minutes. Robinson offered $860 million; Weill felt it should be treated as a merger, not a purchase, and asked for a straight stock swap, running the cost to nearly $1 billion. Weill did not get to be president of Amexco, but he remained chairman of Shearson—renamed Shearson/American Express—and he, along with his top aide Peter Cohen, joined the board of the parent company. The two sides dickered over small points, and Weill reportedly held out for the presidency almost to the last moment. But finally in the early morning hours of April 21, 1981, at Shearson's headquarters on the 106th floor of the World Trade Center, almost a month to the day after Prudential took over Bache, Shearson and Amexco agreed to a deal. They completed the merger by July. For Sandy Lewis, the merger meant a fee of $3.5 million and the realization of a vision. For Sandy Weill, it was an alliance that would keep Shearson a major force in the financial world.

For James Robinson, it was the fourth leg of American Express.

Shearson's people had worried about the effects of a merger with a company as big and as bureaucratic as Amexco, about being swamped "culturally" by the giant. And soon after the merger, American Express staffers showed up at the brokerage firm asking questions and poking around. But Shearson protested, and Robinson called off his men. To tamper with Shearson, he believed, risked destroying it.

The merger, in fact, had much greater consequences at American Express. Amexco's stodgy reputation in the financial world changed radically. It had acquired Shearson's image and identity as well. Amexco now was clearly defined as a financial-services company with Shearson's reputation for adaptability and opportunism, a company that was the embodiment of entrepreneurship in the large corporation. Actually, the change came so abruptly that the public was sometimes confused about who had taken over whom. Had a broker taken over a card company, or was it the other way around? Was it SHEARSON/American Express or Shearson/AMERICAN EXPRESS?

For finally making a major deal, the financial community applauded Robinson and recognized him as a corporate leader. He became a spokesman for the gospel of corporate entrepreneurship, a statesman of the financial community. Wall Street seemed to refer to him less often as Jimmy Three Sticks; he had won the right to James D. Robinson III. He even looked more the corporate leader than the cherub. His forehead seemed a little higher, and more gray appeared in his hair.

But Weill, even without the title of president he wanted, made the headlines, and he did it by leading Amexco on one of the great acquisition binges in American business history. Although it had taken Robinson four years to nab his first big company, and Amexco had typically procrastinated over all major acquisition decisions, Weill continued to look for acquisitions the same way he always had. And when he found them, he opened the checkbook at once, just as he had at Shearson. Beginning at the end of 1981 and early 1982, he picked up two regional brokerage firms—Foster & Marshall and Robinson-Humphrey—to fill in gaps in Shearson's distribution system; total cost was around $150 million. Soon after, he added a real estate packager, Balcor, for around $100 million.

But he and his chief aide, Peter Cohen, had just begun. They made their next move on behalf of the bank. In 1982, Robinson contemplated selling the AEIBC. It appeared in perilous condition, saddled with sizable loans to less-developed countries on the verge of default. It needed to be sold or overhauled, and when Amexco found no buyers, top executives decided on internal change. A study, led by company treasurer Robert F. Smith, argued that AEIBC should stop trying to compete with banks like Citicorp in all areas and concentrate on two high-profit-margin niches, where its office network would be of most value: trade finance and international "private" banking.

Robinson accepted the report, but Cohen offered a typical Shearson suggestion: instead of building the bank in those areas, why not buy an established one and add it to AEIBC? He suggested Amexco try to acquire a leading private bank, the Switzerland-based Trade Development Bank (TDB) controlled by the brilliant, Lebanese-born banker, Edmond Safra. Robinson agreed that Cohen, who knew Safra, should pursue it. Negotiations went on in secret for several weeks; to avoid a premature disclosure that might offend Safra, Cohen, Robinson, and Weill discussed the deal in code. The project was called "Mazel Tov," the Hebrew words for good luck; TDB was called Copper; Amexco, Tiger. By the end of the year, Amexco had a new bank for $520 million in cash, stock and stock warrants, and it had the talents of Safra himself, who agreed to stay on to run the combined TDB and AEIBC.

More major deals followed. Weill pursued Fred M. Kirby III of Alleghany Corp. in order to buy Investors Diversified Services (IDS), which offered life insurance, mutual funds, and financial planning to middle-income customers—a market complementing the more up-

scale one Shearson already reached. Weill bought IDS for $773 million. Then it was Cohen's turn, again. He read in *Fortune* about turmoil at the investment banking firm of Lehman Brothers Kuhn Loeb, and he went out and bought it for $360 million. Altogether, Weill and Cohen spent almost $2 billion on new additions in less than three years. These deals radically altered the size, scope, and image of the company, and by the time the acquisition spree was over, Alva Way had resigned, and Weill became president of American Express.

By 1984, Amexco had become a gigantic corporate institution. Assets had grown from $10 billion to $61 billion, its revenues topped $13 billion, and its stock market value, $8 billion. The company employed 76,000 people in over 2,000 offices. It managed over $80 billion of other people's money and almost $19 billion of its own. It put more money through the U.S. banking system than any single company except for the major banks. AEIBC, which now was recognized as a specialist in export financing, private banking, and merchant banking, had assets of over $13 billion, and in its special areas, it had become an institution of considerable size and weight. Shearson Lehman, with capital swelled to $1.8 billion, only a whisker behind Merrill Lynch, still outperformed most of the brokerage industry in its profit margins and return on equity. In the meantime, because of Gerstner's marketing skills, the card and cheque never stopped growing. In 1984, Amexco sold more than $13 billion in travelers cheques, had 20 million cards outstanding, and processed card charges of more than $45 billion.

Overall, American Express had higher name recognition (75 percent), and was used by more people (14 percent) than any other financial institution in the country. Amexco touched the lives of millions of Americans and millions more people abroad.

Though Weill and Cohen spent some $2 billion for acquisitions in a matter of months and garnered enormous publicity for their efforts, Amexco's explosive expansion arose from Robinson's decision to acquire Shearson for a mere billion. That merger was the key to the whole process of development that followed. Above all, it defined the company. Had he not made the decision to give Amexco an identity as a financial services company, none of the subsequent takeovers would have made sense. He provided the company with a specific focus, and so the acquisitions of TDB, Lehman Brothers, IDS, Balcor, etc. all fell into place. Amexco finally knew what it was, what fit, and what it should buy.

From the time he became CEO, Robinson wanted to purchase a big company. But his decision to buy Shearson, specifically, had nothing to do with the process or policy he started with in 1977. In fact, a brokerage company could not have been farther from his thinking when he and Morley took over. But from that moment on, he led Amexco through a process that underwent changes of direction and followed numerous dead ends: life insurance, Disney, communications, publishing. Only after years of floundering and inconclusive planning efforts did he come up with the decision to acquire a brokerage house—a business that just five years earlier Amexco had gotten *out* of. And even this opportunity arose by accident, circumstance, and the urging of others. Most of all it depended on Robinson's own failures; had he acquired McGraw-Hill or Disney or Philadelphia Life, it is doubtful Shearson would have interested him.

Still, in making the decision, Robinson asserted his own will and leadership in the face of opposition within the company. He had to persuade a reluctant board of directors to go along; the board had misgivings about brokerage and probably would not have endorsed it if Robinson himself had been lukewarm. But he did not simply make a decision to acquire a company. In buying Shearson, he fundamentally altered a sacred policy and a program he had inherited from Clark, and he had to assume responsibility for the consequences.

The effect of his acquisition was electric. It transformed Amexco to such an extent that it seemed an entirely new company. The changes were so radical that some executives could see no precedents in the company's past. Then, too, the company had added so many new people that few *knew* its past. But transformations—both dramatic and subtle—had occurred throughout Amexco's history. From its beginning in 1850, the company underwent many changes of image, of management philosophy and style, changes even of its basic businesses. Each change and each decision for change contributed to the creation of the huge, and hugely successful, organization that exists today. But the process was random. Amexco did not proceed systematically over the years toward a goal of becoming a giant financial services company; the process of remaking Amexco was *not* governed by this or any other end.

Indeed, the circuitous path Robinson took on his way to a decision to acquire Shearson had many precedents in the past. He tried to create a systematic approach and it disintegrated, but at American Express, systems for decision making seldom led smoothly to decisions. In the end, most decisions resulted from the effort and will of individuals working toward their own unsystematic ends. How the people of the company finally made decisions and how, as a consequence, the company evolved into a giant institution, that is the real story of the enterprise called the American Express Company.

THE
TREATY OF
BUFFALO

2

When the American Express Company was founded in 1850, it did exactly what its name said. The express business itself had existed for less than fifteen years, but already it was a vital component of the American transportation and communication system. As the population of the U.S. grew and dispersed into the nation's interior in the middle of the nineteenth century, business followed, and with it the need to move goods quickly over vast distances. The railroads became the primary transportation-communications link in American commerce, and the express rode literally and figuratively on the backs of railroads, offering a new service that combined the high-speed transport of the rails with a delivery system of a post office. Railroads handled bulk freight; the U.S. Post Office carried the mails; the express transported everything else. Actually, the lines between freight, post, and express materials often blurred, and the three systems at times fought over the same business. But the express was specifically designed to carry items that required both rapid transport and safe delivery; the express promised speed and took responsibility for damage and loss.

A limited and informal version of the express business existed before the organization of express companies. Stagecoach drivers used to carry letters and packages from town to town, secreting valuables in their large bell-crowned hats. But stage drivers could not maintain a communications network over such vast and expanding territory. Individually they traveled short routes over a limited range, and carrying packages was never more than a sideline to their driving jobs. Only a formal service based primarily on rail transportation could meet the growing needs of the country. The U.S. Post Office failed to provide it. In the early years of the country, its service proved too expensive and notoriously unreliable.

For a time, merchants preferred to transport packages and money through friends who happened to be traveling in the right direction. And if a businessman could not find a friend, he would hand over the packet to a friend of a friend, or even to a perfect stranger. Throughout the first third of the nineteenth century, on any business day, merchants scoured the wharves of ports such as New York, Boston, and Providence, pouncing on virtually any traveler and stuffing some merchandise into his or her hands. Miraculously, most of the goods ended up in the right place.

But bankers did most to spur a formal express service. In 1836, the federal government dissolved the second Bank of the United States, the Federal Reserve of the day. But when the U.S. bank closed, the only national, interbank, messenger service ended with it. Banks had to handle such transactions themselves, which they did at high cost. A bank hired a special courier to deliver a draft. To cover the cost of transportation and insurance, the bank had to deduct a part of every draft, discounting it by as much as 10 percent. The banks, above all, needed a more permanent system that could reduce their costs.

The express filled that need. It offered to carry for all the banks every kind of financial instrument—cash, securities, and gold—with the same speed and attention as a special courier. Messengers accompanied express shipments every step of the way. But the express proposed to combine valuables with other material needing fast transport— packages (no parcel post existed in the U.S. until the 1900s), fragile items, and perishables. Through economies of scale, the express could lower the cost for banks enormously. In fact, the advent of the express business dropped the discount rate from 10 percent to around 1 percent. Banks welcomed the express, and bank contracts became an important part of an express company's business.

Bank business also had special attractions for express companies. Transportation of money and securities produced the largest return for the expresses because, while they charged for carrying packages by the weight, they charged for shipment of financial instruments by the value. A single messenger could carry a good day's profit in his pocket, or certainly in one bag. It made the express business a natural for ambitious men without any capital. They only needed a bag and a rail ticket to set up shop.

Two bank couriers formed what was arguably the first express operation. In 1834, B. D. and L. B. Earle created a company to carry packages and money on the new rail link between Boston and Providence. But the Earle brothers did not provide a service that covered a sufficiently broad territory to meet the needs of the banking and business communities. A company that had greater geographical scope held an advantage over all others. One organization serving Boston, Albany, New York, Providence, and Philadelphia could handle more at a net lower cost.

The first to appreciate the advantage of a widespread express system was a delicately built, sanguine-looking Bostonian named William Harnden. In 1839, Harnden recognized the potential and hit on the name "express." Then he bought a carpetbag to carry valuables, a ticket for the steamship from New York to Providence and one for the train from Providence to Boston, and launched "Harnden's Package Express," headquartered at 20 Wall Street in New York's financial center. He lost money until he made a deal with steamship operator Daniel Drew. Drew competed with Commodore Cornelius Vanderbilt for east-coast shipping business, and so he offered Harnden a free pass on his boats in exchange for free publicity; Harnden let it be known that he traveled on Drew's line, not Vanderbilt's. Soon, Harnden had sufficient business to run his express every evening, and he usually carried enough to fill whole freight cars.

With his needs for space so great, Harnden negotiated contracts with carriers; the terms would comprise contracts between expresses and carriers—particularly railroads—thereafter. In exchange for a flat monthly fee and/or a percentage of the gross receipts of the express business, the railroads provided cars, transportation (of personnel and goods), and depot facilities. Railroads and expresses leaned toward the gross-receipts formula since it encouraged friendly relations between the two parties: the more business the express carried, the more money the railroads made. At the same time, the contracts usually contained protections for both parties. The expresses promised to keep their rates above bulk-freight rates so that they would not compete with the railroads. For their part, the express companies asked for, and usually were granted, exclusivity—a monopoly right of express privilege over a given rail or steamer line. This was, indeed, the most important clause as far as the expresses were concerned, since monopoly guaranteed high profits.*

As business grew, Harnden expanded his operations along the east coast and up the Hudson River from New York City to Albany. Initially, he failed to gain a contract for express privileges on Drew's Hudson River fleet; Drew held a monopoly on Hudson River traffic and saw no benefit to himself to award a second contract to Harnden. But the Bostonian persisted and finally won it with the help of an acquaintance of Drew's, Henry Wells. After Harnden signed the contract in 1840, he made Wells his first agent in Albany. Wells's entry in

---

*The expresses were not always able to get exclusivity in the early days of the business. However, it became a feature of virtually all express contracts by the 1870s.

the express business began a chain of events that would lead to the creation of the American Express Company.

Henry "Stuttering" Wells was a flamboyant character who dressed in ruffled shirts and in winter always wore a velvet Basque cap with gold tassel. A broad-shouldered six-footer, he was also the physical opposite of the frail Harnden. But like him, Wells was ambitious, and he had tried and failed to make a mark on the world since his preteens. One of his many jobs included schoolmastering at an institution for the "cure of speech defects" (though he failed to cure his own). At the time Harnden found him, the self-educated Wells was thirty-five years old and working as a freight forwarder and ticket agent for traffic between Albany and Buffalo on the 365-mile navigable waterway through the center of New York State known as the Erie Canal.

As it turned out, Wells did not succeed in the job Harnden gave him either; he stayed on only a year. What led to the break was a conflict of business vision between the two men. Soon after he began working for Harnden, Wells urged that his boss put in an express line from Albany to Buffalo. But Harnden refused. "Put people there," the Bostonian said, "and my express will soon follow."

Wells, however, had a better sense of New York State than his employer. Not only had he worked canal traffic, but he also had spent most of his life in upstate New York and had witnessed its transformation after the opening of the canal in 1825. Over the next fifteen years, it had evolved from an area of isolated frontier towns to a prosperous mercantile and industrial region. By 1840, significant population centers had sprung up along the length of the canal: thousands of people now lived in the cities of Buffalo, Rochester, Syracuse, and Utica. Wells saw Buffalo as most important. It contained 18,041 people, a "literary and scientific academy," three banks, and seven newspapers. It also possessed significant port facilities which served traffic on the canal, the Great Lakes, and the St. Lawrence River. Wells recognized that if Buffalo's population was growing, its business would grow, and the city would need better links with the mercantile centers on the Atlantic seaboard.

Already, he had witnessed improvement and development in transportation. The canal had proved an inefficient commercial highway. In winter it froze, and even in summer traffic only crept along. Systems of locks held ships immobile for days. But beginning in 1831, short-line railroads began carrying people around the slowest sections of the canal, reducing the travel time from Albany to Buffalo, and by 1840, railroad companies were joining their track. Once that process was completed, Wells foresaw the promise of year-round, high-speed transport across the center of New York State, and the integration of the region into the mainstream of American commerce. But to participate fully in that commerce, Wells believed Buffalo and the other cities of New York also needed an express service.

When Wells realized he could not convince Harnden of the need, he spoke to a friend, George Pomeroy, and convinced him to start an Albany-Buffalo express line. Pomeroy organized a company in 1841 and began operations, but with the rail line still incomplete, he found the journey from Albany to Buffalo too arduous. He quit after three trips. But Wells still believed strongly in the idea, and he finally came to the conclusion that for an Albany-Buffalo express to succeed, he would have to run it himself. In partnership with investor Crawford Livingston, Wells took over Pomeroy & Co. and began making the run across New York State as the company's messenger. For the next eighteen months, he traveled continuously.

As Pomeroy had discovered, the trip was grueling. Wells traveled only by rail and stage; one way between Buffalo and Albany took him four nights and three days. As he explained in later years to the Buffalo Historical Society, the trains were both slow and dangerous. The cars rode on strap rails, essentially iron bars spiked down to the beds. These rails tended to loosen, causing frequent "run offs" (derailments), or worse, the rails bowed upward in what were called "snake heads," which had the unfortunate effect of ripping through cars and the people inside them. Also, for a good part of the trip, Wells rode in stagecoaches over roads so poorly maintained that the horses could seldom even trot.

As if the journey were not disheartening enough, Wells discovered he had mistimed his venture. Within six months of his first trip, a business depression hit Buffalo and left every bank in the city insolvent. But Wells also proved very lucky. The business community of Buffalo, even more than Wells had anticipated, wanted to maintain this transportation-communications link to other financial and business centers, and consequently, business people nurtured Wells's operation. Wells found they were always "anxious to see whether our list of friends had increased, and whether our trunks seemed well fed by packages."

In time, Wells was making money and he gave up his duties as messenger to concentrate on proprietorship. By 1842, the rail link between Albany and Buffalo was completed, which enormously speeded and simplified the trip. It also led to further growth of the Buffalo region; between 1840 and 1845, the population of the city nearly doubled.

In 1842, Wells hired a freight agent away from the Auburn & Syracuse Railroad and made him a messenger. The man, William George Fargo, then in his midtwenties, was cynical, ambitious, and physically courageous. Like Wells, he had struck out on his own at age thirteen with a strong back and almost no formal education. Also a native of upstate New York, Fargo had already failed as a grocer and appeared to have been just marking time in the freight agent's job. Within a year after he met Wells, however, he proved his value as an expressman, and Wells appointed him the company's agent in Buffalo. By this time, Wells's line, renamed Livingston, Wells & Co., served all of the major cities of central New York, and Wells looked to expand it further.

Wells looked west and formed an express line under Fargo's management that offered service from Buffalo to Chicago via Ohio, Michigan, and Indiana. In creating this line, Wells was gambling on the future of the country. In effect, he bet that the settlers and homesteaders he had seen embarking for the midwest from the Lake Erie port at Buffalo represented growth and development in a new region of the country. Almost no formal transportation system existed through this territory where Wells put his express line. Railroads did not run past Buffalo. Wells recalled that the trip from Buffalo just as far as Detroit could take as long as eight days, and the expense was so high that for the first couple of years he could not make a profit.

But the New York express more than made up the difference, and Wells expanded it continuously. In 1845, after Harnden died (he had worked himself to death at age thirty-two), Wells added the express route from New York to Albany to his line and moved his headquarters to New York City. A year later, he sold all, or most, of his share of the western express to Fargo and William Livingston, Crawford's brother. When Crawford died in 1848, Wells renamed his own company, Wells & Co., though he sold a share of it to Johnston Livingston.* The business grew enormously. Express traffic in New York State increased a hundredfold from 1841 to 1849, and Wells, Fargo, and the Livingstons controlled all of it.

Their success, however, captured the attention of John Butterfield, a onetime stagecoach driver from Utica. Butterfield was a few years older than Wells, and like Wells and Fargo, self-educated and self-made, but by the mid-1840s, probably a good deal richer than both. Butterfield controlled virtually all the stagecoach lines in western New York (which still carried all of the freight and passengers to settlements not on a rail line). He also built the telegraph from Albany to Buffalo (Wells had invested in that venture), and had started a steamship operation on Lake Ontario that dominated traffic along the lake and the St. Lawrence River. Butterfield had powerful friends, too. They included future U.S. President James Buchanan and Erastus Corning, New York's leading railroad man.

The growth of the express business proved a tempting target for

---

*All three men—William, Crawford, and Johnston—belonged to the influential Livingston family, which played a major role in New York State politics and business. But Johnston was only a distant relation of Crawford and William and invested in Wells's company because of a general interest in the express business, not because of a family tie.

Butterfield, and in 1849, he, along with James Wasson of Albany, formed a rival express, Butterfield, Wasson & Company,* to compete with Wells & Company throughout New York State. Wells had a contract with Corning's railroads; the contract gave Wells the right to carry express matter on those lines for a flat fee of $100 a day. Butterfield told his friend Corning that he would pay the same amount for the same privileges, and Corning agreed. What's more, Butterfield cut the cost to customers, making it cheaper for shippers to send express material through Butterfield, Wasson than through Wells & Co.

Competition, any competition, caused extreme alarm among expressmen. They saw competition in social Darwinian terms as a battle for the survival of the fittest or the richest. Of course, this view was not uncommon among businessmen of that era, but expressmen felt particularly vulnerable to competitors. While an individual needed large resources to start a new railroad or an iron mill, he could start an express with virtually no capital and offer the same services as an established company. The expressmen believed then that if they allowed any competition, it would open the way for more and eventually lead to their own destruction.

As a result, the expressmen believed that competition required elimination, and they used two strategies to accomplish it. First, they tried to destroy competitors; Wells had crushed a few upstarts over the years. If that failed, the other alternative was merger. But companies merged only when they agreed that warfare would be too costly and that even the winner would pay too high a price for victory.

Wells set out to crush Butterfield by dropping his own rates below those Butterfield offered. Soon both companies were losing money, but Butterfield's pockets were at least as deep as Wells's. After a few months of losses, and when Butterfield showed no inclination to give up, Wells knew he couldn't win. It was time for alternative two. Sources differ on who called for the merger. Some say it was Wells;

---

*According to one source, the name actually was the Butterfield and Wasson Express Company.

others insist Butterfield took the lead. It might even have been Corning who decided to bring the two men together. In any case, by early 1850, negotiations began, and they concluded in Buffalo at the end of March with an agreement that might have been called the Treaty of Buffalo but was known instead as the Articles of Association of the American Express Company.

The battle between Wells and Butterfield ended with the creation of American Express, but its birth was not simple, nor did the company seem likely to survive. Like many treaties, the one that created Amexco* tried to strike a compromise and balance of interests. But so far from settling conflicts, the agreement created an organization that was divided, contentious, and in some ways virtually paralyzed.

The termination of war did not result in an even balance of power between the two men. Rather the merger marked the surrender of Henry Wells to Butterfield, who emerged as the most powerful figure in the new company. Wells retained some influence and power, but Butterfield wound up with the stronger hand in the business that Wells himself had built.

But American Express was not only the combination of Wells & Co. with Butterfield, Wasson, but with a third company as well. Livingston, Fargo & Co. also joined the new organization, but its presence greatly complicated the power relationships. Why Livingston and Fargo offered Butterfield a stake in their western express remains conjecture. The likeliest reason was that Butterfield threatened to create a rival western express. With his money and connections, Butterfield could have built a company that would have swamped Livingston, Fargo & Co. But Butterfield had not put that to the test and so had little leverage over Fargo and Livingston. As a result, Fargo came to the

---

*The abbreviation "Amexco" was not used at the time of the company's founding. The company was called the "Am. Ex." or the "Am. Exp.," or in discussions of the express business, the "American." To this day, some publications will refer to the company as "AmEx." The company typically uses Amexco, and for simplicity, this book will use Amexco throughout.

negotiating table but would sign an agreement only if it gave him significant power. He and Butterfield together as equals hammered out the form and system of American Express. Henry Wells bowed out of the process. In March 1850, as the talks neared their conclusion, he left for a vacation in Europe. He did not see the final agreement until months afterward.

The reality of the two forces was clearly evident in the agreement that emerged. While the three companies merged into one named American Express, they remained two operating units: Livingston, Fargo & Co. retained its identity, while in New York State, Wells & Co. and Butterfield, Wasson became Wells, Butterfield & Co. (The order of the names did not indicate the relative power, however. Butterfield was named the line superintendent, which made him the operating head of the company. Wells gained no status within Wells, Butterfield.)

These two operating units did not promote a real merger of interests, but rather accommodated and balanced the power of the two strongest members and their respective supporters. As a result, both operating units remained autonomous, and so separate that they did not even report the basic business details of profit and loss to each other, or to the American Express board as a whole. This was not just decentralization, but factionalism, and it guaranteed an adversary relationship among leaders of the company. In other companies directors feuded, but American Express was unusual in that it was *created* around opposition and conflict.

Six men met at Mansion House, the main financial building of Buffalo, on March 18, 1850, to work out the final agreement. Butterfield, William and Johnston Livingston, Butterfield's partner Wasson, Fargo, and Buffalo lawyer James McKay completed the Treaty of Buffalo over eight days. The agreement they signed gave the new American Express Company a lifetime of ten years. That was it. It could be dissolved sooner only by a vote of the shareholders, but after a decade, the company would be forced to disband. Though this clause reflected the mistrust between the parties at Mansion House, it also made business sense. The ten-year limit presented an obstacle against a move to take over the company by one faction or another. Any shareholder would need the cooperation of the others to reconstitute the company at that day in the future when it would be dissolved.

The new company was capitalized at $150,000 (1,500 shares, $100 per share), with each of the three original companies "contributing" $50,000. Most likely, they actually paid in nothing at all.* The men sitting at the table at Mansion House merely decided to value the assets of each of the three original companies at $50,000 and then they created stock for that amount. That number did not reflect real capital assets. (It was questionable whether the tangible assets of the three combined—a few wagons and horses mostly—equaled $50,000.) Rather the "capital" represented an amount for figuring dividends; company officials estimated they could maintain a good return on $150,000, and so they created a mythical capital of that amount. Actually, Butterfield may have paid in some cash, since he was the newcomer to the business and had not built as much "capital." In any event, he wound up the largest shareholder with 225 shares, 15 percent of the company. (Wells and Fargo had about 100 each.)

Because he had the largest number of shares, Butterfield gained more power than anyone else, but also more risk. The American Express Company was not a corporation but an "unincorporated joint-stock association." Stockholders could sell and trade their shares like shares of a corporation, but they had responsibilities of *unlimited* partners. That meant that shareholders were personally liable for the company's debts, even beyond the extent of its capital. If the company lost more money than it had in the till, shareholders could be assessed for what the company still owed, proportionally based on number of shares. So while Butterfield had the most to gain from the success of the new company, he also had the most to lose from its failure.

---

*A company history has claimed that Fargo, Wells, Butterfield, and their associates paid in as much as $100,000. However, in 1909, Amexco's treasurer publicly acknowledged that little capital, if any, was ever paid in.

However, the joint-stock concept possessed advantages that must have appealed to the founders of the company. Unlike corporations, stock associations had few legal obligations toward shareholders. If a stockholder wanted a meeting, he had to request it and put the matter to a shareholder vote. In the normal course of events, stockholders also never received statements of income or assets. * Nor did they vote on directors; the board of Amexco became self-perpetuating. In other words, because Amexco was a joint-stock association, its leaders could do what they wanted in total secrecy. This would have appealed to the two dominant figures of the company, Fargo and Butterfield. In contrast to Wells, who loved to talk and tell stories, they were extremely secretive, private men—Butterfield, for example, kept his few records in his hat and left almost no records after his death—and the company took on their secretive nature. They made secrecy a matter of personal privilege as well as company policy. Even after they had left the scene, the company maintained the policy that the best publicity was no publicity. The less anyone knew about American Express, the better.

Although Butterfield had the most stock, for the American Express agreement to work, control of the company had to reside with the board of directors as a whole. Neither Butterfield nor Fargo could be allowed to dominate. The seven-member board represented three distinct interests: Butterfield and Wasson comprised one faction; Fargo and William Livingston, a second; and Johnston Livingston, James McKay, and usually Henry Wells, the third—what might be called the swing faction. These men had greater loyalty to American Express than to either Butterfield or Fargo and so would thwart any attempt by one faction or the other to gain absolute power. The board, seat of true executive power in the company, operated on an ad hoc committee system that must have been an unwritten part of the agreement in Buffalo in March 1850. The board referred important questions to

---

*In 1876, the New York Stock Exchange asked Amexco to supply information to it for the benefit of shareholders. The Amexco board refused and said that a listing on the NYSE was a matter "of complete indifference to us."

committees, consisting of a member of each of the factions, before the board as a whole made a decision.

Four officers were elected on the same day the board approved the Articles of Association, March 26, 1850. Fargo became secretary; Butterfield, vice president; John Day (who was soon fired), treasurer; and the absent Henry Wells, president. It would be weeks before he would even hear about his election, and four months before he would attend a board of directors meeting.

Like other aspects of the creation of American Express, Wells's election to the presidency owed a great deal to his surrender to John Butterfield. His withdrawal from the field made his election not just understandable, but probably inevitable. Neither Butterfield nor Fargo could hold the office. Since they retained operating control of the halves of the company, the presidency would make either of them the dominant figure. Wells, on the other hand, represented a compromise figure. Over the years, he had been a respected colleague of Fargo and William Livingston, so they accepted him. By capitulating, Wells became acceptable to Butterfield as well. As a result, he could mediate disputes that arose internally. (At times, Butterfield would suspect that Wells was not a neutral party, but Wells generally fulfilled the role assigned him.) Wells did not become chief executive, however, and the board pegged his annual salary at only $1,250. That was not a mean paycheck in an age when $40 per month represented a decent wage, but Fargo earned more for running what, at the time, was the less profitable half of the American Express Company.

Upon his return from Europe that summer, Wells attended his first board meeting at Astor House, New York City's leading hotel. He thanked the board officially for his new job, worked at it for a month, and then announced, without resigning, that he was moving to the upstate New York village of Aurora on Lake Cayuga. This decision removed Wells from the day-to-day affairs of the company. No telegraph reached Aurora; the nearest railroad lay a forty-mile stagecoach ride away (or sleigh ride in winter)—hours of travel time. Wells had moved into the middle of a beautiful, serene nowhere. In Aurora, he built for himself a Tuscan-style villa of blue limestone, and he seemed, at age forty-five, to welcome the semiretirement forced on him by John Butterfield. He decided to devote much of the rest of his life to travel and philanthropy, particularly his pet project, a women's college in Aurora, in the hills above the lake.

He had less of a retirement than he wanted. Company affairs summoned him often. As president for the next eighteen years, he frequently found he had to mediate crises from within and without. On several important occasions, he demonstrated that his loyalty to Amexco transcended factionalism, and he helped keep both Butterfield and Fargo from gaining control of the company.

But he did not make company policy or control operations. Indeed, no individual did. Operational details remained the responsibility of each separate operating unit. Except for an occasional homily against drinking on the job or a threat to go after employees who stole from the cash drawer,* the members of the board and the officers of the company paid no attention to employment practice or policy, nor did they worry about customer relations. The key to profits was not a happy work force or even happy customers, but exclusive contracts and monopoly control over routes. The board constantly fretted about contracts. If they obtained control over routes, they knew they could make all the money commerce could give the express, which was considerable and growing all the time. Any other operating details appeared trivial by comparison.

Executive power resided in the board. The board negotiated contracts with the railroads and the banks, counted the profits and distributed them, mainly to one another. The most difficult problem for management was to keep the power with the whole board, to balance and account for the factions without giving up too much to one or another. Consequently, meetings often proved intense, acrimonious affairs, which produced few results even after hours of exhausting

---

*The board once authorized "criminal means" if necessary to recover money taken by a former agent in Utica.

debate. Although these men had agreed to be partners, they still saw themselves as rivals, too, who did not much like or trust each other. Finally they had to submerge their feelings in order to protect the company from splintering apart. But often they submerged their feelings only after a struggle. Indeed, decision making frequently took on the character of a test of power and will.

The nature of this organization in effect set limits on how much could be accomplished. The company could and did make money through expansion of its express business within its original territorial range. But for Amexco to stay intact, the board needed to satisfy all sides, and that guaranteed paralysis in undertaking new ventures or even significantly extending the limits of Amexco's express activities. Any move could be viewed as a threat by one faction to expand its power. Any new activity offered an opportunity for one side to gain greater authority and leverage. As a result, new ideas had to be opposed.

Satisfying each side—maintaining a balance—remained the preoccupation for the board for eighteen years, because individuals and their supporters did seek to gain control of the board and its executive power. Until 1868, the question of who, if anyone, would dominate the company influenced every decision and the character of decision making itself at American Express.

The system embodied in the Treaty of Buffalo worked well as long as board members accepted its premises. That lasted less than two years. Early on, Butterfield indicated that he disliked the way American Express was constituted. He soured on the prospect of sharing the leading role with Fargo, especially after he found that he could not get basic business information about Fargo's operating unit. In 1851, he forced through a board resolution requiring Fargo to make a statement of losses. It seemed like a small thing to ask since he, Butterfield, was liable for Fargo's losses. But by the next year, Butterfield still had not gained a full picture of the state of the western express. That was not a situation he was willing to endure quietly.

In 1852, Butterfield began playing his hand more forcefully and made clear his dissatisfaction. Ultimately, he got most or all of what he wanted, but to achieve it, he spent more than a year maneuvering, taking advantage finally of a disaster and an internal crisis to advance his cause. The extent and complexity of his efforts demonstrated just how difficult it was to get anything done at American Express.

Butterfield made his first challenge at a board session in Albany. (Meetings were held in different places all along the route of the company—New York City, Albany, Utica, Buffalo, and in summer, Saratoga Springs.) This session produced four days of continuous conflict. Butterfield's first maneuver concerned the matter of who would fill a vacancy on the board—an issue that came up the first day of meetings, February 10. William Livingston, Fargo's partner, had sold his shares and resigned. Butterfield nominated T. S. Faxton, a Utica railroad man and crony who had been a partner in the Albany-Buffalo telegraph venture. * With a hundred shares of Amexco stock (5 percent of the company due to a recent addition of capital), † Faxton held one of the largest blocks. Yet the board rejected his nomination. Livingston had been Fargo's man; Faxton's election would give Butterfield three board seats to Fargo's one, a major shift in the balance of power. The guardians of the Amexco charter, McKay, J. Livingston, and Wells, tabled the nomination, effectively defeating it.

The next day, Butterfield forced a long argument about the dividend by demanding the highest possible payout. As the largest shareholder, Butterfield received the most from any dividend, yet he often felt he was being shortchanged by the others, and he frequently dragged out dividend debates for hours and hours. The debate went to the heart of the conflict. From Butterfield's perspective, power on the board meant money. Butterfield wanted to take as much as he could out of the company, wanted an ally like Faxton on the board to see that he got

---

*In 1820, Faxton had given Butterfield his first job as a stagecoach driver.

†Amexco had expanded its capital to $200,000 to buy with stock a few small local express companies to add to its network.

his money, and wanted to see Fargo's books to know how much he could take. But Butterfield could not get information about the western express, faced a battle every time he tried to get money out of it, and so determined to change the company.

But in the midst of Butterfield's effort, Fargo offered a resolution on February 13 to "extend this line to California." The resolution threw Butterfield suddenly from offense to defense, and he set off a furious debate that lasted a month. Butterfield did not object to a California express because he feared it would lose money. Butterfield, in fact, probably expected it would make money. In 1849, just after the Gold Rush began, he invested in a company that transported freight and people to and from California across the isthmus of Panama. Consequently, he knew better than Wells and Fargo the profit potential of a move further west. The motive behind Butterfield's opposition was the preservation of his own power. Any new venture could enhance one member's power at the expense of another; in this case the western character of the venture would certainly put it in Fargo's domain. Butterfield did not need it spelled out who would win and who would lose. Indeed, he may well have spelled it out himself, probably in obscene terms; he was known to scrape the "sinks of iniquity" in his language on such occasions. And coming on the heels of his defeat over Faxton, he probably felt in no mood to accommodate W. G. Fargo.

The debate over the American Express California operation remained heated at subsequent board meetings. Butterfield opposed everything—in one instance even the minutes of a previous meeting. The debate over the minutes consumed an entire board session. When the members finally voted on the California proposal, they defeated it, four to two. Butterfield, McKay, Livingston, and Wasson voted against it; only Wells and Fargo voted yes. But in reality, only Butterfield and Wasson were opposed. Livingston and McKay performed their duty as swing votes. They must have agreed with Butterfield that this move could affect the balance of power, and to keep the peace in the company, they actually voted contrary to their inclinations. They took the unprecedented step of reading into the record the reasons for their votes. Said Livingston, "The opposition of Mr. Butterfield carries with it a sizable portion of stock, and in justice to those he represents, I am unwilling to engage in a California Express." McKay voiced an identical rationale, although he also noted the opposition of Butterfield's friend T. S. Faxton. Their votes ended discussion of the California express at Amexco, but Wells and Fargo decided to go ahead with a California express on their own. Ten days after the vote, they met with a group of investors at Astor House and formed Wells, Fargo & Company, which became a major express company in its own right.*

The board of Amexco meanwhile continued to be true to the principle of balance. In May, it sided with Fargo in filling the vacancy on the board. On a resolution from Wells, the board nominated and elected E. P. Williams, Fargo's brother-in-law, to fill the slot. Wasson voted against it; Butterfield did not attend the meeting, nor would he attend another for several months. But while he may have taken the Williams election as a major defeat, it was really the modus vivendi for the whole company.

Butterfield had won one and lost one, but on the whole, he remained unhappy and looked for another chance to dominate American Express. He bided his time and got an opportunity quite unexpectedly, an incident that from his own standpoint was both frightening and fortuitous.

On August 20, 1852, the S.S. *Atlantic*, a Lake Erie steamer, sank after it collided with the schooner *Ogdensberg* off Point Albino, New York. On board the *Atlantic* was John Murphy, an American Express messenger. Murphy got himself to safety before the ship went down, but his little safe containing an estimated $50,000 in valuables went to the bottom of the lake. In those days, the loss represented a substantial

---

*Wells, Fargo & Co. was capitalized at $300,000, but as usual no cash was paid in. Directors pledged collateral to acquire the stock. Most of them put up as collateral their shares in Amexco. In other words, they bought Wells, Fargo stock by pledging stock they never paid for.

amount of money—a loss for which the stockholders of the company had ultimate liability. Large shareholders like Butterfield and Faxton were liable for proportionately more of the loss. A month later, Faxton precipitated a crisis more than likely on behalf of John Butterfield.

Faxton distributed to shareholders an ornately printed letter that combined hysteria with fact. After explaining who he was, Faxton got to the point, "After what has occurred on Lake Erie, and what we are *Liable to Daily*, I feel my position to be rather an unpleasant one; and unless something different takes place in the management of our business, I feel I shall be called upon in self-defence, to do something to meet the case!"

He then railed about how there was "not a company in the State of New York . . . that is so badly managed," where directors voted "themselves large salaries [and] heavy traveling expenses, [and who were] receiving pay from other companies to the prejudice of this." Most of his charges were quite true. Board members had just voted themselves a salary increase—Fargo's salary was the highest at $3,600— a fact that Faxton could not have known unless Butterfield or Wasson had told him. Proceedings of board sessions and the details of resolutions were not open to shareholder inspection.

Faxton went on to decry "daily losses" and assets so small that, in the event of a big loss, they would "do little towards paying it." In answer to these charges, Faxton claimed, the company would only say, "we get greater Dividends than many other companies, and therefore have no right to complain."

Faxton offered his own remedy for these problems: a shareholders meeting to "require the present trustees to give an Exposé of their business." Faxton certainly had a valid point when he noted that shareholders did not even know the asset base of the company, a situation, as he said, quite unlike most other companies. He could have added that even Butterfield was not certain of the size of the company's assets, a situation even less like other companies.

Faxton criticized the entire board, but he singled out "one or two of them [who] have more to say about its management than all the others." That he meant Fargo, and maybe Wells, but not Butterfield seems very likely. Wells's friend, E. B. Morgan, believed he saw Butterfield's hand in this. In a letter to another shareholder, Daniel Lothrop, he wrote that "this is a *Utica* movement [Butterfield was from Utica and was its leading business figure] to get control of the company and not designed for your interest or mine." And he defended his friends on the board, "I would rather have Wells, Fargo, Livingston and their associates' *knowledge* of Expressing—as capital than Faxton with $300,000 of capital."

He also offered a curious rationale for opposing a shareholders meeting. "If the shareholders assemble together and have a full exposé of all matters and ask explanations for this and that and the other—get into a warm discussion—a broil and *blowup*—that the whole thing [Amexco] will go to Davie Jones—that others will be induced to engage in the business—and that your stock and mine will hereafter offer *short dividends*." In other words, if stockholders actually find out about the company, they will either get angry and destroy it, or go off and form a company to take its business away.

Yet Faxton won the round. With the help of John Butterfield, Faxton forced a shareholders meeting. The prospect worried other board members, because the exposé Faxton demanded was sure to come to pass, and no one, not even Fargo, knew for sure how much money the western express had. If an audit showed that the company could not cover the *Atlantic* losses, because of deficiencies on Fargo's side of the ledger, Fargo, Williams, and probably Wells, too, faced ouster. The company would surely pass entirely into Butterfield's control.

The directors had no choice but to go ahead with the meeting. On October 19, shareholders gathered at Astor House. They appointed a committee to go over the books of the two operating companies, in effect permitting Butterfield to get an independent appraisal of Fargo's books. At the same time, the meeting did not result in the ouster of any officials. Indeed, Fargo, Wells, and the rest won a qualified endorsement of their handling of the *Atlantic* affair, leaving Faxton's group dissatisfied with the outcome. Fargo's brother-in-law, E. P. Williams, wrote, "Our . . . meeting went off to the satisfaction of *a majority*, leaving a small minority of sore heads to find fault."

While the Uticans won at least a partial victory, Faxton did not wait for the committee report but, rather, planned a new battle. He and several associates began the ultimate attack on American Express: they prepared to launch a new, competitive express company.

Did Butterfield encourage this? Either as a real threat or as a ploy to maneuver himself into a commanding position at Amexco? Butterfield covered his tracks well; his colleagues on the Amexco board thought they discerned his hand but could find no trace of it. But if he did encourage Faxton just as a gambit, he used an extremely clever one. No prospect upset expressmen more than competition, and merely the threat of competition would force the board of Amexco to act. Of course, the directors could have taken various actions, not all of them favorable to Butterfield. But as events unfolded, Butterfield adroitly pushed Amexco along the path he wanted.

Even as a ploy, the competition had to appear serious, and Faxton made it seem very real. The new company, Livingston said, would be capitalized at $500,000—two and half times the capitalization of Amexco—and would start business on March 1, 1853, with lines running all the way to St. Louis, according to Johnston Livingston, "a grand scheme." It seemed real enough to the board of American Express, so they readied the usual tactics. They started with war. "I have written to Fargo and Williams . . . telling them to put up all the bans and lay anchors to the windward," McKay wrote Wells on November 18. "I propose we set to work right earnestly and give these fellows what they deserve."

But Faxton's group was fighting too. Amexco officials soon realized the upstarts had the money and were trying very hard to establish the necessary connections as well. Faxton's cronies began lobbying businessmen and bankers for express contracts, and they went after investors to subscribe to the stock offering of a company they called the United States Express Company.

More ominously for American Express, in January 1853, Faxton went to Albany to try to get the state legislature to pass a bill permitting him to create a state-franchised, incorporated express company. This prospect made Amexco officials particularly nervous; they feared that the bill would create a company with such powerful political support that it would be impossible to compete against. * Johnston Livingston wrote, "The passage of an act of incorporation of this kind, if the capital be large enough, must in time become [a] monopoly."

But Amexco prepared to battle the bill through the legislature. Board members asked E. B. Morgan, a U.S. congressman as well as a shareholder in Amexco, to use his influence. Fargo reported that "one or two friends have promised to keep us advised of [Faxton's] movements." He particularly wanted to engage the services of William Bogart, a Cayuga assemblyman in the pay of Corning's Utica & Schenectady Railroad "to keep an eye to this matter for us."

Meanwhile Butterfield worked on a different plan, what he called a tactic to help defeat "our opponents." But it seemed less that than a tactic to help himself, very likely what he envisioned all along. He offered a "recapitalization plan" that would raise Amexco's own capital to $500,000. Ostensibly, this would allow the company to compete with U.S. Express. But as a plan for express war, it had value only in that it might increase available cash through the sale of new stock. At the same time, the threat of an express war cast doubt on whether the company could even sell the new issue. Who would buy with a money-losing battle looming? The real heart of Butterfield's plan, however, was not a new stock issue, but a stock dividend and a generous payout of profits.

Before the board could act on the plan, Butterfield and his colleagues received another bit of good news: the shareholder committee had examined the books of Amexco and found cash and rising profits in both operating companies. The company had $40,000 in cash on

---

*An incorporated express could have sold shares more easily than Amexco, since incorporation limited the liability of shareholders. In an express war, an incorporated company almost certainly would have triumphed.

hand, almost enough to pay the *Atlantic* liabilities; and since, as the committee reported, profits were rising steadily, the rest could come out of a few months' income. Butterfield had satisfied one of his objectives and learned the financial condition of the western express. The report reduced and perhaps ended the threat of an express war. Now, Butterfield and Faxton had no incentive for war and only wanted to see that they and their friends captured the profits.

Faxton kept up the pressure. Though he had trouble getting his bill through the legislature, he and his men continued to push contracts and sell stock throughout the East and Midwest. But the urge for battle had waned on both sides, and soon Faxton and Amexco were talking merger, based largely on Butterfield's recapitalization plan. The Amexco board endorsed the basic plan in February but, on Butterfield's motion, tabled it so that it could be used in a deal with Faxton's group. By this time, however, the Amexco board no longer thought of war. Instead of preserving resources needed for a fight, the board voted a generous 15 percent cash dividend before settling with Faxton. John Butterfield appeared very much in command.

And what of Henry Wells in all this? In December, when the U.S. Express fight reached its peak, he again demonstrated his habit of vanishing at just the wrong time: he took a three-month leave of absence to go to California and look after the affairs of Wells, Fargo & Co. While his decision on the surface seemed a masterpiece of improper timing, the board, and particularly Butterfield, may have encouraged him to go. His departure could have been a discreet, temporary exit to allow Butterfield short-term control. With Wells gone, Butterfield not only orchestrated events, but he also ran the meetings, and at least temporarily, the board made every effort to accommodate his settlement strategy.

Official negotiations did not begin until March 2, the day after U.S. Express began operations. The new company produced a big, public spectacle, parading red wagons through the streets of New York City. But the company lasted only another week. Just as the talks were ending, Fargo wrote, "I am half sick and worn out with these difficult negociations [sic] and I ashure [sic] you very much confused." Fargo,

Butterfield, and Johnston Livingston negotiated for Amexco, and the deal they struck helped existing shareholders of Amexco most of all. U.S. Express investors agreed to buy the new subscription of 2,000 Amexco shares for $200,000. Half of that money became a dividend for original shareholders; the other half went into the Amexco treasury. Current shareholders also divided the entire remaining profits of the company (from both Wells, Butterfield and Livingston, Fargo) through May 1, 1853, by that time over $70,000. Then to top it off, the company declared a 25 percent stock dividend, giving every share-holder even more shares. The Faxton group also won three new seats on the board.* But Butterfield did best of all. He cleared over $22,000 in cash in four months—in an age when a company president could make as little as $1,250 a year. So in the end, a movement that started with the claim that all American Express could do was pay high dividends was bought off with even higher dividends. Butterfield may have had that in mind all along.

After this affair, Butterfield appeared to spend less energy on Amexco and more on other ventures. Though he remained vice president and a board member of American Express, in 1856 he became mayor of Utica, and in 1857, with the help of his friend President James Buchanan, he won for his company, the Butterfield Overland Mail Co., the guaranteed $650,000 per year government contract to carry the mail to California. He still made his presence felt at American Express board meetings, and he successfully led fights for high divi-dends. Including a 50 percent stock dividend in 1854, original share-holders received about 36 percent annually through 1859, on shares which probably cost them nothing to buy.†

The U.S. Express episode represented the last internal crisis for several years, but the threat of crisis persisted. Board members con-

---

*For unknown reasons, Faxton did not occupy one of the new board seats. If he still held his original shares, however, he made a substantial profit from the settlement.

†Dividends were not the only way board members cashed in on Amexco's profits. The directors also gave each other and their friends low interest loans.

tinued to be wary and distrustful of one another. In terms of feeling, nothing much had changed. Fargo and Wells still disliked Butterfield and referred to him as chief "Ossawatomie." Butterfield felt as hostile toward them.

Balance of power questions still influenced most decisions, and new ideas typically produced long, inconclusive wrangling. The board did agree to one new idea: the company took a large share in the Merchants Despatch, a fast-freight line, something between ordinary freight and express. But this step was safe since it benefited both operating units, Wells, Butterfield and Livingston, Fargo. New ideas came and either went nowhere or died. A steamship ticket agency, for example, though profitable, lasted only a couple months before John Butterfield killed it.

Although the internal company structure could not accommodate new business ventures, the company kept growing. The express had become a vital business in what was a rapidly growing country and rapidly growing economy. As long as Amexco had monopoly control of express traffic over its lines—now extended from New York throughout the Midwest and into Canada—profits rolled in. Within its territory in the East and Middle West, American Express expanded continuously. As new rail lines connected more towns and cities to the transportation system, American Express followed. Its service ran on 6,000 miles of railroad track by the end of the 1850s, and it had become a money machine immune to the squabbles of the directorate that ran it.

The U.S. Express settlement also ended for more than a decade the threat of a serious competitor to Amexco. During that time, only one other large independent express company, the Adams Express Company, operated in the eastern U.S. * But Adams agreed as early as 1851

---

*After Harnden's death, Vermont native Alvin Adams had acquired the express route from Boston to New York, which he developed into the second most extensive express system in the U.S.

on a territorial division with Amexco. The agreement gave Adams free rein along the eastern seaboard and throughout the South while American Express operated unopposed in other parts of the Northeast and in the Midwest. *

For the most part, the express companies cooperated. They not only fixed territory, they also fixed express rates, and Amexco and Adams even formed a jointly owned Union Express Company to handle business in cities where their territories met. To the extent that such collusion was known to the public, the companies faced criticism, but monopoly practices of this type were perfectly legal. Although the two companies experienced periods of tension and even outright conflict, they mostly worked in harmony, and together they would dominate the express business for over sixty years. †

While no competitors disrupted the smooth flow of profits in the 1850s, one other group could and did pose problems for the expresses—the railroads. When railroad men finally realized just how much money the express business produced, they began to regret that they had not absorbed the express for themselves. Because the expresses depended so much on rail transportation, they could not afford a great deal of conflict with the railroads. Yet the rails could not simply have taken over the express business unless all the railroad companies collaborated. If only one railroad decided to absorb the express service on its line, then the big express companies held an advantage: they covered a larger territory than any spanned by an individual railroad. They used several rail lines as well as steamships, and even stagecoaches when necessary. As a result, if a railroad tried to seize local express traffic, the express companies could usually either divert traffic away from that rail line or play the railroad off against its competitors.

---

*Adams competed for a time with Wells, Fargo & Co. in California. A panic in 1855 wiped out Adams's operation, giving Wells, Fargo control of the California express business.

†The companies also had interlocking directorates, which again was not illegal. Johnston Livingston, who invested in many express operations, was a board member of both Amexco and Adams for many years.

Because of the nature of express contracts, railroads benefited more by cooperating with express companies than with fellow railroaders. An express paid a railroad on the basis of gross receipts on whatever it shipped over the line, both materials destined for a customer on the line or for through shipments. Given the network of rails, ships, and roads by the 1850s, an express could usually divert all nonlocal traffic off of a hostile rail line. In other words, a package going from Chicago to Boston could go by way of New York or Albany or Philadelphia or even Montreal. Railroads in fact welcomed the chance to make money at the expense of competitors and so would encourage the diversion of express traffic. The railroads could have overcome the advantage of the expresses only by banding together. According to Charles Francis Adams, Jr.,* several railroad people once approached Commodore Vanderbilt, who by the 1850s had become one of the most powerful figures in the railroad business, to lead a revolt against the express companies, but he declined, saying he was too old. Adams felt that other rail men would have followed the commodore's lead. But no one else possessed the prestige and power to have kept the railroads together in such a venture, and the idea died.

For the most part, though, the express companies and the railroads collaborated, and they developed more than cursory interconnections. The express companies bribed top railroad officials with stock to assure cooperation and favorable contracts. American Express, for example, in the early 1860s passed out hundred-share blocks—very large amounts in those days—to officials of the New York Central, the railroad that had been created by Erastus Corning in 1853, uniting all of the short lines between Albany and Buffalo.

The railroads also went into debt to the express companies. American Express, especially, began using surplus funds to buy railroad stock and bonds. In fact, when a railroad—a capital-intensive business—needed money, it often went to an express company, which

---

*Charles Francis Adams, Jr. (1835–1915), brother of Henry Adams, was an economist, writer, and railroad investor.

provided capital in exchange for interest-paying bonds *and* favorable, long-term, exclusive express contracts. Before long, expressmen had joined directorates of key railroads; both Butterfield and Fargo, for instance, sat on the board of the New York Central for a time. By 1870, Charles Adams believed that the management of the rails was in danger of falling into the hands of the express fraternity. Actually, as he put it the charge was untrue, but express companies had acquired undeniable influence and leverage over America's railroads.

Inevitably, the railroads and the express companies sometimes feuded. In 1854, for example, the New York & Erie—the line from New York to Buffalo through southern New York—summarily kicked Amexco off its line. This presented the fragile Amexco board with a potentially difficult decision: should it try to fight a war against that railroad? But before board members had to answer that question, circumstances dictated an easy solution and indeed a policy: the company invented a "competitor."

The Erie ousted American Express after the railroad was taken over by steamship man Daniel Drew. Drew wanted to keep the express business under his control if not actually in his hands. As a result, the Erie's operating head, Homer Ramsdale, informed Henry Wells that the Erie had no intention of renewing its contract with American Express, that in fact it had already agreed to give the express business to someone else. The news not only rankled Wells, it also perplexed him. Who had the contract? Ramsdale did not say. Was it Adams? It would have been a clear violation of their territorial agreement, a declaration of express war. American Express officials immediately dispatched spies to find out who had the contract, but soon the culprit came to them. He was a friend, Danforth N. Barney, an upstate–New York banker who had sat briefly, in 1853, on Amexco's board. Wells felt better, especially when he heard what Barney had to say. The banker explained that the Erie had asked him to apply for express privileges. He did, and now he had the contract, but he added, "I did not wish to engage in opposition with the American Express and would like to talk it over with the Board of Directors."

In March 1854, Barney and his friends at American Express negotiated a secret agreement. Barney created a new express company which they decided to name after the company Amexco had recently managed to erase—the United States Express Company (the "States" for short),* probably because in the public mind there had briefly been a real competitor of that name. The new company was "capitalized" at $300,000, but the only capital came from American Express. Amexco not only "conceded" the Erie contract, it sold Barney several lines in the Midwest for $150,000, but the sales were as artificial as the concession. They fixed rates, but more significantly, the two companies agreed to pool all express earnings on a 60–40 basis, Amexco obtaining the larger share. Ostensibly this created competition, and railroaders like Drew, if they became disgruntled with one company could turn to the other. But W. G. Fargo explained how Amexco really saw it. "All things considered," he wrote to E. B. Morgan, "I regard it as a favorable agreement for both parties. It will satisfy the Rail Road Co., and place the Express business out west out of reach of further competition for some time to come. We shall be able to make better contracts with the Roads, get a good price for doing the business, and the public will be satisfied because there is *opposition*." As if to show just how difficult this competition was going to be, the board of American Express raised its capitalization to $750,000 with a 50 percent stock dividend.

The idea of the straw competitor had a definite appeal. The next year the company decided to do it again, creating the National Express for business running north of Albany into Canada. Although companies often create subsidiaries, the National Express was unusual. For the next forty years, only a handful of people knew that it actually was and always had been controlled by Amexco.

Amexco's business continued to generate huge amounts of cash. The company had enough extra money to begin buying real estate. In New York, it built a new, redbrick headquarters on the corner of Jay

---

*The States was also a joint-stock company. Fargo's brother-in-law E. P. Williams and James McKay sat on its first board of directors. Other Amexco directors, including Fargo and Johnston Livingston, became large shareholders in the new company.

and Hudson streets in New York, celebrating the completion in 1857 with a parade of American Express wagons through the city's streets.

But for all this good fortune, *because* of this good fortune, Amexco officials had a new concern. A problem loomed, and no one quite knew what to do about it. Amexco was coming up to its tenth birthday, and according to the terms of its original agreement, it had to dissolve—the last thing anyone wanted. The company could reconstitute itself in some form or other, but the danger lay in the loss of the name, American Express, which had gained widespread recognition as the entity connected with Wells, Butterfield & Co. and Livingston, Fargo & Co.

Lawyer McKay studied this issue carefully in early 1859 and determined that if Amexco sold everything else, it could keep the name. The board was delighted. The assets had little value without the name. So at the end of 1859, Amexco announced an "auction" of its assets. A friend of one of the directors came down from Schenectady, New York, "bought" the company for $600,000, handed it back to the directors, and then everyone went to lunch. The directors met again and recapitalized American Express at $1 million, consisting of 2,000 shares of stock at $500 per share, distributed to the original shareholders of the company. This time, while they retained the form of an unlimited-liability joint-stock association, they gave it a time limit of thirty years, and made the association easily renewable by a unanimous vote of the directors.

The same officers and board remained, and the power relationships stayed the same at the new American Express. Wells had not wanted to continue as president. He had been thrown from a carriage in 1859 and could barely walk a year later. But he still represented a compromise between the factions, and influential board members felt he had to stay in office to keep the peace. Johnston Livingston and Butterfield's son-in-law Alexander Holland, now the company's treasurer, met with Wells and finally convinced him that Amexco needed him to mediate between the factions.

They were correct; Wells played a key role in blocking power moves by both Butterfield and Fargo.* Over the previous ten years, Fargo had grown rich and successful; now in his early forties, he suddenly became very ambitious and contentious. He wanted to go to war with Commodore Vanderbilt's Hudson River Railroad over a contract, but his fellow board members said no. He wanted to go to war with Adams Express over territory, but Wells opposed and defeated the move at "the Expence [sic] of being thought a Coward" by his onetime employee. Then Fargo attempted to take control not just of American Express, but in one audacious play, control of Wells, Fargo and U.S. Express as well. Henry Wells thwarted him. As Wells later explained, he decided to "put a stopper to it."†

Though W. G. Fargo lost three times, his ambition had not diminished. Later that year he won something of a consolation prize—the mayoralty of Buffalo. He said he did not want the job, though he appeared to take it up with enthusiasm. At the same time, his main interest remained business. "The mayor-elect [himself] receives the congratulations of his friends . . . with great pleasure," he wrote to his fellow expressmen. "He begs to refer them to the enclosed time table for the purpose of showing how fast the express can run, as for the plunder, that comes hereafter, and is, of course, to be divided as heretofore."

Whether his reference to plunder was serious can only be guessed. But the Civil War had begun, and even he could not have imagined how much plunder there would be.

In 1875, *Harper's* explained how the express companies had profited from the Civil War:

---

*Butterfield had resumed his role as board obstructionist partly in retaliation for his loss of the Butterfield Overland Mail Co. to Wells, Fargo & Co. Early in 1860, Henry Wells, W. G. Fargo and their supporters had ousted Butterfield from control of the Overland.

†W. G.'s younger brother James Congdell [J.C.] had inadvertently revealed the plans to Wells, apparently thinking Wells already knew of it.

> *The source of [the express business's] present vast wealth was the immense business during the war of the rebellion. It has been truthfully said that no person unconnected with the company could imagine the magnitude of its transactions while the States were in conflict. On the nearest and most remote fields the agents of the express were always found, venturing often where a picket-guard would hardly venture, collecting money, letters, and trophies for the soldiers for transmission to "the loved ones at home." Many a thrilling episode might be related of the vicissitudes and perils endured by the expressmen in conveying these articles from the southern frontier to their destination in the North. Where the armies went they followed with the zeal and pertinacity of newspaper correspondents. . . . Around bivouac fires in the stillness of Southern forests they were found waiting for the homeward-bound messages that were hastily scribbled on the torn fly-leaves of prayer-books, or even on scraps of newspapers. Many a time in the thick of a battle a faint voice called them to the side of a fallen soldier, with blood oozing from a death-wound in his breast, and entreated them to remain a moment while he transferred to their care a letter or a locket addressed to a girl in the North. Many a time, too, they saw a noble fellow fall into an eternal sleep before he could finish his message. A romanticist might gather suggestions of countless pathetic incidents from the experience of expressmen who followed the armies during the rebellion. One of the most melancholy duties these brave fellows had to execute was the transmission of the bodies of the slaughtered to their relatives and friends. The delivery at the home office often occasioned heart-breaking scenes, as "somebody's darling," wrapped in a coarse shroud, was presented to the woman who had kissed his handsome face good-bye scarcely six months before.*

The board of American Express rewarded mainly itself for the "vicissitudes and perils" of the men in the field. The record of dividends paid from 1863 to 1866 vividly illustrated the value of this sometimes ghoulish commerce. During that period American Express never paid less than $115 per share per year (over 20 percent). The board also handed out to each of its members bonuses of $5,000, and upped all executive salaries; Fargo earned $7,500 per year from Amexco while still the mayor of Buffalo. And in 1866, the generous heads of the company handed out an 80 percent stock dividend plus $170 per share in cash, a total cash payment of nearly $3 million. Previous stock dividends had made each of these cash payouts especially generous to those who had owned stock before the war. For every share an individual held in 1860, he now had nine. (Capital had grown to $9 million.) Of course, the largest shareholders were the board members themselves. Admittedly, the war produced relatively high inflation, but the directors of American Express more than kept up.

The gentlemen of the express fraternity actually made far more than even the spectacular returns of American Express indicate. They also owned shares of U.S. Express and Wells, Fargo and in some cases Adams Express, and all of these companies paid huge returns. Not surprising, too, the old hostilities among the board members of American Express faded to the background after 1862. Butterfield, Fargo, and Wells still did not like each other, but they were too busy counting money to show it.

Company coffers bulged even after the rich payouts. Amexco had enough cash left over to increase its portfolio of rail stocks and bonds. During the war, Amexco also provided most of the funds for the building of the short-line Oil Creek Railroad, and by 1866, the company had accumulated several thousand shares of its principal carrier, the New York Central.

This incredible record had regrettably, from the expressmen's point of view, received attention. If express business made that much money, and people *knew* about it, they would inevitably want some of it, and soon after Lee and Grant met at Appomattox, others were plotting ways to get in on the express bonanza. The result of this would change the management structure of American Express, and finally end the rule by a contentious board of directors.

The first attack came from a company called the National Bankers

Express. Formed by another group of upstate New Yorkers with good connections and some capital, National Bankers made a public announcement of a new express in mid-1865. But it appeared that this group hoped primarily to be bought out by American Express, and it accepted an Amexco offer without much fuss early in 1866 without ever carrying a package. About the only change that came from this was the addition of banker E. B. Judson to the American Express board.

No sooner had American Express disposed of that problem when another group of upstate New Yorkers got together to form the Merchants Union Express (MUE). This time serious warfare broke out. The Merchants Union began with capital of $20 million, much of it real cash, and it launched an attack on two fronts—both business and public relations. The Merchants Union did not use a delicate approach. Through setup newspaper attacks and posted broadsides, the MUE attacked the old express companies (particularly American Express) for pursuing a policy that "the people are legitimate plunder," and at the same time, the MUE slashed rates, forcing Amexco to do the same. W. G. Fargo's brother, J. C., directed Amexco's side of the war from headquarters in New York. He fired off directives to employees and hortatory letters to colleagues and friends calling on the company "to retain the business of the American Express Company at whatever reduction in price may be necessary, on all routes where the 'Merchants Union' comes in competition with this Company."

The MUE and Amexco continued to fight each other for months, both in the marketplace and in the press. The MUE pressed the publicity war, and it was an extremely effective tactic for the newcomer. Amexco officials detested publicity even when it was good; bad press hurt all the more. The old express companies tried to fight back, forming a committee to "controll [sic] the public press upon Express matters."* But at best they achieved a standoff, which left them in

---

*D. N. Barney's brother, A.H., expected that Amexco could get its message into the press "through the influence of the [New York] Central, the Chicago & Northwestern R.R., and our various Ex. agents."

control of some news organs and the MUE, others. The *New York Daily Tribune*, for one, refused to fall in line with the old companies. It wrote: "The best informed and most comprehensive minds saw that unless [the old express companies] were checked they would absorb to themselves much of the wealth of the country. A full account of the magnitude of their operations, of the extent of their power and the oppressions they afflicted, would astonish."

The *Tribune* made many charges and claims, at least one of which was definitely false. The paper claimed the MUE remained profitable despite a 25–40 percent reduction in rates. In fact, losses mounted on both sides. American Express lost hundreds of thousands of dollars a month; the MUE's losses reached the millions. Yet neither side showed any willingness to compromise; MUE officials actually made a public declaration that they would never merge with Amexco. J. C. Fargo and Henry Wells sent a letter to shareholders saying that American Express intended to reduce the surplus of the company to zero and assess shareholders for more cash if necessary to keep fighting. Neither side considered merger from late 1866 through the first half of 1867.

But by June the losses became intolerable. The American Express board appointed Butterfield, Fargo, and Livingston to negotiate a "consolidation," not with MUE, but rather with Adams and the U.S. Express Co. Amexco officials had apparently decided to pursue a consolidation of the older companies to create an entity with unassailable resources capable of defeating the MUE. But consolidation talks foundered because of reluctance on the part of Amexco's ungrateful stepchild, the States, which opposed the grand merger scheme.

In August, the situation, from American Express's standpoint, worsened. A shareholder of both Amexco and the MUE filed suit against the American Express board, declaring it guilty of mismanagement of the assets of the company, and demanding that the company be placed in receivership and then liquidated. It was not hard to discern the hand of the Merchants Union in this; the shareholder who filed the suit owned five Amexco shares and 900 MUE shares.

American Express blocked the lawsuit but could not stop the losses or the attacks in the press, and some officials finally accepted the fact that they had failed to bring down the MUE. But if confrontation had failed, that left only one alternative—combination. Reportedly, Wells called for pursuing the battle by raising more money through an assessment of shareholders. W. G. Fargo counseled settlement, and the board agreed with him.

What came out of Fargo's initiative was more sweeping than anyone had expected. A Board of Control—a kind of industry-created regulatory body—was established, consisting of representatives from all four major eastern and midwestern express companies: Adams, American, U.S., and Merchants Union expresses. (Amexco's representative was J. C. Fargo.) The control board picked a fifth member to act as head, and the companies surrendered to the board the right to divide and regulate all express business east of the Rockies. "The child is born," reported one expressman. "He has four legs, four arms, and one head."

He was also not to live very long, but he served his purpose. Rates went back up, and everyone went back to making money. But American Express had lost a good deal of its territory to the MUE in the treaty drawn up by the Board of Control, and by the end of the following year, it offered a merger to the upstart. The MUE, despite its promise never to merge, quickly agreed. Together, they formed a company called the American Merchants Union Express Company, capitalized at $18 million, with a charter (still a joint-stock company) to last for thirty-five years. After the creation of the new company, the express Board of Control lost its reason for being and faded out of existence. Despite the merger, some hard feelings remained. "I almost regret the fusing of the Am. and the M.U.," said A. H. Barney, Danforth's brother and now the head of the States. "My feeling is to crush them out, my judgement, not so decided."

The resolution of the fight resembled the one that had led to the creation of Amexco in 1850, but internally it had a very different outcome. Unlike the earlier merger, this one did not lead to a weak executive; one voice had emerged as dominant.

That voice belonged to W. G. Fargo. Each of the merger partners— American Express and the MUE—won six seats on the new board of directors. The company remained a joint-stock association, and W. G. Fargo became president. Somewhere along the line, Henry Wells resigned or was forced out.* Company sources have said he left because of ill health and advancing years; he was sixty-three and had often stated that he wanted to leave office. But at the time he finally departed, he made no request, nor did the board issue a statement reluctantly accepting a resignation and thanking him for a job well done. Given that such letters and statements were almost inevitable, the more plausible explanation was offered by a banker from the Aurora area who knew Wells. The banker claimed that Wells was forced out because he had tried to assess the shareholders for more money to fight rather than pursue peace. Fargo, on the other hand, had taken the lead in settling the feud, and so would have been most acceptable to the old MUE people, as well as to Amexco's shareholders. He was elected as the candidate of compromise, as Wells himself once had been.

But unlike Wells, Fargo took decisive control and put an end to the domination of Amexco by a contentious board. W.G.'s competition had left the company. He had outlasted and outlived the other powers in American Express. Not only did Wells resign the presidency, but Butterfield, after suffering a stroke, first retired and then died in 1869, a year after the Amexco-MUE merger. W. G. Fargo moved quickly to solidify his grasp on power. He appointed his brother J.C. not only a director and assistant treasurer of the company, but also to the key position of general superintendent of all express operations, east and west. Another brother, Charles, became the head of what had been Livingston, Fargo, now simply the Western Department of American Merchants Union Express. (That was changed back to American Express a few years later.) In 1875, brother Charles also joined the board

---

*Wells stayed on the board of Amexco, but for the remainder of his life he concentrated on building his college in Aurora. Because of poor investments after the Civil War, he did not have enough money to complete his dream himself. But his friend, E. B. Morgan, provided the resources that led to the creation of Wells College. Wells died while traveling in Scotland in 1878.

of directors of the company. In fact, W.G. raised nepotism to executive policy, filling the ranks from top to bottom with his relatives. The family's domination of American Express would last almost half a century.

W.G. also made a key organizational change. He created an executive committee which became the true policy making body of the company. It consisted at first of W.G. and J. C. Fargo, Alexander Holland, Fargo crony Benjamin Cheney, and from the Merchants Union, the Civil War political figure Theodore M. Pomeroy. Only three members of the executive committee were needed for a quorum, and those three were usually Alex Holland, J.C. and W. G. Fargo, giving the brothers control of the company. So totally did the executive committee dominate that it soon decided everything from major policy issues to the salaries of employees in Dubuque. J.C. would eventually institute a policy that the executive committee would have to approve *all* expenditures of over $50. Records of the EC show it deciding on such trivial expenditures as pencils and wrapping paper for many decades thereafter.

The board of directors, formerly the seat of real executive power, became little more than a rubber stamp, which met at congenial gatherings to vote another dividend. Probably around 1868, the company began the practice of recording the minutes of board of directors' meetings in advance, a practice continued well into the twentieth century. Since W.G. and J.C. orchestrated those meetings, they did not need to wait for the actual event to record the results.

W.G. had achieved one dream—domination of American Express, and at the time, it was probably a positive step for the company. For once it had stable management. Instead of decision making by squabbling buccaneers, the company now was managed by people who could focus on running it. The old system had been inherently unstable, and either had to destroy the company or solidify it around one figure or one faction. That had occurred, and now American Express had a management that could make decisions and implement them. The price was one-family rule.

Actually, W.G. himself did not devote the bulk of his time to running the company. His success in taking over American Express had not blunted his ambitions, and he sought to become a great railroader. He succeeded for a time: he and a partner gained control of the New York Central, and he later joined financier Jay Cooke in developing the Northern Pacific Railroad. But he finally lost both companies, and after the collapse of the Northern Pacific project in 1872,* W.G. seemed to content himself with diversions: building a great mansion in Buffalo where he continued to live, despite the fact that Amexco kept its headquarters in New York City; throwing memorable parties; and dabbling in companies around Buffalo. But his life was not very happy. Six of his children died in childhood or soon after; only two survived him. In 1880, he took sick, dying in his great mansion in the spring of 1881.

Meanwhile W.G.'s younger brother J.C. ran American Express and did so very successfully. Although the company faced some lean years during a depression in the mid-1870s, it always paid a dividend—no less than 3 percent, usually 6 percent—and by the end of the decade, profits became extremely robust. While the records are incomplete (even in the minute books of the board and EC, statements are left blank), by 1879 profits regularly topped $100,000 per month, and a large surplus remained for the company to continue playing its role as major lender to the rails. Yet it earned its vast sums quietly, without challenge, out of the limelight. The railroad barons, more flamboyant, more visible, more directly threatening to the land, became the targets of nineteenth century populists and reformers, and J.C. and most other expressmen were content to let the rail men hold center stage. The express companies even kept their dividends artificially low so that they would not attract too much attention. Amexco once again slipped

---

*W.G. also lost control of Wells, Fargo & Co. in 1868 after its incompetent operating head, Louis McLane, lost a key express contract. Later, the company changed its name to Wells Fargo & Company, dropping the comma between the names. W. G. Fargo's other business ventures, however, did lead to one enduring tribute: a settlement was named after him and became the city of Fargo, North Dakota.

from the public eye. The press hardly ever ran stories about Amexco (and most of the other express companies) for the rest of the century.

Actually, it was remarkable that the companies achieved freedom from scrutiny. For in the last half of the century, the express became almost as much a part of people's lives as the railroads, the post office, and the telegraph. It was an essential service, and that fact made the secretive American Express Company an increasingly wealthy organization.

J.C., TC, M.F., and MO

3

In 1881, a few months after W. G. Fargo's death, Amexco's board elected his brother James Congdell [J.C.] president; the succession never was in doubt. J.C. ruled Amexco for the next thirty-three years, but the decisions he made affected its destiny for many decades thereafter. Not only did Amexco grow vastly richer under his autocratic regime, but it expanded beyond the borders of the U.S. and the confines of the express business itself. Both inadvertently and by design, J.C. set in motion a process that eventually turned Amexco into a financial institution. He did it with two key decisions—the first, to devise a money-order system; and the second, to create the American Express Travelers Cheque.

When J.C. took over, he found himself in the middle of a battle. But this was different from the ones the company had faced in the 1850s. He and the other major express companies were fighting an opponent that could not be crushed, merged with, or bought off—the U.S. Post Office Department. The Post Office wanted to take the package and money-carrying business for itself, and postmasters general beginning in the 1860s campaigned for the next half a century to persuade the U.S. Congress to abolish the express. Failing that, they wanted permission to compete with it in all lines of business. Congress refused to do either, but did allow the Post Office gradual encroachments into the express business. For example, when Congress voted to create third-class mail, it broke the express monopoly on the transport of magazines and newspapers. But more damaging was the authorization by Congress in 1864 of the postal money order. The money order ended another express monopoly, one in the transmission of small sums of money.

The express companies of course had carried cash from the very beginning, and while they sought principally the business of the banks, they also transported small amounts for individuals. With the rapid expansion of the American frontier and of American commerce, more people had more reason to send money. Personal checking accounts existed only for the wealthy; consequently, many cash transactions traveled via the express. Customers put their money into an envelope, sewed the envelope shut, and sealed it with wax. Since the express provided rapid transport and guaranteed delivery, the system offered speed and safety. Although it was a bit cumbersome, it worked successfully, and the express companies dominated the business for small sums through the Civil War. But afterward the postal money order, simply a kind of check, grabbed an ever-increasing share of the business.

Though the postal money order presented a challenge to the expresses, initially the Post Office Department had not intended it as one. Postal officials created the money order to keep postmen from stealing cash out of letters. At a cost of 10 cents for a $10 order, it was cheap enough to break the express monopoly. Despite express industry fulminations that money orders represented "a prostitution of the mails to illegitimate purposes," the public bought them. In 1880, the Post Office Department sold $100 million worth from 5,491 branches.

The express companies tried to fight the Post Office on all fronts. In the 1870s they met to plan joint action "to meet the serious opposition of the mails." They agreed on an industry-lobbying effort, and they dropped rates on magazines and newspapers to compete with third-class mail. They also fought the postal money order, lowering rates on their money packages. But sales of post office money orders continued to rise anyway.

By adopting its own money order, Amexco decided to take on the Post Office at its own game with a similar product that was better than the original. This was a departure from the industry's usual tactics. Amexco took this step on its own, although express companies usually dealt with the government jointly, in order to bring more resources and more influence to bear than any one company could muster. Also, the expresses had previously used only two methods in fighting the government: they influenced legislation when they could, or lowered prices on competing services. Neither the industry nor any individual express company had tried developing a whole new weapon.

The idea of a money order was not in itself new at American Express. The company could have gotten the jump on the Post Office if it had started a money order system when the idea was first raised at a board meeting in 1857. At the time, board factionalism ruled out the adoption of new products, and a money order became possible only after W.G. took over. Yet when the idea resurfaced in 1868, W.G. opposed it for unspecified reasons. By 1877, he appeared more receptive to a money-order system, but only if it were adopted by the entire express industry. Amexco could not persuade the other companies of the need for a money order, however, and neither W.G. nor J.C. appeared interested in a system belonging to Amexco alone.

J.C. might never have changed his mind but for the persistence of one individual—Marcellus Fleming Berry. Berry had joined Amexco in 1866 as a messenger, and he later moved up to a clerkship in the company's Boston office. In 1880, J.C. appointed him traffic manager at the company's New York headquarters, now located in a nondescript building at 65 Broadway. Berry was a small man, with a cheeky, round face, a thick mustache, and a mostly bald head that he kept covered with a straw boater even at the office. Berry possessed an active business imagination that set him apart from others in the company. And he had something else that allowed him to continue to pursue his ideas, a streak of optimism that made him believe he would get his way in the end.

He needed that attitude to deal with J. C. Fargo. The slightly built, ruddy-cheeked J.C. was not an easy man to persuade. He was an absolute autocrat, a tyrant to many, who assumed for himself more power even than his brother had exercised. J.C., who held both executive and operational authority, tried to control every detail of the company's business, and he did not welcome suggestions from his subordinates. When they approached him, he looked down at them over glasses perched at the end of his nose, and fixed them with a cold, humorless stare. Usually, he greeted new ideas with a sharp, sometimes angry, "No!"—a reaction few were willing to face a second or third time. But if a man could ignore the hostility and rejection and keep trying, he might get what he wanted. J.C. could say no and mean never, but he could also be persuaded.

J.C.'s hostility never stopped Berry. Younger executives recalled that when J.C. snapped at him, Berry would mutter to himself and walk away. Later he would plop down at his desk, a dark look on his face. But after a moment's reflection, his expression would change, and he would announce that, next time, everything would work out all right. Such a rosy outlook kept him pursuing J.C. for months on the money order. Rejection followed rejection. He muttered to himself, but he continued pursuing J.C. until the time was right, and there was no better time than just after J.C. took over. Newly promoted executives have always been especially susceptible to new ideas, and J.C. was no exception.* In 1881, he told Berry to go ahead and create a money-order system for American Express.

Berry believed that he could create a better money order than the one offered by the Post Office. Since the postal order required literacy in English, it presented particular difficulties for the immigrant pop-

---

*In the 1880s, J.C. introduced other innovations, including an "all-express" train and an "Order and Commissions" business. In the latter, Amexco accepted orders for goods, which it purchased at the most favorable price its agents could find, charging the customer a commission and an express charge for delivery.

ulation. Immigrants were arriving in the greatest wave in U.S. history, and the postal money order was the right idea for them, but the system defeated them. Berry claimed that immigrants as well as "stupid persons, or persons who cannot read or write [have] to blunder about [a post office] until some outsider takes pity on them and writes out their application for them."

The postal order presented other complications. To prevent people from buying an order for one amount and forging a higher amount in its place, a postal order could only be cashed at a designated post office, which was notified by a separate advice that an order had been issued. The postal system proved equally troublesome to those wanting refunds on lost orders; the process of fighting red tape could take weeks. But despite its lack of flexibility, the postal money order sold well. That suggested to Berry how successful a more efficient money order system could be.

J.C., too, feared forgery, and he conditioned his acceptance of an express money order on a solution to that problem. But Berry already had solved it. His method, which he later patented, was simple. On the left side of the money order (the MO in company shorthand), he placed nine columns of figures which he called a "protection margin." The figures depicted all 5-cent denominations from $1 to $10, the maximum amount of the first express money orders. When a customer purchased an order, the express clerk wrote the name of the payee and the amount on two stubs, and gave one to the buyer and kept the other for company records. But instead of writing the amount on the MO itself, he cut the protective margin to the designated sum. The customer could not raise the value of the order because the figures simply were no longer there. While the American Express money order changed to some extent over the years, the company retained Berry's basic concept well into the twentieth century.*

---

*Later in the 1880s, when Amexco raised the limit on MOs from $10 to $50, it modified Berry's system. The agent could no longer cut the margin to the exact amount of an order, but only to a round number which served as a limit. The protective margins read, "Good for an amount up to $10, $20, $30 [etc.]" The agent cut the margin to fix an upper limit, and then wrote the exact amount on the order itself.

American Express did not expect to make money at first, and Berry said it was "more a means of advertising our general business than . . . the expectation of making a profit." The company took a sales charge of 5 cents on orders of $5 or less, and 8 cents (2 cents lower than the Post Office) on orders from $5 to $10. If Amexco sold millions of orders, it could earn significant sales charges. But that seemed unlikely. The company had over 4,000 offices, all of which sold orders, but at first only 457 could cash them. Also, the company had offices only in nineteen states; what if someone wanted to send an order into territory controlled by Adams Express? Amexco had not made provisions for cashing orders outside its own lines.

Berry explained his system to the executive committee in January 1882, and J.C. gave it his support; three months later, the first orders reached the market. From the start, the company as a whole made a concerted effort to make the MO work. The EC authorized $5,000 for an advertising campaign, a huge amount in those days, particularly for a company that had little need to advertise its monopoly express service. Soon, ads began appearing in newspapers and magazines throughout Amexco's territory proclaiming Berry's creation to be "The Cheapest, Safest and Most Convenient Money Order System Ever Adopted." Perhaps more importantly, before the end of the first year of the MO, other express companies announced a willingness to cash Amexco's orders, as well as an intention to get into the money order business themselves.* (American Express would honor their paper too.) But, because it was first, Amexco always dominated the express money order business; only the Post Office money order offered significant competition.

The American Express money order caught on much more quickly than Berry expected. In the first month, the company sold 11,959 orders, totaling $51,835.83, with commissions for the company of $559.03. By the end of that first year Amexco had sold 240,000 more of them. And that growth continued; May 1883 saw a 100 percent

---

*Adams did not agree to accept Amexco's MO until the following year.

increase in sales over May 1882. Sales continued to rise and volume grew, especially after 1885, when the company raised the maximum amount of a money order from $10 to $50. By the end of the century Amexco would be selling 3.5 million MOs a year. Seeing that MOs were fast becoming big business, J.C. wasted little time putting the operation into family hands; though Berry had created the business, J.C. called in his brother Mortimer to manage the new Money Order Department, and Berry returned to the traffic desk.

While Amexco made some profit from the sales charges on MOs, company officials soon discovered another, ultimately more important, profit opportunity—uncashed money orders. Customers paid for an order in cash, in full, on a no-interest basis, and the money stayed in Amexco's hands until the order was cashed. This amount fluctuated, of course, but the company realized that it always had an average positive balance of money waiting for redemption. In fact, as the volume of money order sales grew, so did the average outstanding balance. To be sure, this balance ultimately represented company liabilities, but as long as an average existed and could be tracked, the company could invest the money from the uncashed MO fund, the "float," as it came to be called. Actually, it took Amexco officials a few years to begin to realize that they had a substantial and growing investment opportunity, and not until 1891 did the executive committee begin to concern itself with the size of the float and how float funds were invested. But by that time, American Express had an average outstanding balance totaling hundreds of thousands of dollars. The fund was producing an investment income that, although only a small percentage of Amexco's overall earnings, was growing steadily.

Three years after its inauguration, the MO unexpectedly created a new opportunity, which propelled the company into a financial business abroad. As Berry had hoped, the new immigrant population took to the Amexco MO. But Berry had expected immigrants to use orders as a convenient way to pay their bills in the U.S. Instead they were sending them abroad. In Europe, however, Amexco had no financial standing, and money orders sent abroad in the early 1880s could not be cashed.

When Mortimer Fargo, the head of the money-order department, discovered what immigrants were doing, he regarded it as an opportunity. He wrote to his brother J.C., enthusiastically proposing that Amexco plunge ahead with a campaign to sell MOs for use abroad. However, he did not understand the problems and implications. Berry had investigated the question of issuing foreign orders and knew the problems they posed, but Mortimer did not check the records or talk to the MO's creator.

J.C. read his brother's letter on foreign MOs and passed it on to Berry, who blasted Mortimer for his lack of preparation. "It will be a grand fizzle if agents are given to understand that our present forms can be issued payable abroad," he wrote. Berry noted his own investigation and told the brothers Fargo that, if they wanted to have the money order payable in Europe, they would have to make arrangements with foreign banks first.

Mortimer took Berry's advice and went out and established the necessary banking link. On June 15, 1886, Amexco announced that Kidder, Peabody & Co. of the U.S., as representative for Baring Brothers of London, had arranged "for the payment of this Company's Money Orders in Europe." Foreign orders became cashable in thirty-nine locations in ten countries. As the foreign money order business grew, so too did the number of Amexco's foreign banking correspondents, soon reaching the hundreds.*

The need to service the money order abroad was perhaps as important a development as the creation of the money order itself. Purely by chance, American Express suddenly had a network of correspondent banking relationships throughout Europe. This network opened new

---

*Amexco developed especially large correspondent networks in Ireland and Italy because of the number of recent immigrants to the U.S. from the two nations. By the end of the 1880s, Amexco transacted millions of dollars of foreign MOs per month in both countries.

business relationships and made possible Amexco's development as an international financial organization.

In subsequent years, the company continued to move in that direction. Soon, Amexco published circulars giving the exact dollar equivalents of six European currencies, so customers could know how much money their relations back home would be receiving. And in 1891, American Express introduced the Series K money orders, the company's first MOs specifically intended for foreign remittances.* By this time, the company's foreign financial business ran into the millions of dollars per week. To service and guarantee this growing operation, American Express started to put thousands of dollars in cash and securities on deposit in the banks of Europe.

The MO and the foreign remittance MO were launched and doing well, growing year by year. But at just this time, another development led to the most significant, and curious, decision in the company's history.

J. C. Fargo was about to go on a trip abroad.

No other event in company history has quite the legendary status, or quite the importance, of J. C. Fargo's trip to Europe. Yet no one ever recorded very much about it, not even the time it occurred. Some have said it took place in the summer of 1890, but the trip probably came earlier, perhaps as early as 1888. That year the board granted J.C. an indefinite leave of absence to take a vacation in Europe. No one has ever revealed exactly what happened on the trip. Several people, none of whom actually witnessed the events, have described them broadly, usually with fictional embellishments. Nevertheless, the general outline of the tale is the same.

J.C.'s story involved his money. He went to Europe with a letter of credit from a leading American bank. Letters of credit had existed since the Renaissance and were the accepted way for a traveler to finance his

---

*Series K orders contained a space for the agent to write the foreign exchange equivalent of the dollar value.

way abroad. A letter represented a certain amount of cash on deposit at a bank in the U.S. that the user could draw on at correspondent banks overseas. Every time a holder presented his letter to withdraw cash, the bank authorities would compare his signature to a sample on an advice in their files, and they would note on the letter the amount the holder drew down. The letter provided safety for the traveler; no one else could cash it, and he or she could get reimbursed if the letter were lost. The signature system also afforded a measure of safety to the banks.

However, for travelers, a letter of credit often caused considerable delay and trouble. Magazines of the era reported it could take "a half hour" or longer to get cash from a letter of credit. Some banks, to ascertain the validity of a signature, would have everyone "from the charwoman up" scrutinize it.

Letters of credit proved inconvenient to travelers in other ways. Only specific correspondent banks could cash them; in major cities, travelers could get money in only one or two places, and they could not use their letters at all in small towns. Since letters of credit were denominated in dollars (or sometimes British pounds), they also provided no guarantee on exchange rates, which bank officials could determine arbitrarily at the moment the traveler drew his funds. Travelers faced additional exchange problems if they withdrew large amounts of cash at one time and then had to exchange and re-exchange currency every time they crossed a frontier.

J.C. apparently experienced both inconvenience and exchange problems, even though, as the company noted later, he was the president of a major American company. Banks kept J.C. waiting a long time for his cash. As a result, J.C. at the very least went into what one company executive termed a "slow boil." J.C. was also a virtuoso of the towering rage. He had a volatile and easily jostled temper that could flare up even in correspondence. On occasion, he would scrawl on the top of letters: "Tell this person to go to hell!" But however he displayed his anger to the Europeans, he stewed about the events for weeks afterward, and when he came back to America, he had decided that something should be done.

Upon his return to 65 Broadway, he summoned M. F. Berry. "I had a lot of trouble cashing my letters of credit," he reputedly said. "The moment I got off the beaten path they were no more use to me than so much wet wrapping paper. If the president of American Express has that sort of trouble, just think what ordinary travelers face. Something has got to be done about it."

J.C. definitely did speak to Berry, though this monologue, quoted frequently by the company, is largely fictitious, and his expression of concern for the ordinary traveler dubious, or at least misleading. J.C. was a man of deep irrational prejudices. He detested, for example, young male employees ("hoodlums as a rule being a better name for them"), and women employees (he decreed the company would close its doors before hiring any). And he also hated tourists, whom he called, among other things, "rabble" and "loafers." If he expressed any concern for the "ordinary" traveler in his charge to Berry, he did so only because at the time most travelers were not ordinary people. In 1890, European travel still remained a pleasure of the wealthy; the more ordinary travelers became, the more J.C. detested them.

In any event, J.C.'s motivation to do "something" probably stemmed less from what others faced than from his own inconvenience, from the fact that bankers did not accord proper respect to the president of American Express—the largest company in an industry he modestly termed "aside from the railroads . . . the greatest Mercantile Institution in America. . . ." If J.C. was not accorded the treatment usually given to a prominent person, it was partly his own fault. On the one hand, he expected to get attention as the leader of a great company, but at the same time, he did everything he could to keep his company and himself out of the public eye. He just expected people, including Europeans, to *know* his importance and treat him accordingly, but they did not. And so J.C., an intensely proud man, decided to do something, to get the better of the people who had made him cool his heels like a common man.

Whatever words J.C. had used, he gave Berry the task of devising a way to make it easier for Americans to carry money abroad. Berry pondered the problem for months and months. He wanted to create an instrument with the safety of a letter of credit and the convenience of cash, and could not readily come up with an answer. But gradually he began to develop an idea, and toward the end of 1890, he finished his work. He called his new invention the American Express "Travelers Cheque," using the British spelling of "check." The travelers cheque, a device of remarkable ingenuity, was the *only* original product idea ever created at American Express.

Berry's invention, known within the company as the T/C or TC, resembled the old letter of credit in one sense. Its security rested on the double signature: the first fixed in the upper, left-hand corner at the time of purchase, the second written in the lower left when it was cashed. If the signatures did not match, the cheque would be considered a forgery.

But in two other respects, the TC was new and innovative. First, cheques came in set small amounts: $10, $20, $50, or $100. Berry realized that tourists spend small amounts in many places. By carrying books of TCs, tourists could pay for each item individually and would not be stuck with lots of Italian lire or French francs they did not need. Also, Berry eliminated foreign exchange problems. He placed in a band across the center of the cheque its value in all major European currencies. Berry based the amounts on the average rates of exchange over a period of two years, and American Express *guaranteed* that its cheques were convertible to the sums as printed. Because it was an age of stable rates of exchange, the company could take the risk implicit in guaranteed conversion rates. Obviously, though, it became a key selling point since it eliminated the opportunity for bankers and exchange dealers to take huge premiums from unsuspecting American tourists.

The chief executive personally led the drive to make the TC a working business. First, he launched a major effort to sign up establishments in Europe to accept the TC. Amexco started its TC drive with European banks in March 1891 and won widespread acceptance. Because of the MO, dozens of European banks already had correspondent relationships with the company and they were quite willing to accept the TC as well. In a real sense, the MO launched the TC.*

But Amexco wanted and needed a far broader acceptance in Europe than it had for the money order. J.C. wanted an instrument people could use, not only in dozens of banks, but in hundreds of banks, hotels, and shops in every town tourists visited. Its breadth of coverage had to be one of its features. Soliciting entirely through the mail, J.C. and his men pushed hard. J.C. offered commissions to those who sold and/or cashed travelers cheques, and he guaranteed that, if merchants or banking establishments took a loss on a currency exchange, Amexco would reimburse them. More importantly, though, he guaranteed practically without condition to pay cheques. Amexco promised "to assume all risks and responsibilities in payment . . . of fraudulent or forged cheques—you [cashing establishments] to exercise due vigilance and care in payment . . ." And although J.C. told Europeans that, because of money order sales, Amexco had "an established credit rating probably sufficiently good" to leave no questions about its ability to pay, he put additional funds on deposit in major European banks to allay fears that cheques might not be covered.

Amexco's blanket guarantees actually posed a grave danger to the company's existence. American Express suddenly became extremely vulnerable to counterfeit and fraud throughout the world. Although Amexco possessed considerable resources, those resources were limited; for decades afterward, executives would report that they lay awake nights recognizing that a good counterfeiter could bankrupt the company. By offering such a sweeping guarantee, however, Amexco made the TC not just another money order, but rather a kind of universal international currency.

Amexco came to recognize another important point, too: the TC depended on perception as much as reality. In order for the device to work, the company would have to maintain both the appearance and reality of financial solidity. If it promised to pay off frauds, it had to pay

---

*Amexco received some rejections. Pfister & Co., a German bank, for example, refused to accept either the TC or the MO.

off. If it promised to reimburse customers for lost cheques (another of its selling points for users), it had to do so quickly and willingly. If Amexco appeared unwilling or unable to pay, the TC could lose its market instantly.

J.C. continued to solicit the banks of Europe, and beginning in April, Continental hotels as well. With hotels, J.C. and his staff faced a more difficult selling job than they had with the banks, because Amexco had no previous relationship with European hotels, and hotels did not routinely cash financial instruments. What Amexco was asking was unique. Nevertheless, J.C. and his men tried to convince hundreds of hotels across the Continent to cash TCs. In a form letter complete with cheque sample, Amexco promised hotel owners optimistically, that "a very large proportion of Americans traveling in Europe hereafter, will carry with them such cheques instead of other forms of credit." The letter went on to trumpet the size and creditworthiness of the company, to explain how the cheque worked, and to guarantee to merchants and hoteliers that Amexco would pay all cheques without discounting or inconvenience. The letter finally asked permission to list the respondent among the "prominent" hotels accepting the TC.

The campaign to sell the TC made steady progress. By 1892, Amexco published a brochure listing fourteen pages of banks, hotels, and tourist offices (including the worldwide network of Thomas Cook & Son) that had all agreed to accept American Express Travelers Cheques. A traveler could cash the TC all across Europe and into North Africa, Asia Minor, India, Burma, Bermuda, Australia, and New Zealand. Even with this initial success, J.C.'s efforts did not diminish, and he kept company agents actively pursuing more establishments for the TC.

Although Berry had invented the TC for European travel, it did not take Amexco long to recognize its potential for domestic travel as well. In August 1891, B. F. Green, assistant manager for money orders in the eastern region (called the Eastern Department), wrote in a circular letter, "The use of Cheques payable in the United States and Canada will probably be a convenience to Commercial Travelers, persons making long journeys, Excursionists, [et al.]" He advised agents throughout the East to keep hotel managers "fully informed" and to give all rail and ship ticket offices signs and brochures advertising the advantages of the TC.

Green's letter also showed that Amexco had decided to expand its domestic sales force. Fargo and Berry had initially planned to sell TCs through the now 6,000 company offices in the U.S. as well as correspondents abroad, but Green exhorted company employees "to get every Bank, Banker, Broker" to act as branch agents to sell and cash cheques on a commission basis. In Chicago, headquarters of the Western Department, top company officials personally signed up major banks as branch agents for the TC.

While Amexco successfully recruited establishments to cash TCs, much to the chagrin of officials, the company found it could not sell them. Unlike the money order, which sold initially at the rate of almost 2,000 per week, Amexco sold only 248 cheques—$9,120—in all of 1891. Worse, travelers who carried TCs had trouble getting them cashed. J.C. and his son William Congdell (W.C.) traveled to Paris in the summer of 1891, and they took their cheques to the Credit Lyonnais. As J.C.'s assistant Francis F. Flagg later wrote, "They were subjected to an unusual delay at the several times when they went to the bank for this purpose—Mr. W'm C. Fargo at one time consuming over two hours to obtain his funds—seemingly due to a lack of information on the part of the Tellers." Bank director J. Edmond Moret sent his regrets and promised it would not happen again. But it was not an auspicious beginning, and if such problems persisted, they would undermine the raison d'être for the TC.

Within a year, though, the problems cleared up, and the TC began to pay off. Fortunately, Amexco had created the TC just as the American middle class began to participate in what had been largely an upper-class activity. Americans possessed greater wealth and a growing awareness of European culture, and that in turn led to a travel boom.*

---

*Technology aided the growth of travel because travelers needed less time to make a transatlantic journey. New twin-screw steamships cut the time of a voyage to little more than a week.

The company sold more than 21,000 TCs, worth $483,490, in 1892, and by 1896, that volume had more than quadrupled.*

As with the money order, buyers paid a small sales charge to purchase TCs, but the real profit came from the float. Indeed, the TC floated a lot more efficiently and profitably than the money order. While most money orders were cashed in a couple of days, TC use followed a different pattern: typically, a traveler bought a book of TCs, stowed them in a stateroom for a week while he or she sailed to Europe, then cashed them as needed, one or two at a time over the course of weeks, sometimes months. Sometimes buyers held onto cheques for another trip months or years later.† Because travel followed seasonal patterns, the company discovered a predictable short-term float, as well as one based on long-term balances of cheques outstanding. As TC sales grew, so did the two floats and the income they provided.

The TC owed a great deal to chance. Its inspiration was accidental; its success depended on a travel boom no one had foreseen. Indeed, its creation defied business judgment and logic. Unlike the money order, it did not tie neatly into the express business. On J. C. Fargo's whim, Amexco rushed it to market, though no one in the company had the slightest indication that the public would buy the new product. But the TC was wildly successful nonetheless.

At the same time, the TC was an example of creative thinking and determined marketing. Without Berry's inventive mind and J.C.'s tenacious salesmanship, Amexco would not have had a product to exploit the new demand. The TC also owed much to the success of the MO and the growth of Amexco as a financial organization; because of the MO, Amexco's financial paper had instant credibility.

---

*Later, other express companies offered TCs, but Amexco's TC, even more than its MO, dominated the market.

†The TC was good no matter when it was used. Some company officials wanted to put a time limit on each cheque to remove liabilities from the books. But that idea never gained much support. Had Amexco taken that step, it unquestionably would have weakened the TC and left it something less than universal currency. Instead, Amexco's TC gained a reputation worldwide as "blue paper money."

But the TC had another unintended consequence. Even more than the money order, the TC pushed American Express to become an international company. And overseas, because of the TC, Amexco underwent a transformation in its public image and in its corporate identity, alterations J.C. unsuccessfully resisted. By accident, he set in motion a process which he could not stop; J.C. started American Express on a path of fundamental change.

CHICAGO AND PARIS

4

In the 1890s J. C. Fargo decided to send Amexco to Europe. But his decision suddenly embroiled the company in a conflict over a major policy issue: what should Amexco do and be abroad? Should it emphasize its express operations or its new business, the TC? Should it stick to a familiar enterprise and a familiar image, or should it pursue a different opportunity and adopt a new identity? This conflict lasted more than a decade and pitted J.C. against his own man in Europe, William Swift Dalliba. Fortunately for the company, it was a battle that J.C. lost.

On the surface, it seemed improbable that any vision of American Express other than J.C.'s could have mattered at all. Although he could be persuaded to develop something like the money order, J.C. did not intentionally relinquish his authority to decide policy, much less the identity of the company. Indeed, he never gave up his authority, and he made clear over and over again that he wanted Amexco to be an express company in Europe as it was in America; Dalliba simply did not obey him.

The conflict between J. C. Fargo and William Swift Dalliba took on especially striking dimensions because of Dalliba's resourcefulness in fighting his autocratic leader. But his insubordination was actually not so surprising. Although Amexco appeared to be a most rigidly controlled and centralized company, in reality it was not. Internally, the company had split and had two different systems operating simultaneously in two different places. In New York and the rest of the eastern U.S.—Amexco's Eastern Department—J.C.'s rule and rules prevailed. His men operated on the premise that they could try to persuade J.C., but if they could not, they had to do his bidding. In the Western Department, centered in Chicago, men followed a wholly different path. They operated by what might be called the Chicago Rule. It said: J. C. Fargo could be persuaded, and if he could not be persuaded, he could be deceived.

The system in New York stressed J.C.'s authority and was symbolized by the rule book he ordered kept at everyone's side, a large book that covered everything from the technical aspects of the business to employee conduct. The Chicago approach emphasized the individual and his ability to come up with creative solutions to problems. As one western expressman put it, J.C.'s rule book was for "weak men to follow, and strong men to break." The rule book versus the individual. The autocratic leader versus the entrepreneur. Not just different philosophies, but diametrically opposite ones.

The midwesterners were buffered from J.C. in a number of ways. First, paradoxically, J.C.'s personality and imperial style protected midwestern expressmen. J.C. never noticed that his men were getting around him, because it would not have occurred to him that they would try. Of course, they made efforts to cover their tracks. Yet, when he caught someone breaking a rule, which he did once in a while, he always treated it as an aberration. He lectured the wayward employee like a child, telling him not to misbehave again.

97

The midwesterners also benefited from distance: J.C. could not keep watch on all matters in Des Moines, St. Louis, Buffalo, or Chicago from his office at 65 Broadway in New York City. But perhaps most importantly, J.C. must have believed the West lay as completely under his control as the East. Amexco's western express had been a Fargo domain since 1843, and J.C.'s brother Charles still ran it. But Charles, if he did not encourage the individualistic system of the West, at least closed his eyes to it. He had to know that his men routinely flouted the rules, since some of Amexco's most insubordinate entrepreneurs worked directly under him.

Not much is known of Charles. Called a man of "restless energy," Charles followed a step behind his brother throughout his life. J. C. served as agent in Detroit, and when he left it for Chicago, Charles went to Detroit; when J.C. came to New York, Charles moved to Chicago. No one ever recorded what Charles thought of his brother, or even whether they got along. Their business correspondence totally lacked fraternal feeling: they addressed each other as "Sir," and they maintained that formal tone throughout every one of their business letters. However, Charles clearly allowed his men to act contrary to the policies of his brother, and J.C. never knew it. In the process, Charles added the most significant layer of protection for his men against J.C.

In later years, western expressmen told numerous stories of how they employed the Chicago Rule. But perhaps the tale that best exemplifies the philosophy in the West concerned the firing of Howard K. Brooks. The story began in 1882, a year after J.C. became chief executive. The company had just inaugurated the money order, and the Milwaukee office had hired Brooks as a clerk for the new department. Brooks, an imaginative young man, on his own initiative devised a scheme to advertise the MO. He painted on some bed sheets: "To Send Money Away, American Express Money Orders, Safe, Cheap and Convenient." Then he sewed two sheets together and draped them over the backs of the horses that pulled American Express delivery wagons.

The campaign won local attention for Amexco's money order, and a friend of the young clerk thought he would do Brooks a favor. He photographed the horses clad in their ad sheets and sent the picture off to J. C. Fargo. J.C. took one look at the picture and dispatched a wire to Brooks's superior, Albert Antisdel, superintendent of the Wisconsin Division: "Undignified and unworthy of our company. . . . I understand the perpetrator of this is a young man named Brooks. Discharge him immediately." Antisdel read the message and decided to investigate the matter. He discovered that Brooks's office had sold more money orders than any other in the Western Department. Instead of firing the young man, Antisdel transferred him to his own staff and raised his salary. Next, Antisdel assigned Brooks the job of developing other advertising schemes, which Brooks worked on for many years thereafter. All of these ideas, the two western expressmen admitted later, they "carefully concealed from the knowledge of J. C. Fargo." Their deception of the chief executive went on long after Antisdel and Brooks had moved from the Wisconsin office to Chicago where Antisdel became number two for the entire Western Department behind Charles Fargo. (Antisdel later succeeded Charles.) In other words, Antisdel disobeyed J.C. and then deceived him for decades, with Charles Fargo's acquiescence.

In the 1890s, American Express decided to go to Europe, and J.C. chose William Swift Dalliba, a man from the Western Department, to take the company abroad. Dalliba possessed an entrepreneurial spirit, a creative turn of mind, and a willingness to impose his vision no matter what J.C. Fargo told him to do. If Chicago was too far away for J.C. to control, Europe was a lot farther.

Initially, company officials feared a European venture because they recalled a failed attempt in 1846 by Henry Wells to establish offices abroad. But the company could never entirely ignore Europe. At the very least, it had to react to circumstances. Occasionally, in the normal course of business, the company (or the fast-freight line, Merchants Despatch, in which Amexco still held a large stake) carried packages and freight coming through the port of New York to points in the interior of the U.S.

This traffic picked up after the Civil War as America grew wealthier and became more involved with international commerce. Also, Americans began to travel Europe in greater numbers. In 1867, although only the wealthy and professional classes could afford a transatlantic vacation, Mark Twain already found the Continent full of touring Yanks, and they began shipping packages and artworks home via express. Indeed, traffic became so extensive by 1874 that Amexco obtained the status of bonded U.S. customs carrier to permit it to bring "imports from points-of-first-arrival" to other points-of-clearance throughout the U.S.

As a result of the increase in traffic, Amexco decided in the 1870s to develop the potential of the European express business more fully. It established correspondent relationships with a few European freight-forwarding companies such as Dubois Frères in Switzerland. (Forwarders were companies that arranged—without necessarily providing it themselves—transport of freight and packages.) The job of the correspondent forwarders was to drum up some U.S.-bound traffic and steer it to Amexco in return for a commission.

Amexco's freight-correspondent network grew steadily, and at the beginning of the 1880s, J.C. concluded the company's most important correspondent agreement: in exchange for £200 per year, Thomas Meadows & Company, British and colonial freight forwarders of London, Liverpool, Glasgow, Manchester, and Paris, agreed not just to direct traffic through American Express, but also to hire a man whose job was specifically to look after freight and express destined for American Express and Merchants Despatch. In the 1880s, because of the foreign money order, Amexco developed its list of financial correspondents in Europe as well. But even though Amexco's ties with the Continent were expanding, the company developed no clear strategic goals for Europe. J.C. acted cautiously and, as in the case of the money order, usually in response to specific circumstances. Throughout the 1880s, he seemed to treat European business as a sideline with limited potential for Amexco.

In 1890, however, J.C. concluded that Europe was becoming important enough to warrant more careful attention, and so he pulled M. F. Berry from the traffic manager's desk and made him the head of a new "European Department." Soon after, the company began a study to find out whether Amexco should change its role abroad. In December 1891, J.C. and Berry dispatched a representative named James W. Warrack from America to examine the situation carefully and report back to New York. Warrack's study led him to recommend that Amexco set up a baggage-handling business overseas. However, because this business might have put American Express in competition with its own correspondent Thomas Meadows, in violation of their contract, J.C. rejected the idea.

Then, in 1893, Amexco's European business suddenly mushroomed. The Columbian Exposition, the World's Fair, opened in Chicago, featuring hundreds of exhibits from seventy-two different countries. Because Amexco was the primary express carrier from the port of New York, much of the fair's transportation business fell into its hands as a matter of course. But the operation was adroitly handled by the man Charles Fargo and Albert Antisdel chose specifically for the job: William Swift Dalliba.

Dalliba was a natural choice for the job. He began his express career at age twenty-two as Amexco's agent in Marquette, Michigan, and later he became line superintendent in Green Bay, Wisconsin. Though he was rising through the ranks, in 1888 he quit Amexco for a more attractive job. His wife's cousin made Dalliba superintendent of a hydraulic gold-mining operation near Caribou City, Idaho; the post gave Dalliba a vacation throughout the winter, giving him and his wife the chance to travel and visit relatives in the Midwest and East. During his time in Idaho, Dalliba was named an honorary justice of the peace, a fact that in later years, for some reason, Amexco would blow up in order to portray him as a Wild West sheriff.

In 1890, however, Dalliba's wife died after the birth of their son. Now Dalliba wanted to return permanently to the Midwest with his child, and he decided to end his tie to the mining operation and approach Amexco about a job. The company found a place for him within a year. With the Columbian Exposition looming, Amexco needed someone to run the express operation from New York to Chicago and back, and asked Dalliba to handle it. Dalliba probably seemed the ideal candidate. He knew the company's methods as well as anyone, and Charles Fargo and Albert Antisdel wanted an experienced hand to run the operation. Other experienced expressmen failed to qualify for the job on a different count. They tended to be uneducated, unpolished types, not the kind of men likely to hit it off with refined, cultured, European gentlemen. Dalliba's background stood in sharp contrast. He was well-bred and well-connected, an American aristocrat: his mother came from old New England stock, Mayflower society; his father, also from a prominent family, had served as attorney general for the territory of Colorado. Antisdel and Charles Fargo had few others (if any) in their ranks as cultured and sophisticated as Dalliba to handle the sensitive task of the fair business.

Dalliba performed as expected. He coped with the mechanics of moving the often fragile exhibits, and he got along very well with foreign clients. "I made several hundred acquaintances among the European manufacturers and dealers and many among the government officials and others from cities throughout all Europe," he reported. "I found no difficulty in securing [their business at the Exposition] as fast as I could explain our system to them, and many of the firms gave to our company their entire shipments of bulk or weight."

For both Dalliba and Amexco, the fair proved a great success, and at its close in early 1894, he wrote to Charles Fargo urging that the company follow up the groundwork he had done with European shippers. "Many of the European firms not only gave us their business from the World's Fair but promised to continue to consign American shipments to our care from their shops and factories in Europe," Dalliba said.

Almost with one accord these gentlemen urged that our company should have a representative call upon the manufacturers and dealers in their several countries and make clear to them the American system of Express traffic, the routes, rates, customs questions, C.O.D. advantages, etc., so that they might by patronizing our line come into closer touch with American patrons. My experience at the World's Fair leads me to believe that a systematic canvass among manufacturers and dealers in Europe would lead to a steady increase in the number of our European patrons. . . . It would seem to me that if our company should send a representative to canvass Europe, he should be given such title and liberal instructions as should raise him beyond the standing of an ordinary freight solicitor—that he should be allowed such latitude on time as the slow ways of Europe require—and a fairly flexible expense account for such reasonable entertaining as circumstances might dictate as advantageous in the pursuit of business.

Dalliba likely had himself in mind for the job, and his boss Charles Fargo certainly saw him as the man. He wrote brother J.C., "If we are to continue our efforts to secure foreign business from European points, I know of no better man than Mr. Dalliba to represent us. He is thoroughly posted in the traffic and has made a great many warm and substantial friends, foreigners. He is of all men in my acquaintance best fitted to fill the position. He has a fine address and is always vigerous [sic] and pushing in his efforts on our behalf."

But J.C. still did not know what to do next in terms of Europe, and he pondered Charles's letter without arriving at a conclusion. The exposition had undeniably provided a great deal of business and had stimulated the interest of Americans in European goods and culture. But Dalliba's suggestion that the company make a special effort to seek European business posed an internal political problem for J.C. Charles and Dalliba were saying in effect (and later more explicitly) that the existing system for Europe did not work, and that a western expressman like Dalliba could do the job better than M. F. Berry and his New York–based European department. In fact, the suggestion not only implied criticism of Berry, but also of J.C., who had actually made the decisions about Europe and had created the New York department.

Still, J.C. listened to what Charles and Dalliba said, and then he asked several New York officials for their views on what to do about Europe. They expressed no unanimity of opinion, but an unsigned memo to J.C. seemed to swing the debate in Dalliba's favor. It endorsed both Dalliba's suggestions and the recommendation that Dalliba be sent abroad. "I have no question that through personal interview [as suggested by Dalliba]," the writer argued, "we would accomplish much more than can be expected by advertising and correspondence (in which I have little faith)."

Although J.C. had resolved the question of Europe in his brother's favor by March 1894, he evidently still faced political problems at 65 Broadway. He proclaimed himself ready to send Dalliba overseas, but he ordered Dalliba to New York for six months to learn at Berry's knee the ways of the European Department. Charles's reaction heightened the internal struggle. He refused to let Dalliba go, attacked the European Department, and delivered an ultimatum.

> I beg to say that I see no earthly use of Dalliba's coming to New York and staying for a period of six months to become familiar with the methods of our Foreign Department, in a line of business that he is already more familiar with, and can go on there and do better than any one connected with it. I think, however, it would be wise for him to go to New York and stay 3 or 4 weeks, at times discussing the subject of foreign business with you (or if you prefer, with Mr. Berry), but you will find that our foreign management is deadwood, it wants to be overhauled and new men and new methods adopted, and we want Mr. Dalliba's assistance to get them out of the rut they are in, not have them drag him into it. . . . Under these circumstances . . . I will send Dalliba to New York.

J.C. capitulated. Dalliba came east, but only for a few weeks. By June, he boarded a ship for Europe.

J.C. gave his new representative for Europe lots of instructions and several tasks for both the express and TC businesses. He told Dalliba to boost morale of correspondents, sell Amexco's services to shippers, drum up more express business, and sign on establishments, particularly hotels, to cash TCs. J.C. also instructed Dalliba to evaluate the performance of correspondents and advise New York on whether the company should open its own offices abroad. He was less than candid about this to the company's correspondents. In explaining Dalliba's mission to Thomas Meadows, J.C. wrote, "We wish to repeat at this time that it is not our desire or intention by this departure from former methods [that is, having a representative from the U.S. on the scene] to work to your detriment, preferring, as in the past, that our business in both directions shall continue as heretofore to pass through the hands of our regular European Agents."

Actually, if he planned to replace any particular correspondent, it was Meadows. Amexco's relationship with the British firm had deteriorated since the death of the Meadows partner who had nurtured the tie between the companies over the years. After he died, officials at 65 Broadway believed Amexco no longer received proper attention, and J.C. wanted a full evaluation of Meadows from Dalliba.

Dalliba arrived in Liverpool on July 7, 1894, and over the next several months, he moved from city to city, meeting with a continual stream of people: correspondents, forwarders, shippers, hotel owners, and old acquaintances—meetings he reported dutifully to J.C. Dalliba quickly proved to be as effective in Europe as he had been in Chicago. Traveling the continent with a trunk full of brochures, Dalliba was charming, thorough and persistent; he would return to see hotel managers five or six times to try to sign them up for the TC. He quickly proved adaptable to the character and the pace of European business. *

Dalliba impressed European office workers as well as business leaders. John Korthals, who later worked for Dalliba in France and Ger-

---

*Dalliba loved to travel and visited California and Mexico during his winter vacations from the mine in Idaho. It is unclear whether he ever traveled to Europe prior to this. However, he came from a family of veteran travelers and probably heard a great deal about European life from his relatives.

many, recalled how he was struck at once by "Mr. Dalliba['s] striking personality" at their first meeting in Turin. Korthals reported, "I had lunch with him at his hotel, the Hotel de l'Europe, and after lunch he took me up to his room and opened one of his trunks; it was full of American Express Company . . . literature and he allowed me to take any with me as much as I cared." Korthals maintained that these pamphlets and Dalliba's "graphic description of the Express Co.['s] marvellous organization . . . find me with the desire of becoming an expressman."

During the winter of 1894–95, Dalliba returned home briefly, and based on his reports, which criticized several of Amexco's correspondents, J.C. decided that the company would open its own offices in Europe, starting in Paris. But while J.C. approved the idea in principle, he claimed he did not yet want to implement it; the freight and express businesses were "dull," and he feared an exclusive Amexco office could not operate at a profit. But he adopted a strategy that, perhaps deliberately, forced him to create an office anyway. J.C. decided to scold Thomas Meadows into improving the performance of its Paris operations. But J.C. doubted the scolding would succeed. As he told Dalliba, "This will most likely require us to secure an office in Paris and approve an exclusive agent to look after our business. . . . We cannot really afford just yet to set up our own exclusive agency, but if forced, must take the chances."

As J.C. had guessed, Meadows did not appreciate the criticism, and told J.C. that, if he was unhappy, he could break their contract. Having confronted Meadows so directly, J.C. had given himself little choice now that the forwarding company had refused to change its ways, and he exercised his option to terminate Amexco's relationship with Meadows in Paris. (Though Meadows represented Amexco in both England and France, they had signed separate contracts covering the two countries; for the time being, Amexco bowed out of the French contract only.) Amexco had six months to make alternative arrangements.

However, even before J.C. gave notice, Amexco had started looking for an office in Paris. A representative of Amexco's treasurer, traveling abroad in January 1895, inquired about the possibility of Amexco renting space at 2 Rue Scribe, near the Opéra, the center for importers, exporters, and forwarders. Dalliba resumed the search the moment he returned to Europe in the spring of 1895, and soon after, he found an attractive spot at 6 Rue Halévy, a location not far from the Opéra but off the main thoroughfare. He wrote to J.C. about it, and J.C. wired back, "Do not want it."

The debate between J.C. and Dalliba over the Rue Halévy office established a pattern that lasted almost two decades. Whenever Dalliba wanted something, J.C. could be counted on to say no, starting a transatlantic discussion. In fighting for his cause, Dalliba relied with great success on distance. His style was to hammer away at all the difficulties involved in doing what J.C. wanted, talk up what he wanted, overwhelm J.C. with details the chief executive could not check, and then create a sense of urgency and crisis; he'd tell J.C., "We have to act now or we'll lose out, what should I do?" J.C. always started the debate sure of his own position, insisted, and pointed out ways for Dalliba to solve all difficulties, but he could never overcome his disadvantage of being so far away and removed from details and events, and he would usually give in.

In this instance, J.C. wanted to be in the center of freight activity, the Rue Scribe, and when Amexco failed to acquire a space at 2 Rue Scribe, he wanted to buy the lease of the tenant who shared number 4 Rue Scribe with Thomas Meadows. Given the less than friendly parting the two companies had undergone, Dalliba had little interest in sharing space with Meadows. But he mainly wanted to acquire the space at 6 Rue Halévy because he thought it would be a better place for the company's office.

J.C. remained adamant for more than a month that only 4 Rue Scribe would do. Dalliba wanted Rue Halévy, and he wanted it soon so he could be ready for business when the contract with Meadows ran out in the fall. That urgency alone gave him leverage with J.C., but Amexco's president stuck to his position even after Dalliba demonstrated that Amexco could not acquire the lease for 4 Rue Scribe. He pointed out that the colease at that location prohibited the tenant from doing the same kind of business as Meadows—freight forwarding. But J.C. persisted. "Can we not enter into a lease . . . with the understanding that we were to transact a Banking business for the sale, redemption and payment of the Company's Travelers Cheques and Money Orders . . . ?" In essence J.C. wanted Dalliba to lie.*

Dalliba apparently did not test J.C.'s idea and instead relied on his own strategy. He pretended to make a concerted effort to obtain the share with Meadows, but he found ever more problems and snags, while he uncovered greater and greater virtue in 6 Rue Halévy. Finally, toward the end of June, Dalliba began sending panicked messages to J.C. that Amexco would have to make a decision about Rue Halévy quickly or lose the opportunity. J.C. finally gave up and in early July, Dalliba began making plans to open the company's first exclusive office in Europe at 6 Rue Halévy.

As Dalliba prepared for the opening of the office, J.C. filled the mailbags with instructions. He advised Dalliba on employment practices. He warned about specific employees: "Do not like the name 'Cohn,' " he ruminated. "Sounds somewhat Jewish and should therefore advise your looking into his character and business reputation very closely." And he told Dalliba to poach employees of correspondents for other U.S. express companies. He also instructed Dalliba on the kind of behavior Dalliba should demand from his American employees generally. J.C. feared for the moral deterioration of Yanks loosed in decadent, hedonistic Europe. "We want a man to be civil and *agreeable to all* and, *so far as his position and duties will admit* socially attentive to our patrons. It must be distinctly understood . . . that he is not exclusively employed for the latter purpose or will be permitted

---

*J.C. could be devious in this fashion one minute and take a high moral position the next. For instance, in Italy, he objected to a relationship with a local forwarding company because it apparently paid off government officials to help get artworks out of the country.

to go 'bumming' about town during business hours, or at any time of day or night, or in any place, conduct himself in a way to discredit the company." Any American Dalliba hired, J.C. said, had to be someone who could not be "demoralized." What Dalliba thought of such instructions he never revealed. He routinely violated J.C.'s directives on employment practice, including J.C.'s unbending rule prohibiting the employment of women.* But J.C.'s fears about employee conduct must have struck Dalliba as particularly absurd. He had already come to love Europe, particularly Paris, loved the atmosphere and the lifestyle, and his later success probably stemmed in no small degree from his ability to go beyond the provincialism of countrymen like J.C. and to work within the customs and framework of the Old World.

J.C. was also very clear in his instructions about the business activities of 6 Rue Halévy. At least twice, he reminded Dalliba that he wanted the office to advance the freight and "Express business proper." He ruled out financial operations even of the most limited sort (no matter what he told Dalliba to say to Meadows). "It is not at present the intention of the Company to sell either Money Orders or Travelers Cheques at European agencies," he declared. But Dalliba quickly convinced J.C. to change his mind and the European office was soon cashing and selling TCs. In fact, Dalliba put a major emphasis on financial operations from the moment the Paris office opened.

J.C. never stopped giving advice, but, in what was a remarkable and unprecedented step for him, J.C. soon accorded Dalliba an official measure of autonomy. He decided that European operations, which he considered an "experiment," could not be completely controlled from New

---

*Some other managers violated J.C.'s directive on women employees. In small towns, freight and express agents were often outside contractors who ran their businesses as family operations. Often when a male agent died, his widow inherited his business. Amexco's managers found then that they had two choices: either put a woman on the payroll, or stop conducting business in that town. Many chose to put a woman on the payroll and disguised it by listing her name in the books by her first initial only, i.e. a Jenny Barnes became a J. Barnes. J.C. did not find out about this practice until the late 1890s, and relented when the case involved a widowed agent. Dalliba, however, hired women as stenographers, a practice J.C. never approved.

York. In responding to a request from Dalliba to hire a bookkeeper, he wrote, "It is not practicable [for you] to refer here for authority before acting. . . . On account of the great distance and time which would be required for such references and authority, as well as the different surroundings of the same generally, of which we could know little or judge as to what is and is not necessary, greater latitude must be given you for the management of the Company's interests than is allowed or necessary to be given to the General Managers of Company here."

Though this directive seemed very broad, almost a blank check, later correspondence would explain that J.C. meant only to give Dalliba authority over day-to-day details. Dalliba could spend money without prior approval; he could hire the men he needed; he could change correspondents. Basic issues of policy, however, remained J.C.'s province. To the extent that Dalliba wanted to make policy, he would have to apply the Chicago Rule, which, as he would make clear, he had learned as well as anyone from the western express.

The office at 6 Rue Halévy opened without ceremony in November 1895, and at first, business was slow. Korthals recalled that if "we cashed a dozen travelers cheques and delivered about as many packages, we called it a busy day." Nevertheless, Amexco already planned three new offices in Europe. The break with Meadows in Paris had further undermined the relationship of the two companies, and J.C. decided to end it entirely and open offices in London, Liverpool, and Southampton.* Though Dalliba started looking for space in London as early as August 1895, J.C. did not give Meadows notice until early 1896. In September of that year, Dalliba opened Amexco's second European office at 3 Waterloo Place, London; offices in Liverpool and Southampton followed in November. Within one year, Amexco suddenly had not just a foreign office, but a network under the direction of William Swift Dalliba.

---

*Before deciding on a total break with Meadows, J.C. suggested Dalliba spy on Meadows's English operations. J.C. told Dalliba to send in agents to Meadows's offices to see what kind of service they might get. There is no evidence Dalliba followed J.C.'s suggestion.

In 1894, Dalliba left for Europe apparently with the intention of developing the freight and express business as J.C. wanted. His own post-Columbia Exposition memo in early 1894 had focused on that business, and Dalliba never completely ignored European freight-forwarding operations.* Yet over time, his views on the primary focus and purpose of the company's efforts in Europe began to change. First, he placed increasing emphasis on the sale and redemption of the company's financial paper for tourists, business people, and expatriates. Gradually, Dalliba came to the conclusion that finance and particularly the TC offered the greatest opportunity for Amexco abroad. Yet he realized, too, that in order to sell more TCs, the company had to serve the people who used them. Before 1899, Dalliba made up his mind to tie the company's destiny in Europe not to shippers, but to tourists, and through them to the TC. For Dalliba, this conclusion grew logically out of business reality. But to put it into action, he knowingly had to disregard the policies of J. C. Fargo, whose vision of the company in Europe had undergone no changes at all.

Dalliba was not the first person at American Express to propose a tourist business. In March 1896, with the Rue Halévy office less than half a year old, C. O. Smith, the money-order manager for the Eastern Department, prepared an elaborate memo on the subject. "If progression is the order of the day, why is it not an opportune time to promulgate the fact that this Company not only issues Travelers Cheques, payable at any place in the wide, wide world through the most extensive list of correspondents ever published, but is prepared to book tourists for any tour they desire to take in the United States or Europe." Smith suggested making arrangements with existing travel agents and steamship lines, and he even wrote up three proposed circulars, one each for travel agents, steamship companies, and American Express agents.

---

*Dalliba achieved some notable successes in freight forwarding. Most importantly, he arranged to have Amexco serve as the U.S. forwarding agent for the British and French parcel-post systems.

His immediate superior, T. D. Ritson, agreed that the idea "should inevitably be adopted by the Company" but perhaps was premature. Nevertheless, he passed it on to J.C.'s assistant, Francis Flagg, who felt Smith's idea was "all right" except that it relied too much on outside travel agents. "When the time is ripe," he told Ritson, "we will take up the business on our own account." The idea went no further at the time.

Dalliba entered the debate over travel the next year with a modest suggestion to form a joint operation with Thomas Cook & Son in Southampton. Cook's, in its fifty-seventh year, was the leading tourist agency of Europe, with offices across the Continent and throughout the British Empire. It already had ties to Amexco since it accepted the TC, and Dalliba felt a joint operation with Cook's would put Amexco's new, but unprofitable, Southampton office on a self-sustaining basis. A joint office, Dalliba believed, had greater profit opportunities since it could sell tickets, tours, hotel reservations, handle foreign exchange, sell and cash TCs and money orders, and deal with baggage. However, J. C. Fargo failed to see how it would benefit American Express. "[We] would be glad to know upon what you [base this expectation of profitability]," he wrote, and he killed the plan.

Though J.C. had scotched the joint office, Flagg read over the exchange of letters and thought it might be a good time for Amexco to get into the tourist business on its own. He suggested this in a note to J.C., who dismissed it. "Until we can learn what the tourist business is . . . and what benefit there can be in it for the Co., do not think we want to engage in it."

Despite J.C., soon after this Dalliba came to the conclusion that the future of Amexco abroad should be tied to the tourists. What probably turned his thinking was his growing awareness of the magnitude of the American tourist presence in Europe. The tourist boom, which started in the early 1890s and benefited the TC, continued to grow throughout the decade. By the end of the century, even American college students were coming over for the summer, the less well-off hiring themselves on as tenders on cattle steamers (they had to be shipped on the hoof in those days) to pay their way over. European travel, once the prerogative of the wealthy, had suddenly turned into a rite of passage of the young. Dalliba also knew what tourism meant in dollars-and-cents terms: American travelers were spending nearly a quarter billion dollars abroad by the turn of the century, and Americans living in Europe were spending almost that much again. * If Amexco could get a good share of that trade in TCs and money orders, it would make millions.

Dalliba had provided services for tourists and expatriates from the moment he began drawing up plans for 6 Rue Halévy. He ordered a desk for clients' mail and a clients' reading and writing area. These were not radical innovations since banks like Morgan, Harjes & Company, the Parisian banking stop of many wealthy Americans, accepted mail for clients. A reading and writing room appeared harmless, as well, since it provided space for shippers needing to do paperwork as much as for tourists. Although J.C. was by now growing increasingly hostile to tourists, he accepted Dalliba's plans without question.

Amexco's European offices quickly became a magnet for tourists. As more middle-class travelers found the time and money to journey to Europe, Amexco sold more TCs. The TC suited the tourists of all classes. Some wealthy travelers carried TCs, but others preferred letters of credit because of the snob appeal of having a prominent banker abroad like Morgan, Harjes of Paris. Middle-class tourists did not have that option since Morgan, Harjes catered to wealthy clients only, while Amexco sold TCs in many denominations to all comers. Naturally, the new class of American travelers carried TCs, and they gravitated to their overseas "banker," the offices of American Express.

Dalliba pondered the reality of the tourist invasion and decided not just to accept it, but to make it Amexco's primary business activity abroad. Indeed, Dalliba decided that to realize the full potential of the TC business, he had to make Amexco *the* center for Americans abroad. That, in essence, became his vision of American Express in Europe.

---

*Dalliba knew this as fact because he was well connected in the Paris business community; he was one of the founding members of the Paris branch of the American Chamber of Commerce.

He directed his staff to treat travelers kindly, to give them free advice, and to help them find hotel rooms and sight-seeing attractions. Before long, with Dalliba's blessing, the reading/writing area at Rue Halévy swarmed with tourists, and the mail desk became every person's post office.

After a while, Dalliba felt he had to take another step in order to further his goal of creating a company for tourists. Because Paris was the center of European tourism, he wanted to find a better location for the Paris office so that it could become, as he later put it, "the greatest rendezvous for Americans which has ever existed in Europe." But just as Dalliba began his search, he received a jarring demand from J. C. Fargo. J.C. had decided that Dalliba should move himself to *London* and make that city Amexco's European headquarters. Such a move made sense for an express company; London was the mercantile center of Europe. But to implement his own plans, Dalliba felt he had to stay where he was.

He fought strenuously against J.C.'s directive. He wrote letter after letter, arguing that London would ruin his health, and that Paris was actually better located than London from an express standpoint. Because it was on the Continent, it afforded Dalliba much easier access to freight and shipping centers like Rotterdam, Genoa, Le Havre, and Bremen. Once more, J.C. caved in and allowed Dalliba to stay in Paris.

That settled, Dalliba resumed his search for a more prominent location for the Paris office. Dalliba chose to remain in the vicinity of the Opéra because the district not only housed freight and transportation companies, but also the principal hotels, shops, and many tourist attractions. However, Dalliba wanted a more visible office than the one on Rue Halévy, and he visited "every ground floor space" in the area before he settled on two sites that faced each other diagonally across the Place de l'Opéra. One was the establishment of Escalier de Cristal; the other housed the Ferry shoe factory. Dalliba told the landlords of both buildings to let him know the minute a ground-floor lease became available. In the early fall of 1899, Dalliba heard from Ferry's landlord and he began negotiations for the lease at 11 Rue Scribe.

Number 11 was a flatiron building fronting on the Rue Auber and Rue Scribe, at the point where those streets converged and spilled into the plaza in front of the Opéra. * Although painted a dull brown at the time, the ornately decorated building occupied a dominant position in the plaza—in fact, it could be seen "all the way from the grand Boulevard." Inside, on the colonnaded ground floor, the building provided an ample 2,240 square feet (more than double that of Rue Halévy), plus a sizable, basement storage and freight area, and sweeping stairways leading up to a mezzanine where Dalliba planned to put his office.

The opportunity to rent number 11 could not have come at a better time. Dalliba needed extra space more urgently now than ever. The Paris Exposition of 1900 was less than a year off, and promised more express and freight business, as well as an influx of tourists. Though Dalliba had operational control, he could not sign a fifteen-year lease without J.C.'s imprimatur, but the Exposition gave Dalliba an excuse for more space, and even J.C. could not deny the need.

Acquiring the lease for 11 Rue Scribe, however, did not prove an easy matter. Dalliba found that negotiations involved not only Ferry and the landlady, Madame Bogert, but two other parties as well. One of these had actually signed a lease, only to conclude that after the Exposition the space would be too big and too expensive. Dalliba entered into a long, involved, and often frustrating series of discussions. Frequently, one party or another ran off to consult a lawyer, and Dalliba, usually a patient man, twice gave up in despair. "It is impracticable to convey to you in a letter the difficulty one experiences in undertaking to carry through negotiations with the average Frenchman," he complained. "Such negotiations are full of delays, subterfuge and vexations almost beyond comprehension to one used to doing business in America."

---

*Number 11 was a relatively new building. It was built between 1864 and 1874; construction had gone on sporadically during that time, stopping entirely in the early 1870s for the Franco-Prussian War and the Paris Commune.

And if the average Frenchman did not vex him enough, Dalliba faced another problem—J. C. Fargo. J.C. approved the idea of larger quarters, but had his own idea of what and where those quarters should be. Even as Dalliba was struggling to work out a deal for 11 Rue Scribe, he received a message from J.C. telling him not to bother. Sitting in his office in New York, he, J.C., had located what he believed to be the ideal space.

J.C. found the site quite by chance. The president of the Anglo-American Bank, which occupied the building next to 6 Rue Halévy, happened to be in New York, happened to stop in at 65 Broadway, and happened to tell J.C. that he wanted to leave Paris. He said he would be happy if Amexco bought out his lease, which still had fourteen years to run, and J.C. thought it was perfect: by taking the building next door, Amexco would have no need to advertise a move and could take over immediately. All Dalliba would have to do was knock down a wall and presto, a space ready for the Exposition. "You are authorized," he wrote Dalliba, "to make the best bargain with Mr. Sheppard [head of Anglo-American], and go ahead with the changes to be made in interior offices so as to have them complete and ready for the increased business of the Exposition."*

Fearing that J.C. might make some sort of deal of his own with Sheppard, Dalliba cabled the plea, "Await my letter before proceeding." The letter, a hastily written ten-page paean to 11 Rue Scribe, demonstrated again his approach in arguing with J.C. He extolled 11 Rue Scribe and denigrated the combined Rue Halévy space, and then launched into a minute description of architectural detail complete with sketches of the two. Dalliba also claimed that 11 Rue Scribe not only offered larger space, but did so at lower cost as well.

This claim represented a new stratagem—creative mathematics. Though the base monthly rental of Rue Scribe exceeded that of the combined Rue Halévy spaces, Dalliba "proved" the reverse. He added

---

*Given that Dalliba occupied 6 Rue Halévy, in all likelihood he already knew about Anglo-American's plans, but had no interest in the space.

to the charge at Rue Halévy an extra 500 French francs per year for heating because the space had no south windows (though it was also smaller), and he neglected to include on the Rue Scribe side, a FF 75,000 "bonus" Amexco was going to have to pay the landlady up front, in addition to the rent. Also, Dalliba swore he could negotiate down the rent at Rue Scribe; actually, he ended up paying more.* He had by no means exhausted his range of arguments, either. In a second letter, he tried a completely different tack: the specter of competition. He warned J.C. that if Amexco did not take the space at number 11, Thomas Cook & Son would. But J.C. rejected all of Dalliba's arguments and pressed again for a deal with Sheppard.

Dalliba even tried telling J.C. the truth. He admitted his intention to make the Rue Scribe office the rendezvous point for Americans abroad. Such a prediction entailed some danger, since the last thing J.C. wanted was to make Amexco's office a gathering place for the American hordes. But J.C. merely continued to push his own plan for the spaces at Rue Halévy.

Dalliba, however, swamped him with letters and cables. J.C. had trouble keeping up his end of the debate. In response to several thousand words from Dalliba, he cabled in reply, "Against!" Finally, J.C. seemed overwhelmed when he wrote, "Replying to yours of November 17, 18, 21, 22, 23, and 24. . . ." After two weeks, J.C. began to waver and appeared to want to keep both options open, but he told Dalliba to use his judgment. That was all Dalliba needed to hear. He worked out the details of a lease for 11 Rue Scribe by the first week of December. It only needed his and Madame Bogert's signature when he suddenly received a stunning wire from New York. At the last possible moment, J.C. ordered Dalliba to abandon Rue Scribe and reopen negotiations with Sheppard. But Dalliba did not do it. Instead, he put J.C. on the spot. "Others bidding for premises [11 Rue Scribe],"

---

*Before this debate ended, Dalliba admitted to J.C. that the costs for 11 Rue Scribe were higher than for the Rue Halévy spaces. Dalliba argued, however, that the Rue Scribe location would increase business sufficiently to justify the expense.

Dalliba wired. "No further delay and no hope of better terms possible. Have accepted, if no instructions to contrary." J.C. cabled back, "Accept Ferry premises. . . ."

It turned out that J.C.'s last-minute demand had resulted from an error. American Express, obsessed with secrecy, used its own cipher code, and by policy, officials coded virtually all cables, regardless of their importance or confidentiality. According to the message J.C. had received from Dalliba about the proposed lease, the rent for 11 Rue Scribe was pegged at the horrifying sums of "Crisoprasa, Crispabam, Crispassem, and Crepiculis," which translated to amounts over FF 55,000. When J.C. realized that the rent came to only about FF 30,000, he cabled his acceptance, and he wrote the same day, "trust the delay, by reason of this blunder, has not jeopardized our chances of obtaining the premises." Ironically, his telegram had a code blunder, too, and Dalliba spent some time puzzling over it, but when he figured it out, he called on the landlady and signed the lease. Eleven Rue Scribe was his.

Dalliba's prediction of what would happen at the new location quickly began to materialize. By 1905, business grew so hectic during the summer months that Dalliba estimated his mail clerks processed 5,000 letters a day, and at times tourists so packed 11 Rue Scribe that it became almost impassable. Although he told J.C. that he refused service to travelers who were not also customers, Dalliba continued in Paris, and at all other offices in Europe, to be as solicitous to tourists as possible. Meanwhile Amexco's sales of TCs soared: $6.4 million in 1900; $13.2 million in 1905; $23 million in 1909.

Dalliba succeeded in his goal of making Amexco *the* company for American travelers abroad partly by just fostering an attitude and by moving his headquarters to a central location. He helped his effort, too, by persuading J.C. to let him expand his European office network to include locations in many other major cities. But shortly after the turn of the century, he decided to enhance the company's identity still more by developing an active, paid travel business. Adding such a business operation, though, required either the agreement of J. C. Fargo or a remarkable amount of deception.

Henry Wells, W. G. Fargo, John Butterfield: The three founders of the American Express Company. (*American Express Archives*)

J. C. Fargo: President of American Express from 1881 to 1914. He ruled Amexco longer than any other chief executive. Authorized the money order, the travelers cheque, and the company's move into Europe. (*American Express Archives*)

Marcellus Fleming (M. F.) Berry: Creator of the American Express money order and travelers cheque. (*American Express Archives*)

William Swift Dalliba: Went to Europe as the company's first representative to develop the international freight-forwarding business. Despite orders to the contrary, he turned American Express abroad into a company for tourism and finance. (*American Express Archives*)

George C. Taylor: President and chief executive from 1914 to 1923. He instituted a modern management system. Later he ran both Amexco and the American Railway Express. (*American Express Archives*)

Howard K. Brooks: Probably the most innovative mind in the company's history. Developed foreign exchange, tourism, and trade activities, and was the guiding force behind the entrepreneurial period from 1915 to 1920. He saw his vision derailed by the Glass Eye fiasco. (*American Express Archives*)

Frederick P. Small: Succeeded Taylor as president of Amexco in 1923. Turned the company into a travel company, but nearly lost it to Chase in 1929. Remained president until 1944, but was relatively powerless after the Chase takeover. (*American Express Archives*)

Albert Wiggin: Chairman of the Chase National Bank and the Chase Securities Company. He took over Amexco in 1929 and made himself chairman. He actively ran Amexco for only a few months, however, as the crash
of 1929, the Depression, and the merger of the Chase and Equitable Trust
diverted his attention. (*American Express Archives*)

The chances of winning J.C.'s approval did not appear promising. Given J.C.'s loathing of American tourists, Dalliba developed his tourist operations slowly and subtly. In 1902, he persuaded J.C. to let him establish "ticket departments" in many offices to sell westbound steamship tickets. This gave Dalliba an approved operation he could develop on the sly into a much more extensive travel-service business. As one of his agents in Germany later recalled, European employees considered their ticket departments as tourist departments. They used the name "ticket" for home consumption only. Soon, they also sold European railway tickets and eventually tickets for sight-seeing tours. By the middle of the first decade of the twentieth century, American Express offices could arrange virtually every activity tourists wanted.

Although Dalliba had already started a tourist business, in 1905, he thought it might be time to try to win official approval from J.C. for it. He used a letter from a satisfied customer as a way to introduce the subject to the chief executive. The customer wrote to decry the arrogance and inefficiency of Cook's, and to urge American Express to offer an alternative. Dalliba added that he had been talking to former and current employees of Cook's and, yes, they thought American Express could make money booking tours and hotels. Dalliba played on J.C.'s sense of dignity, assuring the aging chief executive that Amexco would never offer cheap tours for the rabble, but rather "all first class" tours for first-class people. J.C. replied succinctly: "We do not approve of taking up the tourist business. We have quite enough and more work than we can manage now—Aside from which we do not think there's any profit in it in the long run."

Dalliba promptly went out and hired the "best tourist and ticket men" to be ready for the 1906 summer season. And when the rabble trooped in again that summer in greater numbers than before, Dalliba told J.C. he was going to have to expand the London and Paris offices to accommodate all the people. J.C. was furious. "[W]e must not increase our rental or other expenses for the mere purpose of accommodating tourists, very many of whom are not even patrons of the Company's Travelers Cheque business, and a large remainder never give us a dollar's worth of express business from one year to the next."

119

He refused to allow Dalliba to expand "solely for tourists' loafing accommodation. . . . Enlarge your organization when the Express and Freight traffic crowds it, but let the tourists crowd themselves."

That summer, when American Express received another letter from an American tourist complaining of having no alternative to Cook's—being a "Cookie," he called it—Dalliba tried one more time. First, he attempted to win J.C.'s approval by playing on his admiration for rich and prominent people. J.C. often fell for this line. His preoccupation with wealthy, powerful people bordered on the mindless, and he was once taken in by a British charlatan because he came recommended by several prominent names. Dalliba had used the rich-and-prominent ploy successfully before, and now he told J.C. that he had spoken to a large number of "influential people," and they supported the idea of Amexco's entry into the tourist business. However, he also admitted that he saw this not just as another business, but as *the* business of Europe. "While I do not lose sight of the legitimate Express business," he said, "it seems to me that our greatest opportunity in Europe lies in the development of our financial and tourist business."

Dalliba was supported this time by Howard Brooks, now a manager of financial activities in Chicago, and J.C.'s son J.F., Amexco's treasurer. J.C.'s answer to the three men was essentially no, no, and never. "There is no profit in the tourist business as conducted by Thomas Cook & Son," he scrawled across the top of his son's letter, "and even if there was, this Company would not undertake it."

J.C. believed that Cook's bore out his prejudices from a business standpoint. He claimed that Cook's was virtually insolvent. Indeed, the British tourist firm had once needed recapitalizing, and apparently this stuck in J.C.'s mind as a permanent condition. Decades later, Amexco would learn that Cook's enjoyed much greater financial stability than J.C. would ever admit.

Actually, J.C.'s opinion of the tourist business was partly correct. (Cook's made most of its money from a banking operation.) The tourist business *itself* never produced substantial returns. But for Amexco, travel fed a very lucrative financial business. J.C. could never acknowledge the obvious link between tourism and the TC, and the potential profit inherent in that relationship. To the end, he remained obsessed with the idea that Amexco's only legitimate business in Europe should be express, that only through express could the company realize a profit. In 1911, over eighty but still autocrat of Amexco, he ordered his comptroller to go over the financial report from the Rome office. J.C. wanted the results for express activities only, which he called the "entire business outside of entertaining tourists." J.C. so believed this, that when the comptroller reported that Amexco handled little express in Rome, J.C. concluded the company should close its office in the Italian capital.

After 1906, Dalliba apparently gave up trying to persuade J.C. of the need to build a tourist business; Dalliba just did it. He continued to add services to his ticket departments and finally did everything except run tours under Amexco's own name. He violated the letter and the spirit of every word on tourism that J.C. ever penned.* He told travelers in 1907 that his ticket men would arrange itineraries for travelers "to all points in Europe," and he booked other people's sight-seeing tours, some of which ran from the door of 11 Rue Scribe and the other European offices. J.C. heard of this and erupted. He would "not have gangs of trippers starting off in charabancs" from Amexco's offices, he declared on more than one occasion. Dalliba had already signed contracts and had no intention of reneging on them. Elisha Flagg, Francis's brother and the agent in London, proposed a subterfuge to get around J.C.; he suggested the "charabancs" leave from around the corner instead of the front door. But Dalliba did not even bother to make this cosmetic change. J.C. was too far away to check up, too old now to make the trip to Europe. Dalliba pursued his own vision and did so with great success. The public increasingly identified the company abroad with tourism, a fact noted by the trade paper of the express business. It declared as early as 1906 that the foreign tourist business was "largely controlled by American Express Companies," this despite J.C.'s firmest convictions.

Perhaps the most intriguing question of all is why J.C. did not fire

---

*Dalliba apparently bore no personal animosity toward J.C. He even considered himself a friend of the Fargo family, although he was closest to J.C.'s son J.F.

121

Dalliba for disobedience. Possibly he never comprehended just how completely Dalliba had set his own course. Then again, J.C.'s restrained response to Dalliba's initiative may have indicated tacit consent. J.C.'s often stated horror of tourists and Dalliba's vision of Amexco tourist offices scattered across Europe clashed so emphatically that J.C. could not have endorsed Dalliba's actions. But with the expansion of tourist services overseas came substantial growth in TC sales; Dalliba's actions may have been generating too much profit to countermand. Possibly, too, J.C. may have enjoyed the transatlantic combat with Dalliba. Though J.C. maintained a cold and formal tone in their correspondence, Dalliba's charm may have worked on J.C. as well; he even once admitted to Flagg that he was looking forward to a visit home from his representative to Europe. But whatever the reason, J.C. never even threatened Dalliba, although Dalliba persistently disobeyed him for almost twenty years.

Dalliba, however, had so thoroughly triumphed over J.C. that, after 1905, he did not work very hard at the game of deception. He concentrated on playing his own chosen role, that of America's number-one host abroad. A tall and now gray-haired gentleman, Dalliba dressed each day in his morning coat and silk hat, wearing on his breast pocket the Legion of Honor* he had received from the French Government in 1906. Although he still did not speak French very well, he insisted on a Frenchified title after 1911: Directeur Général pour l'Europe (Director General to his American colleagues) of the American Express Company. From his rolltop desk at 11 Rue Scribe, he directed his network of European offices in the task he had set for them and for American Express-Europe: tending to his countrymen abroad.

Dalliba had done a great deal to solidify the image of Amexco as the friend of the American traveler, but it took a war to finally stamp that

---

*Many Americans and French business people fought several years to win the award for Dalliba. It was given to acknowledge Dalliba's efforts in promoting business between France and America.

image in the public mind. The same war bestowed on the TC the prestige and stature of a genuine universal currency.

When World War I broke out in the summer of 1914, the banks of Europe abruptly closed to prevent runs; exchange rates, so steady for years, suddenly turned uncertain, and travel became dangerous when it was even possible. The situation left 150,000 Americans—tourists and residents—stranded, some with no hard currency in their pockets. Many went at once to the offices of American Express. At 11 Rue Scribe, some people besieged Dalliba's own office trying to get special treatment for themselves, but the biggest crowd formed at the TC window of what Dalliba now referred to as the bank department. "When our Paris Bank Dept. opened at 9 A.M., a line was formed two, four, sometimes six abreast, leading from the Cash counter through the office, out round the street corner and up the Rue Auber beyond the Transatlantic building," Dalliba would later write. And the people appeared day after day. One customer estimated that while he waited at least 2,000 people crammed into the building, a scene of chaos repeated in London, Berlin, Rotterdam, and half a dozen other cities.

Dalliba, however, had prepared the office network for the outbreak of war. In July, with a crisis in Europe building, he pondered the possible effects on all American Express offices and on 11 Rue Scribe in particular. He decided to bring over to France three million French francs in gold and told other offices to build cash reserves in order to pay every piece of the company's paper, and, if possible, to pay everyone else's paper, too. When the crisis came, leading banks failed to redeem one sou of their own paper, but American Express dispensed chests of pounds, francs, marks, and lire.* Indeed, it was one of the few companies in all of Europe still doing any exchange business. In Paris, Dalliba at one point personally eased fears that Amexco would

---

*In Holland, the government removed all silver from circulation and Amexco's office in Rotterdam ran out of cash. But the office handed out chits that were honored throughout Holland and, of course, by the company.

run out of cash by ostentatiously leading his workers through the throngs at Rue Scribe. As they carried in strongboxes, he waved a revolver and cried out, "Make way for the gold!"

Dalliba had his men scrambling to perform other tasks. They tried to arrange passage for Americans wanting to go home, and they sent out and distributed telegrams and letters, so travelers could remain in contact with loved ones in America. Dalliba's staff worked so effectively in Paris, in fact, that the American embassy sent people to Rue Scribe rather than the other way around. The TC, cashable in the midst of war when almost nothing else was, gained so much stature that Dalliba could report, "Owing to the fact that we had paid out T/Cs in full, I find that hotel-keepers and others were hoarding our T/C in preference to French paper money—with the expectation that they could cash cheques from time to time as required."

Newspapers across America reported on the job Dalliba and his men had done. The *Toledo Daily Blade* commented in an editorial entitled "A Credit to American Business": "The American Express Company deserves a good deal of praise for the success of its European agencies in upholding the integrity of the company's cheques. . . . It is something about which it is entitled to boast all its days." But most of the comment came from the people Dalliba had helped. "I have dealt with American Express Company along these lines for twenty years," wrote one traveler. "But this summer's experience makes a life contract of it." From the company's perspective, after this, according to one executive, "Amexco's credit was never questioned anywhere [and was] more widely known and honored throughout the world than that of any institution."

The image Dalliba created had become fixed in the public mind; the company's path abroad was very much the one he had set. J. C. Fargo, sick and very old, was still alive in August 1914, and though he no doubt heard of what Dalliba had done, he may not have appreciated the consquences. American Express was tied now to the tourist trade; the man he had sent to Europe had changed the company's identity in the eyes of much of the world.

THE DECLINE
AND FALL
OF THE EXPRESS
5

In 1918, the United States Government forced all the express companies out of the domestic express business. This action cost Amexco close to 10,000 offices and 15,000 employees—most of its organization—as well as its primary reason for being. But the actual loss only ended the existence of a business that was already dying. Earlier in the decade, the express business had suffered serious reversals that destroyed it as a profitable enterprise.

The men who had led the express industry to its earlier glory—J. C. Fargo and the heads of the other major express companies—were largely responsible for its decline. Together, for decades, they made resistance to change an industry policy. The policy was so successful that the express business remained an unregulated monopoly into the twentieth century. But Fargo and his peers failed to see that the world was changing.

Express executives were slow to appreciate the new political forces in America—particularly the populist and progressive movements and the reformist ideals they espoused. These movements, which appeared initially after the Civil War, gradually built a consensus in the country in favor of government intervention in business. For the express companies, especially, progressive ideas posed a double threat. First, the movement raised the possibility of government regulation of the express business. But it also threatened the express industry with competition, or even outright seizure. The companies had a special vulnerability to changes in political fortune; a branch of the government, the U.S. Post Office, wanted to create a parcel-post system to compete with or displace the express. If the companies lost political support, they faced a reduction in business or even extinction.

The express companies managed to forestall both regulation and competition for years and, in the process, they grew complacent and arrogant. Even as demands for change grew from the public and the government, the expressmen refused to adapt. The resistance they mounted was both hopeless and self-defeating. Finally, the government forced change on them anyway, and these changes were so drastic that the expresses lost control over most decisions about their business. In a real sense, the express industry died at least five years before the government stepped in to end it in 1918.

During the last quarter of the nineteenth century, before the decline began, the expresses continued to enjoy tremendous wealth and freedom from scrutiny. To get some idea of how rich Amexco had become, in 1903, the company compiled for in-house consumption a comparison of Amexco's capital and surplus with those of leading American banks. Amexco, with a total of about $28 million, came in second behind the National City Bank of New York. Its resources surpassed those of the second largest bank—the First National Bank of New York—by $4.5 million. Amexco's capital and surplus, held in cash and securities, equaled about $150 per share.

Yet, around this time, the stock often traded well below this because people had no idea how much money was in Amexco's coffers. Dividends were kept an unobtrusive 3–6 percent (on capital), but could have been much higher. It has been said that if Wall Street knew how rich the American and Adams expresses were, their shares would not have been available at any price. But investors did not know, because the companies told shareholders nothing; no shareholder meetings were held at any major express company from shortly after the Civil War to the twentieth century.

Five express companies—the American, Adams, Wells Fargo, United States, and Southern—controlled 90 percent of the business. Where the industry as a whole was concerned, no one company or individual made policy. Instead, the top officials of the five together set the course for the express business. Industry action and policy required the consent of J. C. Fargo and his counterpart at the Adams Express— first John Hoey and later Levi Weir—because they headed the two largest and richest express companies. But even Adams and Amexco sought unanimity on most issues. To every extent possible, policies carried on by the industry resulted from a consensus of the major companies.

Because the five had so much money and power, they forestalled any competitive challenges to their control, such as the one the Merchants Union had mounted in 1866–67. Only the richest capitalists in the country had the wherewithal to challenge them, and none did. The five giants treated small rivals with disdain and either squashed them, or bought them off, for amounts so piddling to the big expresses that the money sometimes came out of petty cash. In 1890, for example, Amexco bought a feeder express in Massachusetts for a few thousand dollars, an amount charged off as "a miscellaneous expense."

The five maintained a complete stranglehold over rates. The companies agreed to fix all rates where customers had a choice of carrier; for instance, both Adams and Amexco had services from New York to Chicago.* These agreements remained in force for at least seventeen

---

*Amexco and Adams nominally competed over the New York–Chicago route because both the New York Central (Amexco's line) and the Pennsylvania RR (Adams's line) had service between the two cities.

years after the passage of the Sherman Antitrust Act of 1890, which prohibited price-fixing and "collusive agreements."

Actually, a form of competition existed within the express industry, but it took a different character from any that had been seen before 1870. The competition was not for customers, but rather for the railroads. By tradition, every railroad had an exclusive contract with one express company, and according to those contracts, the railroads received a percentage of the gross receipts for all express business carried over its line—often with a guaranteed yearly or monthly minimum. Any express company wanting to take business from another company only had to offer the railroad a better deal: 45 percent of the gross instead of 40 percent, a guarantee of $150,000 instead of $100,000.

Of course, a company that tried to steal railroad contracts from other express companies violated a tenet of the industry as fundamental as price-fixing—territorial division. That division had never been exact— more a matter of you-take-this-railroad-and-I'll-take-that-one than a strict divvying up of geography—and that inevitably led to disputes among the expresses as railroads expanded to the point where their tracks met those of other lines. Nevertheless, the expresses always considered poaching the exclusive business on a railroad from another company for any reason to be in extremely poor taste, because it was seen as a threat to express company peace. So it was a shock and a bother when in the 1880s one expressman decided he coveted his neighbor's business enough to go after it.

The offender was Thomas Collier Platt. Known as "Boss" Platt, he was one of the most powerful figures in the Republican party of New York State, and of the country as a whole, from the late 1870s until his death in 1910. Although he had had some experience as a railroad executive, the U.S. Express Company hired him more for his political connections than for his management skills. The Post Office yearly approached the Congress with new proposals which threatened the express business. As a result, beginning in the 1870s, the five companies hired executives who could exercise political clout. American Express made onetime speaker of the U.S. House of Representatives

Theodore Medad Pomeroy its first vice president and a board member, although his job was almost exclusively political. In 1879, the U.S. Express invited Tom Platt to become secretary, general agent, and its chief political lobbyist. Six months later, though, Platt had gotten the notion that he should run the States himself and maneuvered his way to the presidency of the company. Once there, he proved as adept at office politics as he was at the other kind. He made himself a virtual president-for-life of the States and used nepotism to establish a loyal executive corps around him. His grip was so firm that he was able to retain his post as president from 1897 to 1909 while he served as a U.S. senator from New York.

But Platt had another notion—that he could compete with his fellow expressmen. Within a year after he had taken command of the States, Platt had ended the old profit-sharing arrangement with Amexco, and over the next decade and a half, Platt went hunting for Amexco's railroad contracts. He caught a few—much to the rage of J. C. Fargo and associates—and tried for others. Platt also went after Adams's business, and in 1889, scored his biggest success when he used his political contacts to win from that company the exclusive contract to carry money shipments for the U.S. government.

Yet the company hurt most by this combat turned out to be the States itself. Platt was adept at power games but not at management, and a few of the deals he made with the railroads resulted in unprofitable contracts. By 1895, the States had to suspend its dividend—always the very last resort of any express company. So in May of that year, Platt agreed to end the competition.

The other companies were pleased, although Amexco officials expressed skepticism about whether Platt would live up to any agreement. Wrote Pomeroy to Amexco attorney and board member Lewis Cass Ledyard, "I suppose it was best to enter into it and take the chances of his observing it, notwithstanding his bad faith toward all Express agreements heretofore."

Two years later, Platt signed a new territorial agreement (also contrary to antitrust statutes), but by this time his rivals had the upper hand, and they decided that a truce was not enough. In 1901, Adams and American each bought 10 percent of the stock of the States and, with the help of allies, particularly J. P. Morgan, gained control of the company and began to bleed it. J. C. Fargo and Levi Weir, president of Adams, installed themselves on the States board of directors (at a salary of $3,600 per year), in violation of the States' charter, and soon after, Adams "won" back half of the government's money-carrying business, and Amexco wrested three major railroad contracts from the States, in what it claimed was "the normal course of business." Fargo and Weir protested that they had not abused their position at all, an assertion which no one took seriously, but which for some time no one—including the U.S. Express's other stockholders—could do anything about.

Tom Platt himself did not come out of this badly. While Fargo and Weir pillaged his company, they left Platt and several of his family members in office and even raised their salaries. Profits returned to the States with the help of a prolonged economic expansion. Though the board raised the dividend first (to the benefit of Adams and Amexco, the two largest shareholders), there was enough surplus left over so that the States could put up a new $3 million headquarters, built by a company in which one of Platt's sons had an interest. The losers in this were the other stockholders of the States, whose company was being bled without their consent; there had not been a shareholder meeting of the States since 1862.

The expresses played some of their own games by their own rules, but in much of what they did, they usually had one important ally, the railroads. True, some railroads exploited the competition Tom Platt had engendered between the expresses, but on the whole the two industries cooperated. In fact, they formed such extensive and important links that it was hard to tell just who was really calling the shots. They seemed to be calling them together as part of what was termed a "community of interest," and they both profited handsomely.

For the express companies, ties to the railroads were a form of insurance since their business required at least the cooperation of railroads. The express companies had loaned funds to the railroads in the 1860s to win contracts. Later on, express companies discovered that, through financing, they could dictate the terms of the contracts to the railroads. Railroads were very capital-intensive, and new or undercapitalized companies often had trouble raising money through normal channels—the bond market or the banks. But the expresses had both a great deal of money and a reason for lending specifically to the railroads.

The express companies soon realized that they could dominate a railroad with a weak credit rating by providing financing to it. They negotiated concessions that included guaranteed express contracts of ten years or more and control over every move the railroad made. When Amexco purchased $200,000 of a new preferred-stock issue of the Bangor & Aroostook RR, for example, it obtained a long-term express guarantee, veto power over any increases in the railroad's capital stock, and the right to approve any agreements of any kind that the B&A might make with another railroad.

With the Louisville, New Albany & Chicago Railway, in exchange for a $200,000 loan, Amexco won a ten-year, guaranteed contract, plus a personal, written pledge from the chief executive of the LNA&C that Amexco would have the contract "so long as I remain an Officer or Director of said Railway Company." American Express also collected the market rate of interest on the money it loaned and had the right to suspend express payments if interest on the loan became overdue.

Of course, the B&A and the LNA&C were a cut below blue-chip rail companies, and from an investment standpoint, their paper was speculative. But Amexco risked little since it ran the express business on both lines, which was bound to pay off even if the railways could not.

The large, wealthy railroads, like the New York Central, did not need cash from the expresses. Still, the express companies wanted to keep all their contracts on the most favorable terms possible, and so they found a way to exercise considerable influence even with the largest railroad companies in the country. The express companies dipped into their cash reserves and bought blocks of stock in the major railroads—particularly the railroads with whom they had large and lucrative express contracts.

American Express had three big holdings: the Central, the Chicago & Northwestern, and the Boston & Maine. The last of the three offers a good illustration of what such stock ownership meant in practical terms. In the early 1890s, Amexco held an exclusive express contract with the railroad and about 30,000 shares (10 percent) of the Boston & Maine's stock. In 1894, however, that troublemaker Tom Platt approached the management of the Boston & Maine. He promised them a better deal if they would sign on with the States after their express contract with Amexco expired.

Boston & Maine officials said no to Platt, and that was the end of it—until a few years later. In 1901, American Express was embroiled in a court case on a totally unrelated matter, but prosecutors were interested in knowing just how Amexco made and kept its contracts. They took a deposition from Amexco's lawyer, Lewis Cass Ledyard, who represented American Express's holdings on the board of the Boston & Maine. Just why, they wanted to know, did the railroad reject Platt's clearly superior offer? Ledyard explained, "It was the opinion of the Board, so the president stated, that the United States Express Company would not give their road anything like the business that the American Express could." Such a claim was certainly dubious. From the railroad's standpoint, one express was as good as another; Amexco or the States—the volume of business was likely to be the same, because the public had no alternative to the express carrier a railroad chose.

Ledyard—who, besides serving on the boards of Amexco and the Boston & Maine, was a director of three other railroads—proceeded with an unorthodox legal maneuver: he cross-examined himself at this hearing. He asked himself, "Has the ownership by the American Express Company of Boston & Maine railroad stock ever been used by the American Express Company to promote or further its interests in the express business upon the railroad or to promote or further the procuring of a contract for the doing of such business?"

"Never!" he answered himself.

Later, government officials had the opportunity to compare the Boston & Maine's contract with American Express and the one offered it by the States. They concluded that the Boston & Maine lost at least $10 million because it stuck with Amexco—news that sent the railroad's shareholders running to the courthouse. But for more than a decade, American Express held a favorable contract and collected dividends on its 30,000 Boston & Maine shares.*

Although the expresses benefited from the railroads, in return the expresses provided the roads with one tremendous advantage: a means to enormous profits in ways that circumvented government regulations. For years the railroads had fought brutal freight wars and engaged in price gouging and price discrimination. But in 1888, the U.S. government finally said enough and created the Interstate Commerce Commission (ICC) to regulate the railroad business. The act, however, left a loophole big enough to drive a train—an express train—through.

When the ICC was formed, the commissioners ordered all "common carriers" to file rates and other statistics. ("Common carrier" was a legal definition that referred to transportation companies. A common carrier was obliged to provide services without discrimination to anyone willing to pay.) The railroads, the target of the act, had no choice but to comply. The courts had declared express companies common carriers, too, and the ICC demanded they comply as well. But the expresses refused. The companies argued, first, that they were not guilty of the excesses of the railroads, so the act was not meant to apply to them; second, that the rates for express were exceptionally complicated and so beyond the limits of the small ICC staff to understand;

---

*The other express companies also had large holdings of railroad stock. The Adams, for example, owned 35,000 shares of one of its principal carriers, the New York, New Haven & Hartford RR.

and third, that expresses were only "contractors" with the railroads, and the law as written did not apply to them. The commissioners regarded the first two arguments as absurd, but they were persuaded by the third. Until Congress amended the law, the ICC agreed that express companies were exempt. For the rest of the century, the ICC's statisticians would plead with Congress to bring the expresses under their authority.

But ICC officials did not achieve their goal. Until the 1900s, national political leaders were reluctant to tamper with the free-enterprise system. Most politicians and the majority of voters believed that the only thing worse than big business would be a government decision to interfere with business.

Actually, some political groups advocated more extensive government regulation of business. The Populist movement of the 1870s and 1880s endorsed the idea of government control over all transportation companies—the railroads and the expresses. However, the Populists, a largely agrarian movement, though they did pass some state laws, could not put their program into practice on a national scale. The urban middle class regarded the Populists as radicals, and the movement remained outside the mainstream of American political thought. American voters saw regulation as a last resort, to be applied only after abuses became extreme. The abuses by the railroads had become intolerable, bringing about the creation of the ICC. But the public did not place express practices in the same category and so, generally, did not support its regulation.

Probusiness sentiment in the country made it easy for Boss Platt and his friend Senator Chauncy Depew to hold the Republican majority in Congress in line. Throughout the late nineteenth and the early twentieth centuries, they managed to quash all moves to bring the expresses under the jurisdiction of the ICC.

Consequently, the expresses never had to report anything about how they made money. The railroads reported everything to the government: freight rates, profits, passenger traffic, even how much they made from their express contracts. But they revealed neither the substance of those contracts, nor the nature of express-business practices.

But for the rails, an unregulated express meant they could profit by proxy from the kind of abusive and discriminatory practices that had gotten them into trouble in the first place. The express industry had created a system that allowed discrimination to go virtually undetected. Express rates, based on a mix of weight, value, and distance, were too complicated for the public to follow. As a result, express companies could raise rates on a whim, with almost no public reaction. The system worked like this: J. C. Fargo once heard that grape growers in one region of the country had a good crop;* although Amexco stood to benefit anyway from an increased volume of traffic, J.C. almost doubled the rates on the shipment of grapes coming out of that particular region. The same quantity of grapes traveling an even greater distance from another area could be shipped for less. The growers might have recognized that their charges had increased, but they could have proved discrimination only by investigating the entire market and performing an enormous number of calculations.

This complicated and unregulated system allowed rates overall to rise continuously, and since railroads by contract received a percentage—at least 40 percent, and up to as much as 60 percent—of express gross receipts, they made more money the higher express rates went. In fact, by the late 1800s, express rates averaged four times the rates for freight. This produced a perverse situation: railroads made twice as much money by encouraging people to use express instead of their own freight service. †

The public remained largely ignorant of express rate practices and express company ties to the railroads. Most people knew the companies

---

*Fruit growers had no real alternative to the express. Because they shipped perishables they depended on speed, and clearly the expresses took advantage of that fact.

†Some of the major railroads profited from the expresses in another way. Just as the express companies owned railroad stock, the rails, in turn, owned express-company shares. By the beginning of the twentieth century, the New York Central owned about one sixth of Amexco, and from 1900 to 1910, the railroad earned more than a quarter of a million dollars annually in dividends.

only through personal experience, which produced a widespread dislike of the entire express industry. Alvin Harlow, who as a young man worked in the express business and later wrote a book about it, said that nowhere else were people more brusquely treated than at express offices. John Hoey, the flamboyant president of Adams in the early 1890s, even joked about this. On the free passes the company gave out to friends he emblazoned a mock coat of arms bearing the motto, "Diligenter nequaquam" ("By no means diligently").

Because the companies enjoyed the status of unregulated monopolies, there was not much that dissatisfied customers could do.* They could complain, of course, but only to the company, and in the event of damage, they could file claims. The expresses promised to make good on losses, but the average customer confronted red tape more typical of government than private industry. A loss claim could take months to process and review. Thousands of people hauled the expressmen into court, but that was distinctly to the latter's advantage. There, a plaintiff had to confront the know-how of top law firms such as Carter & Ledyard (later Carter, Ledyard & Milburn), which was on retainer to Amexco for $12,000 a year to take all suits—even when they were for just a few dollars. Occasionally, Amexco's attorneys *appealed* court judgments of under $50 (the legal fees for the complainant would have been much higher), and they dragged out some trivial cases for a decade or more.

Despite what amounted to continual conflict with the public, the express companies succeeded in maintaining a policy of almost total secrecy into the twentieth century. Few businesses in those days were open about their affairs, but no other industry imposed the kind of blackout on information managed by the express companies. As unincorporated associations, they could legally deny shareholders and

---

*In 1886, the Supreme Court declared the exclusive express contract legal; the court ruled that a common carrier, such as a railroad, did not have to be a common carrier of other common carriers, i.e. express companies. This ruling effectively legalized the express monopoly.

anyone else information about the size and profitability of their business. In 1880, the companies even refused (and were not challenged) to give information to the U.S. Census Bureau. Still, the suppression of information that they achieved was surprising. Virtually everyone used the express; every town in America had at least one express office. But people did not even know which company was which. In 1897, Amexco's general auditor, W. E. Powelson, told J. C. Fargo candidly, "To show what the public know about express affairs I will say that I have been asked many times if Wells Fargo & Company were not owned by the American; and I blush to say that one apparently level headed man once asked me if the United States Ex. Co. did not own the American." Even express employees knew little of company affairs. In the same letter Powelson doubted that "one in ten of our own employees" was aware that American Express owned National Express. *

Only the government offered hope for any redress, but the expresses fought both national and state government for years to forestall any kind of intervention. The companies battled not only against regulation and competition, which really threatened the industry, they also fought against taxation, which did not. At first, they won. But their early victories and clever ploys for circumventing government action led to complacency and made the companies slow to accept change when it became inevitable.

While the companies always triumphed in Congress in the nineteenth century, they fared less well against state legislatures. The individual states were seldom interested in regulating the express business, and since the express was largely an interstate activity, the states could not have regulated many aspects of the business even if they had wanted to. But state officials saw the expresses as a potential source of

---

*Even top executives did not know of all the connections between the companies. William Swift Dalliba, for example, once launched a vigorous campaign to win business away from a U.S. Express office abroad. He appeared unaware of the fact that Amexco owned 10 percent of its competitor. When company officials in New York heard of the campaign, they told him to stop it at once.

revenue. Since taxes could always be passed along to customers in the form of higher charges, the express companies had little to lose but a principle: the right to keep their affairs private. The expresses believed the principle important enough so that they battled every attempt to tax them.

As they did in the U.S. Congress, the companies banded together to fight the states. They divided the states into spheres of influence; whichever company had the largest express business in a state became the leader of all legislative combat for the industry in that state. But all the companies paid a share of the cost of battle and had a say about tactics and policy. One company could, and often did, veto a plan of action.

The form of these actions varied. In 1870, in New York State, legislators introduced a bill which the companies killed, reportedly through outright bribery of the Tammany crowd that controlled the legislature. Encouraged that the companies were so willing to hand over cash, New York State lawmakers tried again in 1871. The board of American Express agreed to pay its share—$2,500—but Adams, perhaps feeling that this sort of extortion was a bad precedent, balked, killing the idea. At American Express, the directors resolved to let the matter "take its course," and if necessary to use its influences to persuade the governor to veto the measure. Probably Pomeroy was dispatched, as he often was, to "explain" the situation to his friends in office. The second bill died too.

How often the express companies resorted to bribery is not known, though such activity went on for many years. But there are literally dozens of unelaborated references to "legislative expenses" in the minutes of Amexco's executive committee. Sometimes these noted Amexco's share in many thousands of dollars—at a time when a couple of thousand would buy the services of a law firm to take a tax case from legislative hearings through to the Supreme Court. There is no doubt that some of the expenses were simply for lobbying activities, but other expenses may have been to put legislators on the payroll at least temporarily.

The expresses openly handed out one type of gift to hundreds of government officials. The companies dispensed free passes—"franks"—to just about everyone of importance. In 1899, American Express gave passes to, among others, the president and vice president of the United States as well as the secretaries of state, treasury, interior, agriculture, and navy, and both the postmaster and attorney generals. Key House and Senate figures had franks on all lines, and American Express had a whole category of "South Dakota legislative franks" for a long list of legislators, in a state where the express companies regularly had to fight off tax laws. Some reformers considered franks a form of bribery, and they tried to curb them even before the Civil War, but "franking" went on into the 1900s before it was finally stopped.

Despite such gifts, the express companies could not keep all laws unfavorable to the business—especially tax laws—off the books. This was especially true in states where there was a strong Populist movement, usually in the farm country of the Midwest. But when legislators enacted a tax law, the companies had other strategies to keep the tax collector at bay.

First, they used the we-aren't-a-corporation-so-your-law-doesn't-apply-to-us gambit. Indeed, the expresses were joint-stock associations, not corporations, and if a state erred in that regard when drafting a statute, the companies denied it applied to them. When a governmental body sought to tax express capital, they denied there was any of that either. As Alexander Holland told the New York State legislature in 1882, when it tried to impose a tax on Amexco's capital, "[American Express] has no Capital paid in or secured to be paid in." That claim, however, clashed with other statements made by Amexco. The board, for instance, routinely paid dividends on what it called the "capital stock" of the company, and the company even printed "Capital $18,000,000" on the top of its stationery.

But the story of how Amexco and Adams handled a tax law in Indiana provides the best illustration of the rearguard actions the companies fought against governments. In this battle, the Populist "granger element" in 1881 forced through the Indiana legislature a tax on the gross receipts of express companies. In response, Amexco and Adams adopted another ploy: the intrastate-expenses-receipts game.

The Indiana tax required the expresses to pay 1 percent of their gross receipts on business within the state. Amexco officials at first wanted to challenge the law in court on the grounds that most express business in any state was interstate, and only Congress had power over that. But a court challenge had the danger, as Amexco's lawyers explained, that the Indiana legislature would just go and write a different law that would stick.

On careful examination of the law, however, someone recognized that they could beat it, if they complied with it—sort of. The law allowed the expresses to deduct substantial expenses, so the companies figured out their gross receipts on intrastate shipments and then deducted virtually all of their expenses, whether they were connected with inter- or intrastate business. As a result, while in fact both Adams and Amexco were making hundreds of thousands of dollars in Indiana, they managed to show a loss *every* year.

Who was the clever soul who figured this one out? It may have been the resourceful Albert Antisdel, number-two man of Amexco's Western Department. J. C. Fargo did not know about this form of pseudocompliance until 1889, when Antisdel told him that over the eight years the law had been on the books Amexco had not paid a dime. But at just that time, Indiana legislators put an end to the express companies' ploy and pulled a trick of their own. To circumvent any attempts at bribery and other forms of "heavy pressure," the anti-express forces introduced and passed an amendment to the tax bill on the last day of the legislative session.

But the expresses tried another game: the "compromise tax." The idea was that the companies would declare some figure for "gross receipts" that would sound reasonable and would lead to the payment of an amount of tax satisfactory to state officials. Though American Express used this approach before in Maine and Michigan, for unexplained reasons J.C. opposed it in Indiana. In 1890, he directed Antisdel to file the usual report—a loss. This time state officials sent it back.

Indiana officials reacted mildly compared with the top brass at Adams. Adams had, through its agent in Indianapolis, John J. Henderson, a direct line to the state attorney general, and Henderson had been trying to work out a compromise. As Levi Weir, at the time the line superintendent of Adams, explained to J. C. Fargo: "I believe our agent has been of service to [the attorney general] in some way which is regarded as an obligation." At Weir's behest—he feared a harsher law if the expresses could not make a deal—Henderson cashed in his obligation and achieved a compromise tax. Adams planned to pay about $1,000, an amount Weir estimated would roughly equal the sum the company would have to pay a good lawyer to contest the case in the courts. Weir even calculated a good round number for Amexco— $1,140.

Fargo agreed on one condition: That the state attorney general pledge "in writing" that he would not try to collect the "balance of tax called for by the law." Obtaining such a written pledge was extremely unlikely, as Fargo must have known. An attorney general guaranteeing in writing that he would not fulfill a law? The Indiana attorney general did not provide it, and J.C. did not pay.

When tax time rolled around again Antisdel, after conferring with J.C., reported to the state a loss of $37,000. Weir was not pleased. "The trouble about the Indiana tax is that your company made a return [according to which you] would not be obliged to pay anything," he wrote to J. C. Fargo. He suggested strongly that Amexco should pay about $1,500 to satisfy state officials, and he also reminded J.C. of his duty to the express fraternity to stick together; he noted in a postcript that one other express company had agreed to play Adams's game. Fargo passed the letter on to Antisdel, who was not completely swayed by Weir's arguments, but did recalculate gross receipts in Indiana and came up with the company's first profit: $11,082.51, for a tax of $110.82. The state did not accept this figure either and told American Express to try again.

Amexco and the other expresses decided then to challenge the law in court. The litigation lasted into the twentieth century and in the end, the expresses lost. Amexco alone had to pay court costs, back

141

taxes, penalties, and other expenses totaling $28,207. Amexco's cost of fighting the tax was far more than the tax itself.

This kind of skirmishing with government persisted into the new century. The expresses managed to win some fights, delay others, and maintain their status and power, but by the middle of the first decade of the 1900s, their fortunes reversed, and the decline of the express business began. New political and social forces helped bring this about. The Progressives movement had supplanted the Populists as the leading reformist political group, with far greater impact. Muckraking journalists like Ida Tarbell and Upton Sinclair formed public opinion—particularly the view that big business equaled bad business, or at least unfair business. In time, the public came to accept, even demand, that government had the right and duty to make the free-enterprise system give everyone what the leading Progressive of the day, President Theodore Roosevelt, called a "square deal." The politicians and the muckrakers attacked the big, visible monopolies. They started with companies like Standard Oil, but inevitably, they soon focused on one of the most secretive and most obvious targets of all, a monopoly business in every town in America, the expresses.

Beginning in 1905, the expresses finally came under legal pressure both from the various governmental bodies and from the companies' own stockholders. For their manipulation of the U.S. Express, Fargo, Weir, and Platt were hauled into court by shareholders. The States directors—including Fargo and Weir—responded characteristically: they raised the dividend to buy off the dissidents. But shareholders refused to end their legal action, and the case piqued the interest of the attorney general of New York. When he threatened to bring an antitrust action against Amexco and Adams, the companies sold their stock in the States to railroad man E. H. Harriman. Government threats also forced the expresses to cancel the territorial agreements they had lived by for more than half a century.

Meanwhile, the companies could no longer escape publicity. In 1905, an article by Frank Haigh Dixon in *Atlantic Monthly* spelled out for the first time how little was known of this vital enterprise.

Dixon concluded, "To require of express companies reports similar to those required of railways would seem to be the immediate duty of Congress. The express business is, from every point of view, an industry which should be subjected to the principle of publicity." It was the first critical article on the expresses since 1870.

By 1906, Congress got the message. The Republican majority in the Senate followed Depew and Platt and voted once again to exempt the express companies from ICC oversight. This time, however, Democrats, led by Mississippi Congressman John Sharp Williams, raised a strong objection and threatened to turn the exemption of the express companies into a partisan issue. Williams declared that if the Republicans exempted the express companies, then the Democrats would retaliate by turning Republican support to the express companies into a campaign issue. The Republicans backed off, unwilling to run as friends of the expresses. As a result, the progressives won a victory over Depew and Platt in Congress. The Hepburn Act of 1906 at last placed the express companies under the authority of the ICC, but it did not mandate any particular form of regulatory action. The ICC had to investigate the expresses first, and the commission promptly demanded that the companies submit their schedule of tariffs. U.S. Express reported it would need *six months* just to compile all its rates. Amexco said its filing would include 18 million separate rates, and Wells Fargo said it had 11 million. They had, if anything, understated the clerical problem of putting together a list of rates.

Besides the power to examine rates, the ICC had the statutory right to demand statements of earnings and of securities held; they could finally find out how much money the express companies had. This prospect provoked a sudden, eye-opening move by Adams. To the amazement of Wall Street, Adams announced a dividend of $24 million in bonds, equal to 200 percent of the company's capitalization. It looked, correctly, like an attempt to distribute the company's surplus before the ICC forced Adams to reveal just how wealthy it was—a revelation likely to produce stockholder outrage and even lawsuits. Most of all, the surprise dividend suggested that all express companies had much greater wealth than anyone had realized. Adams's largess put pressure on the other companies to open their treasuries. Stockholders threatened Amexco with a suit, forcing J. C. Fargo to raise the dividend. J.C. still seemed to feel that he could buy people off this way indefinitely. When the shareholders' action ended, he noted smugly that the rise had put "these chaps" out of business.

But the power and prestige of expresses continued to weaken. The ICC provided a forum for complaints against the companies that had been accumulating for half a century. There were so many—most of them from businessmen who felt they had been discriminated against—the ICC finally decided it could not hear them all separately. As ICC commissioner Franklin Lane wrote later, "So numerous were the complaints made to us informally as well as formally of the unreasonableness of express practices and rates that we found it impracticable to deal with express conditions over the line of a single carrier or within narrow territorial limits." Instead, in 1909, Lane launched a comprehensive investigation of the whole business; it would take him and his statisticians three years to finish it.

Before the ICC could finish its study, the expresses suffered a debacle of an entirely different nature. In October 1910, express helpers in New York City walked off the job. Soon drivers and other express workers followed, demanding higher wages, shorter hours, and the right to unionize. The companies had fought labor actions for years, mainly by hiring scab workers and firing union members. While such tactics had succeeded in the past, this time they only produced violence. As the rioting escalated and undelivered express material mounted, New York's mayor, William Gaynor, stepped in and threatened to impound express wagons driven by scabs, and finally, he forced a settlement. Initially, the strikers gained little: they were guaranteed their jobs back (unless they had engaged in violence), and they won a promise from the companies to negotiate their grievances. In dollars and cents, the expresses were not hurt badly; Amexco lost about $30,000. But the companies suffered a more serious blow to their reputations. As the press investigated the causes of the labor action, it reported another aspect of express-industry abuse—abuse of their workers.

In the early twentieth century, people routinely worked long hours for low pay; yet when the press detailed the lot of the express worker, the public was shocked. Wages for wagon helpers were especially low, as little as $17 per month and never higher than $50. Drivers who, the express companies explained, ran "express offices on wheels," made $65–75 per month. By the standards of the day, neither helpers nor drivers made enough to live on. Drivers had a maximum income of $900 per year, while U.S. mail carriers earned a minimum of $967 and as much as $1,183. The earnings of express helpers were, on average, $100 a year below those of the lowest category of railroad employees. Routinely, helpers and drivers put in fifteen-hour days, and were required to work on holidays and one Sunday a month. There was no overtime pay.*

The companies maintained that they looked after their workers. The express companies gave employees assurances for their retirement— something not every business provided in those days. From 1875 on, Amexco paid a pension to all longtime employees—payments that chief auditor W. E. Powelson noted were not charity but were designed to "foster a feeling of fraternity and oneness" among employees.

Yet the darkest side of the labor story was never reported in the press at all. In 1884, the express companies had made a cartel arrangement on labor, just as they had on prices and territory—a cynical pact in view of their antiunion bias. (It is not clear if the agreement was still in force in 1910. Amexco's records do not indicate that it was terminated, but by this time, the companies, under pressure from the government, had abandoned most of their pacts.) Under the agreement, the companies had assumed "absolute control of the welfare of an

---

*Also employees had to grant the companies unconditional release from liability and had to pay a few dollars out of their salaries to become bonded. In most cases, the bonding companies were wholly or partly owned by the express companies.

employee in so far as his employment in the express service of any of the [major express] companies is concerned." No employee could switch jobs from one company to another without "a written document setting forth the fact that such application is made with the knowledge and consent of the company employing him." A Wells Fargo vice president did suggest that this pact was "onerous and unjust to employees." But the others, including J. C. Fargo, disagreed, noting that a free labor market was "expensive to the joint interests" of the express companies.

Still, what the public did learn during the strike was bad enough. And another blow followed soon after—a long exposé by muckraker Albert Atwood. His four-part piece in *American Magazine* on the express business outlined all the interconnections between the expresses and the railroads, rehashed all of the labor issues, and concluded with a plea for a government parcel-post system. After the Atwood article appeared, the public image of the express companies hit bottom.* But for the express companies the worst news was still ahead. The business was about to face what expressmen had always dreaded: regulation on a vast scale and competition they could not suppress.

In 1912, Lane and his ICC staff finished their investigation of the express business, and their conclusions were devastating. In a 600-page report, Lane called for a total overhaul of the business. The commission had concluded that "the evils [were] so fundamental it has been deemed necessary not only to criticize and correct existing rules and rates, but to build from the very bottom by outlining a national system stating rates, a rational classification of express freight, and to enter into the minutiae of the billing, routing, and other details."

Lane concerned himself mainly with rates, which he found so incoherent that they guaranteed abuse. It was not exactly certain how

---

*In light of the bad press the expresses received in the U.S., Dalliba's performance in Europe took on even greater importance. It did not counteract the negative press Amexco received at home, but rather created a separate, positive image for the company abroad.

many different rates there were nationwide; Lane's staff found 600 million to examine, but by another reckoning the expresses had 200 *billion* separate rates. Expecting any single human to be able to apply all of them accurately was ludicrous. Yet express companies expected their agents—some of them in the $50-per-month category—to do that every day. (They had to learn *every* company's rates since packages often had to travel through or to another company's territory.) Lane, in an experiment, asked the same express company the rate on the same package to the same destination three different times on the same day. The company quoted him a different rate each time.

Incorrectly calculated rates led to an enormous number of over and under charges. Lane's men detected 4,000 errors in one day at just one company; they examined another company and found 3,000 errors. Not even the most aggressive muckrakers had guessed the magnitude of the problem before.

One of the main reasons for the "overs" was the double collection: customers paid all charges when they dropped a package off, and the company collected again on delivery. Since a willful overcharge was a criminal offense, few agents collected double charges deliberately. The problem stemmed from a vague, complicated waybilling system that often left unclear whether charges had been paid or not. Since employees were personally liable for shortages in the till, they preferred to err on the side of a double charge rather than a missed one.

The expresses knew about overs and unders, and several years before the ICC findings came out, an auditor at American Express, Frederick P. Small, devised a new waybill system that would prevent them. Small took the initiative and had his waybills printed up, but J. C. Fargo discovered Small's innovation, and he told the clerk, "You tend to your business and don't try any monkey business on American Express. And I'll see that you don't." Small gave in without a fight. Just what irked J.C. is a puzzle. J.C. knew of the unders and overs and must have realized that the waybills would solve the problem. The possibility remains that he just did not want anyone tinkering with a system that worked so badly so well.

The remedy Lane had in mind was more drastic than a new waybill. He intended to overhaul the whole rate and billing system from the ground up—and he did it in dramatic fashion. He chucked all the millions of old rates and substituted a zonal system with a fixed per-pound rate from zone to zone. Any changes in rates from the ones he set would have to be approved thereafter by the ICC.*

Lane had high hopes for his system. Not only would it make express rates rational and comprehensible, he believed it would lower inflation. Lane was wrong about reducing the cost of living, but his system did indeed lower express rates, and of course express-company profits as well. The companies complained that the ICC's ruling had cost them revenues of $26 million in 1913, but they had only one recourse now: they went hat in hand to the ICC asking for rate relief.

In 1913, they needed that relief more than ever. Congress at last authorized a government parcel-post system. The Post Office finally won its victory because the expresses had lost all credibility with the public, and their support in Congress had evaporated. (Tom Platt died in 1910.) Because of the parcel post, express profits fell by another two thirds in 1914. The decline was so dramatic that some of the same businessmen who had complained about the express companies, now went before the ICC to plead the expresses' case. Many business leaders saw the ICC regulations as an example of government overkill, and supported the companies' demand for rate relief. But it did not come quickly, and profits remained extremely poor.

The United States Express, in fact, posted a loss in 1914, and its directors decided to liquidate the company. American Express took over 12,000 miles of express lines and 2,400 offices from the States; Adams and Wells Fargo divvied up the rest. But with the new rules and the new competition, these routes were not the plums they had once been.

---

*Lane cracked down on other express practices. He even set up rules for the maintenance and destruction of express records. In the course of a few years, the express business changed from an industry with no regulation to become one of the most tightly regulated.

Initially, American Express faced the new era of competition and limited profit without a leader. J. C. Fargo, at eighty-four in 1913, still ruled as chief executive of Amexco, but his health was failing. After 1912, he ran American Express in name only; loyal Francis Flagg, now first vice president, took charge, but only as a caretaker. J.C. did not designate a successor or delegate power, much less resign. Yet his absence from business and Flagg's lack of real authority left the company powerless to make decisions. The board of directors refused to undertake its most urgent task—to force J.C. out. Instead it waited for the old man either to resign or die—neither of which he seemed prepared to do.

Though the board was unwilling to oust J.C., it did take the matter of succession into its own hands around 1912. From the outset, the directors decided to end family domination of the company. All the bad publicity had demoralized the company, and the Fargo-family rule had become a source of increasing resentment among senior managers. The board apparently applied three criteria in choosing the next chief executive. First, he had to be a good manager and a good negotiator. Second, because of the labor troubles of 1910, he needed to be in touch with rank-and-file employees. And finally, he could not be a Fargo.

The man they settled on was George Chadbourne Taylor, the head of Amexco's Western Department. Taylor, in his mid-forties, was the epitome of the self-made expressman. A broad-shouldered man with a boundless store of energy, he had worked his way through college and up from the very bottom of the express business. Like J.C., he had an explosive temper, and even one of his admirers admitted he could be "outspoken, unruly and aggressive." But for the most part, he was quite the opposite of the imperious Fargo. He possessed a good sense of humor, an "eye for the ladies," an open, friendly attitude toward his fellow executives, and a fun-loving spirit. Once, as an executive, he swore he could drive a team as well as ever, and when challenged, he leapt into a wagon and drove at top speed down the street. He also had a good deal of bluff in him. When he went before the board to accept the presidency, he told the directors he had one condition and handed them a sheet of paper—his resignation, to become effective, he said, the "first God Damn time anyone in this group tries to tell me how to run my job."

When J.C. finally resigned in June 1914, the board named Taylor president partly because he was the best negotiator in the company— a good bargainer with a personal style that opponents found winning and tough. At the ICC hearings in 1912, for example, Taylor admitted no wrongdoing, and provided a seemingly clear explanation of how the express companies operated. Then he deflected an aggressive question from Commissioner Lane on the partnership between the express companies and the railroads with a polite evasion and praise of the "honesty" of the railmen. Such diplomatic skills had become especially important. In the new, regulated environment, the chief executive would have to seek the most favorable deals possible from the railroads as well as from the ICC.

Taylor had also won the respect and even love of employees throughout the ranks of the company. Executives in New York had bungled the strike of 1910 in large part because they maintained a relationship to employees described as "telescopic," but Taylor, though personally antiunion, was seen as someone who could restore and maintain labor peace. Indeed, Taylor often felt more comfortable with drivers and messengers than he did with board members, who he once contemptuously dismissed as "these bankers, lawyers and others, none of whom had ever bent his back to pick up an express package." Taylor knew dozens of employees by their first names, and on inspection trips, he often stopped to greet the lowest-ranking employees before he saw the managers. At 65 Broadway, employees considered him the kind of boss "anyone could go up and see." He learned the names of the clerical staff, a breathtaking change after J. C. Fargo, who never spoke to some people in his own office for decades. Taylor even called on sick messengers and dipped into his pockets to help employees in trouble.

Though the board had apparently picked him as early as 1912, his elevation took the company by surprise. Expressmen in the field must have expected one of J.C.'s sons—J.F., vice president and treasurer, or W.C., secretary and director—to get the nod. When the board announced the appointment of Taylor, people throughout the company called it "an inspiration."

In Taylor, the directors and the company actually got more than they understood or bargained for. Taylor was very much a western expressman—a protégé of Albert Antisdel and the other western entrepreneurs, and he surrounded himself with like-minded people. He was not simply a modern manager for his time. He was a manager for our time, with a style that emphasized planning, marketing, and a level of creative thinking never before permitted at 65 Broadway.

When Taylor took over in the summer of 1914, his first task was to put the express on a paying basis again. The company was losing money—over $500,000 in 1913 and $600,000 in 1914. Flagg had done nothing to stop the losses. In fact, Flagg's thinking showed how the old guard could not, as one younger executive put it, "really adapt themselves to their environment." In response to the losses, Flagg was all for mounting a battle against the ICC. But times had changed, and lawyers advised that the tactic would create "adverse publicity." Without the possibility of war, Flagg had run out of ideas.

Taylor on the other hand plunged into the problem. He ordered expenses cut, and while he included the salaries of all employees, he started with executive salaries, cutting them on a sliding scale—20 percent for those making the most money down to 5 percent for those making $2,000 a year. Then he cut the dividend to $1 per quarter, half the rate of the year before. In the past, the dividend was cut last, and executive salaries next to last. In 1908, for example, in the face of a reduction in business, the executive committee had ordered cuts in *pension* benefits, and at the same time raised the dividend.

Taylor's leadership turned the company around by 1915, when the company recorded a profit of $500,000. However, the express business itself still lost money. Amexco earned enough from its various financial and foreign operations to obscure its problems in the express business. One executive even proposed to Taylor that Amexco split off its domestic express into a separate company to make plain to the ICC how bad business really had become. But the plan was shelved when Taylor and the heads of the other express company, with the help of many business leaders, managed to win a rate hike from the ICC. The next year Amexco's total profits topped $3 million, the first year the express business itself had made money since 1912.

Next, Taylor launched an effort to keep Amexco profitable. He began a marketing effort to compete with the parcel post. Under J. C. Fargo, the company had founded a "publicity bureau," but in 1915, Taylor upgraded it to a full-scale advertising department, headed by a newcomer, S. Douglas Malcolm.

Malcolm began running an extensive advertising campaign to sell the public on the express business. But he also needed to persuade express employees to become more accommodating to customers. Toward that end, Malcolm created a house organ, *American Express Service*, that first appeared in 1916 with advice and lectures on salesmanship. Articles bore titles such as "Selling Ourselves To Ourselves," and contained warnings against rudeness and sloppiness because, as the magazine said, the "boss" might be checking up. The company's effort, mirrored at other express companies, had the intended effect. Wrote Alvin Harlow, "A great change was now observed in the atmosphere of express offices."

J.C. did not live to see the next item on Taylor's agenda. J.C. died early in 1915, and Taylor immediately began purging the company of Fargos. W.C. resigned within two months of J.C.'s death. Charles's son, Livingston Wells Fargo, retired though he was only in his early fifties. J.F., meanwhile, remained treasurer but was stripped of his vice presidency, his influence, and half his salary; it must have been a deep humiliation for him after thirty years of service, and he was the last Fargo with any status in the company at all.

Taylor also reversed some of J.C.'s long-standing policies—he ended the ban on women employees—and he went on to sweep out a good portion of the New York operation. Flagg, for example, stayed on for a few more years without power or influence, and the head of the

Eastern Department and the general traffic manager both retired by 1915. Only a few New York executives remained after the purge. F. P. Small of waybill fame became an assistant to Taylor and later took over as company secretary from W. C. Fargo. Harry Gee, successor to M. F. Berry at the European Department, also remained and soon rose into the top ranks of management.

Long after the Fargos and their supporters had been eliminated, Taylor displayed a hypersensitivity to nepotism and "influence." Into the 1920s, Malcolm's house organ denied that advancement depended on contacts rather than accomplishments. Taylor himself once refused to allow his western manager to promote his brother C. S. Taylor. "No one is going to say that I pushed my brother along," Taylor said. "Let him stay where he is or get out."

Though Taylor's efforts had improved morale, image, and profits, life had gone out of the express business. With competition from the parcel post, Amexco struggled continuously to make ends meet.

In 1917, with America's entry into World War I, the express business remained marginally profitable and even picked up for a time. But late in the year, the U.S. rail-transportation system dissolved in chaos. The military made demands on the railroads for freight haulage that the rails could not meet. Freight backed up, and essential materials lay on sidings for days. Most express material traveled on passenger trains and was not affected at first. In fact, some shippers who normally used freight sent goods by express instead to make sure their shipments arrived.

By autumn 1917, the freight situation had become a crisis. The trouble lay in the rail system itself; the independently run railroad companies did not have the mechanism or the will to coordinate their efforts effectively. As a result, strategic industries lacked the materials they needed to operate. Finally, the ICC called the heads of the major railroads together and formed the Railroad War Board to deliver the nation's freight. By December, however, the board had failed in the effort and resigned. President Woodrow Wilson felt he had no choice

153

but to seize the entire American railroad system, every car and mile of track, and he made Secretary of the Treasury William Gibbs McAdoo director general of the entire system. After the takeover, however, the government did not honor the contracts between the railroads and the express companies.

The blow disrupted the express business and company cash flow. Suddenly red ink again filled the bottom line of the expresses. For his part, McAdoo did not seem to have even thought of the predicament of the express companies. He had larger worries: getting the freight rolling again, and as treasury secretary, providing the money to finance the war effort. But the express companies needed to restore their business as quickly as possible. Soon after the railroad takeover, representatives of the express companies met to discuss strategy. They were in a delicate position. Protesting would only draw bad publicity if they were seen putting themselves and their profits above the war effort. But they were losing thousands of dollars every day.

On January 10, 1918, Taylor and executives and lawyers from the other major companies met with McAdoo in Washington. Although the results of the meeting were not made public, it appeared that the director general made no concessions to the expressmen, except a promise to begin negotiations for a solution to their problem. McAdoo placed the negotiations in the hands of ICC Director Charles A. Prouty.

Prouty began talking with express representatives soon after. He also consulted state railway boards and other public officials, including the postmaster general, for opinions on what to do with the expresses. Within a few weeks, Prouty had narrowed the discussions to four possible actions. First, the government could do nothing and continue to pay the expresses on the basis of their old contracts; but Prouty and the companies opposed the idea. Second, the government could seize the expresses, as it had the rails, and pay the companies a fixed sum for the duration of the war—and then return everything to the *status quo ante.* But Prouty dismissed this alternative because he felt the expresses asked for too much money.

The express companies proposed the third alternative. They wanted

154

to negotiate a uniform contract with the government, covering all the railroads. At the time, because every railroad had the right to conclude whatever deal it could get from its express carrier, when a single shipment passed from railroad to railroad the express companies had to make ever-changing calculations. A uniform contract would prevent confusion, eliminate bookkeeping expenses, and improve operating efficiency. The companies would pool earnings, and at common points, facilities. As F. P. Small said later, "Instead of two wagons with half a load, there could be one wagon with a full load." Then at the end of the war, the expresses could easily reclaim their separate identities.

Prouty, however, firmly opposed this plan too. Instead, he wanted a single government-regulated express entity—a private company to be "the agent of the government in the transaction of express business upon all railroads operated by the government" (a regulated, private, national company something like the old AT&T, although in this instance a company with a government-owned competitor—the Post Office). This new company would combine all of the express assets of the old companies, and some capital in cash from them as well. In return, the old companies would receive stock and dividends. "It secures complete unification of the express business," Prouty explained, "without risk or trouble to the government and it leaves the conduct of that business in such shape as to be readily controlled by the government."

Before Prouty raised this alternative with McAdoo, he posed it to the companies. They were dismayed. Prouty was planning a general merger and consolidation of the business—a combination of facilities, the merging of assets, the creation of a new corporate entity with its own name—that would be almost impossible to unscramble at the end of the war. The companies argued against the plan, but Prouty let them know that what they wanted did not matter. As he told McAdoo, the companies eventually "assented in a general way."

In February, Amexco's board gave Taylor permission to do what he thought best, and the companies began three months of nonstop ne-

155

gotiations with Director Prouty to work out the details. One important concession came from the government: Prouty agreed to a government guarantee of a 5 percent dividend on the new company's stock. Other details produced not just hard bargaining, but hard feelings. Taylor and Wells Fargo chief executive, B. D. Caldwell, nearly got into a fistfight, and Carter, Ledyard attorney Edwin deT. Bechtel had to step between them. No one recalled years afterward what brought the men to blows, but the expressmen argued principally about the division of the stock in the new company and the unfunded pension liabilities of the old companies—liabilities that totaled hundreds of millions of dollars.

They worked out the details in May 1918; at the end of the month, a new company, first called Federal Express and then American Railway Express (ARE), was born. American Express emerged with 40 percent of the stock, at a cost of about $11 million—stock that paid a government-guaranteed cash dividend of about $550,000 a year. Amexco turned over to the ARE assets the company had accumulated strictly for the express business, such as garage facilities for express trucks, but Amexco kept 65 Broadway and the company's large liquid surplus.

Taylor was elected president of ARE while remaining head of Amexco. Executives from Amexco and the other express companies filled the upper ranks of the new company's management. The ARE opened for business in July 1918. In only six months, American Express had lost the business that had been the reason for its being for the past sixty-eight years. *

Most of the express companies were essentially put out of business; Adams became simply an investment trust. At Amexco, employees felt that the company's "guts had been ripped out." But for American

---

*Amexco attempted to retain its status as a transportation company by keeping express contracts on two small intrastate railroads. The company took the step because of a New York State law that said only banks and transportation companies could sell their own TCs and money orders. By keeping the lines, Amexco at least confused regulators and kept its financial paper business.

Express, the action of the government was in many ways a blessing. Though Amexco was now much smaller, it had lost a business that had turned into a financial albatross and remained a public relations problem. Amexco was also ready to become a different company. Because of the efforts of people like M. F. Berry, William Swift Dalliba, and others, the company had vast new opportunities. Most of all it had the TC, a product that was large, growing, and consistently profitable.

It also had a new spirit. Soon after Taylor came to power, American Express had a strong impetus for change and growth. Taylor had gathered around him men of vision, and by 1918, they were already remaking American Express in dramatic fashion.

THE
AGE OF
ENTREPRENEURS

6

Shortly after the government expropriated Amexco's domestic express business, the company's chief executive, George Taylor, confidently declared that "separation would make us bigger and stronger" in the long run. Given the fact that American Express had just lost most of its organization, Taylor's statement was extraordinary, but there was good reason to believe he was right.

Three years earlier, Taylor had removed J.C.'s son, J. F. Fargo, as the company's chief financial officer and replaced him with Howard K. Brooks. No appointment had greater importance in the company's history. A small, bespectacled man, Brooks was a visionary who set in motion a radical transformation of the American Express Company. In late 1914, while Europe lay shattered by the conflict of World War I and most of the world became inaccessible to commerce, Brooks announced his intention of turning Amexco into a company that would provide "Round-the-World" service. He envisioned a colossal international organization offering a full range of shipping, foreign trade, and tourist services. Yet the company he planned to create would, above all, be dedicated to finance. He intended to make American Express a worldwide banking organization with a breadth and scope unlike any other in America, "with branches in every important city in the world" providing every type of banking service. For three years before the loss of the domestic express business and for some time after, Taylor gave Brooks the opportunity to make this new company a reality.

But Brooks not only remade the company's business activities. He also changed the way American Express made decisions. For the previous thirty-three years, J. C. Fargo's arbitrary and autocratic style had focused all official power in himself, though J.C.'s most enterprising executives found ways around his unbending stance—indeed, some simply went behind his back. But with Taylor's encouragement, Brooks instituted a more systematic process for making decisions. He believed in analysis, planning, and market study. He asked for ideas from staff, and he listened to the answers. While Brooks masterminded a new American Express, he and Taylor created a management system based on the philosophy of individual initiative, which they had both learned when they worked in Chicago for the entrepreneurial Western Department.

Even before Brooks came to the New York headquarters in 1915, his ideas had expanded Amexco's financial business and added hundreds of thousands of dollars annually to Amexco's profits. From the 1880s on, during the years that Brooks worked in Chicago, his innovations reached throughout the nation and across the seas. Of course, Brooks was not the first man to take Amexco into new financial territory. His own efforts built on the work of M. F. Berry. Berry's TC and MO provided Amexco with ongoing financial operations. But Brooks more than anyone else pushed Amexco to become a financial institution.

He affected Amexco's course before 1915 through a combination of genius, tenacity, and the support of Albert Antisdel and Charles Fargo. Brooks's position in Chicago was unique. For nearly thirty years after he was "fired" in 1882 by J. C. Fargo for the bed sheet ad campaign he had invented, Brooks wielded influence in the company out of all proportion to his official status. For most of that time, he held the rank of clerk, or assistant money order manager, and drew a small salary. (It took him twenty-three years to reach the rank of manager of the western financial business.) Yet Antisdel, the assistant superintendent (and later superintendent) of the Western Department, relied on Brooks more than he did most of his senior managers. Brooks, a dapper dresser and a lover of nightlife, even became the Chicago office's offical host. As another executive later described it, "Distinguished guests from anywhere who wished to see Chicago were referred to Brooks who became their cicerone with an unlimited expense account. . . . Nothing but an assistant cashier at $100 a month, but better than anyone else with the big shots." Far more importantly, Antisdel gave Brooks a practically unlimited opportunity to think up ideas and implement them. He applied his active imagination partly to the matter that had won him his reputation: advertising and promotion. But above all, as Antisdel put it,. Brooks was "prolific" in ideas for developing the company's financial business.

Brooks not only thought up financial schemes, he proved that he could manage them capably as well. In Chicago in the 1880s, Brooks created the most extensive network of money-order sales outlets in an American city. He signed on hundreds of branch agents mainly among drug, grocery, and book stores, providing money-order service for ordinary people in places they frequented every day. The basic idea of expanding the branch network was not Brooks's; J.C. and his brother Mortimer Fargo had encouraged their men to sign up "leading stores." But Brooks interpreted those instructions liberally in applying them to the corner druggist. Antisdel did not restrain him in the slightest; in fact, he even gave Brooks a separate express wagon for his collections.

Brooks's next idea built on his branch network. Since nearly everyone was in reach of a money-order branch, and since everyone also had to pay utility bills—mostly gas, some electricity—Brooks envisioned a way to combine the two—sell money orders to pay gas bills, providing receipts for the bills to customers and a collection service for the utilities. Brooks first took his idea to Samuel Insull, the man who controlled Chicago's electric and gas utilities. Although at the time, Brooks held the lowly title of assistant manager for money orders for Chicago, he nevertheless knew Insull on a first-name basis. When Insull heard the scheme, he approved it and even suggested Brooks quit American Express and take up the business for himself.

But Brooks stayed loyal to Amexco, and he instead brought the idea back to Antisdel and Charles Fargo, both of whom endorsed it. Antisdel also assumed the burden of approaching J. C. Fargo. Typically, J.C. rejected the idea at first, but Antisdel pressed him for a month, until the chief executive relented and let Brooks try it for a short period. After the business started, however, Brooks made it profitable in Chicago and convinced J.C. to adopt it in every town where Amexco could get a franchise from a local utility. But nowhere did it prove as profitable or as thoroughly managed and promoted as in Chicago under Brooks. Utility collections in Chicago alone were more than twenty times greater than those of the entire Eastern Department. By the turn of the century, profits on this business in Chicago reached about $35,000 a year (less than 1 percent of the company's total net profit, but consistent and growing steadily) and utility collection earnings in other cities provided several thousand more.

A few years later, Brooks applied his talents to another new business, and this time he chose an enterprise that brought him into the realm of international finance. Brooks taught himself foreign-exchange trading and made it a business activity for Amexco; indeed, he was so successful at it that by the early 1900s, foreign-exchange operations produced almost as much profit as all of Amexco's other financial operations combined.

The TC and the foreign money order had made Amexco retail dealers of foreign exchange. Every company office converted MOs, TCs, and, as a courtesy for tourists, actual currency as well.* Amexco

---

*Amexco had the exchange concession at Ellis Island for a number of years.

161

took a small profit on the exchange, of course, giving the tourist less currency per dollar than the company could get itself. Amexco never speculated in currency transactions; indeed, the acceptance of the gold standard throughout the western world permitted exchange rates to vary so little from year to year that such speculation was really not possible.

But foreign-exchange *trading* was a different kind of business, one conducted mostly between banks and other financial companies, and Amexco officials never displayed interest in it. Brooks, however, learned how money was made in exchange trading. While countries had agreed on a fixed value of gold bullion, an exchange transaction also involved costs of transport, interest on the time involved in shipment of the currency, insurance, and so on. These costs (which, unlike gold, did fluctuate), not the exchange rates themselves, provided the opportunities in the exchange-trading market of the late nineteenth and early twentieth centuries.

Most exchange trading involved drafts used in import-export transactions.* To take an example that Brooks used, when an American grain dealer sold a shipment of wheat to an English firm, the U.S. grain dealer attached a bank draft to the invoice for acceptance or outright payment by the British importer. After acceptance of the draft, the importer usually had thirty, sixty, or ninety days (depending on the terms of the agreement) to pay it. But since a transatlantic commercial transaction could take months to complete, the exporter often preferred to sell the draft in America at a discount to someone else who would take on the burden of collecting from the English importer. Although a British pound might command $4.86 officially, and a tourist might get $4.82, a local U.S. buyer of a draft might pay the exporter at the rate of, say, $4.80—more or less per pound depending

---

*In several major European cities, there were trading centers where drafts and other negotiable "bills of exchange" were traded. In London, foreign-exchange traders met every Tuesday and Thursday at the Royal Exchange in the "City," London's financial center.

on how quickly and how reliably he could collect from the English importer. Of course there was always a risk for the buyer of a draft; he could wind up with paper that the importer could or would not redeem. And profit margins tended to be fairly low because competition was keen between foreign-exchange traders for drafts from, and to, reliable firms. Nevertheless, following the Columbian Exposition of 1893, the increasing trade between the U.S. and Europe generated a tremendous amount of export-import business, and so exchange trading could be quite lucrative for an aggressive company with a competent staff.

Although Brooks had virtually no formal education, he possessed a scholarly bent and a deep intellectual curiosity about the financial world, and he taught himself the essentials of exchange trading. It was not an easy self-study program. Foreign-exchange traders were very clubby and tended to guard their secrets. Brooks, in fact, later found it difficult to hire knowledgeable people to help in the exchange business. He discovered that even after a couple years of experience in bank For/Ex departments, junior employees often had not learned what exchange trading was all about. Yet Brooks penetrated the secrets of the traders' club so thoroughly that he wrote two books on the subject, lectured at the University of Chicago, and gained recognition as one of the foremost authorities on exchange trading in America.

There is no record about how he started the exchange business for American Express, or when or why J. C. Fargo let him do it. However, Brooks began the business probably after 1895 (the year the company opened its first office abroad),* and he may have conducted it without telling executives at 65 Broadway for a year or two. However, after he demonstrated its profitability, trading became an accepted part of the company's financial business, and by 1898, the New York office pub-

---

*Amexco's exchange trading business inevitably involved the new foreign offices, which were in position to trade, or collect on, drafts purchased in the U.S. As Brooks's business grew, the company's offices abroad were drawn increasingly into these financial operations.

lished a circular saying that both New York and Chicago were "always in the market" for foreign drafts.

New York and Chicago may have been equally "in the market," but Chicago was far more active and aggressive in pursuing exchange business than New York. In 1900, Brooks engaged in 41,788 transactions, a total volume of $6.6 million, and a profit of $16,000, ten times the amount earned by the Eastern Department. The real growth in the business came over the next few years. By 1907, exchange-trading profits throughout the company—still mainly in the Midwest under Brooks—had risen to over $400,000 a year. The operation Brooks created now generated nearly 10 percent of total profits for the company; it was more profitable than either the TC or the MO.

Brooks believed that he could make still more money in exchange trading, but only if the company took an important step first: it needed to reorganize all its financial activities and create a bank. Brooks on his own could not have convinced J.C. to create a bank, and Brooks had lost his most important backers in the company. By 1906, both Charles Fargo and Albert Antisdel had died; to get J.C.'s approval now, Brooks allied himself with the company's treasurer and chief financial officer, J.C.'s son, J. F. Fargo. J.F. agreed with Brooks about the need for a bank, and in 1907, J.F. formally proposed one.

He and Brooks believed that a bank was now not just timely, but urgent. After years of indifference to the express money order, the American Bankers Association suddenly launched an attack on it. The group decried the fact that banks were subject to regulation while the expresses conducted their banklike business "contrary to justice and law," and in late 1906, the ABA formed a committee to take the issue to the ICC, which now had power over the expresses. The association also proposed legislation to make it illegal for common carriers to sell money orders, letters of credit, or TCs—legislation that made it onto the docket in Missouri and Illinois in early 1907. Amexco officials were deeply concerned; the money order business alone did a volume of over $40 million per year, and the company did not want to lose it. But if Amexco formed an actual bank, all of the legislation would become moot.

As Brooks and J.F. reckoned, Amexco also had enough financial business to justify a banking operation. Financial operations had expanded to such a degree that they had become a sizable enterprise. Gross financial business in 1907 reached $280 million, and profits, more than $1 million. For his part, Brooks wanted a bank especially to enhance his competitive position in the foreign-exchange business. He told J.F. that the exchange trading would grow if the company could take deposits, an activity open only to banks. Large foreign-exchange transactions, he explained, were mostly between banks, and banks preferred to do business only "with concerns with whom they carry a balance as it avoids the necessity of transferring the funds on settlement." (Any transaction could be instantly credited or debited to the account, saving time and the expense of transporting large sums of money.)

Amexco did not face any barriers in establishing a banking subsidiary. Wells Fargo had already done it in 1905, successfully merging its financial operations with the Nevada National Bank (creating the forerunner of the Wells Fargo Bank that exists today). In pointing to that as a precedent, one of J.F.'s assistants said that the Wells Fargo Bank had developed into that company's "most important asset," and he suggested a bank would prove equally valuable to Amexco.

J.F. decided to bring the idea to his father, a prospect he must have dreaded. J.F.—Jimmy—Fargo was a man of some imagination in his own right and, like Brooks and Berry, thought up ideas for expanding the company's financial business. But J.F. had a difficult relationship with his father, and he was terrified of his father's reactions to new ideas. J.C. was reputed to be "mad all day" whenever J.F. had an idea. On a few occasions, J.F. asked Brooks to present J.F.'s ideas for him so that if J.C. hated them, Brooks would take the heat. J.F.'s terror translated into incompetence. He appeared unable to present an idea to his father that the old man could reasonably accept. Indeed, if the bank idea was an indication, J.F. had a way of making even the most logical idea sound harebrained.

J.F. broached the subject to his father, who told him to put it in writing. The American Express Banking and Trust Company, as J.F.

described it in a memo in late February 1907, would be a wholly owned, incorporated subsidiary of the American Express Company. The bank would take over all the financial business of the express company and would take deposits, make loans, and place securities. (Such brokerage activities were standard banking operations until 1933.) But J.F. conceived a particular and unelaborated idea connected with this bank that made it a vastly different sort of business from the one that Brooks wanted. The bank, J.F. wrote, would cater "especially to those of moderate means . . . to transact a so-called mail order banking business through the medium of the Express Company."

J.F. submitted the proposal, not only to J.C., but to four executives involved in the company's financial operations. Brooks, of course, was one, and he quickly endorsed a bank in principle, though he stressed his own foreign-exchange operation, and had no comment on the "mail-order" concept. Of the other three, all advocated an increase in banking activities, and two of them endorsed the principle of a separate bank subsidiary. Said Harvey Gay, chief accountant, "It would seem that the evolution into a separate Financial organization should at this time be the logical outcome." None of these men appeared interested in a "mail-order" bank either, and that may have killed the specific proposal at the time.

For his part, J.C. said "no," but he did not crucify J.F. for the idea, nor did he preclude the possibility of establishing a bank in the future. As a result, J.F. felt emboldened to try again in 1908, offering two alternative proposals: Amexco could start a bank or buy one. J.F. had an acquisition candidate specifically in mind—The International Banking Corporation, a bank that possessed a charter that contained, as J.F. put it, "generous powers" to conduct an express business as well as banking in the U.S. and abroad. Also, the basic idea fit well with the existing financial operations of the company, including the TC and Brooks's foreign exchange-trading operations. But J.F.'s presentation was awful. He had not done his homework and knew nothing about this company beyond the powers granted in its charter. He did not even know if the bank was solvent. He admitted, "We do not know the actual conditions of this company."

Although J.F.'s proposal for the bank acquisition lacked preparation, his second proposal—for an internally developed American Express Bank—lacked coherence. In fact, it was so convoluted one could begin to understand J.C.'s frustration with his son. The American Express Company, J.F. declared, should become "a holding company pure and simple," with not only a bank subsidiary, but also a realty company, a foreign company (to handle all aspects of Amexco's business outside the U.S.), and an incorporated express company. His explanation, however, of how the parts would work together sounded more like a riddle than a management plan: express offices would become branch banks, sort of, even though they would be express offices; the bank would handle the express company's bookeeping and accounts, but there were exceptions; the bank would receive a commission for paper sold by the foreign company or work out a "private arrangement," while the bank would pay some salaries of workers in the foreign company in some financial activities, but maybe not others under the auspices of the foreign company. With each sentence, J.F. made it more confusing. It may have all made sense in J.F.'s head, but he presented it in such a way that the savvy businessmen in Amexco's directorate, including his father, could not possibly have endorsed it.

While board members turned down J.F.'s specific plan, they actually supported the basic principle of separation of the company's financial business. But the directors never came up with a satisfactory alternative plan of their own. They were stymied by the fear that a banking organization would have to come under the regulatory oversight of some state banking authorities. J.F.'s plan had called for the incorporation of "a State Bank under the general laws of New York." The financial men of the company—J.F., Brooks and Gay—had agreed the year before that an American Express bank was going to have to play by the same rules as other banks, but the directors seemed less inclined to do this. Indeed, one director, E. B. Judson, Jr., who had some sympathy with the idea of splitting off the financial business of the company, pointedly called for "a change [which] would not be under the National or State Banking Laws . . ."

The idea of a bank died, although J.F. kept trying to revive it. He clipped articles and sent little notes to J.C. on branch banking and the like, even though J.C. never showed interest, except for one brief period in 1911 when he feared that "public clamor" might force the company out of the express business. Yet even then it was not certain if J.C. was serious. He told J.F. to draw up another proposal but, curiously, asked for a plan that emphasized J.F.'s most peculiar and as yet unexplained notion: a mail-order bank. J.F. concocted a bizarre and elaborate proposal to sell bonds on the installment plan to the little guy. After one long memo to his father, the idea went back into limbo. This was the last bank plan submitted to J.C. during his term in office.

After his father had effectively left the scene in early 1914, J.F. presented the idea again to first vice president and caretaker chief executive Francis Flagg. Why J.F. thought he could get anywhere with Flagg is a mystery. Flagg had no power; the board had already designated Taylor as successor. By June, J.C. resigned at long last, and Taylor soon began to assemble his own team, which pointedly excluded any and all Fargos, and J.F. was never a factor in company policy again.

Six months after he became president, Taylor appointed a replacement for J.F. as chief financial officer; Taylor chose Howard K. Brooks. Brooks, almost seventeen years older than Taylor, was nonetheless closer to the new president than any other colleague. They were friends, not just office comrades. They spent their Sundays together, went out on the town together, and frequently golfed together. (Brooks loved the game but was so bad at it that he invented a counter to keep track of his score.) Although Taylor outranked Brooks at the office, Brooks was the new president's mentor.

Taylor made Brooks a vice president in charge of financial affairs but gave him broad powers over all the company's nonexpress activities. Brooks had always managed to bring about change and development anyway; now, while Taylor reserved for himself the chief executive's right of final decision, he gave Brooks virtually a free hand to do what he wanted. This was a fateful appointment; the most visionary man in the company's history now possessed the one thing he had always lacked—power.

But Brooks did not wield power autocratically. He encouraged initiative throughout the ranks. He sought ideas and advice, not only from senior managers, but from all employees. If their advice appeared sound, he took it; for example, he agreed to set up an entire banking operation for American soldiers during World War I on the advice of a young traveling auditor. Both Taylor and Brooks also delegated authority and responsibility—especially over operating details—to others. If a manager could not make up his own mind, as one executive noted, the two leaders "got someone else who would. . . ." The management style they imposed, by its nature, encouraged entrepreneurship. Not surprisingly, it led to a burst of creative development, unprecedented in the history of American Express.

By the end of 1914, even before he was officially named VP, Brooks set off the planning and development process through a letter he sent to Harry Gee, the foreign traffic manager. Brooks's letter outlined his vision of a "round-the-world" company that provided global services in trade, banking, and tourism—an extraordinary leap of imagination, since the company had only the barest outlines of what he wanted in trade and banking and had no formal tourist bureau, only Dalliba's unapproved operation abroad. So to get what he wanted, Brooks would have to create most of it himself.

He started in November 1914 by delegating a planning task to Gee. Brooks told Gee and his men of the Foreign (formerly European) Department to provide ideas in the area of their greatest knowledge and expertise: trade services. The Foreign Department already offered two trade services: international freight forwarding and a small program in trade finance. In one of M. F. Berry's more remarkable acts, he had created a program to supply short-term trade credits, what he called "advances-against-invoices." The remarkable feature of this operation was that he apparently developed it in secret around 1905 and ran it without the approval of then president J. C. Fargo or the board for the better part of a decade. (He maintained secrecy by keeping it small and

169

by operating it out of the company's office in Rotterdam, Holland.) Brooks intended to expand these existing operations but wanted to go well beyond them, and he felt the Foreign Department could provide the ideas about what additional trade services might become viable businesses. As Brooks noted, Gee's department not only engaged in the business but "had a line on all the principal exporters and importers."

As for travel and finance, Brooks was preparing to cope with these himself, starting with travel. Discussions on a formal tourist business had of course been in progress for nearly twenty years and had picked up later in 1914. Shortly after the outbreak of World War I, Thomas Cook & Son, as a British firm, had refused to honor its paper in enemy territory—Germany and Austria. As a result, Cook's not only lost business but a good deal of prestige as well. Since America was still neutral, Harry Gee wondered if Amexco could go into Germany and Austria and pick up the tourist-service business Cook's had lost. Dalliba, Francis Flagg, M. F. Berry (in his last months at Amexco), and Taylor himself all agreed that there was merit in Gee's suggestion, but they only discussed the issue and made no attempt to put a plan into motion.

When Brooks came to New York in January 1915, however, he quickly developed the idea far beyond what Gee had proposed, and he wasted little time in proposing a full-fledged world tourist service. In March, after consulting with Amexco executives and outside experts, he wrote a four-page letter to Taylor advocating the creation of a travel department at once. He noted some obvious points. Dalliba's efforts in Paris had already put the company in the tourist business. The only parts missing were what Brooks called the most remunerative: eastbound ocean-liner tickets, hotel vouchers, and, most importantly, tour packages. Brooks also argued that the time was right. In the summer of 1914, Dalliba had scored a public relations triumph. "The prestige of this Company among American travelers has had a remarkable increase and emphasis . . . [that] will be a permanent asset and will serve most effectively *now*." (Brooks's italics.)

But Brooks felt that most important reason for a travel department was to support the TC. TC sales hit $30 million in 1913 and topped $20 million in 1914 despite the war; the long-term TC float had reached some $10 million, providing a steady income of around $500,000 a year. But in spite of the prestige Dalliba had won, Brooks saw a real danger that TC sales would flag. Competition in the traveler's check business was, he said, "developing to a tremendously strong degree." Some banks and steamship lines sold their own checks now, and Amexco's market share, at one time 100 percent, had slipped steadily. But, wrote Brooks, "if we, by supplying *all* the needs of travelers succeed as we unquestionably will, in bringing persons who contemplate European or foreign trips, to our offices *first*, to arrange their itineraries, steamship accommodations, railway tickets, etc., we will have *first* call upon their credit business instead of last call, as at present."

Within days of writing the memo, Brooks obtained Taylor's approval for a travel department, and soon after, Brooks hired Ralph Towle, an experienced tour and travel man, to run it. With World War I in progress, Amexco could not have chosen a worse time to start a travel office. The western and eastern fronts were not exactly hospitable to sightseers. In fact, with U-boats plying the North Atlantic, all of Europe was essentially out-of-bounds. That eliminated the biggest travel market. As Towle pointed out, Americans did not go to South America or the Far East for vacations. He suggested a chartered cruise to the West Indies, but Brooks found that with the war on, he could not even find a boat.*

While Towle wrestled with the problems of travel, Brooks moved on to other tasks. In mid-April, he returned to foreign trade. The previous November he had charged Gee with the task of providing concrete

*Amexco also faced a boycott from the major steamship lines. Travel agents feared Amexco with its giant network of express offices—this was 1915, before the consolidation of the domestic expresses—would gain a monopoly of the travel business, and they pressured major steamship lines into denying Amexco agency privileges. Cunard broke the boycott in 1917, but some steamship companies did not grant Amexco agency rights until the 1920s.

suggestions on foreign-trade services, but Brooks did not wait for Gee to offer a formal proposal. Instead, in a memo to Taylor, Brooks repeated his idea that round-the-world service would have to depend on a significant expansion of banking and trade services for commercial customers and listed thirty-four possible trade-related businesses. These suggestions covered almost every conceivable need of importers and exporters from trade brokerage to claims adjustment, to credit reports, and to publishing of a "foreign trade bulletin." However, Brooks admitted that he did not know which of these were viable business ideas, and he recommended to Taylor that the company try to find out what trade services manufacturers wanted before initiating any of them.

But if Brooks hesitated over what services to offer, he knew on what basis they should be chosen. The most extraordinary aspect of his round-the-world concept was his idea of "interlocking services." Whatever trade services Amexco chose, they had to tie in with the other businesses of the company. So commercial customers might come to the company for export-import shipping services but also get a trade loan and steamship tickets for business travel. Travelers might come in to book a tour but would also use Amexco to act as a freight forwarder for sending home items purchased abroad, to buy TCs, and maybe to develop a bank or brokerage account. Banking customers might start with a personal account, but then use trade services for business, as well as travel services for both business and pleasure. Brooks actually projected a company that would be a combination of leading bank, travel agency, export-import company, and shipping company, all in one unified, world-spanning organization—a multinational company—before there was such a thing—without parallel in the world. Brooks's concept was distinctly modern. It was suited to a world growing more accessible to American business and tourists, a world growing increasingly interdependent.

Of course, round-the-world service also required a round-the-world office network, and Brooks got down to business on that issue, too. On April 15, a few days after making his trade proposal, he told Taylor he wanted to open new offices as soon as possible in four locations: Honolulu, Manila, Hong Kong, and Buenos Aires. Though small-scale, this expansion would give the company offices at strategic points around the globe. Brooks made clear that he intended to make the network truly world-spanning over time.

Brooks returned to the foreign trade issue again in May. In keeping with his idea to find out what manufacturers wanted, he launched what was probably the first formal market survey in Amexco's history. He began "an exhaustive investigation" of trade, including a survey of the needs of 4,000 U.S. manufacturers who engaged in various forms of export-import business.

Before Brooks reported the results of the survey, however, Harry Gee voiced skepticism about involvement in a broad foreign-trade operation. He liked the idea in principle but opposed trade brokerage and large-scale trade finance "until we grow up to it, so that there may be no mistakes or putting the company in a wrong position which could easily be done in a thousand and one ways." He suggested a minimal effort—a trade information and credit report service only. Brooks favored a more extensive operation but deferred to Gee. As Brooks wrote later, "I had too little knowledge of the business to do other than except [sic] [Gee's] views." Brooks scaled back his plans. Instead of a full-blown international trade bureau, he created the modest Foreign Trade Information Bureau to promote trade, aid shippers and manufacturers, and prepare and sell credit information.

The man Brooks chose to run the Trade Information Bureau was Donald Frothingham. Brooks seems to have discovered Frothingham from a series of articles he had written abroad—mostly for the *Chicago Tribune*—on world trade conditions, and Brooks hired him in the fall of 1915. Brooks may well have seen in the young Dartmouth graduate a well-educated version of himself. Frothingham was, according to a contemporary, a "brainy type" and a "wielder of imagination." But the young man generated a remarkable amount of antipathy at 65 Broadway. Some saw him as slick and glib, even a "wild man." The real problem for Frothingham might have been the fact that he was, as the same contemporary noted, "singularly unlike" any expressman the company had ever seen, an Ivy League graduate in a world of self-made men, a youngster in his twenties thrust into top management, above others who had worked for the company for decades. But however other employees felt about him, Frothingham enjoyed a favored position beside Howard Brooks, the company's number-two executive. And for the next six years, Frothingham would be a leading figure in the company, a force pushing American Express toward the vision Brooks had outlined.

In October 1915, Amexco formally announced to the press all the changes Brooks had made since the beginning of the year: the formation of the Trade Information and Travel departments and the opening of offices in Buenos Aires, Manila, and Hong Kong. (Honolulu was shelved for a while.) Curiously, the press seemed most surprised by Amexco's decision to go into the tourist business, which, the company declared, was nothing more than a "legitimate extension" of what it was already doing. Buried in the press reports, however, was a more important assertion about the future of American Express: all of this new business activity, the *New York Times* reported, was "merely the beginning."

In his first ten months in New York, Brooks had created two new businesses and expanded the office network to three new countries and throughout had maintained a brutal schedule, working nights and weekends. He put in such long, exhausting hours that on occasion he would have to lean against a wall and hold himself up to keep from collapsing.

He was not finished by any means in planning his round-the-world company. But he did not sustain the momentum of 1915. This resulted partly from the new management system. While J.C. could authorize the TC on a whim, Brooks and his men prepared studies and held numerous discussions first before implementing their ideas, slowing the progress of development. Indeed, the more they talked, the more possibilities they could envision, and the less they did.

But the process slowed, too, because Brooks's attention was diverted. As chief financial officer, he had to run his department and cope with immediate details that sidetracked him from planning and development. In 1916, distractions cropped up often. For instance, because of the uncertainties of the war, exchange rates fluctuated, and he spent a considerable amount of time on the question of whether or not to remove the printed conversion rates on the TC. Also, the war presented Amexco with opportunities, and Brooks had to decide whether or not to take them. He and Dalliba looked into, among other war-related enterprises, the "financing of war supply measures" and the expansion of the advances-against-invoices program to involve war shipments.* (That program was in the open now. In 1917, Gee's Foreign Department even calculated the profits of the advances program from the previous five years. The total came to $106,000, a small amount to be sure, but the profits were consistent at a time when the express business often lost money.)

Indeed, with Brooks so preoccupied with other matters, in early 1916, Harry Gee and his staff took over the planning effort. Gee was actually working on two issues, which he subsequently combined in one report. The first idea would have split off the express business from the rest of the company in order to make express earnings clearer to ICC. The second continued Gee's planning work on trade issues. Even though the Trade Information Bureau had started to operate, Gee began thinking ahead about how to expand its services in the future.

Gee had many thoughts on both matters, which he sent directly to Taylor. By April 1916, the president, overwhelmed by the volume of it all, threw up his hands. "If there were 48 hours in each day instead of 24, I could not personally find the time to get through with some of the detail necessary in order to form any positive clear cut conclusions," he wrote to Gee. He told Gee to form a long-range planning committee to report a consensus of opinion "to me in the fewest

---

*Brooks expanded the advances-against-invoices program for trade through neutral ports, particularly in Scandinavia.

possible words." Taylor suggested a committee of Gee, Brooks, Frothingham, Dalliba—who was in the U.S.—and whomever else Gee might choose "to produce something that would really cause us to make an effort."

Gee did not form such a committee, however. Instead, he held extensive meetings with his own staff at the Foreign Department. Gee was a bit of an eccentric, with a curious habit of writing notes to himself on his shirt cuffs, and he must have left those meetings in the spring of 1916 with notes up to the elbows. Two weeks after receiving Taylor's plea for brevity, Gee produced a report, which, so far from the fewest possible words, was, Gee admitted, "somewhat the opposite." The report, ten single-spaced pages, called for the creation of two affiliated companies, domestic express in one company, everything else in the other (with Brooks as president of the second). But it included numerous suggestions for other "extended activities," mostly connected with freight and trade: a marine insurance company; a fidelity and surety company; and an export business with its own chartered ships, and loading, provisioning, and warehousing facilities. But for all its length, the proposal led to no action other than the one Taylor had called for earlier: the creation of a planning committee including Brooks, Gee, Dalliba, and the company's lawyers.

This group met during the spring and summer of 1916 and revised Gee's proposal. The final product bore the hand of Howard Brooks as much as or more than that of Harry Gee. Though Gee's earlier scheme had called for two companies, after he ran the proposals through Brooks, the scheme included *at least* five affiliated companies under the American Express banner. The American Express Company would remain the domestic express arm and a holding company. But under the holding company, there would also be American Express Shipping Corporation, for cargo haulage and freight forwarding; American Express Commercial Corporation, for all other aspects of trade, including full export-import operations such as trade brokerage; American Express Travel and Tours Corporation; and American Express Financial Corporation, which would be both an international banking organization and a fidelity and surety insurance company. If the company decided to add a warehousing operation or a marine insurance company, these would also be separate subsidiaries. Of course, this plan was predicated, as Gee put it, "on normal times—or in other words, to be made effective at the close of the present great war the preliminary details to be worked out in the interim."

For some time, however, officials could not work on the "preliminary details." Brooks, Gee, and the rest of the company faced another distraction: the company had decided to put up a new twenty-one-story building at 65 Broadway, and while construction proceeded, top executives were scattered in temporary quarters throughout lower Manhattan. But soon after the new headquarters building opened in April 1917, a committee, called the Post-War Planning Committee, under Brooks's direction began to meet regularly to work out the details of what was always referred to as "after-the-war expansion."

But before the committee could take concrete steps, the effort was again sidetracked, this time by a crisis. On January 1, 1918, with the seizure of the railroads, planning became uncertain since the future of the company was unknown; for a time, planning stopped. Then in February, ICC Director Prouty made it clear that Amexco was going to continue to exist but would lose its domestic express business, and Amexco's planning resumed with a new urgency. Executives believed that with the loss of its main business, the company needed to expand what was left or it might die.

By early March, Harry Gee made a formal proposal that appeared to be a panicked response to the loss of the express. Gee, who had favored "growing up" slowly and conservatively in foreign trade, proposed that trade services "should be *at once* expanded" and "aggressively" pursued. Gee's new proposal was in line with the ideas he and Brooks had proposed as the American Express Commercial Corp. Ltd.* Gee called for an international trade organization to conduct all manner of trade and freight business, with a special emphasis on trade finance. "*Credit*

---

*Without the domestic express, Brooks and Gee saw no need to create a holding company with separate subsidiaries, and trade services simply became a department of the American Express Company.

is the underlying feature, without which the [Trade] Bureau or those connected with it cannot properly proceed," he wrote.

Brooks and Taylor appeared to be swept up in the urgency of the moment as well. While they had usually waited for careful analysis, they now endorsed Gee's idea at once. They delayed implementation of the plan for only a few days, but not because of a disagreement over the basic idea, rather over Gee's management scheme. Gee suggested that the new Trade Department should be jointly managed by his office and Brooks's—his, because he and his men knew shipping best; Brooks's, because he and his men knew finance best. Gee suggested a chain of command and the names of two men to run the new department.

Brooks objected because neither of the two recommended was Donald Frothingham. Gee, in fact, did not mention Frothingham, but Brooks came to the young Ivy Leaguer's defense. Brooks told Taylor that not only had Frothingham's Trade Information Bureau done "excellent work," it had already succeeded in starting the business Gee wanted to get into, obtaining "direct orders for the purchase and sale of goods." Brooks made it clear that, if Amexco created a trade department, he wanted Frothingham to run it.

This dispute quickly turned into a test of power. Gee stubbornly stuck to his joint-management proposal. But Brooks, who did not often need to demonstrate his clout within the company, held the upper hand. After the two men presented their arguments to Taylor—each wrote two separate memos—Taylor sided with Brooks. Taylor named Frothingham general manager of the new Foreign Trade Department and gave him full authority to run it under Brooks's supervision. Frothingham and Brooks expected business to boom. With the world emerging from war, with the company's round-the-world network taking shape, the potential for growth in trade seemed enormous.

After the creation of the trade department, the time and energy of top executives was again diverted by the impending loss of the express, which overrode all other planning considerations for the next six months. It occupied not only Taylor's efforts, but Brooks's as well. For him, there was one issue of tremendous importance: to protect the TC and the money order businesses. There seemed a real danger that the loss of the express would kill both. In losing its express business, Amexco stood to lose 10,000 branch offices, a possibly fatal shrinkage of its sales network.

Instead Brooks and Taylor figured out a way to *expand* Amexco's sales forces. First, they bought for Amexco the traveler's-check and money-order businesses of the Wells Fargo, the Southern, and the Adams express companies. * These three companies sold out readily because they felt that with the loss of their own express office networks to the ARE, they could no longer sell and service their TCs and MOs properly. The move made Amexco's the only express paper left in the country. Next, Brooks and Taylor sat down and "negotiated" a deal between Amexco and the new American Railway Express. Brooks negotiated for Amexco; Taylor donned his ARE cap and represented it. They exchanged a couple of solemn letters and met a few times and soon reached an agreement. As a result, the ARE offices became sellers of Amexco's TCs, MOs, and later, tour tickets. Instead of losing 10,000 outlets, Amexico *gained* over 10,000 new ones. † The agreement that Brooks and Taylor worked out did not simply save Amexco's TC and MO, it helped both businesses to pick up in 1918, and they grew steadily and dramatically for more than a decade thereafter.

Once he had settled the TC and MO question, Brooks returned to after-the-war expansion plans, focusing on the last and most crucial part of his vision: the creation of a banking operation. He wanted nothing less than a full-fledged international bank (and/or trust company) that would allow Amexco to offer all banking and brokerage services.

Brooks intended to acquire banking charters around the world and

---

*Taylor and Brooks feared that if any one of the express companies defaulted on its paper, it could cause a run on express TCs and MOs generally.

†After this, Brooks reported Amexco's entire sales network at over 70,000 outlets. This included corner drugstores and supermarkets that sold MOs.

organize a global banking business. In fact, Amexco had already obtained banking rights in some countries in order to conduct a TC and MO business. For example, when the company opened its offices in Hong Kong, it discovered that to do any financial business it needed a banking charter, and as a result, it now had the legal right to take deposits and make loans on collateral. In fact, in Hong Kong and later Shanghai, where similar laws prevailed, the company was perceived generally as a banking company. But the company also had bank charters in several European countries, and Brooks intended to tie them together into an international banking organization. His plan was not a revival of J. F. Fargo's confused American Express Bank plans. Brooks had a clear idea in mind of a bank that offered traditional banking services and built on its existing operations in trade finance and foreign exchange. The idea of a bank made more sense now than ever; with the loss of the express, Amexco really had no other business.

Brooks began to create and expand banking operations at offices throughout the world, but he also wanted a bank name for the company abroad—a symbolic gesture that he regarded as increasingly important. He had support for that view. R. A. Foulks, one of Brooks's protégés and head of the offices in the Orient, reported that while customers regarded Amexco as a bank, government officials and other bankers were unwilling "to recognize as a banking organization an association engaged primarily in the transportation business." In Shanghai, the company's lack of clear banking identity led to its exclusion from the Foreign Exchange Bankers Association. This was a blow to business since the company's main banklike activity at this point was foreign-exchange trading. As a result, in the autumn of 1918, Brooks began lobbying for a banking name worldwide. Taylor referred the matter to the company's lawyers.

The question of the name had not been settled when the Armistice came in November. Brooks and Gee went to Europe in December 1918, arriving before Woodrow Wilson did, and the two men began restoring and expanding the European offices, a network devoted, according to Brooks's plans, to banking, trade, and travel in that order.

On his return home, Brooks assigned F. P. Small (back at Amexco after a volunteer stint with the Red Cross during the war) to continue the effort abroad. Small was named first vice president and was given full administrative power over the foreign office network. He made several trips in 1919 and 1920, including one lasting eight months. In that time, he opened six new offices, and when Small finished, Brooks announced plans for at least a dozen more in Europe, the Middle East, India, and South America.

But Brooks could not persuade Taylor to let him register a bank name for use abroad. In late 1918, Brooks proposed the creation of the American Express Trust Company, established under the laws of New York State with its main focus on international finance. Taylor balked and told the board that if the company was going to do a full-fledged trust business he wanted to acquire an existing trust company to provide a nucleus of organization and expertise. Brooks accepted that argument for only a few months. By early 1919, he had grown impatient and again asked Taylor to adopt a banking name for the company.

He won a partial victory; while he was still in Europe, the company split off a wholly owned, incorporated subsidiary to conduct business abroad. But Amexco did not call the company a bank or a trust, but simply, American Express Company, Inc. (known as the Inc. Company). While Amexco made the point to the press that the Inc. Company's primary business would be international banking, neither Brooks nor his man in the Orient R. A. Foulks was satisfied. In February 1919, Foulks wrote attorney Edwin deT. Bechtel pleading for a bank name. "As to foreigners, when the term 'Express Company' carries to them any distinct impression it is of transportation, whereas the term 'Bank' is almost universally understood," and he suggested the creation of the American Express Bank, with the company's freight and travel left under the banner of American Express Company, Inc. He added in a letter to Taylor, "I think we have for some years been feeling more and more the need of a true banking organization, and perhaps the time has now arrived to give effect to it." This was of course in line with what Brooks had wanted, and he picked up the argument. Just after the creation of the Inc. Company, he sent out a letter to what was known as the Committee on American Express, Incorporated suggesting a simple name change from the Inc. Company to American Express Banking Corporation.

A few weeks later, he raised the idea at a planning committee meeting attended by Bechtel, Foulks, Brooks, and representatives from the offices of Gee and Small. Brooks did most of the talking. Not only did he reiterate the idea of his letter, he even posed an alternative—the American Express *and* Banking Corporation, which he said "might be more descriptive of the operations carried on." Though the freight and travel offices feared the name would discourage their customers, in a show of power, Brooks moved that the Inc. Company be renamed American Express Banking Corporation, and the motion was seconded and passed. The motion was written up and sent along with a letter to Taylor on July 21.

Taylor did not consent. For a long time, Brooks could not even get an answer, much less approval. The two men, Taylor and Brooks, were still on good terms, and Brooks was more surprised than anything else by Taylor's delay. Nevertheless, by mid-September Brooks complained, "May we suggest again the desirability of an immediate decision about changing the name of American Express Company, Incorporated to American Express Banking Corporation? As Mr. Small is about to leave for Europe, we believe it would be very desirable that a decision to change the name should be reached in order that when he is talking to our officers and men in Europe, he can speak of the proposed name and of the policy of expansion which the name naturally suggests." But Taylor either said no or nothing, and Small sailed with instructions to organize offices in the name of American Express Company, Inc.

Taylor overruled Brooks, apparently on the advice of lawyers from Carter, Ledyard & Milburn. They feared a change in the name could change the company's legal status. Although it had lost the domestic express, Amexco retained its status as an unincorporated stock association, which by definition spared it from what the lawyers called the "annoyance or interference of disgruntled stockholders," and regulation of its "quasi-banking" activities. Since that form of organization still protected the company from many laws and prying eyes, the lawyers considered it the company's "most valuable asset." They strongly urged Taylor to do nothing that would jeopardize that status.

Yet at the time, a name change seemed not a visionary step, but a simple reflection of business reality. In all financial operations, the company was posting exceptional results. Even though Americans could not get to Europe, they were traveling around the U.S., to South America, and even Asia, and taking TCs with them. Sales hit $51 million in 1919, almost double the best previous year, 1913. And they were heading up. In 1920, the company sold over $80 million.

But Amexco made its greatest profits in the business Brooks had personally developed—foreign exchange. Because of the economic turmoil caused by World War I, the For/Ex business had changed from the days when Brooks had entered it. Back then, exchange rates were nearly immovable, based on widely recognized values of gold. But rates which had grown unsteady in 1914 fell apart at the war's end. European governments debased their own currencies by printing too much paper money. Exchange rates changed by the day, or even by the hour. The volatility of the market finally forced American Express to remove its conversion rates from the front of travelers cheques (with no negative effect on sales of TCs).* But more importantly, the value of most European currencies fell dramatically against the still steady U.S. dollar. Even the world-standard British pound dropped 3 percent against the dollar; other currencies fell much further. This had two consequences: a new and active wholesale currency-trading market, and an unusual profit opportunity for companies that sold dollar-based foreign remittances.

Traders engaged in a more lively currency-trading market, buying and selling currencies through forward (future) and spot (present-day) contracts. Exporters and importers and financial institutions used con-

---

*Amexco officials agonized over this decision, but after Dalliba's efforts in 1914, travelers recognized that TCs offered important attractions beyond exchange rate guarantees.

tracts to protect themselves against swings in currency values; others used the trading to speculate on the direction of currency values for a quick profit. In these hectic markets, currency traders faced the risk of equally rapid losses, and they needed to keep up-to-the-minute with the latest exchange rates to establish and cover positions. Amexco participated actively in all aspects of market trading, and market activity became a significant contributor to the company's earnings.

Still, for Amexco, foreign-exchange profits came less from the currency-trading market than from sales of foreign money orders and other forms of foreign remittance. More than ever before, the country's millions of immigrants were sending home money to relatives in not yet rebuilt Europe; back in the old country, people needed the money to keep from starving, and their American relatives came to Amexco for foreign MOs. This increase in business, coupled with the fall of exchange rates against the dollar, provided Amexco with a unique opportunity.

The company made money on three separate parts of each transaction. An individual intending to send money abroad came into an Amexco office and bought a foreign money order (or cable transfer) at the exchange rate of the moment. However, as Howard Smith, then an assistant to F. P. Small, remembered, "The operator in New York was slow in finding out exactly what the sales were and equally slow in covering the sales . . ." By the time the operator actually got around to purchasing the foreign currency to cover the order—maybe a few hours later—the value of the foreign currency had fallen, and he covered at a more favorable exchange rate. That produced enormous profits in itself. But every transaction produced earnings in two other ways: the initial conversion rate carried a small profit for Amexco, and also, the customer paid a service charge for each remittance order.

The business was not only very profitable, the volume of it was enormous.* Amexco handled transactions worth at least half a billion dollars each year from 1918 through 1920, and the profits were pro-

---

*In 1919, the office in Athens alone processed $160 million in remittances.

portionately huge. No one apparently ever knew how much money Amexco earned on remittances in the years immediately after World War I; the books were poorly kept. Income probably reached more than $10 million annually. Once, when Small asked how much the company was earning from exchange operations, he was asked in return, "How much do you want?"

Much of the credit for this business belonged to Brooks, of course, the founder of the business. But he was no longer the active manager of foreign exchange, and the tremendous profits it generated threw the spotlight on the young man Brooks had put in charge, Alexander B. Johnson. Johnson's tremendous success had elevated him into the highest ranks of the company and marked him as a leader of the future.

There are no records of the qualifications Johnson brought to the job or even when he was hired. On June 1, 1918, he appeared in the records as a foreign-exchange trader at a salary of $500 per month. This point marked the start of an incredible rise through the ranks. Within nine months, he won three raises to $833.33 a month. Less than a year after that, he was awarded a bonus of $10,000 and had another raise to $2,083 a month. A month later his salary rose again to $3,000 a month, about $1,000 more than first VP Small's and almost double that of Harry Gee's. Two months later, the board elected Johnson a vice president, and at the end of that year, his salary was set at $40,000 per year and he was awarded a bonus of $25,000. No other individual in the company's history had risen so fast.

Johnson's ascendance—and his youth—marked him, not just as a leader, but as heir apparent to Taylor. This was especially true now that the company was being transformed into a financial institution; no one else at Amexco had the qualifications to run it. Brooks felt the future of American Express belonged to men like Johnson and Frothingham. As he said in 1919, "At the rate these young men are moving now, a 40-foot stone wall will not stop them. . . . They are the ones who will plan and carry out our future progress. I believe they will do wonderful things."

If Johnson was the future, some people at American Express were not looking forward to it. The most vivid picture of Johnson was provided by Small's aide, Howard Smith. One day, while Smith was sitting with his boss Small, in the latter's office, Johnson barged in unannounced and probably uninvited. "Johnson did not sit down in a chair or take part in the general conversation," Smith remembered. "He simply sat *on* the table at which Mr. Small was working and reached over and took a cigar from Small's box." Smith said later that he thought these "were almost acts of disrespect"—which was a charitable equivocation; Johnson treated F.P. like an underling.

While Brooks still could not get Taylor to let him call the banking operation a bank, he kept aggressively expanding financial services anyway. He launched a securities brokerage business here and abroad specializing in foreign bonds. And to complement that service, he thrust Amexco into investment banking, participating in foreign-bond underwriting. Also, Brooks added TCs denominated in French francs and British pounds.

Brooks felt confident of the future, and in 1920, for a group of company trainees, he spelled out what he expected American Express to look like in 1925, 1930, 1940: he invited them all to daydream with him. He said in "his fits of imagination" he had pictured Amexco in the future, and

> the picture I have before me is something like this. . . . A full fledged incorporated banking institution with branches in every important city in the world; its banking activities principally international, although it does some local business; its foreign trade activities are so developed and systematized that a large portion of the world's trade was conducted through some one or more of our various branches of service. Its travel service so complete in all its details that very few thought of traveling except under its care and guidance. Its foreign shipping accommodations were so extensive no one undertook to handle their foreign freight transactions themselves. Its marine insurance

department, savings department, investment department, surety bonding department and every class of banking operations were all very busy making money.

In 1920, this scenario was superficially plausible, but there was a flaw in it: the expansion Howard Brooks had brought about was in the right direction for the company, but Brooks had placed people in positions of responsibility who were long on enthusiasm but short on experience. The organization of American Express was far more fragile than anyone realized.

A
DIFFERENT
VISION

7

Around 1920, Americans developed a fascination with things Chinese. The game mah-jongg became a rage; Chinese objects and motifs popped up everywhere. At Donald Frothingham's foreign trade desk at American Express this fad was viewed as a unique opportunity. Frothingham and his men arranged for the purchase of a boatload of Chinese baubles for sale to a merchant in America. But soon after the trade department concluded the deal, the cultural and economic environment suddenly changed. The Chinese fad trailed off, and the world economy fell into depression. Before the cargo reached the U.S., the American buyer declared bankruptcy, and the cargo became unsalable, leaving American Express with a warehouse full of Chinese trinkets including mah-jongg sets and 50,000 glass eyes.

The deal, which had once made some sense, now appeared absurd, the result of too much spirit and not enough experience in the Foreign

Trade Department. And, indeed, this was not the only bad deal the trade department made. But it was those 50,000 glass eyes that people remembered—a blunder that symbolized not only the failure of a department, but the failure of Howard Brooks to build the company he wanted. The foreign trade debacle was the beginning of a series of reversals over the course of a year or so, a period nicknamed in later years "The Glass Eye Era." The cost to American Express was probably about $2 million, maybe even a bit more, but the events had implications more far-reaching than its cost in dollars and cents. The Glass Eye debacle put an end to the entrepreneurial experiment Brooks had started just six years before.

The losses began in the trade department in late 1920. In a very short span of time, Frothingham and his men had involved the company in five dozen deals that were either total or partial losses. As Frothingham lamented, "Business contracts have been cancelled, drafts refused, and goods rejected, often on the merest pretext. As a result large quantities of merchandise, originating in many countries, lie unclaimed in foreign ports, in many cases deteriorating in value."

Most of the deals were for goods with far greater utility than mahjongg sets and glass eyes. Frothingham's efforts had won for the company a load of saccharine in a Shanghai warehouse, bales of cotton duck in Britain, tons of wolframite (a tungsten ore) financed way above market price, and tapestries sitting unclaimed on the dock in Buenos Aires. In all, Frothingham's department cost the company at least $250,000.

Despite the cost, some executives were delighted to see Frothingham make such a mess of things. And they were even more delighted by the other failure of the Glass Eye Era, Alexander Johnson. Johnson, now a vice president with the second highest salary and the largest bonus in the company, fell as dramatically and as quickly as he had risen. In early 1921, just weeks after the board of directors awarded him $25,000 for making so much money, the young VP had to report a loss of $710,000.

Actually, the loss was not Johnson's fault—except in that he failed to control exchange-trading operations outside of New York. The loss occurred in China, which had one of the most difficult and vigorous exchange markets in the world. Johnson probably did not understand it, and his men in China clearly did not. Not only were there several currencies in China at the time (it was a period of fragmentation and continual civil strife), but most of the currencies were pegged to the price of silver, which fluctuated far more radically than that of gold. Inexperienced men, operating without apparent limits, had speculated heavily in this market and had lost—crushing Alex Johnson's reputation as a miracle man in the process.

The loss of $710,000 did not threaten the company's survival; its surplus and reserves still topped $15 million. But because of the magnitude and suddenness of the loss, it appalled George Taylor and Amexco's directors more than all the losses in foreign trade and led to an air of crisis at American Express. Taylor cabled F. P. Small, who was abroad surveying and expanding the branch network, and told him to return to New York at once. In the meantime, the executive committee met in an emergency session devoted primarily to the foreign-exchange setback. At the end of the meeting, the committee had declared that henceforth foreign-exchange transactions would take place "only within such limits as may . . . be authorized by the Executive Committee of the Board of Directors."

The executive committee made one other decision: Taylor and the other members of the committee decided to elevate Small to a higher level of authority. When he returned from abroad, they gave him the mandate and the power to clean up the mess in both foreign exchange and trade. Brooks remained the chief financial officer, but because it had been Brooks's men who had failed, Small was in effect given Brooks's power. Small gained a greater level of authority; even Taylor, who was perhaps tainted himself by his close relationship with Brooks, deferred to Small on nonexpress matters.

The decision to appoint Small was as fateful as the one to appoint Brooks, and it led to change that was no less dramatic—although in the opposite direction. Small set in motion a massive reduction in the size, scope, and above all, the ambition of the American Express Company. Much of what Brooks had done, Small tried to undo. Small did not dismantle everything Brooks had built; by this time that would have meant dismantling the company.* But when Small finished making changes, only a few parts of Brooks's vision remained. The impact of Small's policies would last for decades.

Small could have opted for reform instead of massive reduction, but his decision for drastic action was perfectly consistent with his character. He was a taciturn New Englander who never showed much emotion or got unduly excited. He was careful to the point of obsessiveness; he would take down in shorthand every telephone call and most personal conversations he had. Although he appeared a little colorless—a reporter once tried to do a story on Small's rise from stenographer to the top, but gave up and exclaimed, "I can't find that you ever did anything!"—he inspired confidence in the ranks of old expressmen. He was one of them, a member of the express class, mostly self-educated and self-made. And his reticence came as a welcome relief to many old express people after the flamboyance of Frothingham and Johnson. But there was another side to F. P. Small that made him the exact wrong man for the job—a side not so well known. Small was the kind of man who interpreted a charge so literally that he left no room for compromise. If he was told to clean up a mess, he would take the broadest broom to sweep it up. Though conservative in style, his actions were radical, and whatever direction he chose, he pursued with a vengeance.

Small had shown signs of these characteristics when, as a company auditor, he invented a new waybill system. Before it went into use, of course, J.C. found out, destroyed Small's invention and warned him not to perpetrate any "monkey business" on the American Express. J.C. sent Small back to auditing, and Small, though he admitted later

---

*In 1950, Ralph Towle still felt that Brooks had had a greater impact on the company than anyone else in its history. He said, "[American Express] today is a creature of Howard K. Brooks."

to feeling crushed, went quietly. But there was a coda to the story of the Small waybill: soon after J.C. vetoed Small's innovation, the ICC attacked the expresses for "overs and shorts," the very thing Small's system was designed to solve. J.C. looked for a solution and his traffic manager, J. H. Bradley, reminded him of the Small waybill.

J.C. at once told Bradley to get Small back to New York "to come here and put them in." But the curious part of the story came next. After Bradley called and explained the circumstances, Small refused to come back, refused to reinstitute his waybills, and using J.C.'s own words told Bradley, "I'm just tending to my auditing and no monkey business." In the end, Small returned, but only after Bradley on behalf of J.C. practically begged him. This waybill proved enormously beneficial to Small. The system he instituted gave him a claim to fame and a boost to his career.

In 1921, however, the choice of Small for a top leadership role was not dictated by character; it resulted from a process of elimination. Small was the highest ranking official untainted by the failure of the Glass Eye Era. He set to work at once "cleaning up the mess" and made abundantly clear from the outset that he intended to make Frothingham, Johnson, and to a lesser extent, Brooks bear the responsibility for the debacle.

Small dealt with Frothingham first. In the summer of 1921, Small suspended all trading operations outside of New York, and a few months later, he abolished the Foreign Trade Department altogether, despite a protest from Brooks. Small did not respond to the protest and, in fact, ordered Brooks to send out the announcement of the department's demise—which was Small's decision entirely—over Brooks's own name. Frothingham was made head of the "New Business" Department, but since Small wanted no new businesses, the job was a shell, and Donald Frothingham had no influence or authority for the remainder of his time at American Express.

As for Johnson, he was not so easily displaced. Johnson had been a hero from 1918 to 1920—every executive received large bonuses because of Johnson's efforts—and one or two slips did not warrant a demotion. However, Small asserted his control over foreign-exchange trading, and in 1922, although Johnson remained the nominal head of the operation, Small took some of the trading activity out of his hands entirely. He vested it instead in a new company called Kennelly, Wirth & Co.—a wholly owned subsidiary of Amexco run by Small's protégé Louis Wirth.

In 1922, the company posted a profit again. Had Small solved the problems of the company? The better question was: had he even identified them? And the answer to that was no. The company profited less from Small's efforts than from the end of the postwar depression and a boom in TC sales, which reached the hundred million dollar mark in 1922—a mark Amexco surpassed every year after. Profits for the year stood at about $1 million before dividends, notwithstanding a few hundred thousand in write-offs from old trade and exchange losses.

But the real problem at American Express was not trade or foreign exchange, but rather personnel. Small did not see that Brooks's greatest shortcoming was in his choice of people for positions of authority. Brooks never failed under J. C. Fargo when he had to assume management control himself; he made money with gas collections, with foreign exchange, with all the financial businesses he directly managed in Chicago. But he did not always manage to distribute responsibilities wisely. Of course, Small felt that Brooks had chosen badly in Johnson and Frothingham, and Brooks had. They were not qualified for their jobs.* But Small did not see the choices as a problem in principle; he thought Frothingham and Johnson were bad choices because he did not like them. He dismissed Frothingham, for example, as nothing more than a "glib promoter."

Small was convinced that the real problem lay in the businesses

---

*In 1918, Harry Gee had warned Brooks and Taylor of the possible consequences of putting someone as inexperienced as Frothingham in charge of trade. "The Company must not expect too much at once in the way of results from men of our organization many of whom have had no experience in these special lines of work, and the 'precarious' or 'dangerous' transactions that are bound to develop . . . must be met with . . . a stern negative. . . ."

themselves—that foreign trade, especially, was a bad business for Amexco to be in. Few other executives in the company saw it his way. Most agreed with the executive who said that a trade operation "if properly handled would have been very profitable." There was much evidence to support that. For all of Frothingham's mistakes, when he did complete a deal, he made a substantial return.

George Weston, who was later company treasurer, felt even more strongly about the value of a trade operation. He pleaded with Small to revamp the department, not abolish it, and he argued that it was a vital service—one the company needed to offer. "May I also inject a suggestion about the need of the Foreign Trade Department. . . . We must have some experienced man or men at New York to take care of [trade transactions] because they are profitable from every angle—financial, exchange, insurance, shipping and foreign trade. To be sure, they take a good deal of time, but the earnings are usually compensatory. We could not live on Foreign Trade Department earnings but we need that service to complement our other services." But Small refused to listen. There is no indication that he bothered even to reply. There is merely the scribbled "Noted by F.P.S." on Weston's letter. Small had decided that such businesses were, as he later termed them, "adventures" and "fancy things," and not only did Small abolish the Foreign Trade Department, he suspended indefinitely the advances-against-invoices commercial-credit program, which M. F. Berry had created, and which had been profitable since its inception in 1905.

As for the personnel problem, so far from solving it, Small actually compounded it. If Brooks's failing was an inability to see the true abilities of his men, Small's was an inability to see the value of any other quality but loyalty. Small had charge of staffing the foreign offices from 1919 on, choosing in particular the managers of each office. He made his choices on the basis of one criterion: ten years of service to the company. As he explained, "Faithful service for the Company and the knowledge of its policies and ideals are most valuable assets for the men who are to direct our affairs in the future . . ."

In later years, Small claimed he was following a policy set by Taylor after the merger of the expresses. To every extent possible, Taylor decided, the company would take care of employees. They could go to ARE or join the foreign service of American Express, and they had the first call on available jobs. This policy, which Small practiced to the letter if not beyond, was a noble one, and it engendered a feeling of family among employees.

But it was as wrongheaded as it was noble. It was even irrational, and it left the company with incompetent managers throughout the world for years afterward. The problem lay in the fact that Brooks had indeed remade the company to such a degree that most loyal stalwarts no longer understood its businesses, even after Small's cutbacks. Small appointed package, freight, and money-order men to do the work of bankers and export-import men and sent them to run offices in parts of the world they had never even seen before.

Many of these men were unqualified by any measure, but Small's organization of the foreign offices made it difficult for even the most competent among them to succeed. Each manager was a local chieftain who supervised everything: banking, trade (while it lasted), investment, freight forwarding, travel, administration. Often he had to run all of these activities personally since, initially at least, many offices operated with limited staffs and small budgets. George Weston, as early as 1907, had argued that the company could not hope to find people with such all-around talents anywhere, much less from the ranks of old expressmen. Twelve years later, as Small began his staffing efforts, R. A. Foulks, head of the Far Eastern offices, voiced similar concerns and claimed that the evidence already proved that managers could not adequately fulfill multiple roles. He maintained that managers could not successfully combine the jobs of bankers and freight men, much less travel men and administrators, too. "We have tried to build up men equally capable of handling both [banking and freight] departments, but not with any high degree of success," Foulks said. "Office managers generally turn out to be either financial men or transport men—not both." He argued therefore that the company should organize along product lines—create a bank run by bankers with branches worldwide, and a travel service staffed by travel people worldwide. Small ignored this advice.

Actually, on some level, Small recognized the difficulty his system posed, but his response was simply to try to reduce the job to the man. Small once said, in explaining why he abolished foreign trade, that foreign office managers extended credit for grain export deals but did not know "number one wheat from barley." This was true, but the obvious point was to find people who did know the difference. Small abolished trade instead.

Small's thinking on personnel became especially clear in 1920 during his search for a manager of the new Constantinople office. Brooks, who still made policy at the time, had decided to create an office in Constantinople almost exclusively for banking and told Small to set it up. Although Small had authority to choose any manager, he asked for suggestions from Brooks and from Dalliba's successor in Europe, W. J. Thomas.

Brooks found three candidates—outsiders—who had experience in Turkey, and Small had the New York personnel office investigate one of them, a V. D. Tchertchian.* The report on Tchertchian was overwhelmingly favorable, although it did allow as how the Armenian gentleman should have "proper supervision, owing to the make up of the Oriental mind." If the "Oriental mind" was too much for Small, he had another alternative. Thomas had uncovered an Englishman with the quintessential WASP name of E. Saxon Napier, who had had banking experience in Constantinople before World War I, and who spoke five languages including French, Turkish, and modern Greek, the commercial languages of the city.

Small rejected Tchertchian, pondered Saxon Napier for a while, and then rejected him as well. He informed Thomas that only a ten-year company man would do. Thomas was dismayed; in his view, there was no company man conceivably qualified for the job. "The fact is that I do not see that we have anyone amongst our employees in Europe who could possibly fill the bill at Constantinople as satisfactorily as would a man of the type of Mr. Napier, who is so familiar with conditions in Constantinople," Thomas said.

---

*The personnel office was in itself another innovation of Howard Brooks.

Small, in reply, lectured Thomas on company personnel policy. "The new offices . . . will be headed up by men who have been in the company's service for from ten to twenty years, who are not necessarily experts in Banking or Exchange nor do they possess any knowledge of the customs or languages of the countries to which they were assigned." (Thomas had reported that French at least was *essential* for anyone in Constantinople.) In the end, Small appointed company man R. E. Bergeron. Bergeron, a ten-year man who was in Japan at the time, at least had a "thorough knowledge of French," as Thomas noted with relief.

Elsewhere, Small made appointments that were far worse. Adhering to his basic principle, Small picked company men and sent them abroad, and few of them succeeded. Some offices lost money year after year. Calcutta, for example, lost money in twelve of nineteen years between 1921 and 1939. Small juggled the offices—closing one here, opening another there—and he changed managers (there were three different managers in Zurich during its first two years), or he merely shuffled them among offices. Paul Whipple Bradford, the one manager who made money in Calcutta, went from Calcutta to Shanghai and back to Calcutta again. Bergeron went from Yokohama to Constantinople to Athens in less than a decade. But these moves had little impact on overall profitability.

Yet the poor performance of the foreign offices and office managers never endangered Small's own job. Part of the reason was that the red ink appeared in small amounts—$1,000 here, $5,000 there, $250 somewhere else. Small was never taken to task for the losses as long as the company overall made money, which it did. That was a turnaround from the Glass Eye disaster—a turnaround most people in the company credited to Small. Even board members regarded him as the man who had saved American Express. As a result, they certainly would not quibble with the loss of $500 in Calcutta.

Small's authority and influence grew steadily through 1922 and 1923. Now reports that once went through Brooks and his men went to Small and his. Small had assembled a team of young men ("a bunch of boys" one called it), who had worked under him at the Red Cross during the war. Most senior was John K. Livingston, until he met Small, an employee of the telephone company. Howard A. Smith, a genial, lovable Irishman, was next in line. Then there was foreign-exchange man Louis Wirth, comptroller R. C. James, and his assistant and later successor, Ralph T. Reed. By 1922, none of these men had more than a couple years of service. They were young and wide-eyed with admiration for Small, whom they saw as a man of "vision and judgment," an ideal cadre of aides for a leader who valued loyalty above all. With Frothingham and Johnson fallen, Small's young men had suddenly become the company's future.

Despite the changes in the lines of authority at the top, and despite the controls Small had put in, losses reappeared in exchange trading in 1923. It was no one's fault, really, but it was Johnson's responsibility. The losses stemmed mostly from the great inflation in Germany. Johnson and his men had actually guessed right about the market, yet they still dropped more than $200,000 when three German firms went bankrupt and failed to pay off their forward-exchange contracts.

Then another crisis struck American Express. In November, George Taylor died suddenly of overwork at age fifty-five, and the only possible candidate to succeed him was Frederick P. Small. Others were, like Brooks, discredited, or like Dalliba, dead. So Small won the job. Brooks remained, but possessed little power. Small, meanwhile, settled into office and settled old scores. A quarter century later, he boasted that the first thing he did as president was fire Frothingham and Johnson. * There was only one trouble with the story: Johnson had resigned in disgrace the previous February. It was a measure of Small's resentment that he recalled having sacked him. By 1924, Brooks's two rising stars had departed. Livingston, on the other hand, was elected corporate secretary, and Small's other protégés were also promoted. Small, his men, and his point of view commanded American Express.

---

*Johnson and Frothingham were almost entirely expunged from the record. In 1950, Alden Hatch was ordered not to mention either man in the one hundredth anniversary book. Little information about them remains in the company archives.

Although Small now possessed the president's title and chief executive authority, he made no change in his basic approach of restricting the scope of the company. The company, he declared, would "stick to our knitting." However, that principle begged a basic question: in 1924, just what was Amexco's knitting? Arguably it had lost its knitting in 1918 when it lost the domestic express business. There was of course the international freight-forwarding and package-handling business, which might have been considered the company's knitting, but Small did not have that in mind.

Then, too, banking—TCs, money orders, foreign exchange—could have been construed as Amexco's knitting. Before the Glass Eye Era, Small himself had declared that the company's "greatest opportunity is in banking and exchange operations." The New York office still handled millions of dollars in transactions a day, and from 1918 through 1920, the company made huge amounts of money on the remittance business. Amexco did a volume of more than $100 million a year in remittances and more than $100 million in TCs.

But banking was not what Small had in mind either. In fact, Small now considered banking one of those "adventures" of Brooks's that the company should abandon. Instead, Small determined that the company's "knitting" was a business it had been in officially for only eight years—the travel business. In 1919, Brooks and advertising manager Douglas Malcolm had created a company slogan, "World Service." Although they had included world banking and trade, Small applied the slogan almost exclusively to travel.

Small himself loved travel. His men described him as "a clipper ship captain born a generation too late." Each year, he sailed away on world tours, paying calls on offices around the globe: Singapore, Hong Kong, Alexandria, Calcutta. He would be away for months at a time, leaving Livingston in charge back in New York. (Curiously, while he insisted on ten-year men for branch offices, he routinely left a six-year man in charge of the company.) The concept of the romance of travel began to appear in company advertising and in articles about Amexco during the 1920s. "Romance had ambushed the American Express

Company under the sober business guise of travelers cheques," wrote *Forbes* magazine in a 1929 article that was mainly an interview with Small. "But in its travel service, the company frankly extends the hand to romance and makes it a partner. . . . '*Voyage* [sic] *c'est vivre*—To travel is to live.' "

The company's own publications touted travel in purple prose and even poetry. The soberly named *American Express Travel Bulletin* rhapsodized: "It is a normal desire in men and women to travel; to wander far from home and then to return to its increased sweetness:

> For it's there I store my memories
> and there I tend my fire,
> And there I'm always dreaming of
> *new* ports o'heart's desire.

In fact, the company went beyond romance in its pitch. Travel was a matter of self-fulfillment and self-definition, even "the most effective method of promoting civilization."

Small argued, too, that he had business logic behind him. Because most travel operations did not require outlays of large sums of money, he considered the business risk free. But it was also profit free, since competition and overhead—advertising, as well as such Amexco specialties as a free post office and interpreter service—made any real profits next to impossible.

The only travel profits were in the TC. Brooks, Dalliba, and most other Amexco officials had supported a travel business as an adjunct to the TC, but the TC itself they saw as a part of banking rather than travel. Small disagreed. In his view, the TC belonged to travel, and by making that identification, he was able to support the TC and at the same time undermine all other banking operations.

After 1924, Small always referred to banking operations with the qualifer "so-called," but he did not eliminate banking outright, because he found that his most radical steps could have serious consequences. His suggestion that the company get out of banking in Zurich in 1922 devastated employee morale and drove away customers to such an extent that he had to reverse his decision. So Small did not abolish American Express worldwide banking operations; he merely savaged them so severely that he appeared to his men to be determined to make them fail.

Though Amexco never had an office called a bank, a banking operation most certainly did exist. Before his own fall, Brooks had directed Small not only to make banking a function of all offices, but also to set up some offices exclusively for banking in major financial and commercial centers. The most important of these was on Lombard Street, in the "City" of London, the financial center not just of England, but of the world. The company also established important banking offices in Brussels, Zurich, Genoa, Constantinople, and Athens; in the last of these, Amexco enjoyed for a time the status of being the *only* American bank. These offices engaged in all kinds of banking activities—deposits, loans, securities trading, and foreign exchange. Foreign exchange was especially important. Remittances, TCs, and exchange trading for commerical firms often combined to make American Express one of the leading players in local exchange markets. In Constantinople, Amexco stood number two or three in all clearances.

Even before he became president, Small began his assault on the banking offices. He started by putting severe limits on operations—limiting the value of exchange contracts the company could carry with any bank or firm, the amount of cable transfers, the value of positions in silver trading, the size of overdrafts, and the size of time (loaned) letters of credit. He continually tightened these limits until some offices could barely function, and others had little hope of profitability. In the commercial city of Genoa, for example, the company office tried to play an active role in trade finance. But Small made it virtually impossible for the Genoa office to extend commercial credits to anyone. Not only did he impose strict limits on the amount any one company could receive, Small—along with a "Credit Committee" in New York—passed on all loans of even modest size. This system hampered business. Small and the committee knew little about conditions 4,000 miles away, yet they often turned down what men on the scene considered perfectly sound transactions. As Dennis Harmon of the Zurich office protested, "Business which other banks accept at a moment's notice is after lengthy correspondence, often refused by us or is in the first place lost because of our inability [locally] to decide."

Small also placed severe restrictions on loans to banks. Even in that bastion of banking solidity, Switzerland, Small made transactions nearly impossible. He allowed the Zurich office to make interbank loans to the largest Swiss banks but with such strict limits that according to Harmon, "they do not require the amounts which we can offer." Meanwhile, Small forbade loans to even moderate-size Swiss banks. And in less stable countries, Small prohibited transactions even with the very largest banks. He vetoed a London office request to handle exchange contracts with the major banks of central Europe—even though these banks were clearly solvent and economic conditions in the countries, by Small's own admission, were good. Often, too, he ordered that surplus funds abroad be kept exclusively or largely in local, short-term government securities. These were safe enough, but at times led to such small spreads between what Amexco paid for deposits and what it earned, that no profit was possible after expenses.

In clamping down on the banking offices, Small would sometimes hide behind the authority of the board of directors or the executive committee. As he wrote to Thomas with reference to currency trading with central European banks: "I am not inclined to re-open this matter with the Executive Committee. Their attitude was that from every standpoint this was not a desirable class of business for us to undertake." This protest is not wholly believable. At American Express, presidents dominated the EC. Small almost certainly could have gotten the executive committee to see the desirable qualities of central European bank transactions if he had wanted to. In fact, he did not indicate to the board that any kind of bank transaction was desirable. Year after year, Small spoke to the executive committee and the board about the dangers of banking. Each year, he prepared a report on his voyages, and in the reports from 1924 to 1926, the refrain was the same: Expand travel, limit banking—even to the point of keeping at low levels "the amount of money placed at the disposal of the Foreign Offices" lest they get carried away in their banking activities.

In support of his policy, Small was able to show the directors that the banking offices were unprofitable. But he had cooked the books. The banking offices carried a disproportionate share of overhead for all of Europe while other offices—more travel-related—were credited for some banking profits. By the time everything was added up (or not added up) the banking offices showed a loss.

The most egregious example of book manipulation was in Lombard Street, London, an office headed by a Brooks protégé, G. P. Kenway. In 1924, Kenway reported a loss of almost £400 (a little under $2,000). Late that year, Small wrote a letter decrying the poor performance of Lombard Street and warning that, if results did not improve, "we may wish to discontinue Lombard Street activity . . ."

In a reply to Small, and in another letter addressed to Thomas in January 1925, Kenway protested and accused Small of rigging the numbers. Kenway claimed that so far from losing £400, Lombard Street by any fair measure made money, at least £7,000! First, the office had a capital of £200,000, loaned to it from the parent American Express Company. Lombard Street paid New York 3.5 percent interest on that money. That took £7,000 off the top that could not be credited as earnings.

Lombard Street also had to pay £7,900 in indirect "administrative expenses" incurred by the company throughout Great Britain and the rest of Europe. Almost £1,000 of those expenses went for overhead of the office of the general manager for Britain. But the general manager had almost nothing to do with banking, not after 1923 in the era of F. P. Small. "As you are no doubt aware," Kenway said to Thomas, "the services of the General Manager for our territory naturally chiefly benefits the Travel side of our activities in this country. Why then would a financial office have to bear such a large proportion, 45 percent, of this expense?" By contrast, Kenway pointed out, the Amexco office in Haymarket, where the general manager had his *physical office*, paid only 35 percent of his expenses. Kenway also noted bitterly that the financial offices paid 57 percent of the overhead of the European organization though they constituted fewer than a third of the offices. With this burden, Kenway figured he had to earn 7.5 percent on primary capital (well above market interest of the day) just to break even—a level of return "not often exceeded by even the very finest institutions."

At the same time, Lombard Street performed a range of services gratis for other parts of the company. Kenway and his staff processed remittances from New York, with the profit credited to New York. They also cleared all sterling transactions for other British offices without charge. And while other British offices were allowed to charge New York a commission for sales of TCs denominated in British pounds, Lombard Street could not.

Small did not listen to Kenway's protests. Later in 1925, he resumed his attack, ripping Lombard Street and the other "so-called banking operations," for turning in very little revenue, and for bombarding him with wild "proposals calling for our establishing large limits for credit risks." Ironically, at almost the same moment he was lambasting Kenway, Small received a protest from Zurich like the one he had heard from Lombard Street. Harmon lamented that, between interest on capital (4 percent in this case) and indirect expenses, he had to earn 10 percent to break even.

Although the banking offices paid the highest share of expenses, Small charged travel offices very little. Kenway complained that they were able to report "their profits almost gross." This of course was the point. In a blink of the books, Small made travel a money-maker and banking a loser. He could show the board a travel business that was growing and a bank that drained profits, and board members would surely then endorse his decision to expand travel and stifle banking.

His position was revealed in another way at this same time. Small regularly demanded that the banking offices pare expenses. They all complied, cutting personnel and other expenses wherever possible. Kenway, in fact, tried to cut one of his largest expenses, his rent. He did not want to leave the City of London, because that was the center of banking, and as fortune would have it, he found a desirable location in the City, actually better sited (a ground floor instead of upstairs) and cheaper than Lombard Street. To Kenway, it seemed ideal, but Small said no, a rejection that Kenway took as a reflection of Small's priorities for the company. Kenway protested that Small was not interested in improving the bank's profitability at all, but rather was waiting for the moment when "our travel business will have assumed such large proportions that the banking business will no longer be required or necessary."

The true situation in the foreign offices was quite different from the way Small represented them. Throughout the world organization, travel did not make money for the better part of the next half century despite all of Small's loving care. Small continued to lie about this even to his own board of directors. As he told them, "We have an increasing volume of [travel] business yearly with satisfactory net returns." But actually, if the company had given up the TC and the money order and relied strictly on travel, it would have lost money consistently.

In the few instances when a foreign branch office made money, the profits actually came from banking. In Athens, for instance, the office, even with all the restrictions, remained one of the largest exchange traders, handling accounts for the major American tobacco companies, who needed drachmas to buy Turkish tobacco. This commerce produced net income in several years. Other offices also profited from financial operations. In offices that Small established to handle all businesses—travel, freight forwarding, and financial operations—finance often brought in more money than the other two combined. This was true even in Paris, the travel center of the world. During a six-month period in 1922, when the office figured separate tallies in travel, freight, and finance, financial revenues were four times those of the other two combined. Few knew of these figures, and in fact, for most of the next forty years, company offices did not report separate totals for finance and travel.

Still, some managers knew where the money was coming from. In the Far East, both Paul Bradford in Calcutta (and for a time, Shanghai) and Frank Groves in Bombay recognized that their profits came from banking. As Groves put it, "We never made any money on travel . . . the banking business is what made the money." Groves and Bradford had an advantage over their European counterparts, however. Small paid almost no attention to them. Because of time and distance (and the fact that profits or losses were fairly small in any year), he let them have almost unchallenged autonomy and seldom sent them more than a Christmas card.

Small never acknowledged the instances when offices posted profits from banking, but he harangued managers whenever financial operations lost money. Usually, personnel caused these losses, not the businesses themselves. The worst case, one almost comical in its twists and turns, occurred in Genoa, which posted a serious loss one year. Sherman Boyce, a former route agent from Oregon, headed an office set up largely for trade and banking. Boyce faced difficult problems from the outset. He ran a commercial credit operation, which he knew nothing about. He tried to cope with the falling value of the lira, but that was not his field. But the most serious problem arose over securities trading, another field unfamiliar to Sherman Boyce. In 1925, one of his men, a Mr. Lasciata, went on an unauthorized, speculative binge that resulted in fraudulent records and a sudden loss for Amexco of something like 200,000 lire (about $10,000 in those days). Boyce was away from the office when his number-two man, Robert Tennenbaum, uncovered the fraud. The number-three man, Mr. Schiaffino, should have caught it since he was in charge of securities trading. A. G. Dennis, chief auditor for Europe, was dispatched to Genoa to investigate and found the whole securities operation in disarray. "The records were inaccurate and poorly kept," he reported, "errors having been discovered in the records dating back several months. Mr. Schiaffino, while absolutely honest is not the type of employee to have charge of securities as he showed every indication of being stupid."

Dennis had it wrong; Schiaffino was both stupid and dishonest. He was not even Schiaffino. That was an alias. In 1913, he had run into some personal trouble and had taken a job at Amexco under an assumed name. He kept it and his job for twelve years. Once the truth came out, the logical response would have been to send the man packing as fast as possible—perhaps off to the police. But Small's reaction was quite different. When Thomas reported all the details, Small wrote back that "the man's work had been *entirely satisfactory* over a period of twelve years [and so] we should not be too hard in dealing with him." (Italics added.)

Despite such episodes, the company made money each year. The profits came exclusively from the TC and the money order, particularly the former; TC volume hit $200 million in 1926. Of course, the company made its money, not on the sales of TCs, but on the float which was quite competently managed during the 1920s by Howard Smith and George Weston. The short- and long-term TC floats reached a total of more than $50 million and produced regular profits, not huge amounts, but enough to pay through 1928 about $1 million a year in dividends and add another million to surplus.

The strangest aspect of the float was that few outside the company knew about it and fewer still appreciated its importance. Nearly every Amexco employee worked in travel, which made no money, while a handful of staffers, led by Smith and Weston, made all the money and labored in total obscurity as far as stockholders and the general public were concerned—almost as though their activity was a dark secret. For the next thirty-five years, no one in the company talked about the float publicly for fear that banks and other travel companies, realizing how lucrative it was, would get into the business and take Amexco's market share. That share was substantial: in the 1920s, around 50 percent.

Meanwhile, Small succeeded in redefining the image of American Express as one of the world's premier travel companies. From the mid-1920s on, Amexco's only identity was as the American's friend in foreign places.* Novels and stories of the day, such as Sinclair Lewis's

---

*There was some public confusion about the relationship between American Express and the American Railway Express (ARE), because of the similarity of their names. Throughout the 1920s, and even in later years, Amexco received complaints about lost packages entrusted to the care of the other company.

Dodsworth, took that perception for granted. Lewis had no need to explain why a character, a confused tourist in a strange port of call, found the words American Express Company "thrice golden." Small had given the company an exact identity—as exact as it had been in the old express days. More than a few people must have wondered why a travel company would be named express. But it did not keep them from the doors of 11 Rue Scribe and the other travel offices around the world.

After Small had finished cutting Amexco down to the size he wanted, he showed no inclination to add to it. Except for opening some new travel offices, he was content with the status quo. A few ideas for new or expanded business drifted around 65 Broadway but never went anywhere. Small even rejected the opportunity to build the travel business into what would have been unquestionably the dominant travel company in the world. In 1923, Brooks heard that Thomas Cook & Son was for sale, and he suggested to Small that Amexco buy it to keep it out of the grasp of Bankers Trust, which sold a traveler's check that was the main competition to the TC. As things stood, Amexco's travel department gave the company a competitive edge in TC sales—an edge that Brooks feared would evaporate if Bankers Trust took over Cook's. Small said no, however, and a few years later Cook's was sold to Wagon-Lits, the Belgian builder of railway cars.

Small sat back, encouraged his own travel division, limited banking operations, and totaled up the profits from TC sales, money orders (Amexco sold over $200 million in money orders as well), and the related float. Later, Small and his men took credit for saving the company—twice. First, they claimed to have saved it by getting out of the "fancy" things in the early 1920s. And then they claimed they saved it in the 1930s because Amexco had not committed itself during the 1920s to businesses that suffered in the Great Depression.

The latter claim was, and is, impossible to evaluate. But the assertion about the early twenties is highly debatable. In making it, Small and his men presupposed an either/or choice. Either reckless banking and trading or nothing. Small chose nothing. But while trade and banking carried risk, there was no reason why Small could not have used the lesson of the Glass Eye Era to build conservative and effective banking and trading departments under experienced people.

How successful could an operation in banking, especially one run by qualified people, have been? A useful illustration is the record of the Guaranty Trust Co. It is apt for several reasons. First, Brooks, Gee, and others pointed to the Guaranty in the 1910s as an example of the kind of bank they wanted Amexco to create. Such a banking operation was not far out of reach for American Express. In 1916, Amexco's capital and surplus almost equaled those of the Guaranty. Also, the Guaranty had begun a vigorous expansion into foreign banking, especially trade finance, and had established offices in London, Paris, Liverpool, Le Havre, Brussels, and Constantinople. The Guaranty makes a useful comparison too, because, unlike many other banks of the period (Continental Illinois, Equitable Trust, etc.), its growth was purely internal and did not rely on mergers with other institutions. Finally, the Guaranty suffered reversals as bad as the Glass Eye debacle at the same time. The Guaranty lost several million dollars and had to set up a $15 million contingency fund out of surplus and profits to bolster its loan-loss reserves. The Guaranty handled those reversals by instituting more measured and conservative banking practices—reform rather than reduction. In 1922, these reforms produced $900,000 in profits. Thereafter, profits increased steadily. By 1928, profits topped $10 million per year.

In the meantime, Amexco grew much less dramatically. In 1927, revenues were around $7 million, actually 10 percent *lower* than they had been in 1922. Profits rose from around $1 million in 1922 to $2 million in 1928, but the 1922 figure included write-offs from bad deals made during the postwar depression, while Small could only manage $2 million in profits during an economic boom. That amount was nowhere near what the company had made from exchange trading just before the Glass Eye fiasco, and its rate of growth fell far short of banks like the Guaranty during the 1920s.

Small did keep the company solvent, but he also made it substan-

209

tially smaller in scope. During the 1920s, he rented out half of 65 Broadway; the company did not do enough business to fill it. Few on Wall Street appreciated that Amexco had become a small company with a large image. That, however, satisfied F. P. Small.

In 1925, Howard Brooks retired as VP, and the same year, J. F. Fargo finally departed. Small elevated his people in name as well as in fact. Before long Livingston, Smith, and Reed were all vice presidents. They were in many ways competent men; Smith and Reed, especially, provided quality work with investments and accounts respectively. But there was little force for change within the executive ranks of American Express. Small had plugged in loyalists, some incompetent, who took their cues from their president. Small was standing pat, and who were they to say otherwise?

If there were to be any substantive changes, they would have to come from outside American Express.

SAVED
BY THE
DEPRESSION
<u>　　　　　　　　　　　</u>
8

In the summer of 1929, American Express neared the end of its existence.

The Chase National Bank and its securities affiliate, one of the largest financial organizations in America, had just completed a tender offer for Amexco's stock and now owned over 97 percent of it. This purchase was the first step in Chase's strategy to absorb all of the profitable parts of Amexco, discard the others, and turn American Express into a Chase trademark.

It was on the verge of happening, it should have happened, and it did not happen—more or less by accident. Chase's timing was all wrong. Chase had blundered into historical circumstances—a chain of events brought on by the Great Depression, which seriously damaged the bank's reputation and curtailed its freedom of action. And Chase's bad luck was Amexco's good fortune. American Express had done nothing to save itself. Chief executive F. P. Small had made no move to stop the original takeover and could not have prevented the absorption. Although Chase had developed an elaborate offensive strategy from the outset, Small had no defense. From the time of its acquisition to the day it regained its freedom, Amexco was entirely passive in the transaction. But by sheer luck, it emerged from this episode independent and buffered from other takeover attempts for years to come. In a very real sense, American Express was saved by the Depression.

None of this would have happened but for F. P. Small's policies of the 1920s, without which Amexco might not have needed saving in the first place. As matters stood, he presided over a company with great, untapped growth potential—a potential that made it a very desirable target. At the same time, since his policies had not produced much growth, Amexco was an easy target because it was not very expensive. It was an easy target, too, because Small's American Express possessed a dramatically different character from the company of the past. Beginning in the 1880s, Amexco was led by fighters. Dalliba, Berry, and Brooks worked for change through and around whatever system was in place. But the aggressive spirit of those men was replaced by complacency. Small consistently rejected innovation—all "fancy" ideas or adventures—and he emphasized saving money and avoiding risk. He asked for nothing new and warned his people abroad not to try anything original because, he told them, he would find out through "the grapevine."

As a result, so little happened at Amexco from 1923 to 1928 that when Alden Hatch sat down to record the accomplishments of the era in a 1950 company biography, he could identify only two: a better accounting system (actually devised by the comptroller, Ralph Reed) and an "Inspector's Office" to track down TC and money order counterfeits. (This latter innovation helped put Bugs Moran behind bars.) But the spirit—or spiritlessness—that produced no significant advances in five years, spilled over into the company's approach to a possible takeover: it formulated no plans; it undertook no defense.

Although Small was content with what Amexco already had, people

212

outside the company recognized its vast undeveloped potential. One of these outsiders, Albert Henry Wiggin, had enormous resources at his disposal. Wiggin was chairman and chief executive of the Chase National Bank (the CNB, for short) and its brokerage and investment banking arm, Chase Securities Corporation (CSC). During the 1920s he had built Chase from a relatively small bank to one of the giants of the financial world. From 1918 to 1928, the bank's capital had increased eightfold to $80 million and its surplus had quintupled to $77.5 million.* The CSC meanwhile had grown from a $1 million organization at its founding in 1917 to a $28 million company eleven years later. Wiggin had achieved this tremendous growth in large part through acquisitions of banks and other financial institutions and through an aggressive and successful investment strategy that placed the Chase among the leading stock market players of the 1920s bull market.

Wiggin focused mainly on shares of companies he knew best—banks—but around 1927, he developed an interest in express companies. He sat on the boards of the Adams Express (at this point an investment trust) and the American Railway Express (ARE). His fascination with the express companies rested on their investment portfolios and on ARE shares themselves, which carried a government-guaranteed return. (Adams owned almost 30 percent of the ARE.)

Because American Express was a different kind of company, with a travel business as well as the TC and money order, Wiggin showed little interest in it at first. But in 1928, he was persuaded to consider a takeover of American Express for one of its underused assets: its international branch network. Wiggin's son-in-law, Lynde Selden, head of the Foreign Department at the CNB, had studied Amexco and realized that it had banking charters in countries around the world. The network and its charters could prove invaluable to Chase. Only one U.S. bank—the nation's largest, the National City Bank—had offices in so many places. Chase, though a domestic financial power, had next to no world organization, and Selden, who envisioned turning Chase

---

* Chase actually had lower capital and surplus than Amexco in 1918. Ten years later, Chase had six times greater resources.

213

into a leading international bank, argued that Amexco's network could provide Chase with instant status and credibility in international finance. * Selden thought, too, that Chase could acquire Amexco for a bargain price—perhaps as little as $36 million (its market value).

After Selden brought this proposition to his father-in-law, Wiggin decided to investigate Amexco for himself. What he discovered only increased his interest. Wiggin learned that, in addition to having an international office network, American Express handled a huge amount of cash—he estimated it at $300 million annually, including by his guess $100 million in TCs—cash he wanted for deposits in his bank and for stock-market activities. In fact Wiggin underestimated Amexco's cash volume. Turnover was closer to $500 million and TC sales well over $200 million, but even his low estimates made Amexco an attractive takeover candidate on a cash-deposit basis alone; with the office network added in, Amexco was worth far more than $36 million. On two counts, then, American Express made an excellent addition to the Chase organization, and in the summer of 1928, Wiggin decided to mount a takeover.

In 1928, it should be noted, a raider did not have to report a 5 percent holding to the Securities and Exchange Commission (which had not yet been created), or make public tender offers to take control of a company. The usual acquisition technique was to get as much stock as possible—preferably enough to gain control—as surreptitiously as possible, typically by buying shares on the market through several separate accounts so activity could not be traced to one source. Only later would a raider announce his intentions. Often officials of a target company would not know of an acquisition until they saw the price of their company's stock soar.

In August, Wiggin told Chase officials that the normal technique of buying control of Amexco on the open market would be difficult.

---

* Initially Selden wanted to use Amexco's office network to build an international merchant bank. Merchant banking involves the identification and development of investment opportunities, and such an operation would have allowed both the CNB and the CSC to expand internationally.

Ralph T. Reed: President of American Express, 1944–1960. Rebuilt the company after the war and made the key decisions to start the charge card and revitalize the international bank. (*American Express Archives*)

Robert C. Townsend: A major force at Amexco in the 1950s, pushing the company toward adoption of the charge card and revitalization of the company's banking operations. Left Amexco to head Avis. (*American Express Archives*)

Howard L. Clark: Chief executive officer from 1960 until 1977. Led Amexco out of a scandal and oversaw a period of remarkable growth. (*American Express Archives*)

James D. Robinson III: Became chairman and CEO in 1977. Expanded Amexco enormously in financial services, beginning with his acquisition of Shearson Loeb Rhoades. (*Peter Kaplan*)

Robert L. Clarkson (*front row center*): Became chairman of Amexco in 1935. Along with Albert Wiggin, he ran the company until 1944 and remained chairman until 1960. This photo was taken at the 1957 Officials and Managers Conference. Also pictured, all in the front row, are: Olaf Ravndal (*third from left*), P. W. Bradford (*fourth from left*), Ralph Reed (*fifth from left*), Howard Clark (*sixth from right*), Frank Groves (*fourth from right*), Robert Mathews (*third from right*), and Robert Townsend (*second from right*). (*American Express Archives*)

11 Rue Scribe: William Swift Dalliba fought vexatious Frenchmen and his own chief executive to get the lease for this building. As he intended, it quickly became a mecca for American tourists abroad and has remained one ever since. (*American Express Archives*)

65 Broadway: Amexco's headquarters building from 1874 to 1917. (*American Express Archives*)

65 Broadway, rebuilt in 1917: Remained the company's headquarters for almost 60 years. (*American Express Archives*)

American Express Tower: Headquarters as of 1985 in the World Financial Center in New York. By the time Amexco moved in, the new building was already too small. (*Korrine Nusbaum*)

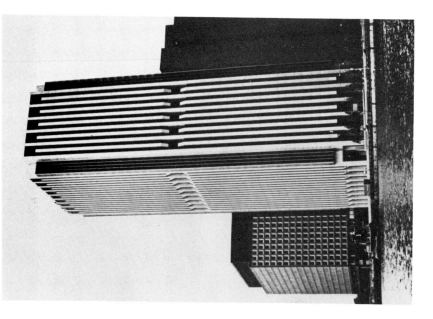

American Express Plaza: Modern Amexco moved into this building in 1975 and left 10 years later. (*American Express Archives*)

Amexco's 180,000 shares were "widely distributed," making the acquisition of a controlling block of stock in the market uncertain at best. But Wiggin had identified a few key blocks of stock, which he thought might be available and could provide Chase with a sizable base before it began open-market activities. After some discussion, Chase decided to go after one particular block—15,900 shares belonging to the New York Central Railroad.

Chase officials thought the railroad should sell at a good price: the Central had originally bought Amexco stock because of the ties between the express and railroad businesses, but the only link that Amexco now had to domestic transportation was through its shares in ARE. However, earlier in 1928, the railroads had decided to buy the ARE's express business and run it themselves as the Railway Express Agency. (The railroads held the contractual right to exercise this option unilaterally.) Once that occurred, Amexco would have no further association with domestic transportation, and the Central would no longer have a rationale to keep its stake in Amexco.

Wiggin and his men agreed that Chase's best chance of obtaining the Central shares lay in getting a friend of the railroad to make the offer, and they settled on financier William T. Hoops. Hoops, a leading investor of the twenties, was an associate of A. H. Smith, onetime president of the Central. Hoops and Smith had in fact formed an investment company together, LCL Corp., of which Hoops was now president. Chase executives thought Hoops would be especially interested in a deal since he owned a block of Amexco stock himself (4,500 shares), and since he talked openly in the investment community of his dissatisfaction with Small's management, in particular, Small's "lack of interest toward enlargement of [Amexco's] scope." Chase officials hoped they might win Hoops over by promising him substantive development at Amexco.

Wiggin designated CSC executive Medley G. B. Whelpley to handle the negotiations with Hoops, and Whelpley met with the financier soon after the August meeting. Hoops was initially skeptical: he had been studying Amexco's operations for years and was contemplating taking control himself. He added, in case Chase had any doubts, that he had enough of his own resources to implement his plans.

215

By the end of the meeting, however, Hoops was persuaded that Chase would develop Amexco's growth potential. He agreed to set up in partnership with Chase; for the time being, he would hold on to his own shares and maintain a joint account with the CSC to buy up more stock, including the shares held by the Central.

Hoops handled the negotiations with the Central, and as Wiggin had hoped, Hoops simplified that process enormously. The financier soon purchased the Central's 15,900 shares at $225 each—not a bad price from Wiggin's perspective, considering that in July 1928, in the normal course of trading, the price had gone as high as $207.75.

With 20,000 shares now under his control—Hoops's 4,500, along with the 15,900 from the Central—Wiggin started market operations from several accounts, the most important of which was a joint account with Hoops managed by Whelpley. For all the accounts, Chase employed "dependable brokers" who would neither leak information to the public nor try to doublecross Chase by playing broker/dealer, that is, by buying up shares for themselves and selling them to Chase at a high premium.

Around this time, Wiggin also formed another alliance—this time with Eugene W. Leake, an investor and attorney. Leake's motives for joining such an alliance were straightforward: he was a director of both the ARE and Adams express companies, and he wanted the ARE. The ARE was about to receive $32 million from the railroads for its express business. Leake planned to liquidate all of the ARE's cash holdings and vest the money in the Adams Express, which he controlled.* Wiggin offered Leake the chance to buy the largest single block of stock

---

*Leake also needed Wiggin's support inside the boards of Adams and the ARE, but it's not clear if he ever got it. Leake was challenged for control of Adams by Charles Hayden of Hayden, Stone & Company. Hayden wanted to turn the ARE into an investment trust, while Leake planned to liquidate the express company. In the end, Wiggin sold Amexco's ARE shares to Adams, but the ARE became an investment trust as Hayden wished. Both Leake and Hayden remained officers of Adams, but Hayden won the battle. Interestingly, Hayden then joined the board of Wiggin's Amexco; Leake and Hoops (who had joined Leake's faction in the ARE fight) reportedly felt they had been betrayed by Wiggin.

in the ARE—130,000 (40 percent) owned by Amexco. In return, Leake pledged to Wiggin not only to sell him Adams's shares in Amexco, but also to use his influence on Wiggin's behalf, even before the takeover was complete, by taking a seat on Amexco's board of directors.

By the autumn of 1928, American Express officials should have realized something was up. Already, there were signs of unusual activity in Amexco's stock; the price of a share had nearly doubled in a matter of weeks. Brokers all along Wall Street heard rumors about a battle for the control of American Express.* Indeed, the battle was being waged not simply on the stock exchange, but inside the company as well. The investment community talked of "turmoil" on the board of American Express. That assessment was accurate; conflict existed in the persons of Hoops and Leake. The two men (though they did not reveal their connections to Wiggin) made it known to Amexco's management that they held sizable positions in the company. Amexco believed that Hoops now owned the stake formerly belonging to the Central and when he demanded seats on the board, the board complied; Hoops also took a seat on the executive committee. Amexco's executives should have known—since nearly everyone on Wall Street did—that these men had not joined the board to support the status quo. Hoops, especially, had his own agenda. But Small and his men responded by doing nothing. In general, they pursued a policy of standing still; in this strange episode, they pursued a policy of standing in concrete. While Chase officials worked out an intricate strategy of market maneuvers and business alliances, Amexco's leaders did not try to cut a deal with anyone else, did not seek a white knight, did not dip into surplus and buy back 50,000 or so of their own shares to forestall a takeover.

Chase's market operations had netted Wiggin only about 50,000 more shares, giving him overall control of about 40 percent of the

---

*There were also rumors that Amexco planned to liquidate, but the rumors were unfounded.

stock. That was a large stake but not the decisive interest he wanted. As a result, on November 9, 1928, Whelpley and Wiggin met in another strategy session. Whelpley reported that he was finding it harder and harder to buy shares in the market; Wall Street knew a takeover was in progress, and those with Amexco stock were holding tight expecting the price to go even higher. Whelpley despaired of getting the rest of the stock through trading operations, and he recommended that Wiggin make a tender offer.

Wiggin reluctantly agreed, but he felt that before making an offer for the outstanding shares, he would have to buy out Hoops. When he met with Hoops, though, the financier balked at handing over his interest. Hoops did not preclude a deal, but neither did he accept one, and negotiations went on throughout the winter.

In early 1929, Wiggin engineered his own election to the American Express board and executive committee, undoubtedly with the help of his two men inside the board—Hoops and Leake. Two weeks after his own election, Wiggin increased his influence by arranging an expansion of the Amexco board from eleven to thirteen. The two men picked for the new seats were Fredrick Ecker and Newcomb Carlton. Though the former was with Metropolitan Life and the latter with Western Union, they were both board members of Chase and friends of Al Wiggin. Wiggin now controlled five of the thirteen votes of the board, giving him considerable power even before he consummated his takeover bid.

Then, he prepared his final assault on Amexco. He finally succeeded in buying out Hoops early in 1929, at $300 a share, and he completed negotiations with Leake over the disposition of Amexco's shares in the ARE. Then, his men drew up the terms of a tender offer, and on April 5, Wiggin presented them to Small at the new Chase headquarters on the corner of Pine and Nassau Streets.

The two men met in Wiggin's fourth-floor corner office. Small only had two alternatives: to accept the bid, or to reject it and probably end his association with American Express. He accepted it and apparently felt convinced that it was a good thing. As he wrote to his managers,

"THERE WILL BE NO CHANGE IN THE NAME, POLICIES, IDENTITY OR PERSONNEL OF THE AMERICAN EXPRESS ORGANIZATION. . . . I consider that we are in an extremely fortunate situation to have as a result of this affiliation the support and assistance of such great organizations as those of the Chase National Bank and the Chase Securities Corporation." (Small's capitalization.)

Small was not simply trying to put a good face on a deal he could not stop; a memo drafted a few days later and passed among Small and his top advisers indicated that he really believed what he told his managers. In the memo, Amexco's top executives looked not at the dangers of their new affiliation, but at its usefulness for expanding Amexco's business, especially the travel business. Small initially hoped that the Chase tie might help Amexco get agency agreements for passenger tickets and freight-forwarding arrangements with all the leading eastern railroads. He nowhere indicated a fear that Chase might eventually tamper with its new subsidiary.

Small endorsed the takeover plan as well. The deal called for Chase to give Amexco shareholders five Chase "units" (a combination of CNB and CSC shares in a fixed proportion) for each share of American Express. In a press release, Small called the offer "fair and equitable."

Small believed it all, but Wall Street knew better. Wiggin wanted Amexco's cash and office network; he wanted to make Amexco an adjunct facility of the giant bank. As B. C. Forbes wrote in the *New York American*, "[The acquisition of American Express] gives the Chase Bank a tremendous network of offices and outlets here and abroad. It will add greatly to the importance—and profits—of the Chase Securities Company [*sic*]. Wiggin now will have a department store bank."

Chase and Amexco shareholders approved Wiggin's plan and on July 1, 1929, Chase traded its own shares for 92,719 American Express shares, and Amexco became a subsidiary of the CSC. A little later Wiggin received another 7,613, giving him over 97 percent of the stock. Actually, he needed the missing 4,702 shares more than he knew, but on the surface he seemed to have what he had sought: absolute control of Amexco.

Wiggin's plan for the takeover of American Express had been well conceived and well carried out. But 1929 was not a good year for making deals.

Wiggin waited until early October before he took personal control of Amexco. At the beginning of the month, he had himself elected to the post of chairman—the new chief executive office—and nine days later he began to implement his program. He authorized two Chase officials to study Amexco's investments, and on the same day, he appointed Whelpley and Small to study whether American Express should establish a bank. The bank study was a mere formality. The first reason for buying Amexco was to use it as the center of an international banking operation, although initially Selden had wanted simply to incorporate the branch offices into Chase's international operations (and ultimately, Chase would return to that plan). Apparently he and Wiggin had decided instead to create a separate banking subsidiary to capitalize on the name and goodwill of American Express. For that strategy to work, Wiggin and Selden believed that Amexco needed a banking identity in the U.S. So Wiggin assigned Small, who had spent the previous eight years closing down Amexco's banking efforts, to rubber stamp a bank under the American Express banner.

Wiggin returned to 65 Broadway less than two weeks later to effect more changes. Wiggin proposed to print under the American Express name in the center of the TC the notation, "Affiliated with the Chase National Bank." This change was only the second revision of the TC in thirty-eight years. Small and his predecessors had found reasons why every previous attempt at alteration would have been a bad idea, but this time Wiggin made the decision and the board ratified it.

Wiggin had other worries in the next few days. Legend has it that on October 24 as he sat watching his stock ticker, he leapt from his chair with a cry and headed for the NYSE, recognizing that the market was in the grip of a panic. In the days that followed, Wiggin spent most of his time working with other bankers and financiers to stabilize the financial markets.

Despite the market Crash, he found time for American Express on

October 30. He had relaxed about the stock-market situation and told the executive committee—which now included Whelpley, Selden, and two other Chase officers—that the Crash presented a buying opportunity. He liked convertible securities especially, he said, and he ordered Amexco to buy them. The executive committee voted $5 million for the purpose, and soon Amexco made its first purchase: $250,000 in convertible bonds of General Theatres Equipment, a company which owed Chase millions and would shortly go bankrupt with almost $20 million in unpaid debts.

Wiggin only compounded this mistake when, a few weeks later, he launched a program of aggressive investments with Amexco's money. This strategy would have made sense in 1925, but not late in 1929. Nevertheless, at a meeting of the board attended by F. P. Small and seven Chase officials, the directors voted Wiggin a free hand to invest all of Amexco's surplus funds.

Wiggin did not simply expropriate the company's cash and securities. He and his staff at CSC created an account—called Account #50—for the CSC to play with. The account was limited to $20 million, with Amexco contributing 45 percent. A slight ambiguity in the wording of the account agreement, however, allowed CSC officials to claim several months later that what they really meant was not that the *account* was limited to $20 million but that Amexco's portion was limited to that sum. In all, the CSC took over $13 million from American Express for Account #50 and used it to buy stock during the worst market collapse in history. Most of the money in Account #50 went for shares in the Corn Exchange National Bank, and the losses finally incurred made those of the Glass Eye Era seem like pocket change.

Wiggin continued to implement his plan. In late November, Small and Whelpley reported to the executive committee that Amexco should indeed create a bank. Wiggin accepted the report. The bank, to be known as the American Express Bank & Trust, was capitalized at $10 million, with $6 million in additional reserves. American Express agreed to take 54 percent of the shares in the AEB&T; the CSC took 26 percent; and 10 percent of the stock was reserved for the new bank's officers and directors. Since the CSC owned 97 percent of Amexco, it controlled the AEB&T, but the plan allowed Wiggin to pay for it with Amexco's money. Whelpley was named president of the new bank, which had its headquarters at 65 Broadway.

Despite the Depression, the bank proved to be a money-maker. Whelpley pushed his bank into the forefront of trade credits and acceptances, and within a year it was ranked among the top one hundred banks nationwide in that area. As others before Whelpley had guessed, the American Express name was a valuable asset in international trade finance. By late 1931, through its efforts in trade finance, the bank was earning about 8 percent on its capital—not a bad performance during one of the worst periods in economic history.

Small raised not a word of protest over the draining of his company's treasury or the creation of a bank. He did nothing to forestall Wiggin's agenda, but began developing a program of his own. The alliance with Chase, Small hoped, would allow Amexco to gain "control of the tourists [sic] business throughout the world."

It took Small about eighteen months to make a definite proposal. In the interim, he tried to sell Chase officials on the travel business. He persuaded Chase to put travel desks in bank branches, and he talked up travel every chance he got. His best opportunity came in March 1930, when he gave a lecture to officials of the bank and the securities company. Small set out to present a general picture of what Amexco was and did, but the way he saw the company was reflected in the weight he gave each topic. The twenty-four-page talk (complete with pictures) contained three pages of history (with as many errors as facts), three pages on the money order and TC, one page on freight forwarding, then eight pages on travel, and nine pages of counterfeiter and forger stories.

The specific message of the lecture was travel. "This Company is yours," Small said cheerfully.

> *You are always going to need a service unit for your customers and your correspondent banks and it is going to be a real*

asset to you in the years to come. We naturally want you to help us in our efforts for business. We do not expect you to do much. All I am asking of you to do this evening is to give us leads of people who intend to travel. . . . I have prepared a little blank put up on pads which I would ask you to take away with you and use. This blank simply gives to our sales organization information as to prospective travellers. We would like to have each of you send us one or more per day. Try and do it. It will be greatly appreciated.

But all the lobbying Small did for travel proved futile. In 1930, Wiggin had no time for or interest in his subsidiary's little plans. He faced more pressing concerns. First, there was the economic situation. Though American banks had weathered the Crash and early days of the Depression surprisingly well, the rest of the economy was in severe trouble. Companies failed; the stock market continued to plunge. Wiggin extended himself to do what he could to bolster the American economy. He spoke at every opportunity with "sublime confidence" in the future, and he put up his money, loaning some $300 million in new funds to cash-strapped customers in a show of courage, loyalty, and bad judgment. It was a noble effort—it won him the reputation as "the most popular banker on Wall Street"—and because Chase was so wealthy, it did not threaten the solvency of the bank. At the same time, Wiggin had to cope with the reality of an increasing number of bad loans and red ink on the bank's balance sheet.

But Wiggin did make time to conclude his own deals for Chase. Even as Small was trying to sell travel, Wiggin was overseeing a merger that would create the largest bank in the world. In late 1929, Chase ranked number three in total resources among American banks. But in December of that year, Chellis Austin, the dynamic fifty-three-year-old chief executive of the billion-dollar Equitable Trust, died suddenly. The Equitable's largest and most important shareholder was John D. Rockefeller, Jr., who wanted a successor to Austin who would look after his family's interests. Rockefeller turned to his brother-in-

223

law, attorney Winthrop W. Aldrich, and asked him to take over the Equitable. Aldrich did not want the job but agreed on one condition: he would take it for a maximum of one year, and in that time, he would try to find a merger partner.

Aldrich picked Albert Wiggin and his Chase National Bank as that partner. Negotiations began early in 1930 and concluded in the spring when Aldrich agreed to merge the Equitable into Chase. Wiggin retained control, while Aldrich reluctantly became president of the CNB, again to safeguard family interests. The bank became the world's largest: it held deposits of more than $2 billion, with capital and surplus of nearly $300 million.*

Although the merger delighted Wiggin, it was a logistical nightmare. The two banks employed 8,000 people spread out in some 400 offices, with administrative departments (often duplicated) scattered all over New York City. Chase bank executives were preoccupied for weeks afterward putting the pieces of the two organizations together.

But Wiggin barely paused before embarking on his next big deal, the purchase of the investment-banking firm of Harris Forbes, which he added to the CSC. In the course of one year, with help from Aldrich, he had created and was now consolidating the greatest financial institution, not just the biggest bank, in the world.

In the midst of this financial empire building, Wiggin heard from F. P. Small, who wanted to buy Thomas Cook & Son. Though he had turned down the chance to buy Cook's at least twice before, Small had now changed his mind. He learned that Wagon-Lits wanted to unload the travel company and that the Canadian National Railroad was interested in buying it but probably could not for political reasons. In a memo to Wiggin, Small suggested that Amexco/Chase buy Cook's for about $10 million and sell a minority position to the railroad. This idea had the utmost urgency for Small, who peppered Wiggin and other Chase executives with memos for weeks. Wiggin, who had just

---

*Wiggin controlled the Chase, but the Rockefellers became the largest shareholders. Thereafter the bank would be known on Wall Street as "the Rockefeller bank."

completed the deal of the decade, showed little interest in Small's scheme; nonetheless, he assigned a Chase VP to investigate. Chase actually approached Wagon-Lits with an offer, but Wagon-Lits' rejection spelled the end of the matter as far as Chase was concerned. Small did not give up. He had his men abroad keep him posted on developments with Cook's, and in turn, he kept Chase officials informed. They ignored him.

In the long run, it was extraordinarily lucky for Amexco that Wiggin did not have time to focus his attention on his subsidiary. His plans for Amexco did not include making it the world's premier travel company. He wanted to use American Express to help build a financial empire dominant throughout the world, but, preoccupied by Equitable and Harris Forbes, he delayed thinking about Amexco for a year, a year in which the banking world moved from calm to crisis. By the time Wiggin was ready to turn to Amexco again in 1931, the economy had so far worsened, along with the public image and financial position of the banks, that whatever plans Wiggin had had for Amexco were impossible to put into practice.

In the winter of 1931, Wiggin, Selden, and Aldrich began to consider a strategy for the absorption of American Express into Chase. They had essentially three goals: "to vest a substantial part of the liquid assets of the Express Company in the Chase Securities"; "to vest in the Chase National Bank . . . the Travelers Cheque and Letter of Credit business"; and to convey Amexco's foreign branches and banking charters to the Chase Bank, the international banking arm of the CNB. Wiggin must have initiated this discussion, but he did not have much to do with the negotiations and planning that followed. Selden and Aldrich handled the details.

The two Chase officials discussed "various plans," seeking advice from lawyers at Milbank, Tweed, Hope & Webb. In spite of Chase's dominant 97 percent stake in American Express, there were a surprising number of problems. The most important one was that, although Chase had most of Amexco's shares, it did not have all of them.

225

Aldrich and Selden did not know exactly what problems the minority-shareholder issue entailed, and they asked Milbank, Tweed for clarification of that issue. Even before the lawyers prepared a formal memorandum, they warned the two Chase officials orally that the shareholders could pose a substantial barrier to Chase's plans. On April 28, Selden and Aldrich agreed that the most prudent step they could take would be to buy up all 4,702 outstanding shares of American Express. Selden was put in charge of the effort, and he made his first report a few days later. He found the situation discouraging. Of the shares outstanding, over 3,000 were in the hands of people who believed that the initial Chase offer had been unfair. A thousand or so more shares were in the hands of new owners whose feelings were unknown. That left only several hundred within reach. Nevertheless, Selden and Aldrich did not consider abandoning the hunt for all the stock, and Selden appointed assistant cashier of the CNB W. A. Pierce to work with the brokerage firm of J. K. Rice & Company to buy all outstanding shares.

Several days later, Lawrence Bennett of Milbank, Tweed detailed just how big an obstacle the holders of those 4,702 shares could be. The problem—and Amexco's good fortune—lay to a great extent in the form of organization of American Express: it was not a corporation, but a joint-stock association, a factor Wiggin probably had not closely investigated in 1928 when he launched his takeover bid. The company's articles of association and an 1894 New York State law governing such associations made it likely that the minority shareholders would fight Chase's plans in court on any one of several grounds.

First, an outright merger of Amexco and CSC was out of the question, in Bennett's opinion. The articles made it plain that Amexco could merge only with another express company or a transportation company. To get around that difficulty, Bennett wrote, Chase would almost certainly have to get "unanimous consent" of the shareholders. If Chase owned 100 percent of the stock, a change in the charter would be easy; without it, virtually impossible. An alternative, Bennett felt, was for Amexco to sell its assets to Chase Securities, but in that case minority shareholders who objected to the price and terms might well head for their lawyers. The problem persisted even if Amexco only "sold" the TC to the bank. "A minority stockholder of the Express Company could object to being 'frozen out' of the business taken over by the Bank," Bennett cautioned.

Even if minority stockholders could be persuaded "to go along," as Bennett said was their right, there was a problem, from Chase's side this time. What would Chase give them? Chase could offer cash, but what if a stockholder wanted to maintain his or her minority participation? Chase stock was unusual: it took the form of units, each share of the bank balanced by a proportional amount of Chase Securities stock. (The stock certificates showed CNB stock on one side, CSC on the other.) The problem with Amexco was that it was owned by the CSC alone, and so if a minority shareholder wanted stock in the company that held Amexco, he or she should get shares in the CSC alone. But if Chase gave out single-sided certificates, it would have to reorganize its whole capitalization structure.

Bennett emphasized that while Chase owned Amexco the two could not merge easily; to absorb its subsidiary, Chase would have to come up with a complicated scheme. This news did not deter Aldrich and Selden, who, with Bennett's help, laid out steps for the absorption of American Express. An unsigned May 15 memo, probably the work of Selden, outlined a plan that would let Chase acquire the TC and the overseas offices, and would leave an American Express—a shell of its former self—devoted solely to travel and freight, with a modest capitalization and little hope for profitability.

The plan consisted of several parts. First, Amexco would sell effective control of the TC and the money order to the CNB. American Express would retain the rights to both products, but Chase would take over management of the two. Amexco would convey to the bank all the assets and liabilities connected to outstanding TCs and money orders, about $54 million. The bank would also pay Amexco $424,000 in cash to make up the difference between assets and liabilities. In effect, Chase planned to buy the *float* for less than half a million dollars; it generated gross income of around $3 million annually.

Next, CSC would purchase all of Amexco's securities for $36.35

million in cash. How much cash would actually go into Amexco's coffers? Next to none since Amexco then would declare a "liquidation dividend." The shareholders would divide the cash assets of the company and since the CSC owned 97+ percent, most of the money would go back into the hands of the CSC. About $35 million would make the round-trip from the CSC to Amexco and back.

Although the "old" American Express would be liquidated, the company would be resurrected, chartered in Delaware with a capital of about $5 million. This company would retain the right and title to the money order and the TC, but the business would stay in the hands of the CNB. Amexco would enter into a contract with the CNB for the sale and distribution of both types of financial paper "under the CNB's guarantee or acceptance of responsibility for payment." The meaning of this was spelled out more fully: "The new company would therefore operate the travel and freight forwarding business only . . . [although] the CNB would use the branch offices of the new American Express Co. to sell and distribute the Travelers Cheques, Letters of Credit, Money Orders, etc., on an agency basis." In fact, Amexco's name would really be a Chase trademark, with Chase deriving the income from Amexco's most profitable products. The only money American Express would earn from the TC and MO would come from commissions for selling its own creations for the CNB.

The Inc. Company would be disposed of in a simple fashion: it would merely convey all its "assets and liabilities to The Chase Bank" for an exchange of stock—the basis of which would be determined later. That would finally put all the overseas branch offices at the disposal of the Chase.

The proposal also offered solutions to both the minority shareholder problem and to Chase's capitalization problem. Minority shareholders of the old company would first obtain their share of the cash in the liquidation dividend. For the remaining value of their holdings, they would get a choice: they could take cash or stock in the new Amexco; if they wanted Chase stock, they could get a certain number of CNB/CSC units, preserving Chase's capital structure.

Small was called in to see Aldrich some time after this plan was drafted. Aldrich gave him the proposal and invited him to express his views. Small's initial response was not recorded, but he must have been appalled. The implications of this plan must have been all too apparent: Chase wanted all of Amexco's money and its money-making businesses. Small would still have travel, but without the TC, the good results he often claimed for travel would be exposed as a sham. Black ink would turn to red, and the company would become either a charity case—something Chase would keep going to maintain sales and viability of the TC—or a corpse. Of course, as Small had said, the company belonged to Chase and, in the end, the owners could do whatever they wanted with it.

Small, distinctly alarmed, told only his top men what Chase had proposed. In a memo he drafted on June 4 and presented on Friday, June 5 to Bennett, Selden, Ralph Reed, Edwin Bechtel, Robert L. Clarkson (president of the CSC), and another Chase official, Frank Callahan, Small argued for eleven pages against the plan. He posed dozens of questions and hinted at all kinds of dire consequences if the Chase plan took effect. He tried to paint a horrible picture of "thousands of tourists" descending on Chase banking offices, of a bewildered public, and of a hostile banking community. Many of his arguments were absurd. He asked, for example, "could we avoid disturbing public confidence" in the backing of the TC, while in fact the change would mean that the TC would be backed with $2 billion in assets instead of $70 million. Small also wondered "what excuse" Chase could give to the public for such a move when Chase owned Amexco anyway and had now simply made it offical.

Chase rejected all of Small's arguments. Aldrich dismissed several points with marginal comments. "No fear!!" he scribbled next to Small's worry that the public might not trust Chase as readily as Amexco. "No," he put next to Small's query as to whether other banks would refrain from selling a Chase-backed TC. Actually, the plan still called for no change in the form of the TC. The American Express name would remain alongside the Chase name. Since the Chase name had been on TCs since 1929, Small's case was feeble in the eyes of Aldrich and Selden, and they rejected it completely.

While Selden worked on a formal rebuttal to Small's arguments, he heard discouraging news. Pierce and the brokers at Rice were not making much headway in acquiring outstanding stock. On the NYSE, the price had become a distorted $190 bid, $250 asked. Personal contact with shareholders had revealed, however, that some wanted a price even higher than $250. Pierce had managed to buy a mere fifty-four shares to date and had concluded that there were only two ways to get much more.

One was to delist the stock, take it off the board, and go after the remaining shares privately, without the distraction of market quotations that everyone could see. Faced with that kind of uncertainty, some of the holdouts might be persuaded that $250 was indeed a good price. As a tactic, this option made sense, and it was a common practice when so few shares were outstanding.

His second idea was more devious. Pierce suggested that he go into the market himself as an individual buyer (though really as "nominee" for the CSC) and buy all shares at current prices. At the same time, Chase would enter the market as a "seller," selling the shares to Pierce of course. As holders saw Chase "unloading," they might be stampeded into selling themselves. They might even be willing to sell out at a price below $250. Pierce recommended a test to "prove one way or another as to whether or not we are up against an impossible situation."

Chase never tested the idea. Aldrich, who hated such market sleights of hand, may well have vetoed the idea personally. At the same time, neither he nor Selden called off the efforts to acquire through normal market activities the 4,648 shares still outstanding.

Selden was ready with a reply to Small's objections at a meeting on June 15. In his memo, Selden answered every substantive point the Amexco president had raised. He also argued that the issue really boiled down to one key question: which company, American Express or Chase, was better able to run a financial business? And on that question the answer was clear. "My belief is that so long as the goodwill of the name 'American Express Company' is maintained," he said, "the Chase as a financial institution is better equipped to handle economically the financial activities of the American Express Company, than the American Express Company is itself." And he added, "[American Express] is thought of as a tourist office like Thomas Cook & Sons [sic], and I am afraid it would never be considered a real bank."

As Small readied new counterarguments, W. A. Pierce filed another discouraging report. He sent Selden a detailed list of the shareholders Rice had managed to contact, representing people who held about 1,000 shares in all. It appeared dubious that Chase could get any of them. A hundred shares, for example, belonging to a "shrewd jew" named Myron P. Nathan, were for sale at perhaps $300 each. Constance Coleman, on the other hand, wanted $400 for each of her one hundred shares, and Harry Germanow would part with his one hundred for $500 each. Others like William Vaughn, who owned a mere ten shares, told Rice their stock was "not for sale at any price." Though Pierce had reported nothing but bad news for a month, Selden sent him back into the market and told him to keep trying.

Selden had sole charge of the project now because Wiggin and Aldrich were dealing with a far more urgent matter. In May 1931, Germany, burdened by debt and war reparations, threatened to default on its foreign loans, which in turn imperiled the already battered world economy. Along with the government and other business leaders, the two top Chase officials devoted most of their time to solving this problem. In June, they even drafted a plan of their own to head off the default. The negotiations, which ended with a debt-payment moratorium, were to occupy Wiggin (and Aldrich to a lesser extent) all during the summer of 1931, and for much of the remainder of the year.

Small, for his part, probably thought of nothing but the Chase proposal. After the June 15 meeting, Small must have realized that Selden had not bought a single one of his arguments. He decided to try again, rephrasing some old arguments and adding a few new ones.

Over the next couple of weeks, he drafted another nine-page, single-spaced memo.

In it, he pressed the minority shareholder issue—the issue on which Chase seemed most obviously vulnerable. Small cleverly used the troubled economic times to bolster his case. He noted potential suits and "the resulting bad publicity," which at that time must have seemed as likely as they would have been unwelcome. By the end of 1930, a wave of bank failures crossed the country. Some of these brought such negative publicity that the integrity of all banks and bankers was called into question. Although the Chase proposal actually offered minority shareholders fairly generous terms, shareholder suits against Chase could have played to the negative feelings about banks and bankers; the suits might have portrayed the Chase offer as an attempt by a financial giant to cheat the little guy—an image Chase certainly did not want. While this line of argument was strong, it was also pointless. Selden, Bennett, and Aldrich had considered the minority shareholder issue for months and had decided to confront it.*

But one new argument in Small's memo did catch Selden's attention. Small now faced the reality of a travel business without the TC. The changes, he admitted, would destroy the company's ability to function, and as a result, as he put it, "would affect the spirit and the morale of our key men." He argued further that the men would see this as a prelude to the dissolution of American Express and "would become discouraged and start to drift away from the organization."†

The whole argument covered less than a page and appeared to be a bit of an afterthought. Yet of all the points Small raised, it alone

---

*Small also tried a bizarre line of reasoning. He argued that Chase would save a lot of money by *not* absorbing the Inc. Co. According to Small, if Chase wanted to turn the foreign offices into banking operations, it would have "to spend considerable money to keep pace with" the National City Bank. But Chase wanted to compete with the National City Bank, and only by using Amexco's vast network could it do so on a relatively equal footing. If anything, Small provided the best reason *for* absorption, not against it.

†Selden may have worried about Small's personal effect on morale. The men in the field were loyalists in most cases and might well have taken their cue from him.

concerned Selden. He had studied American Express closely. He had gone abroad and visited many of the branch offices, and he had looked carefully at the company's operations. As a result, he recognized the potential problem. As he explained to Aldrich in a note, "If the Amexco as a travel and freight company only has no esprit de corps, is unprofitable (which it probably will be), and the threat is always present that the Travel and Freight business will sooner or later be discontinued, the financial paper will not be serviced properly, and the goodwill will be lost at a considerable cost."

Selden therefore advised that Chase should not push its plan for the absorption of American Express. Small was told that the plan had been dropped, and no further word of this matter appears in Amexco's archives. But Selden actually had not abandoned the basic idea. Small's arguments had made him cautious, and he proposed an alternative plan to effect amalgamation gradually, and at the same time, to remove the minority-shareholder issue by acquiring the outstanding shares. He directed Pierce and Rice to remain in the market, and he kept them active throughout the fall and winter of 1931 and into the next year.

To begin the gradual absorption, Selden also suggested that Chase offices abroad merge with those Amexco branches that maintained a banking component. Selden focused on Hong Kong, Shanghai, and Tientsin, where Chase had acquired a significant banking presence through its merger with the Equitable. Selden suggested a merger of all the Chase and Amexco offices in China (or perhaps in just one city) as an experiment. If it avoided morale problems, then the experiment would answer Small's objections. Selden clearly expected that, if the test proved satisfactory, he would merge other offices until virtually all of Amexco's world network was a part of Chase.

Chase did not put this idea to the test but did not abandon it either. Chase people also continued to bring up other ideas for gradually merging operations with Amexco. Over the next year and a half, Chase officials met with Small to discuss ways of "coordinating the various functions of the affiliates," and the Chase agenda included such ideas as new joint offices abroad, a joint cable depot abroad, and the consolidation of credit departments, actually an attempt to give Chase the power to make credit decisions for Amexco's limited banking operations.

But Chase never started its gradual merger program and never finished its efforts to acquire outstanding Amexco stock. Depression-related crises came so frequently that Chase executives had little time to worry about anything other than disaster control. After the German debt crisis came the utility crisis. Chase, which had loaned heavily to investment bankers who had financed utilities, found itself facing big losses when a few leading utilities neared insolvency. Other major corporate customers collapsed as the Depression finally caught up with them, Al Wiggin's loyalty and money notwithstanding. By the year's end, Chase had to write down $77.2 million of bad loans and posted a net loss of over $5 million.

Wiggin sloughed off the problems and, ever the optimist, looked forward to improved conditions in 1932. But there were still more crises: hundreds of bank failures, corporate failures, foreign government debt, Detroit debt, New York City debt. Wiggin no longer had time for American Express. He seldom attended board and executive committee meetings now; he was chief executive in name only. Aldrich, too, had his hands full. His calendar for the period showed him devoting most of his time to crisis meetings, and playing an increasingly important part in Chase's affairs. In May he was elected vice chairman of Chase, suddenly heir apparent to Wiggin. Meanwhile, profits continued to decline; surplus at the bank would fall by almost another $100 million over the next four years.

The CSC lost proportionally more. With the market plummeting, Chase Securities filed for a reduction of capital from $90 million to $40 million, and then to $37 million. One of its losing investments was the Corn Exchange Bank, which Chase had bought through an account it held jointly with Amexco. By late 1932, Amexco and Chase had a book loss of $8 million each on the Corn Exchange investment.

Business also sagged at American Express. In 1932, TC sales slumped to $123 million, the lowest level in nine years, and barely half the 1929 peak. Remittances, cruise business—everything was off. The surplus dropped, and the company spent 90 percent of its contingency reserves, leaving only $500,000 in the till. Investment practice, which Wiggin had tried briefly to make more daring, became ultraconservative again. Already American Express had lost so much money that any further large losses would have seriously imperiled its ability to pay off the millions in outstanding TCs and money orders.

Exhausted by the strain of negotiations and, according to some sources, nudged by the Rockefellers, who apparently wanted brother-in-law Winthrop Aldrich in command, Wiggin announced his retirement. At the end of the year, after Aldrich delivered a brief statement of thanks, Wiggin left the Chase with a pension of $100,000 per year.

But a final blow to Wiggin, the blow that ultimately freed American Express, came from the U.S. government. The stock market, Wiggin's playground of the 1920s, had never recovered public esteem after the Crash of 1929. Revelations in the press about market manipulation and "bear raids" gave people the impression that Wall Street had caused the Depression and was somehow preventing economic recovery. In 1932, President Herbert Hoover asked the Senate Banking and Currency Committee to launch an investigation of securities dealings prior to the Crash. Those hearings began in February 1933 under the direction of chief counsel Ferdinand Pecora, and one of the first major figures to take the stand was Charles ("Sunshine Charley") Mitchell of the National City Bank in New York. His testimony proved sensational. Pecora brought out that Mitchell and the National City's brokerage operation had participated in market-manipulation pools. It was a common technique of the 1920s; a group of wealthy investors created a "pool" of money to bid up the price of a stock using numerous accounts to give the appearance of widespread buying interest. When the effort generated buying from outsiders, however, the pool sold short, forcing the stock price down and giving the pool players a profit on both ends of the deal. Mitchell's participation in pools in the stock of companies such as Anaconda Copper discredited him, the National

City, and by association all of the leading New York bankers. After he left the witness stand, his successor at the National City decided to abolish the bank's securities affiliate.

In the meantime, the national banking crisis had reached a climax. Runs at bank after bank—often provoked by mere rumors—were rapidly destroying public confidence in the banking system. By February, several states felt compelled to declare bank holidays and to restrict withdrawals by deposit holders. But even these measures were not enough, and Franklin Roosevelt declared a national bank holiday to take effect shortly after he became president in March 1933.

Although Aldrich did not know exactly the extent of Wiggin's involvement in market games, the revelations of the Pecora hearings worried him. Because banking was a business that depended as much on public perception as reality, Aldrich felt the need to help restore confidence in the banking system. In early March 1933, he delivered a tough public statement advocating bank reform and calling for the separation of commercial and investment banking. In an indirect swipe at his predecessor, he also denounced the "spirit of speculation" at the major banks. Then he decided to make a gesture of his own. In April, he wrote a letter to stockholders announcing plans to rid the Chase bank of its securities affiliate. He reduced the capital of the CSC again to $7.4 million and changed the name from the Chase Securities Corporation to just the Chase Corporation. The only significant asset it still held was American Express, but Chase officials could not decide what to do with Amexco. For months, Aldrich and his aides discussed variants of the 1931 plan, giving the TC and the foreign offices to the CNB, and spinning off a new American Express for travel and freight. But as Aldrich pondered the matter, Chase was hit by a final blow that would force a different decision about Amexco.

In October 1933, Albert Wiggin took the stand in the Pecora hearings—and his testimony was the ultimate embarrassment for Chase. Pecora laid out all of the market manipulations in which Wiggin and the CSC had participated and exposed the threads of interlocking companies that Wiggin had employed for his market activities. Pecora revealed that Wiggin owned six private companies, three incorporated in Canada to avoid taxes. These companies, along with the CSC and its subsidiaries, had also participated in market pools, including pools that dealt in the stock of the Chase itself. Still, the most damaging testimony was a disclosure that Wiggin's investment companies had made a profit of $4 million by selling Chase stock short at the time of—and for a while after—the Crash. The fact that Wiggin had also personally lost a lot of his own money later, in a futile effort to prop up Chase share prices, did little to mitigate the picture of the banker who had made money through his company's misfortune.

The effects of these revelations were predictable. As Pecora himself recalled afterwards, the "storm of popular disapproval was so great that Wiggin felt constrained to renounce [his $100,000 a year] pension." The storm also had more far-reaching consequences. A stockholder group filed suit, charging the officers and directors of the bank and the CSC with engaging in unsuitable transactions that "never should have been undertaken," and that led to tremendous financial losses. The lawsuit named virtually every one of the CSC's operations among Wiggin's dirty deals, including his acquisition of American Express.

Wiggin's testimony and the stockholder response made it clear that Aldrich had to make a total break with Wiggin to keep any credibility at all. The ex-chairman gave up not only his pension, but also his seat on the Chase board. Wiggin still held a huge block of Chase stock, however, and even a hint of any continuing influence in the company had to be erased.

Though Amexco was a Wiggin legacy, Aldrich seemed reluctant to part with it. A new Federal banking law, the Glass-Steagall Act of June 1933, compelled Aldrich to do what he had already promised: to divest the CNB of its investment banking and brokerage operation. But as late as December, Chase executives were still considering a plan to absorb the Inc. Company and the TC. In fact, they contemplated using Amexco to pay off some leftover debts of the CSC. The idea was that the CSC would sell the lucrative parts of Amexco to the CNB for enough money to pay off what the CSC owed.

But Aldrich found a better use for Amexco: he would give control of it and the rest of the CSC to Wiggin in exchange for the ex-chairman's shares in the Chase. This would complete the separation from Wiggin. *
It was announced with considerable fanfare and approved by shareholders in the spring of 1934. The remnants of the CSC were spun off into a company called the Amerex Holding Company with Albert H. Wiggin as the largest shareholder. Amerex consisted of four things: debts, lawsuits, near-worthless investments, and American Express.

Aldrich and his men were relieved to be rid of Wiggin and his legacy, but sorry that the price had had to be Amexco. In 1946, with the Depression a memory and the bad press forgotten, Chase tried to get it back—and again in 1949. Chase's lawyers drafted an elaborate plan with the support of the Federal Reserve, which Wiggin refused to consider; eventually, he sold his shares in Amerex with the proviso that Amexco would not be broken up, and that it would not wind up in the hands of Chase.

So American Express was saved by the Depression and gained its freedom without a fight. Despite the paralysis of senior management, Amexco was independent again. Because Wiggin owned so much of the stock, its autonomy was assured for a time.

It had the same basic components as the day Wiggin took over. It was, of course, poorer; five years of Wiggin's management and economic depression had reduced the company's surplus and reserves to only $3 million, its lowest level since the nineteenth century. But the TC still assured the company of a certain source of income. Sales had dipped to $123 million in 1932, but rebounded to more than $191 million in 1935, and remained high thereafter.

The TC's market position had actually strengthened during the

---

*Prior to this, the American Express Bank & Trust was merged into the Chase organization and dissolved. Despite Whelpley's good start, in the end, it also proved an embarrassment to Chase. The Pecora hearings revealed the bank had loaned hundreds of thousands of dollars to Chase employees and friends, with Chase stock as collateral.

Depression in large part because of one event: the Bank Holiday of 1933. Through Aldrich, Small persuaded the Treasury Department to permit Amexco offices to remain open during the holiday to cash TCs and MOs. What developed was a situation not unlike that of the early days of World War I in Europe; the American Express TC became the only negotiable paper with guaranteed convertibility. As a result, the TC received a boost at the expense of the competition. In fact, its main competitor, the American Bankers Association traveler's check, folded about a month later, leaving Amexco with a virtual monopoly of the traveler's check market for the remainder of the 1930s.

Although Small won a notable victory during the Bank Holiday of 1933, he never regained the authority he had once held. He stayed on as president after the separation from Chase, but the new chairman and chief executive was Wiggin's protégé, Robert Livingston Clarkson. Clarkson, a round man who at Amexco worked at a round squire's desk, had been a boy wonder of the financial world. In 1928, at age thirty-six, Wiggin named him president of the CNB. But a year later, Clarkson took sick, an illness that proved extraordinarily lucky. Because of his health, he had to give up his stock-market activities and take a vacation, and he sold a good deal of his holdings a few months before the Crash. He returned to Chase some months later still rich, but he suffered a demotion. Aldrich was given his old job as head of the CNB, and Clarkson took over the CSC instead. After the Pecora hearings, Wiggin remained under a cloud, and he did not regain the chairmanship of Amexco. As the last head of the CSC, Clarkson became the logical alternative for the post.

Wiggin retained influence, however, and he and Clarkson together made policy. These two men, who had been among the most aggressive investors of the 1920s, instituted a program which was as conservative as Small's. They adopted an investment policy which stressed saving, rather than making, money and they succeeded in maintaining modest profits each year.

Clarkson and Wiggin wanted guaranteed profits because they needed Amexco to pay off the CSC's leftover debts. At the end of 1934,

Amerex had debts of more than $11.5 million. By the end of 1935, despite the persistence of the Depression, Amerex managed to reduce its indebtedness to a mere $3.5 million. The money for that reduction came in large part when Clarkson and Wiggin sold 5,700 shares of Discount Corporation of New York to Amexco for a price "in excess of $4.5 million."

This sale produced some wry commentary over at Chase. "From reading the attached clippings from the Times on the Annual Report of the Amerex it makes me think that the wang doodling process is on," wrote one of Aldrich's lieutenants. "If I were the Amexco I wouldn't want [Discount Corp.] at any price let along [sic] the price they must have paid for it."

Amexco paid for the shares not just by draining its funds, but also by embarking on a program to cut expenses drastically. The economy drive Clarkson instituted in late 1935 forced many longtime, loyal employees, including W. J. Thomas, head of Amexco in Europe, into early retirement, and it required departments throughout the company to cut salaries and overhead. This kept profits high enough so that Amerex could bleed its subsidiary for the million or so in dividends it needed to keep paying down its debt. By the end of 1936, without more egregious "wang doodling," Amerex paid off another $1.2 million it owed.

In the midst of this belt-tightening, which grew more stringent as the Depression wore on, F. P. Small effectively put an end to his own career. With others taking pay cuts or retirement, and with his own salary at over $60,000 a year, Small asked the board for a raise. His motives mystified executives at 65 Broadway. The deflation of the Depression had increased the purchasing power of his salary, and he did not appear to need the money. His request amounted to a confrontation with the board and with Clarkson, and it infuriated other executives at corporate headquarters; in that one act, Small had undermined his influence even with his most loyal men.

Clarkson and Wiggin promptly removed Small from any significant role in the company's affairs and elevated comptroller Ralph T. Reed, one of Small's men, to the new position of executive vice president, in effect the chief operating officer. * Reed was the logical candidate: he was the best numbers man—the best "bean counter" some called him—at Amexco. But after Clarkson made Reed number two in the company, Small, as one executive put it, was left "without a damn thing to do." Often he would come into the office and spend the day poring over his stamp collection. Most important business was routed through Clarkson, Reed, or Lynde Selden, who left Chase in 1936 and became head of the Inc. Company.

Reed came from extremely humble origins: born a poor Philadelphia boy, he worked his way through the Wharton Business School of the University of Pennsylvania. With a reputation as a "green-eyeshade" type, Reed lacked social grace and refinement, and Clarkson began transforming him into someone who could mix with the right people—Clarkson's people. Clarkson moved Reed out of his home in a middle-class neighborhood in Queens, New York, to an apartment in the Park Lane Hotel, a fashionable Manhattan address. He had Reed invited to the right parties, to meet the right people, to play golf at the right clubs.

Soon, people began to see a change in Ralph Reed, and thought it not entirely for the best. They saw him turning into Clarkson. Clarkson had a reputation for being as "tough as nails," but also a "glad-hander," a man with a polished, insincere manner, a practiced informality (he signed all of his letters "Bobby," even to underlings) that paradoxically tended to reinforce a sense of his social superiority. Reed suddenly was acting like a glad-hander too and seemed to love his new social status.

On the job, however, Reed continued to pursue his unglamorous mandate to count the beans. One economy drive followed another as Reed continually pared expenses. He controlled costs with the help of

---

*Why Clarkson did not fire Small is a matter of conjecture. N. F. Page, an assistant secretary of Amexco at the time, suggested two reasons. First, Wiggin liked Small and Wiggin still held a great deal of power. Second, Clarkson wanted someone looking over Reed's shoulder, at least symbolically, for a few years until Reed could assume the presidency and Small could be quietly retired.

three associates—a group of men known collectively as the Four Horsemen of the Apocalypse for the pink slips and other bits of bad news they passed out. Clarkson gave Reed no room for experiment and innovation. The period of 1935–38 was one of the dullest in the company's annals, a time of limited growth and limited opportunity. But the company did have relative stability and consistent earnings, which held out the prospect of growth in the future when the economy improved.

World War II threatened the company's stability, however. Fortunately for American Express, senior executives recognized the possibility of war in Europe and planned for it before it happened. Because of their analysis, when war finally came, the company was, for the most part, ready to close down in an orderly manner the parts of the operation that could no longer function and to keep the rest going profitably.

The company began to prepare shortly before the signing of the Munich agreement in 1938. Reed and Selden (with Small also playing a part in this instance) developed elaborate plans and procedures to move people, papers, and money in the event of war. They established procedures for destruction of TC blanks and voucher books, and for storing securities and valuables. By the summer of 1939, R. E. Bergeron, who had replaced Thomas as director of American Express in Europe, had his people "carrying preparedness to the nth degree." As he told Selden, "It is a fact that we seem to be spending most of our time working for, or because of, Adolf and Benito but I do not see that we can do otherwise." Bergeron reported that he had no doubt that his "boys in the field" were cursing him because he not only laid down a long set of procedures, but also had his people conducting regular rehearsals of what to do in the event war broke out. He wanted "nothing less than perfection" if it did.

By August 1939, Selden was keeping a running record of events in Europe. Office managers in every European city were required to report larger political and economic events as well as the status of the local offices. At 65 Broadway, executives discussed each report and ordered managers to take steps in accordance with local conditions.

242

When war finally came, the company's plans worked smoothly. Offices functioned as long as they could and then closed with few losses of money or records.

Still, even with all the planning, managers found themselves having to improvise on occasion as the war engulfed Europe. Probably the most resourceful was C. R. "Dick" Merrill, the intrepid office manager in Berlin in 1939. Among other stunts, he "worked [an unspecified] shenanigan" to get all of his money out, and developed his own network of "spies" in the German government, so he could have advance warning of all developments. For a time, he also managed to have the only financial operation open in Germany—keeping it going even as the bombs were falling. He maintained his operation until Hitler kicked him and all other Americans out in June 1941.

While the company was completely successful in winding down— or where they could, keeping up—the European organization, Selden and Reed were caught off guard in the Far East. Selden had concluded that the Japanese threat was a bluff, and Frank Groves, who was in charge in the Far East, agreed. This error led not only to the seizure of company records, but also to the internment of several Amexco employees, including Groves, who was caught in Manila when the Japanese invaded. He, along with two other employees, spent the next three and a half years in a Japanese camp at Santo Tomas. The Japanese also captured Max Eliot, manager in Singapore, and sent him off to work on the Burma Railway—the story of which was recounted in the movie *The Bridge on the River Kwai*.

There was of course nothing Amexco could do for them except wait. In America, employees left by the hundreds for war duty, and the company itself launched another economy drive to keep expenses as low as possible. Business did not end completely. TCs still sold. Amexco advertised them to GIs as "torpedo proof," and sales remained well over $100 million for the duration. The TC float still produced income (though some of it was invested in government securities paying less than 1 percent) and remained the major source of Amexco's earnings throughout the war.

There were enough sales so Reed could report yearly profits to his bosses at Amerex. It soon became clear that for all its disruptiveness, the war posed no threat to the survival of American Express. The last threat to its existence had ended in 1934, and with a great deal of luck Amexco had pulled through. In 1941, it could look forward to the end of hostilities. Reed had no doubt that, when the end came, the opportunities for the reborn American Express would be greater than ever.

THE POOH-BAH
AND
THE CARD

9

On January 4, 1944, Clarkson decided to have the board make official what had been in effect for eight years: F. P. Small, age seventy, was retired and Ralph Thomas Reed, fifty-four, was elected president, beginning one of the most eventful periods in the company's history.

Extraordinarily enough, the succession came as a surprise to most people at American Express. Employees, including senior executives, had speculated on who would succeed Small and had all believed the board would choose J. K. Livingston. How such a misperception came about is a mystery. Those who remembered that event insisted merely that "Livingston was senior," in other words, he had been in the company longer than Reed and therefore was entitled to the presidency. But as the lone executive VP, Reed was higher on the company ladder; he socialized with Clarkson, the chief executive, and had played a noticeably larger role in decision making than Livingston had from the mid-1930s on. Every important memo passed through his hands; only selected bits of information went to "Jake" Livingston. *

The reason so many employees had figured wrong must have had a great deal to do with the way Clarkson and Wiggin (who was still influential in company affairs) conducted business in the years after the Pecora hearings. Because of the horrendous publicity they received during the hearings, they both became extremely secretive; they kept their plans and ideas to themselves, confiding in few others in the company, and seldom putting anything on paper. (Both men were known around 65 Broadway as "no file" people.) As a result, not even company executives seemed to know that, by 1936, Clarkson and Wiggin had decided to make Reed the next president of American Express.

Staff members were wrong about the succession, but not generally disappointed. They knew Reed had his faults: he could be tyrannical and imperious, a "Little Caesar" who never admitted fallibility and who, according to one secretary, could fly into a rage "over a paper clip." But he had a softhearted streak. Like Small, he believed that Amexco was not just a company but a family, and he forgave everything except disloyalty. He seldom fired anyone, not even people who clearly could not do their jobs. During his presidency, for example, at least three of his senior managers had serious drinking problems, but he never fired or demoted any of them. "You smell too bad," he would say to one. "Go stand in the corner." Incompetents also stayed at their desks; the thought of getting rid of them never seemed to occur to Ralph Reed. The important thing was that they had stood by the company, and now he was standing by them.

Reed had also shown himself a highly competent manager who had straightened out the books and had guided the company through dif-

---

*So far from winning the presidency, Livingston was effectively demoted. Livingston was the only senior executive who did not receive a promotion. Selden was named vice chairman and Howard Smith, executive VP.

ficult times. He had demonstrated, too, the kind of drive, forcefulness, and dedication needed to run the company (he routinely put in fourteen-hour work days). After the war, Amexco would have a massive rebuilding job to do, and the company needed a man who could grasp the details of a problem, make a decision quickly, and then implement it effectively. Whatever people thought of Ralph Reed, they believed he would get the job done.

Clarkson gave Reed equal powers with himself, and they divided the company into two areas. Clarkson held authority over the money-making part of the company, the investment department, but it was isolated from the rest of Amexco. Reed, on the other hand, controlled operations. So while the two men theoretically shared power, the arrangement allowed Reed to dominate Amexco, to become the sole chief executive, in fact, if not in name. He eventually became the single most autocratic chief executive in the company's history. He reserved for himself the right and the duty to make every decision, no matter how trivial. A director once said of Reed that if the company bought a "broom in Cairo," Reed had to know about it and approve it. He had to endorse every merit pay increase, and he even oversaw the window displays for the travel office on Fifth Avenue.

And like another company autocrat, J. C. Fargo, Reed presided over one of the most productive periods in the company's history. Reed also made two fateful decisions: to resurrect banking and to create the American Express Credit Card. Reed's decisions, like those of J. C. Fargo, would have as much or more to do with the character of the man who made them than they would with the business of American Express.

For the first three years of his presidency, Reed was notably receptive to new ideas. Even before he took office, he began the company's first active planning process in more than a decade, looking for new business opportunities. In the early autumn of 1943, Reed assigned assistant VP Dennis Harmon, formerly head of the Zurich office, to investigate possible ventures for the postwar period. On October 19,

247

Harmon brought Reed a suggestion for a new business that seemed promising: an obscure enterprise called field warehousing.

Field warehousing permitted companies with poor credit ratings to borrow against their inventory: a company needing credit would contact a field warehouser and sign a "storage contract." This contract would give the warehouser control over the portion of inventory the company wanted to borrow against. After the warehouser took control, it would certify that the inventory existed and that it was of a certain value, and would write out a receipt for that value. The company needing credit could take this receipt to a bank as a guarantee of inventory and get a loan. Field warehousing was peculiar in that the warehousing company did not take actual possession of the inventory. Instead, the warehouser segregated inventory on the borrower's own property and then hired a "trustworthy employee" of the borrower's company to act as custodian; the warehouser made its profit simply through "storage fees" paid by the borrowing company on its own inventory. A warehouser carried one risk: it guaranteed a quantity of inventory and was liable if the actual inventory was less than the amount certified.

Reed discussed the idea with his men for several months and finally gave a go-ahead. Despite the lengthy discussion, the business seemed likely to become only a small sideline.* But it was to play a major role in the history of American Express, because as the company would learn, the business was notably susceptible to fraud. Because the warehouser left everything in the borrower's hands, the inventory might be removed or wrongly declared, especially if the "trustworthy employee" was more loyal to the creditor firm than to the warehouser who hired him.

This susceptibility was a fact neither Reed nor his men fully appreciated. For the most part, they saw in field warehousing a low-risk

---

*The creation of a warehousing subsidiary was a forward-looking step. Because of the war, the government had imposed inventory controls on manufacturing businesses, and as a result, Amexco's new subsidiary could not even operate.

operation that might enhance Amexco's goodwill with the banks. As the new treasurer Olaf Ravndal noted, through a warehouser's services, a bank could take on loans it otherwise would avoid. In other words, if Amexco took on this business, Ravndal suggested, bankers would make some money, and their goodwill would benefit American Express.

This argument sold Reed because, by the 1940s, nothing was more important to Amexco than the goodwill of the banks. The company depended on the banks to provide retail outlets for the TC, still by far the company's most profitable business. Over the years, the TC's competition had dwindled, and the company felt enough faith in the public's loyalty to cut advertising to a minimum. But the banks were under no obligation to market the Amexco TC. The company's preoccupation with cultivating the banks' goodwill persuaded Reed to announce, in the summer of 1944, the formation of the American Express Field Warehousing Corporation, a wholly owned incorporated subsidiary, with capital of $1 million.

But field warehousing was only a small part of Reed's post–World War II plans, and he waited until Allied troops invaded Europe in June 1944 to begin his most intensive planning effort. At almost the same time the Allies were landing on the beaches of Normandy, Reed held a conference at 65 Broadway attended by all current and some former officials. The conference ended with general agreement that the company's prospects, once the war ended, were bright, especially in travel. Reed and his men based their assumptions on their experiences after World War I. There had been a boom in travel in the 1920s and Reed and his men guessed it would happen again. They anticipated growth in air and business travel, and they plotted a strategy to meet that growth, mainly through a rapid resurrection and a vast expansion of Amexco's office network, as well as an expansion of travel services. In an August issue of the company house organ Reed said: "In truth we can look forward with confidence to Post-War success in all our activities. The opportunities will be worldwide. . . ."

The expansion came even sooner than expected, only a couple of months after the Allied landing, when the U.S. military gave Amexco the chance to establish a base of operations in Europe. That base provided Amexco with two opportunities. First, it allowed the company to develop businesses with the military itself. And more importantly, the military helped put Amexco in a position to take advantage of the travel boom Reed and his men had accurately foreseen.

In August 1944, the military asked Amexco, along with a few other companies, to open offices in Europe in order to act as a "depository" of U.S. military funds. But by the time R. E. Bergeron put 11 Rue Scribe back in business in January 1945, the armed services wanted American Express, instead, to set up a program of sight-seeing tours in Europe for American service men and women on leave.* B. E. "Bert" White, an Amexco executive who at the time was a major in the army, handled the negotiations for a military travel service and concluded an agreement "in principle" in late 1944. (The final agreement was delayed by the Battle of the Bulge and was only completed, according to company legend, after a personal meeting between General Dwight D. Eisenhower and Reed.) By the winter of 1945, Bergeron traveled to the south of France and opened offices in Nice and Marseilles to serve troops in what the military had designated the United States Riviera Recreation Area.

At the same time, Bergeron took advantage of his presence on the Continent to pursue the plan developed at 65 Broadway. In early 1945, he opened an office in Stockholm, and by early summer, a couple of months after the German surrender, he had Amexco operating in Holland and Belgium as well. Soon, Reed sent freight-forwarding executive Gerald K. Berkey to Europe to continue the job that Bergeron had started. Over the next ten months, Berkey not only reopened old offices, but also tracked down former staff members, and prepared for a renewed freight-forwarding business. Before the end of 1945, Amexco

---

*Both B. E. White and Gerald Berkey claimed credit for setting this project in motion. Both were company men on leave to help the war effort, and they had connections in the military and the Department of War.

had almost fully reestablished its Continental network. The company even had offices inside Germany, at the request of the military, to extend its R and R services to the occupying forces.

In the Far East, too, Amexco worked to rebuild the network. In February 1945, an emaciated Frank Groves emerged from internment camp in the Philippines. A few months later, he was huddling with Reed in New York, making plans for a new office in Hong Kong, and by December, he was already back in the Far East overseeing reconstruction efforts throughout the region. Reed was the catalyst in the effort both in Europe and the Far East. He made decisions quickly, authorized spending large sums of money, and even absorbed losses to put the network back into operation.*

By 1946, Amexco had rebuilt its worldwide system, although it remained eager to find something to do besides entertaining the troops. While overseas civilian travel was still restricted, the company's presence in Europe and the Far East allowed it to take advantage of a different kind of opportunity that it had not considered—banking for the military.

Although military banking would prove to be Amexco's most important new activity, the company probably would never have gotten into it were it not for one individual, John Dowrick. In January 1946, Reed appointed Dowrick head of operations in Germany. Dowrick was an imaginative individual who intended to make the most of his promotion. Even before he left for Germany, he wrote a memo listing five ideas for new business: to create a German express business; to manage an air transport service; to ship souvenir pistols home for service men; to open banking offices for American civilian personnel and German businesses; and finally, to act as chief railroad-ticket agent for the army.

After two months in Frankfurt, however, Dowrick had decided to

---

*Overall Amexco's expenses rose over 50 percent from 1945 to 1946, and they rose another 25 percent in 1947. These increases were largely attributable to the rebuilding of the world network.

focus on banking for the troops. He saw enormous potential in TCs for R and R activities, in money orders, in deposits and loans—in a full banking service for the hundreds of thousands of Americans stationed abroad. On June 7, 1946, he proposed a military banking operation to Reed. Because of the still unsettled condition of Germany, the letter took three weeks to get to 65 Broadway.

Reed was not convinced at first. Like his predecessor F. P. Small, Reed feared risk and seemed to live still in the shadow of the Glass Eye Era, acting as though anything to do with banking was doomed to catastrophe. (Under Small, Reed had charge of auditing the branch offices, making sure they kept to the strict limits Small had established.) Now faced with a proposal to get into military banking, Reed seemed initially to be torn by his desire for development and his wariness of banking, and for a few weeks he pestered Dowrick with questions. Reed's final decision both was and was not a departure from Small's policies. He decided to undertake a banking business, he told Dowrick, but only if he could hold risks to a minimum. In his mind, that meant Amexco had to obtain what was in effect a government subsidy: the right to invest money in special high-yielding Treasury bonds—the *high* yield then was a grand 2 percent—and a promise from the military to place some of its funds on deposit. By early September, the government agreed in principle to Reed's demands that a military bank would be conducted on very safe terms—if and when the U.S. officials agreed to license one. The government had not made that decision yet, but since the probable terms suited him, Reed backed the idea for American Express.

Creating a bank, however, was not going to be easy. Amexco needed a license from four different government organizations: the departments of the Treasury, War, and State, and the U.S. Forces European Theater (USFET). Reed launched an intense lobbying effort on two continents to win the necessary approvals. Reed, Howard Smith, and Dennis Harmon handled the lobbying in the U.S., and Reed traveled to Europe to join Dowrick in lobbying the generals overseas. It proved a frustrating battle against red tape, competing governmental departments, and bureaucracy. In Washington, Harmon and Smith had to cope with the peculiar bureaucratic logic that found Amexco's proposal "timely" but decided "nothing further could be done at this time."

Despite the contradictory signals, Amexco officials pressed ahead. By early December, Reed thought Amexco had won its license, only to have the War Department send the idea back to USFET for another review. As Reed lamented to Dowrick, "We now feel that the matter is right back where we started the first part of September." But then the outlook improved. Reed called on General William Draper, director of the Economic Division of the military government of Germany, and came away feeling reassured. "Based on the tone of the discussion," he reported, "I feel the American Express is being favorably considered."

His reading was correct. After another two months of dickering with the various bureaucracies, Amexco obtained a license to operate banking facilities for military personnel in Germany and Austria. In March 1947, the first office opened in Frankfurt, and later others appeared in the occupied areas. By the following November, Amexco had $34 million in deposits, and by 1949 was reporting banking profits of $100,000 per quarter. And its growth continued. Over the next several years, Amexco gained a large percentage of military banking business throughout the world—from Germany and Austria to England, France, Morocco, Saudi Arabia, and Okinawa. From modest beginnings—some early offices were located in Quonset huts—military banking became a major activity in the 1950s and made a significant contribution to the company's income throughout Reed's years as president.

For all the interest Reed showed at the end of the war in developing new activities, it was an old one that engaged most of his attention—travel. There was a tremendous, pent-up demand for travel, civilian as well as military, and by 1945, Reed went all out in pushing tourism to the public and preparing the company to meet the demand. First, he began an expansion of the office network—from fifty foreign offices during the war, to 139 soon after it ended. Simultaneously, he set into motion a massive publicity campaign. In January 1946, although overseas travel restrictions were still in effect, Reed sought to whet that appetite for travel in an article he had published under his own name in the *American Magazine,* entitled "Now You Can Go Places." Once restrictions on European travel were lifted, Amexco took out full-page ads in major newspapers across the country. Later, the company sold foreign travel as an extension of the Marshall Plan, as a way in which ordinary Americans could help the economy of the Western world. Travel, the company maintained, was "a social, political and economic force . . . a powerful instrument of helping foreign nations gain needed dollars. . . ."

The travel business expanded more quickly than even Reed had predicted. Millions of Americans were going abroad for the first time. The wartime creation of fast, safe transatlantic aircraft suddenly opened Europe to anyone with a week's vacation and a middle-class income. For these travelers, as for Americans of previous generations, Amexco's offices became a gathering point and a refuge. Tourists overwhelmed some of the offices. In Paris, sometimes 12,000 people a day showed up at 11 Rue Scribe, and the company hired fifteen people just to staff its free information service.

Amexco profited enormously from the travel boom—not through travel itself, a business still burdened by high costs and low profit margins, but as always, through the TC. The TC sales explosion began in 1945, the last year of the war. That year, Amexco sold a record $522 million in cheques, and sales just kept rising thereafter. In 1947, Amexco sold over $800 million; $900 million in 1951; $1.1 billion in 1952. The float expanded as well; average outstandings passed the quarter-billion dollar mark early in the 1950s and grew rapidly for the rest of the decade.

Increasingly, there was a split between what the company seemed to be, and what it actually was. In the public eye, Amexco appeared to be a giant travel agency. Reed fostered that image. He always told reporters the company had one main business, travel, and two other important operations, freight forwarding and field warehousing. In fact, none of these businesses made money. The profit came primarily from the Investment Department, which Clarkson had turned into a professional organization run by skilled money managers and experienced securities analysts. Investment was, however, a small operation; during Reed's era the department never employed more than a handful of professionals and it remained largely hidden from the public.* In 1950, Reed commissioned a book on the company to mark its one hundredth anniversary. Only one paragraph out of almost 280 pages discussed the Investment Department. Of course, it lacked the glamor of travel. It made its money primarily through safe investments in tax-free municipal bonds and short-term government and commercial paper. For his part, Reed kept a respectful distance from the investment people. Occasionally, he would call up the money managers with a request: he might ask them to increase capital gains in a quarter, for example. But typically, he kept hands off and let the department go about its money-making business.

Reed's approach to the rest of the organization was exactly the opposite. He controlled everything and everyone. In the one hundredth anniversary book, he told author Alden Hatch that he was developing "a whole group of leaders at American Express, not just one," but he was not telling the truth. Indeed, he had hired several competent managers, but (with the exception of the investment people) he allowed them, no matter how senior, little authority. Not even Chairman Clarkson had much say. Clarkson's office was on the thirteenth floor, only one above Reed's, but he was in effect miles away from the decision-making process concerning operations. Reed monitored every piece of information going up to the thirteenth floor and made sure the chairman received only what Reed wanted him to receive. Clarkson had previously exercised most of his power through

---

*The float was not so secret anymore, but its import was still hidden from the public. As late as 1959, a magazine article on Amexco reported that it made most of its money from sales charges on the TC.

the board of directors, but in a skillful bit of political maneuvering, Reed won the support of the board for himself, guaranteeing his own control of the company. Reed had cultivated and developed the board, beginning in the 1940s, and then in 1949, he saw a crisis brewing and he turned it into an opportunity.

The crisis developed because Albert Wiggin was old and dying. He owned 24 percent of American Express and he, Clarkson, and Reed all feared that, when he died, his stock would wind up in the wrong hands. The Chase National Bank had made it clear that it wanted to buy the stock back, but Amexco's leaders opposed a Chase bid. They wanted, instead, to place the stock with investors who would keep Amexco independent, and it was Reed who personally found buyers— two investment men, Brownlee Curry of Equitable Securities and Joseph King of Union Securities. Curry and King had a better idea than most people of how Amexco made its money because Equitable and Union sold and underwrote municipal bonds. In 1949, after a round at the Augusta National Golf Club with Reed, the two men agreed to bid on Wiggin's stock. There were a few other parties, besides Chase, interested in bidding on the shares, and King and Curry actually offered Wiggin less for the stock than anyone else. But they alone accepted the conditions Wiggin set down: namely that they would not break up the company. With the stock in friendly hands, Clarkson and Reed dissolved the Amerex Holding Company and distributed Amexco's stock to Amerex shareholders, a total of 2.5 million shares at an initial price of $10 per share.* American Express once again became an actively traded stock, listed on the over-the-counter market.†

Reed's sponsorship of the deal proved a great personal victory. Curry

---

*King sold most of his holding soon after buying it, but the company bought back the shares and created its first employee stock-option plan. King remained an influential director until 1974.

†Amexco was delisted from the New York Stock Exchange in 1939; at the time, Amerex owned 99 percent of the shares and there was not enough stock in circulation to warrant a listing.

and King became enormously influential members of the board of Amexco (although Curry died soon after and was replaced by his brother-in-law Ralph "Peck" Owen, who also played in that fateful golf game in 1949). They agreed with Reed that only he could run the company, and they even believed that he had somehow saved it. "I doubt [Amexco] could have survived [without Reed] the first six or seven years after we bought it," Owen said in later years. "It took a strong arm and Mr. Reed was a very strong armed man." Just what he thought threatened Amexco is a mystery, but such support from key board members clearly gave Reed a mandate to be as "strong armed" as he wanted to be. Actually, Reed increased his support on the board in the years immediately after King and Curry joined. Reed recruited outsiders, including General Lucius Clay, who became Reed backers, and the chief executive added loyalists from within the company such as senior VP and secretary N. F. Page. In the early 1950s, the majority of the board backed Reed; his grip on the company was unassailable.

Reed became more authoritarian and autocratic in his style of management. On his desk in his twelfth floor corner office, he had a panel of push buttons connected to buzzers in the office of every senior official at 65 Broadway. When he pushed a button, executives were expected to come running, even if they were meeting with important clients at the time. One senior manager began to stutter as soon as his buzzer went off. Others reacted to the sound as if it were a fire alarm, bolting out of their offices and fighting into their suit jackets, as they raced through the corridors to the twelfth floor.

When they arrived at Reed's office they might well find themselves facing a furious chief executive. Reed sometimes ranted, bellowed, and cursed at them, but he expressed his anger most often with what one executive called "the glassy eyeball," a cold hostility that left subordinates shaken and convinced they had performed badly. Reed blew up at subordinates mostly in the privacy of his office, but occasionally he exploded at meetings. One branch manager recalled with deep embarrassment a dressing-down he received from Reed in front of a client. When he was not chastising his men, Reed frequently behaved like a drill sergeant. He lined his subordinates up outside his office door and called them in two to six at a time for ten-minute sessions to give them their marching orders. His more routine Monday Officers' Conferences were less demeaning but resembled orchestrated recitations more than genuine exchanges of ideas.

Reed not only assumed the role of absolute ruler in the business of the company, he also used his position to surround himself with the trappings of kingship. This was particularly evident on his yearly tour of Europe, an event popularly known around Amexco as the Reed Circus. Each year, he set sail for Europe—he *never* flew—with an entourage including his wife, daughter, and devoted secretary, Eleanor Williams. On the Continent, they traveled superdeluxe for a time in a private railroad car built for Hermann Göring, and through Egypt, they traveled on a train built for King Farouk. Reed threw lavish parties and once booked the whole first floor of London's Savoy Hotel to hold a cocktail reception for 500 people. The Circus was mainly an occasion for Reed to hold a major conference for European office managers in one or another European city or resort area, and a time, too, for Reed to visit some of the branch offices, where he would poke through the records and greet the staff.

Reed, who was insecure enough to wear elevator shoes, relished his role as king of travel. With the help of his European staff, he received perks that fit the role and that he especially craved: medals from European governments, including the Cross of the Legion of Honor in France, which he often displayed on his lapel. He was also awarded honorary degrees, and he dined with the kings of England and Greece and other titled figures on the Continent. His personal ascendency over the travel business was capped in 1956 when he appeared on the cover of *Time*, dubbed by the magazine the "Grand Pooh-Bah" of travel.

But Reed's kingly style, along with his autocratic management practices, frustrated the younger generation of executives who had come into Amexco after 1945 (most were war veterans). In many cases, they had trained at top business schools in modern concepts of marketing and management, and they found Reed's company a corporate dinosaur. While some businesses like the First National City Bank (later Citicorp) created "think tanks," pioneered long-range planning, and developed sophisticated marketing strategies, Reed increasingly discouraged real planning, discouraged individual initiative, and discouraged new ideas. After the burst of postwar development that led to field warehousing and military banking, Reed rejected most new ideas out of hand; even when staff members presented ideas for increasing travel, he reacted warily. He wanted no tampering with his system or his authority.

Reed reverted more and more to being the bean counter of old. He reasserted Small's policies from the 1920s and took the company away from making money to saving money; he started deflecting new ideas with the comment, "we have to live within our means." The nation was in the midst of a period of sustained economic growth, but the thinking of the Glass Eye Era and the Depression dominated at 65 Broadway after 1948.

This kind of attitude inevitably discouraged more than a few staffers, and some of the more able young men left. Others stayed because they felt that Reed, who turned sixty in 1950, would not be around much longer, and that when he left, they could develop the company's great potential. But he showed no inclination to leave and continued to block innovation.

At the same time, Reed hired and kept in the top ranks of the company a few men of imagination.* They also proposed innovations, and Reed opposed them. But these men had ideas they believed in and the will to fight to put their ideas into effect despite the resistance of the chief executive. They had a considerable impact on the history of American Express from 1955 on.

Three individuals played especially important roles in the company: Paul Whipple ("Pete") Bradford, Howard L. Clark, and Robert C.

---

*Reportedly, the board pressed Reed to hire and retain young men of ability for the company's future.

Townsend. All three were chief executive material.* Two, Bradford and Clark, expected at one time or another to succeed Reed; Townsend apparently believed he *should* succeed Reed. But all were strong-willed enough to fight Reed's autocracy and find ways to influence the major issues of the 1950s.

Howard Clark had a good deal of influence throughout the company though actually of the three had the least influence with Reed. He had come to Amexco in 1945 with outstanding credentials—both law and accounting degrees—but Reed's rigid system and Clark's own slow promotion drove him to join W. R. Grace four years later. He was wooed back in 1952 by Amexco company directors; Clarkson, vice chairman Lynde Selden, and finally Reed himself called and asked the thirty-six-year-old Clark to return. Clark was named a senior VP, given a 10,000-share stock option, and had the real expectation that he would one day be chief executive of the company. But Clark had committed the ultimate sin: disloyalty. Once back at 65 Broadway, he did not find Reed happy to see him. He found instead an angry Pooh-Bah with no intention of turning his office over to Clark. Because of his strained relations with Reed, Clark tended to work toward his goals quietly; if he could not persuade Reed, he influenced others, including his allies on the board, to keep important issues alive.

Bradford also had some expectation of becoming chief executive, in part, some believed, because he had dramatically proven *his* loyalty to Reed. In the late 1940s, Reed set sail for Europe, but before the ship docked in Southampton, England, Reed was struck with an attack of acute appendicitis. Bradford, manager of English operations after 1945, received a message about Reed's illness and had an ambulance waiting at the dock and the royal surgeon standing by ready to perform the operation. In China and India in the 1920s and 1930s, Bradford had demonstrated that he was a highly competent executive, but after this

---

*Around 1950, Amexco had another possible heir to Ralph Reed. Tom Clark, no relation to Howard, was only in his late thirties and was already VP and company treasurer. However, he died of cancer in 1952 at age forty-one.

show of loyalty, Reed insisted he come to the U.S. Bradford left England reluctantly; he liked his job and his authority in England. But Reed led Bradford to believe he would succeed to the presidency after Reed retired, probably in 1955. Reed remained grateful and supportive of Bradford, made him a senior VP, and treated him as well as, or better than, anyone else. But before 1955, Reed had changed his mind about retiring, and Bradford, then fifty-five, may have felt he would be too old ever to become Amexco's president.

Robert Townsend, on the other hand, probably never expected he would make it to the top of American Express. He was a bright young man in the investment department, but also a brash nonconformist who disturbed some of the older executives. B. E. White, for example, remembered him disapprovingly for wearing pink shirts. Townsend was the kind of individualist who pushed his ideas with the tenacity, as one colleague described it, of "a dog with a bone," and he did not mind antagonizing people, including board members, in the process. But Townsend exercised influence because he maintained a good relationship with the man who made the decisions. Reed appeared to have a special fondness for this accomplished scion of a prominent New York family, and his support gave Townsend an important role in the company's affairs.

All three of these men were aggressive and talented and largely underused. But they were persistent, and on one issue, they all brought their influence to bear. The three men pushed Reed to make the company's most important decision of the twentieth century: to create the American Express Credit Card.

In the 1950s, Americans fell in love with credit cards. There were two kinds: charge cards for specific stores or companies, which had existed for years, and the universal travel and entertainment charge card, which was created in the fifties and had enormous importance in the history of American business.

The idea of a travel and entertainment card had emerged in 1949 out of a moment's panic in the life of New York businessman Frank

McNamara. McNamara had just finished a meal at a restaurant when he realized to his dismay that he could not pay the check. At that instant, McNamara thought of a device that would have allowed him to cover the bill, and later he joined forces with lawyer Ralph E. Schneider to turn his idea into reality: a universal restaurant charge card that would be accepted in all major New York restaurants.

When Schneider and McNamara tried out their idea on restaurateurs, they were almost universally turned down. Schneider wanted his card company to get a percentage of every charge. As one restaurant owner told him, "The people who'd use it come in here anyway and then we'd have to give you a share. What good is it to us?"

Schneider said later that if none of the first ten restaurateurs had encouraged him, he would have given up. But one loved the idea. So Schneider and McNamara pressed on and within weeks had signed up a hundred New York establishments. Schneider then borrowed $30,000, and in March 1950, his company began operations under the name of The Diners' Club* with Schneider as chief executive.

He and McNamara made up the business as they went along. Cardholders charged a meal, and the restaurant collected from the club, minus a discount of 5–10 percent. Diners' Club guaranteed payment to the restaurant and took on itself the task of collecting from cardholders. In the card, club members had blank-check, interest-free charge privileges and a notable convenience. Cardholders received a single bill for all charges once a month. Schneider expected that most members would be individuals, such as sales people, who needed to keep track of expenses. In fact, he recruited the first club members from a mailing list of 5,000 sales managers.

Since the concept seemed so simple, Schneider and McNamara had no inkling of the kind of trouble they were getting themselves into. Paperwork and billing procedures quickly overwhelmed the club's offices in that precomputer age. As the club grew, so did the headaches.

---

*In its early years, the club was officially The Diners' Club. Later, it dropped the apostrophe and is now simply Diners Club.

After losing only $80 in its first year, Diners' Club lost nearly $60,000 its second. Worse, the company was gaining a bad reputation among restaurant owners. As paperwork backed up, so did payments. If it were not for the fact that an increasingly large number of people were using this new device, Diners' Club might have lost all its service establishments. However, within only two years, many restaurateurs felt they had to honor this card or lose business to other establishments that did.

Still, many people doubted that the company would survive—not because of the bookkeeping problems, but because of an inherent danger. A store or even a chain of stores could check previous purchase records before allowing a customer to continue using a charge plate. But the Diners' Club card was honored in hundreds, later thousands, of unconnected establishments. That increased the risks enormously. If someone decided to abuse a card, there was no way the club could stop him until it was too late, and the club was committed to pay whether its cardholders did or not. A large number of card abuses would bankrupt the Diners' Club.

Those who saw disaster lurking in a universal card were of course far off the mark, primarily because the 1950s had become the age of the corporate expense account, and the universal entertainment card became an invaluable tool for business people. More and more businessmen signed up each year. Soon, ordinary consumers, too, were drawn to the convenience of the card. To take advantage of its broadening membership, Diners' Club went beyond restaurants and signed up florists, gourmet shops, motel chains, and in a big coup, the Hertz Rent A Car company. Membership in the club grew rapidly. In year two of the club's existence, members charged $1.1 million on their cards, and over the next eight years volume increased a hundredfold. In year four, Schneider assessed a $5-per-year membership fee, and Diners' Club posted a profit for the first time.

By that time, Diners' Club had competition. *Gourmet* and *Esquire* magazines were among twenty different companies that launched restaurant cards, but most folded within a year or two. Diners' Club bought out one competitor, Alfred Bloomingdale's California-based

Dine 'N Sign; Schneider not only added new cardholders through the purchase, but also made Bloomingdale the new president of the club. *

Other types of cards were growing in popularity as well. Just as Diners' Club began to branch out into other areas, companies introduced cards for every aspect of travel and entertainment. By 1955, with a handful of cards, it was possible to charge meals, airline or train tickets, oil, gas, tires and every other gas-station service, and tickets to plays or movies. Credit cards had been a part of life for years, but by the mid-1950s, they were beginning to become a *way* of life.

Amexco executives had noted the buy-now-pay-later trend in American life even before the birth of Diners' Club. Various ideas to sell Amexco's services on some sort of credit basis had been floating around the corridors of 65 Broadway since the 1920s. Initially, proposals centered around personal loans for travel, but these ideas did not go very far. Small opposed them, and after his unofficial ouster in 1935, any credit plan seemed too risky during the Depression.

But after the war, when Reed had officially taken control, he received the first suggestion for an American Express Credit Card. In July 1946, an unnamed airline executive approached assistant VP Louis S. Kelly and suggested to him that American Express issue a travel charge card for use only by business people. Reed, who was never so receptive to new ideas before or after, liked the basic concept and assigned William Eichelberger, sales manager for travel, to study it and report to B. E. White, the head of travel operations. Late in 1946, Eichelberger proposed a plan, calling for the creation of a corporate travel card. According to Eichelberger's plan, companies would deposit money with Amexco—$400–500—against possible default or abuse of a card. Then they could use the card to book all aspects of travel, either directly with carriers (if they agreed to accept the card), or through Amexco travel offices. Eichelberger estimated 5,000 firms would take the card, which would produce revenue of $20 million per year and profits of $1 million, no small amount for a company which

*McNamara left Diners' Club shortly after its founding.

in 1947 had net profits of about $2 million for all its businesses. Eichelberger was unequivocal in his support of the plan. "If we go into it wholeheartedly," he wrote in his final report, "we could materially increase our gross business and net revenue."

Reed studied the plan and, at first, appeared ready to approve it. The only worry he had was that the card would hurt TC sales. But Reed leaned toward the view, endorsed by Eichelberger, that business travelers were not big buyers of TCs. According to Eichelberger, businessmen and women already paid for one of their largest travel expenses, transportation, with airline and railroad credit cards.

However, the proposal faced opposition from most of Reed's staff. Executives noted the dangers of the business, especially the credit risks, and argued that Eichelberger was overly optimistic in expecting 5,000 companies to take the card. Their fears had an effect on Reed, whose support began to waver. However, he sought advice from outside the company, from an executive of an aviation company. The executive strongly backed the concept, claiming that Eichelberger was actually a *pessimist*; he predicted a yearly gross of $50 million, not $20 million. He supported, too, Eichelberger's contention that business travelers did not buy TCs and wanted a general travel card in place of a hodgepodge of rail and air cards. Reed once more seemed ready to implement Eichelberger's proposal and informed his men: "I will discuss [this idea] again at the Officers' Conference, June 1st."

The idea came up at the meeting and it died there. As a Reed assistant noted, the card idea was put "in indefinite suspense." Reed, who had been in favor of the card concept, had changed his mind for unknown reasons. Amexco had lost a chance to beat everyone to a universal charge card, and afterward Reed was no longer receptive to the card idea or any other new idea.

Nevertheless, discussion of credit cards resurfaced at Amexco soon after the sudden emergence of Diners' Club in 1950. Though executives talked about credit cards, few initially wanted to involve American Express in that business. They thought of Diners' Club, according to one executive, as a "schlock" company that had alienated many customers because of billing and bookkeeping problems. The reputations of the other card operations such as Esquire's were no better. To most company officials, who saw Amexco as a "high prestige" company, the card business was unworthy.

Yet by the mid-1950s, some Amexco executives, particularly the younger men, discerned two trends: first, more Americans than ever were acquiring credit cards; and second, people were using cards for travel-related services. The first trend represented a business opportunity, but the second posed a threat. If people were using cards for travel, then eventually they would use them in place of the TC. This situation presented Amexco with what a few executives realized was one of the company's most important business dilemmas ever: how to protect the TC market, which made all their money?*

Just how quickly the credit card business was growing became apparent in late 1955. On November 16, Diners' Club made a public offering of 150,000 shares, a one-third interest, at $8 per share. The prospectus showed that the club had increased its membership from 40,000 in 1951 to 200,000 in 1955. Annual charge volume topped $20 million; profits, $500,000; and both were rising. Despite its poor reputation, Diners' Club was, in fact, expanding at an astonishing rate. As Howard Clark noted, such growth might encourage other "prestige companies" to issue travel and entertainment credit cards of their own, thereby increasing the threat to American Express.

But Reed continued to show no interest in credit cards, until the matter surfaced again in the spring of 1956, when American Express was suddenly presented with the chance to buy Diners' Club. This offer began a Byzantine decision-making process that continued on and off for almost two years. It was a process that included countless meetings, memos, proposals, and deals, nearly all of which would lead nowhere.

---

*Amexco's money order still produced revenue but its importance was fading rapidly. By the 1950s, personal checking accounts became more readily available to individuals, and the MO had increasingly less importance in Amexco's business thereafter.

The process began when a board of directors meeting was breaking up. As most of the directors rose from the table and made their way to the door, director Joe King collared Reed and Howard Clark. King, an investment banker with numerous contacts in the financial community, said he had received a message from Ben Sonnenberg, a publicist and corporate marriage broker, that Ralph Schneider and Alfred Bloomingdale wanted to sell their shares in Diners' Club to American Express. Since the two men owned two-thirds of their company, this offer was tantamount to a full sale. Despite their public offering, the two men had actually been trying to make a deal for some time. They had sounded out Amexco through Pete Bradford, who had turned them away, and subsequently they had unsuccessfully shopped the club to Western Union. Now, through King, they were trying Amexco once again.

While Reed ignored proposals from his staff, he listened to directors such as King, and consented to King's suggestion that Howard Clark pursue the matter with Sonnenberg. On May 7, both Clark and Robert Townsend had lunch with Sonnenberg and Belmont Towbin, an investment banker at C. E. Unterberg & Towbin Company. Towbin had handled the Diners' Club public offering and was himself on the board of Diners' Club. He reported that Schneider and Bloomingdale were interested in exchanging their shares for shares of Amexco and would support a tender by American Express for the shares in public hands.

Clark returned from the luncheon clearly enthusiastic about the proposal and wrote a lengthy memo to Reed. He addressed what he knew would be the biggest objection to a card business: that a credit card belonging to American Express would undercut its own TC market. Clark did not dispute the idea that a card would hurt TC sales. Rather, he argued that cards were going to cut into those sales anyway, and the best offense would be to get a share—the biggest share—of the credit-card business. This idea became the basic premise of the procard argument. But Clark's argument was by no means universally accepted. To some officials, the idea of undercutting the TC seemed like lunacy.

Clark also thought Amexco could get Diners' Club at a good price, and he argued in the terms most likely to win a favorable response from the old bean counter, Ralph Reed: small and cheap. Clark estimated that Amexco could acquire the whole of Diners' Club for 120,000 shares of Amexco, a total market value of $4.32 million and a dilution of around 5 percent. Even at $5 million Clark thought Diners' "a real buy." Clark's figures were perhaps overly optimistic since, on a market basis, Diners' Club would have cost $8.6 million, which Clark considered too much. However, he noted that even at that price Amexco would realize 40 cents a share in pretax earnings immediately.

Clark also discussed creating a separate American Express card, which he saw as the only sensible alternative to buying Diners' Club. But Clark argued against it. First, he considered it a "cheaper substitute [that would] 'downgrade' our quality product," the TC. And he thought Diners' Club already had too large a share of the market and was too well established in the business. Buying Diners' Club would offer instant profitability, while Amexco would have to take losses if it started the business from scratch. Clark recommended pursuing Diners' Club, but he proposed some interim steps before Amexco made an offer: continue the discussions with Diners' Club representatives; talk to Western Union (which Clark thought might be interested in a card business) about joining forces for a takeover; get an opinion about the potential legal problems of such a bid; and consider an outside survey to assess Diners' Club and the impact of cards generally on the TC.

Reed read the memo and passed it on to Pete Bradford, who promptly and thoroughly attacked it. On H.M.S. *Queen Mary* stationery, Bradford expressed his low opinion of Diners' Club, and of Schneider and Bloomingdale, and pronounced himself "VERY LUKEWARM" to the proposal. Reed concurred with Bradford and dispatched a memo marked "urgent" to Clark: "I would not continue your discussions with Messrs. Schneider and Towbin of the Diners' Club because there might be some implied commitment of you to carry these discussions further."

Reed had two objections to Diners' Club, and both were more a reflection of Reed's prejudices than his business judgment. First, he did not want to purchase and operate a business that did not have the Amexco name attached to it. The fact that, once he owned it, he could change the name to American Express Diners' Club, or anything else he wanted, seemed to escape him. It was as though he wanted to make some kind of symbolic point—or perhaps he just used this as an excuse to bolster his second reason. He did not want Schneider and Bloomingdale to own a large block of Amexco stock, even though they would have no real power. As Clark noted, the stock they received could have been put in a voting trust, giving them stock, but no power to use it. Also, although Towbin talked stock, there was no evidence that the two men would not entertain a stock and cash offer, or just a cash offer.

Reed never explained why he did not want Schneider and Bloomingdale to own Amexco's stock. Bloomingdale did have a reputation as a playboy, and Reed was known to disapprove of such behavior generally, but some of the younger men at Amexco wondered whether Reed was motivated by anti-Semitism (both Diners' Club men were Jewish). Amexco officials were virtually all White Anglo-Saxon Protestants, and the company's relations with the Jewish community were poor at the time.* But whatever the reasons for Reed's decision, significantly, he did not discuss the TC or any other business issue in opposing the Diners' Club offer.

---

*In January 1956 the company decided to close its office in Tel Aviv, in what appeared to be compliance with the Arab boycott, and this led to denunciations of Amexco from some American Jewish leaders. The company always denied it had complied with the boycott and noted that in the autumn of 1955, Bradford, Clark Winter, and Frank Groves advised Reed to shut down Amexco's money-losing operations in Israel. But Reed did not act on this recommendation, and when Saudi Arabia told Amexco either to close its Tel Aviv office or get out of Saudi Arabia (where Amexco had a military bank), Reed resisted. He and several aides tried to persuade Saudi officials that Amexco's Israeli office was merely for American tourists and should be exempted from the boycott. But the Saudis gave him no option, and Reed decided only then to shut the Tel Aviv office. The Arab League subsequently claimed Amexco as a boycott success, but by 1958 the company reestablished operations in Israel.

The Diners' Club proposal was dead for now, but the credit-card issue was not. In the same letter in which he attacked Diners' Club, Bradford urged Reed to consider an American Express credit card. Bradford, an enormously opinionated individual, possessed a self-confidence that bordered on arrogance. While still head of the London office, he had the distinction of being one of the few people to get Reed to admit an error (on a small business detail, but the admission was unusual nonetheless). Now, in arguing the case for the card, Bradford proved far more forceful in disputing Clark than Clark had been in making his proposal. Bradford could "not see how an Am. Exp. card would 'downgrade' our TCs." An Amexco card, he argued, would "have prestige and would be honored everywhere." As for the difficulty of a start-up, he called it a simple business. "I could organize it," he boasted, "so could Dennis Harmon." For starters, he revived the 1946 idea, a card for commercial travelers. "After some experience, we could decide whether to expand it."

Reed was not ready to go ahead, but he was persuaded to continue discussion. He told Clark to form a committee with Bradford, Townsend, treasurer Olaf Ravndal, secretary N. F. Page, and Robert Mathews (formerly the head of advertising and now in charge of money orders and utility collections) "to spell out how American Express can get into [credit cards] as an American Express activity."

Clark gathered his committee together, and over the next month, they wrote a report. It called for the creation of a credit card strictly for domestic use to limit competition with the TC. The report projected losses of about $500,000 over the first year and a half, and a net of $500,000 per year on a volume of $32.7 million by year five. The committee figured cardholders at 48,000 in the first year, rising over five years to 196,000. These figures were largely guesses and could just as easily have been half or twice the size; as the report itself noted, all the figures were "rough" and "unchecked." Ultimately, the main recommendation from Clark's group was to get another recommendation—from an outside consultant. Reed agreed, and Clark chose

Cleveland-based Robert Heller & Associates.* In August, Reed approved an expenditure of about $30,000 for a credit-card study.

On October 22, the consultants submitted to Reed a summary of their report, which strongly opposed the creation of an American Express card. According to the summary, credit cards were going to have "a substantial adverse effect on Travelers Cheques in the near future," and there was "little opportunity for [Amexco] to operate a credit card plan on a profitable basis." The Heller consultants based their dire predictions in part on a supposition that the American Automobile Association (AAA) was about to get into the credit-card business. According to the consultants, this card would be used by middle-income people who ordinarily bought TCs. The Heller study estimated that the AAA card would cost Amexco 10 percent of its TC sales, about $147 million annually. Projecting the profitability of an Amexco card, the Heller group examined Diners' Club and some department-store charge divisions. They concluded that Amexco's own study had overstated costs but inflated revenues and profits. When they refined those numbers, they concluded that a card would lose money for two and a half years and in the fifth year would earn only $185,513; Amexco would still not have earned back its initial investment. As a result, the consultants determined that an American Express card would be a bad business proposition.

Though the Heller study seemed to destroy any hope of a card operation at American Express, Reed asked his own people for comments on the report. Before he received them, another complication made a card even more unlikely. On November 8, the American Hotel Association (AHA) announced the creation of a new card, The Universal Travelcard, in what was termed "an all-out fight against encroachment of outside credit card schemes into the hotel and res-

---

*Clark also considered using McKinsey & Co., but Heller had the inside track. It had already studied Amexco's travel operations and had made several recommendations for changes in the organization, including the addition of new products and services (suggestions Reed did not implement). Heller had also studied the credit card business for Western Union.

taurant fields." Said Seymour Weiss of the AHA, "these outsiders are trying to chisel into the hotel business as 7 percent partners." Amexco ran the risk that, if it created a card, hotels might refuse the TC and damage sales severely.

Despite this latest bit of bad news, Bradford attacked the Heller report and continued to press for some form of card. He argued that, because of continued economic growth in the U.S., there was room for both a robust card business and a TC. He again endorsed the idea of a business-travel card and added a new wrinkle: an overseas credit card. With its worldwide office network, Amexco had a tremendous advantage over Diners' Club abroad.

Reed heard other dissent both inside and outside the company. Publicist Fred Rosen and the company's advertising agency, Benton & Bowles, both believed that, although cards could have an impact on TC sales, the impact would be nowhere near as great as the Heller people had predicted, and Benton & Bowles seconded Bradford's opinion that a card and the TC could coexist side by side. Townsend joined the debate with a new plea to buy Diners' Club, if not the whole company then a minority interest of 40 percent. He thought it would work out as long as "we approach the Diners' Club with admiration and enthusiasm rather than condescension and reluctance." His was a lone voice this time.

Other Amexco officials, including Howard Clark, supported the Heller argument against a card. Clark attacked Townsend's proposal, opposing a purchase of less than 75 percent of Diners' Club, and he now rejected any acquisition involving Amexco stock. He also argued against an American Express card and suggested following Heller's advice, which was to develop other sorts of new business to make up for the expected falloff of TC sales.* Company secretary

---

*Clark, Bradford, and Ravndal proposed hedging the company's bets with respect to the AAA card. They suggested going to Washington "to attempt to dissuade [AAA officials] from entering the credit card field." They even drew up a position paper listing all the reasons why AAA should stay out of the business; this self-serving program was, however, never implemented.

N. F. Page opposed an Amexco card, too, and seemed uninterested in anything other than "expanding and developing the travelers cheque business."

The report and the disagreements it engendered bolstered Reed's own opposition. Only Bradford seemed determined to press on with the card, at least the overseas version. But Reed no longer showed the slightest interest in any card proposal; the Heller report had for the time ended formal discussion.

By June 1957, the Diners' Club discussion was revived. Bloomingdale, apparently without Schneider's knowledge, asked the investment banking firm of Goldman Sachs to arrange a takeover of Diners' Club by the American Express Company. Bloomingdale made his request in a letter to Gustave Levy, Goldman's managing partner, who passed it along to Robert Townsend. Townsend arranged a meeting between Reed and Bloomingdale for July 10, but first he had an inspiration: before Reed had a chance to talk with Bloomingdale, Townsend proposed that Amexco acquire not just Diners' Club, but also the Hertz Corporation.

Through one of his many contacts on Wall Street, an investment banker at Lehman Brothers, Townsend had begun discussions on a joint Amexco-Hertz project. Reed's attitude to Hertz at this point appeared cool. Townsend, in a memo just before the Bloomingdale meeting, scolded Reed: "Every time one of the top men of these two organizations [Hertz and Diners' Club] makes an effort to see you, you should advantage yourself of the opportunity to learn their ideas about travel and how American Express can profitably apply these ideas either in combination with Hertz and the Diners' Club or alone." But Townsend really wanted a "three-way merger" in which Amexco would buy the other two with an issue of 2.6 million new shares, more than doubling the current total. He tried to catch Reed's attention by putting the idea in the context of travel. He told Reed, correctly as it turned out, that both car rentals and credit cards were going to be big factors in the travel market, big enough that travel's Grand Pooh-Bah should not ignore them. But if Townsend believed he could convince Reed of an idea this vast, he was mistaken, and he soon abandoned his grand plan.*

Reed's first and last face-to-face encounter with Alfred Bloomingdale went ahead as scheduled. On July 10, Bloomingdale, Levy, and Richard Fay, also of Goldman Sachs, met with Reed and Townsend in Reed's office. Bloomingdale started out by explaining why he wanted a merger: Diners' Club was undercapitalized. The company needed a bigger bankroll to cover the cost of a new billing system using IBM computer equipment; it needed the support of a company with resources like those of American Express. Bloomingdale wanted Reed to take two steps: acquire at least a majority of the shares of Diners' Club, and then give the club a loan of $6 million for the IBM equipment. To show that the loan was a sound business idea, Bloomingdale noted that the equipment would lower overhead 30 percent, or about $1.1 million a year, allowing Diners' Club to repay its new parent company quickly and with interest. But Bloomingdale could not have picked a worse line of argument for the old bean counter, Ralph Reed.

Reed said nothing, and Bloomingdale went on. He painted a picture of a Diners' Club–American Express card used by ten million people for every service and product imaginable. Already, he reported, there were nearly 500,000 cardholders, and profits and revenues were rising. (Schneider told security analysts a few days later that charge volume had reached $7 million per month.) When Bloomingdale finished, Reed had two questions. Did Bloomingdale have a detailed proposal? No. Did Bloomingdale and Schneider intend to stay on in the event of a merger? Bloomingdale said yes for himself, but thought Schneider, who had had a heart attack recently, might want to step down. That of course would have killed the idea for Reed; he had said from the very beginning that he opposed keeping either of them.

---

*In later years, some of Townsend's colleagues wondered if he had not proposed this scheme simply to shock and amaze Reed. One said Townsend liked to play the role of company "nettle." However, the memo seemed serious, and Townsend remained in the forefront of encouraging ties between Amexco and Hertz.

Twelve days later, Reed met with the finance committee of the board, at The Recess, an old luncheon club of the financial community. The committee members took their places around a table in one of the back rooms: Robert Clarkson, Howard Clark, Joe King, Ralph Owen, Howard Smith (retired as a VP, but still a member of the board and the finance committee), financier and board member James Lee, and of course Reed himself. Four others sat around the table at Reed's invitation: Robert Townsend and three other young men from the Investment Department.

Reed began by explaining that there were two parts to the agenda: a proposal for a joint Hertz-Amexco overseas car-rental operation, and a discussion of a takeover of Diners' Club. Reed was ready to accept the car-rental idea, which surprised some staff members; it was the first significant new venture he had approved in years. Townsend was able to sell the deal because it was the kind Reed could accept: travel-related and relatively small and cheap, about $2–3 million.*

Diners' Club, however, was another matter. Reed had spent the previous week putting some numbers together. By his reckoning, 80 percent of Diners' Club would cost $20 million, four times what Clark had thought Amexco could pay for the whole company a year earlier. Reed would never have agreed to an expenditure that large. Clarkson wondered if Amexco should not take $20 million and start its own card. Reed, Clark, and Townsend countered that Diners' Club was too far ahead for Amexco to start its own card operation profitably.

Townsend alone defended the Diners' Club deal. He began after Lee asked, "Why are we interested in Diners' Club anyway?"

Townsend launched into a description of the growth and potential of Diners' Club. "Earnings," he said, "are increasing, conservatively speaking, at a rate of 50 percent per annum and there doesn't seem to be anything to reverse the trend." As for the price Amexco would have to pay, the cost would be in the range of $20 milion, but if Amexco would issue 400,000 shares of new stock "it would not cost us any

---

*Hertz–American Express International began operations four months later in November 1957.

money." For an outlay of zero dollars, Amexco should realize a return of at least $6 per new share before taxes. Though this new stock issue would give Bloomingdale and Schneider each some 6 percent of American Express, he noted, the shares could be placed in a voting trust to prevent the newcomers from instituting an agenda of their own.

When Townsend finished, Reed objected that he had forgotten the $6 million loan. But Townsend had a ready answer. Diners' Club had established a $4 million line of credit through Chase, its principal bank; to date, the club had taken out only $400,000, so more than half the money for the new equipment could be financed out of the proposed new subsidiary's own resources.

There may well be a gap in the record of the meeting at this point—a missing question—because Reed volunteered that "our people do not feel that Diners' Club competes with Travelers Cheques." Perhaps his statement was simply a non sequitur, but in any event, it was both important and also false. Several executives, including Clark and Townsend, were sure that the Diners' Club card did or would compete with the TC. The Heller group agreed.

No one challenged Reed on this point, however, and the discussion resumed. What about the Diners' Club people, James Lee asked, "Do we want *these kind* of people [Schneider and Bloomingdale] in the American Express Club?" Townsend, who did not suffer fools gladly, shot back, "I thought American Express was a profit-making enterprise rather than a country club." Lee, probably embarrassed, suddenly pronounced himself ready to go ahead and see "what kind of arrangement could be worked out." Clarkson agreed and so did Howard Smith. Townsend appeared to have won cautious support from the committee for a takeover.

As the discussion wound down, however, Reed decided to summarize: He "sensed" enthusiasm for the deal with Hertz, but as for Diners' Club, "Since that Committee does not have much enthusiasm for [it], I'll tell them we don't want to talk any more."

Townsend at first refused to accept Reed's version of the outcome.

As the meeting was breaking up, he said he would vote to buy Diners' Club, and the next day, in a memo to Reed, he claimed "there was no real objection to pushing the discussions with Diners' Club further." But to Reed, the issue was "filed."

To an outsider with no understanding of Amexco's internal structure and politics, the meeting's resolution might seem incredible. Although only Townsend was wholeheartedly in favor of a deal with Schneider and Bloomingdale, the consensus clearly favored continued discussion. Clark was in favor in principle. Lee, Smith, and Clarkson wanted to keep talking. King expressed no view but had brought the matter to Reed in the first place. In fact, only two people at the meeting definitely opposed a deal: Owen and Reed. They carried the day two to five.

The meeting appeared to finish off the card idea, but a few people in the company were not willing to let it go. Despite Reed's rejection, cards were going to take business away from the TC, and the only way to cushion the blow was to be in the card business.

Bradford and Townsend continued to push the hardest. Bradford bulled ahead in trying to win support for his overseas card. From May 1957 through the early summer, he polled managers in European offices, many of whom supported the basic idea. Harry Hill wrote from Paris, "I would like to stress that I feel very strongly that something must be done for New York to get into this picture. There are too many people coming abroad with their Diners' cards and we are losing business. . . ."

But in New York, only Townsend, who had abandoned his hopes of acquiring Diners' Club and had turned to the idea of an Amexco card by default, endorsed Bradford's scheme. He saw it as a first step toward a worldwide card. "I agree with Harry Hill that the real question is not whether American Express should have a credit card but how long we can afford to delay. I for one would move immediately." Other executives continued to worry about doing harm to the travelers cheque business, and about something called a "negative float." With the TC, Amexco collected money, floated it, and paid it back over time. With

a card, the order changed: the company had to pay the service establishment first and then collect. If it could not collect, the card company would have to take a loan to pay off the service establishments.
A long-term average of negative outstandings could build up—a negative float. The prospect of a negative float did not appeal to people
who had lived by the TC so long.

While Amexco executives continued to have doubts about a card,
more and more *outsiders* thought a card would be a natural addition to
American Express. In September, Amexco received another proposal,
this time from Arthur Roth, president of the Long Island–based
Franklin National Bank. Roth met with Clark and Townsend, and
suggested that Amexco start a card, handling only promotion and sales.
The Franklin, which had more experience with credit matters, would
handle all the credit checks and the rest of the bookkeeping. The
response at Amexco to Roth's proposal was mixed: Reed, however,
displayed no more enthusiasm for this deal than he had for any other.

Meanwhile, Bradford kept pressing Reed on the overseas card. Finally, in late September the chief executive told him to get together
with nine senior executives and produce a definitive recommendation
one way or the other. Reed had a system of "concurrences" which
required everyone who might be affected by a decision to sign off on
it. Reed seemed to use this system at his convenience since he reserved
for himself veto rights over every decision. But in this case, the system
would put Bradford's proposal to rest since opinion was far too divided.
Reed said nothing himself, but then he did not have to; his system
killed Bradford's plan.

But Townsend kept up a stream of memos backing the Franklin
scheme. On November 19, he told Reed that he and treasurer Olaf
Ravndal had made a lunch date with Roth at The Recess on November
27. Would Reed talk to Roth? The answer was no, but Townsend was
allowed to go, and Clark, Ravndal, and Bradford, who had conceded
defeat on his own plan, went along. Roth repeated his offer to take over
the bookkeeping for an American Express card, and he reported that
Amexco could acquire the entire membership list of the Gourmet

Club for next to nothing.* Since the problems of running and marketing a universal credit card made Gourmet eager to get out of the business, Roth thought they might sell their membership for as little as $2,000. Roth noted that buying Gourmet's list would give the proposed Amexco card 40,000 members who had already proven creditworthy. It all sounded good to Amexco's executives, who asked Roth for a formal proposal. Townsend and Bradford returned to 65 Broadway and advised Reed to wait for Roth's response before making a decision.

Reed did nothing of the kind. Five days later, on December 2, at his regular Monday Officers' Conference, Reed addressed the card issue once and for all. Present at the meeting were most of the senior officials of the company: Clark, Groves, Bradford, Page, comptroller Paul Ross, Townsend, Ravndal, White, and VP George Shirey.

Although this was to be Reed's chance to announce his final decision, he played out a little scene first. He gave his executives one last chance to state the things they had said repeatedly over the previous two years. One by one the executives raised all the old issues; Townsend tried to rebut the objections. No one had changed his mind.

Then it was Reed's turn. He started out like the bean counter of old: the costs of launching a program, he lamented, "could be extremely heavy," and he saw no way of limiting the issuance of the card and so limiting the risk. As a result, he concluded, "we probably have to go all out as long as the cardholders are creditworthy." Most of the people in the meeting were stunned, waiting for the other shoe to drop, something like, "we would have to go all out, so we won't get involved." But Reed was finished. He had reversed himself. He had given a go-ahead.

From that day onward, Amexco executives wondered why—why had Reed changed his mind? There was no definitive answer. Reed

---

*The Franklin performed bookkeeping tasks for the Gourmet Club and so already had a system in place. Some years later, of course, the Franklin National Bank became insolvent in one of the most publicized bank failures of the post–World War II era.

apparently had heard a rumor that Diners' Club was planning to enter the travel business through a new outfit called the "Intercontinental Express Agency." Bloomingdale planned to use this new agency to put together tours for travel agents, and perhaps, to offer traveler's checks. Reed probably took the news as a personal attack and decided to fight back by invading the club's territory. Such a scenario would have been completely in character for Reed.

Perhaps his reversal was more the result of the continuous lobbying he faced for two years. That Reed had permitted the debate to continue suggests that he was still considering the issue. However strong his resistance was, he clearly changed his mind over time, perhaps because the most forceful arguments came from the two men he liked best, Bradford and Townsend. But finally, the reasoning behind the most important decision for the company during the twentieth century remains a mystery.

So Reed made the decision to create the American Express Card, but the new venture was to have a difficult birth. Amexco was totally unprepared for this business and was unable to learn from the experiences of Diners' Club and the other card companies. American Express suffered from a belief that this was a simple business over which the venerable American Express would easily triumph, as Bradford had once claimed. But the card operation became so chaotic that before long, many executives would regret that Reed had changed his mind.

In early February 1958, Reed appointed Robert R. Mathews to head the start-up of the card division.* He was joined on the project by in-house troubleshooter Clark Winter. A few months later, assistant VP Michael Lively, who had been working on the Hertz–American Express joint venture, became the third executive of the start-up project and was named the future general manager of the new card division.

---

*While Mathews developed a new division, he was still required to act as head of the money-order and utility-collection operations.

Reed also designated Bradford and Townsend to advise the card operation. While all of these men had proven themselves competent executives, none had ever had anything to do with a credit-card operation. Lively even admitted that his knowledge of such cards was "limited to a layman's evaluation . . . hearsay and conjecture." But that was sufficient for Reed, who never thought of bringing in someone who knew what the business was about.

At this point, no details of the card operation had been decided. Amexco still considered the idea of having the Franklin Bank handle the paperwork, an option not finally rejected until March. The question of buying the membership of Gourmet or some other club to get a nucleus of cardholders was also up in the air and would hang there for months. At the same time, Reed made one thing clear: he wanted to get this project moving swiftly. Mathews was as committed as Reed. He wrote, "We are convinced without reservation that we should get in to this business as quickly as possible." Long before most issues were resolved, in early March, Reed set the launch day for October 1, 1958.

Mathews, Winter, and Lively faced promotional details, organizational details, management details, credit details, policy questions. They had to decide whether or not to charge for the card and how much; what kind of contract to have with service establishments; what discount rate to charge; whether there would be a uniform rate or different rates; what the card would be made of; what the card would be called; and so on. Winter and Mathews sat down one day and filled sheet after sheet of yellow paper just enumerating the questions that had to be addressed. Both men began putting in long days, working until midnight or later, seven days a week. It was not enough. By April, they were still grappling with basic questions like the cost of the card, and whether it would be made of plastic or cardboard. To be sure, they were beginning to get some of the issues in hand. They knew they needed a credit department, a sales department, and a collection department, and they began sketching out a rough organizational plan.

On many matters, Reed gave Mathews and Winter an unusual degree of autonomy and authority. They could simply make decisions without the need to write lots of memos or get concurrences and were required to advise only Reed—with whom they dined one or two nights a week. The card-division heads were able to maintain their autonomy in part because the new division operated out of the old 1858 redbrick building on Hudson Street, out of sight and oversight of headquarters.

But Reed took one matter out of the new division's control entirely. He settled the question of who would handle the accounting: it would be neither the card division nor the Franklin Bank. Instead Reed gave complete authority to the company comptroller. His decision was not surprising. Reed continued to draw on his own experience as company comptroller, and he always maintained tight oversight of the company's operations though his comptroller, Paul Ross. In this instance, however, the paperwork was of a different character and a different order of magnitude. By its very nature, a card business involved an enormous burden on an accounting operation. Although the company brought in an outside consultant to help set up new accounting procedures, the comptroller's office never hired the personnel to manage the volume of work the card would entail. The people in the office knew nothing about credit cards and made no apparent effort to learn.

Through April, preparations for the card went on in relative secrecy. No one, not even Diners' Club,* knew what Amexco was planning. But Mathews, Winter, Lively, and other employees could not keep the operation quiet for long. Out of necessity they had to let an ever-widening circle of people know what they were planning. They had to advise managers in the field, sound out some service-establishment owners, and talk to bankers (to make certain the card would not cost Amexco their goodwill), and so the secret inevitably got out. By early May, B. E. White received a message from his friend Seymour Weiss of the American Hotel Association and its Universal Travelcard. Weiss

---

*Amexco had good intelligence reports on Diners' Club. Travel agents reported contacts with club officials, and Hertz kept Amexco abreast of its meetings with Schneider and Bloomingdale.

wanted to talk to White for unknown reasons. But White surmised correctly that it had "to do with our entrance into the Credit Card Field."

White expected that Weiss would be angry about the card. But actually, Weiss offered assistance on two fundamental concerns of the card operation: recruiting cardholders and signing up service establishments. Weiss wanted to make a deal. The American Hotel Association, Weiss's organization, had gotten into the card business to battle Diners' Club and the other travel and entertainment cards. But while the AHA had 150,000 cardholders and 4,500 participating hotels, member establishments were still losing business to other cards. Consequently, the hotel association decided to end its war against outside cards and form an alliance with one of the card organizations. Weiss and his group picked Amexco and offered the latter all AHA card members and service establishments. At once, American Express had 150,000 cardholders, and its card had credibility as a *travel* and entertainment instrument widely accepted in U.S. hotels.*

Mathews, Winter, and Lively achieved other notable successes in the search for both service establishments and card members. In the summer, the New York Central Railroad, an old friend of Amexco, agreed to allow passengers to charge tickets on the card. Amexco bought the Gourmet card's membership list, adding more than 40,000 members. That list, combined with the one Amexco had acquired from the AHA, brought the number of holders of the still-to-be-issued American Express Card to over 190,000. Two years earlier Howard Clark's committee had projected 196,000 holders after five years of operation; instead, Amexco had that two months *before* operations began.

---

*Amexco made a concession to win the AHA. It allowed association hotels to use the American Express Card strictly as an ID so that they could bill customers directly and avoid paying a discount to Amexco. This system led to complications such as this: a hotel billed a customer, but the customer did not pay quickly, so the hotel decided to collect what it could and rebilled the customer through Amexco. In the meantime, the customer paid the hotel's original bill only to get a new bill from American Express. After a few years of confusion and ill will from this system, Amexco decided unilaterally to break the contract, and the courts sided with American Express.

Actually, Amexco had many more cardholders than that. In May the press had begun to report rumors about Amexco's plans for a card, and so many reports appeared that the company felt it had no choice but to confirm that the rumor was true. The response to the news was both overwhelmingly positive and just plain overwhelming. With the card still in a very formative stage, Mathews, Winter, and Lively were deluged with appeals from people who wanted to be cardholders. This response demonstrated how much goodwill the company had built up over the years. But it was more a distraction than anything else; people clamored for cards, and Amexco still had not even decided how much to charge for them.

Nevertheless, a few weeks later, Amexco decided to give people a more formal opportunity to apply for a card. Mathews, Winter, and Lively put ads in twenty-three newspapers that included a return coupon so that people could apply for the card. Lively recalled how he and Mathews were told that some mail had arrived, and they went to take a look, expecting a few dozen responses. Instead there were *thousands* in a dozen mailbags. Two days later, the three card-division heads were forced to assign eighteen people to work in the mailroom going through these letters—some of which not only asked for a card, but wanted special favors such as "lucky" card number. The problem for the card division was that each one of these letters required not just a polite note in response; they required credit checks, entries into a billing system, a printed card (if they qualified), and then some letter of response complete with cardholder rules and obligations. Working day and night, the card operation tried to accomplish all of these tasks, and by launch date the company had issued more than 250,000 cards. But the division was still behind in its correspondence, and new applications were arriving at a rate of thousands per week.

The pressure on the card division not only to approve cards, but also to sign up service establishments grew enormous as October 1 drew near. Mathews, Winter, and Lively dispatched their representatives from New York, briefcases filled with contracts to sign up as long a list of service establishments as possible. Amexco managers around the world got into the act soliciting restaurants and hotels. Other service establishments actually came to Amexco unsolicited, in part because they valued the American Express name and the goodwill it enjoyed. As the colorful restaurateur Toots Shor said, "[Amexco's] got a reputation for being clean and decent, and it'll probably lend some class to my place." Shor called Reed directly and told him, "Ralph, ya bum, I'm going into business with ya—put my joint down for them credit cards of yours."

By opening day, Amexco had signed up 17,500 establishments. It charged its quarter-million cardholders $6 per card, one dollar more than the Diners' Club card to emphasize that it was a higher prestige item. The cards were made of paperboard—a lightweight cardboard—and had a purple border over a purple-tinted beige field. On the left side, it had, in purple, a familiar decoration: the head of a centurion, a symbol that had been added to travelers cheques in the early 1950s to make them harder to counterfeit. The card numbers were printed in red, and the old slogan, created by Howard Brooks and Douglas Malcolm, "World Service," was watermarked into the card's background. Reed presented the new creation to the world, as promised, on October 1 at a packed press conference. Already, the American Express Credit Card, as it was officially called, rivaled the Diners' Club card in size and scope; on the surface, the American Express Card appeared a smashing success at birth.

But initially, the card was the most paradoxical development in the company's history: its success nearly destroyed it. While no product or service ever received such a warm reception, no product so greatly threatened the company's goodwill, or so drastically drained its treasury. Part of the trouble stemmed from Reed's decision to put the comptroller's office in charge of accounting. The comptroller just did not get the work done. As Mathews and Lively tried to explain to Reed, "There was no accounting going on." Relations particularly with service establishments suffered. The card business depended on their goodwill, but they were not getting paid on schedule. Complaints poured in to a company that had not heard more than a handful in any one year since it lost its express business. Although they tried, Mathews and Lively could not make Reed believe that the accounting operation endangered the entire venture. They went to Reed's office to explain, and Reed immediately called in the comptroller who reported that "everything was in hand." Reed threw Mathews and Lively out of his office. For a few more weeks the work backed up, and the complaints mounted. The comptroller fell at least two months behind. Finally, Mathews and Lively sent the outside accounting consultants in to see Reed and explain the problem to him. Then the card division heads went back to the chief executive's office themselves. Reed acknowledged at last that the problems were serious, and he accepted a recommendation to take the billing system out of the comptroller's hands and give it to the card division. But the paperwork would not finally be brought up-to-date for years.

Lively, Mathews, and Winter adopted a positive philosophy about such problems. They remained determined to forge ahead and clean up the messes as they went along. As a result, growth in both card members and service establishments continued at a rapid pace. But the complaints persisted, and far more important, the card lost money—lots of money, on the order of $4 million in the first two years, a total of perhaps $14 million by 1962.

Some of the losses resulted from organizational problems such as accounting. But actually most of Amexco's losses stemmed from the behavior of cardholders, from a combination of card abuse and slow payment. The company had done a poor job in evaluating credit risks, which was understandable since it had no experience with handing out blank-check credit, or any credit for that matter. Beginning with the Glass Eye Era, Amexco had made a policy of denying credit; now it suddenly shifted policy and handed it out to hundreds of thousands of people. Mathews, Winter, and Lively recognized the potential of card abuse, and they hired a few people from other card operations who had some experience in credit evaluation. But these people did not know their business very well; indeed the card operations they came from had similiar problems. Amexco just had the problems on a bigger scale, a roster of cardholders that quickly topped 500,000

286

Some of the losses arose from a deliberate abuse of the card. But many other people just did not pay on time. This was partly due to the way Americans had traditionally settled their debts. Travel and entertainment cards were new, and Americans were not used to the idea of paying off bills like clockwork every thirty days. Amexco pledged to settle with service establishments in ten days, but many cardholders squared their accounts only after ninety days or even six months. When Amexco pressed cardholders, they often reacted indignantly. American Express compounded the problem with a reluctance to crack down on the deadbeats. Reed, especially, despised the idea of dunning customers. Pressing people for money built ill will, and the company was only used to creating will of the good kind. After a couple of years, Lively tried a gentle approach to both educate and threaten; he dispatched a seven-stanza poem allegedly from a remorseful cardholder that included lines such as:

I let your bills go much too long—
The oversight, I know, was wrong.
It roused your righteous indignation
And brought about my cancellation.

The poem appeared to have some effect, but prior to it, the amount of money due from cardholders—"receivables"—increased steadily, a negative float grew, and the card lost more and more money. In 1959, Reed told the *Wall Street Journal* that the card was "pulling out of the red as fast as expected and should begin to show a profit next month." Reed was not telling the truth. Profitability was nowhere in sight. But having committed himself to the card, he now showed no signs of backing away from it.

Such support was typical of Reed; once something bore the American Express name, he believed in backing it out of what other executives termed "corporate pride." At the same time, his support for the card was unusually tenacious and personal. He appeared to tie it to his own future, as well as the future of the company. He was

287

nearing seventy now and board members, including his supporters and friends, began to suggest to him that he should choose a successor and retire. Reed did not want to go, and he appeared to use the card's struggle as a means of hanging on, an excuse for delay. He had told Mathews and Winter that they were not to tell his likely successor, Howard Clark, what was going on in the card division. Since Clark's office was across the hall from Reed's—their secretaries faced each other—Reed could see any disloyalty. Winter and Mathews felt extremely awkward about this order; they were faced with the choice of disobedience to the boss or denial of vital information to the second-ranking official in the company, the man likely to be chief executive soon. But that seemed to be the point; Reed wanted to forestall the possibility that there would be a next chief executive.

In the midst of his personal struggle, Reed suddenly made what turned out to be his last major decision: he agreed to the resurrection of the international banking organization. The decision about the bank was as simple as the card decision had been complicated. But in the process, Reed reversed a policy that Small had set down and that Reed himself had followed throughout his presidency. In the late 1940s, Frank Groves had brought to Reed the idea of developing an international commercial bank.* Groves told Reed that in places such as Hong Kong and Singapore, there was plenty of money and nothing to spend it on, and Groves wanted to loan money especially for trade. Reed said no; then and throughout his first fifteen years, he consistently limited banking activities just as Small had done. He once responded to a report that one of his managers had earned extra money in foreign-exchange trading by asking nervously, "Is Max within his limits?"

Yet Reed turned aside decades of tradition and did so after a period of discussion lasting only a few days. Reed was in fact persuaded by

---

*Bradford had also suggested developing banking activities but Reed turned him down.

one long memo from Robert Townsend. Townsend, along with two consultants, had studied the company's banking operations for several months, and they concluded that Amexco had vast, untapped potential as an international bank. Of course this was the same conclusion reached by Groves, by Lynde Selden and Albert Wiggin, by Howard Brooks and R. A. Foulks. It was not a view that Reed had shared.

But Townsend tried to convince him anyway. By this time, he appeared to understand Reed better than anyone else in the company and knew how to approach him. In February, he wrote a twelve-page memo urging Reed to expand and revitalize Amexco's banking operations. He put the proposition this way: "By spending $100,000 now for additional experienced banking personnel at New York," he wrote, "we can produce $1,000,000 *more of interest* income in 1960 than is currently blueprinted for 1959." In other words, spend next to nothing and make a great deal. Other executives regarded the argument as extremely simplistic. But it was a Reed proposition if there ever was one, and the chief executive accepted the idea at once. In part, Reed bought the small and cheap argument, but he also appeared to back it as a vote of confidence in Townsend, who was to become head of the new bank. The speed and tone of the debate amazed other executives. As one would later say, "It's an interesting footnote to corporate history that a major decision like that would be made on such a basis."

Though his approach was tailored to the man rather than the business, Townsend was confident he could deliver on the promise of a substantial increase in income. The company had accumulated about $100 million in deposits, mostly through its military banking. But Amexco had a small loan portfolio, and all loans were doled out only after microscopic scrutiny. Townsend planned to loosen and expand loan activity and to make much better use of the vast world office network. Amexco, he noted, still had banking rights in dozens of countries that it hardly used. In some places, like Karachi, Pakistan, Amexco was the *only* U.S. banking operation, but thanks to policies set down by F. P. Small, the office hardly did any banking. *

But Reed's approval did something far more fundamental to American Express than just expand a business line. By endorsing Townsend's plan, Reed had agreed to the first change in the branch-office system since Small had created it. Small had established the system of offices with local chieftains responsible for everything, a structure Reed had maintained. But Townsend's plan would establish a centralized international-banking authority under his own management. † He would hire professional credit managers, professional loan officers, and build a true banking operation. His Overseas Banking Division, as it came to be called, was to be organized along broad geographical lines, with its own officers responsible for all banking activity in a given region. In other words, these officers would take authority over all banking from the branch-office managers. Not surprisingly, local managers opposed the plan, and Harry Hill, onetime manager of 11 Rue Scribe, urged Reed not to rush into this scheme. But Reed ignored him and instructed Townsend to create the banking division. ‡

As Townsend predicted, banking business picked up immediately. By the end of 1960, deposits topped $169 million, and the company's loan portfolio more than doubled to $48.5 million. Whether he made good on his promise to spend $100,000 and make $1 million, no one exactly knew since company accounting procedures could not determine it. (For the one-year period between 1960 and 1961, Townsend claimed a net of $1.047 million.) Whatever the true figure, most agreed it showed that banking could make a significant contribution to Amexco's earnings, although for the next twenty years, Amexco offi-

---

*Townsend also saw new opportunities in international banking because of the birth of the Common Market in Europe.

†Associates of Townsend felt he wanted to create a banking operation mainly to make a challenging job for himself, since he had little chance of succeeding Reed.

‡Because the bank was separated from the branch-office network and system, it remained something of an outcast organization, definitely not part of the "family" Small and Reed had made of the rest of the company.

cials would continue to debate whether the company really needed a bank after all.

If Reed hoped that the addition of banking as well as the card would make him seem the more indispensable, he was mistaken. In fact, these new activities highlighted how archaic and inadequate his system was; the branch-office network, which had trouble sustaining travel and freight, could not manage travel, freight, the card, the TC, Hertz-Amex, and other minor operations. Nor could Reed make decisions on all the little trivial details anymore. Other officials found themselves making decisions because neither they nor Reed had time to go through all the old decision-making procedures. Reed was the victim of his own success; the company had grown literally beyond his control, and now the structure of American Express needed drastic overhaul.

Soon after Reed approved the bank, the board decided on its own to end the Reed era. Some of Reed's friends such as General Lucius Clay tried to persuade him to step down voluntarily. But when he would not, General Clay and a few other directors formed an ad hoc nominating committee to appoint a new chief executive. Eventually, the committee met informally with Reed and told him emphatically that they wanted him to retire, and they asked him to name his own successor. Bradford, at sixty, was too old; Townsend, too brash. Reed named Clark, the man the board wanted as well. Soon after, the board went through the ritual of electing Howard Longstreth Clark, forty-four, president and chief executive.*

Reed and Clarkson were named to powerless jobs as chairmen of the executive and finance committees respectively, but Reed was permitted one remaining trapping of power. The board voted him the right to visit offices of the company throughout the world as a kind of roving eye of the board. This right produced one of the more painful moments in the company's annals.

---

*Ralph "Peck" Owen was elected chairman, but the post did not give him operational authority. Through a change in the bylaws, the chairman was no longer an officer of the company.

In the spring of 1960, Reed and Clark traveled together to Europe. It was to be the swan song of the Reed Circus and the beginning of a new era. Office managers from around Europe assembled at the Ritz in Paris to say farewell to Reed. Clark made a speech, and then Reed stood up. "I want to tell you," he said, "while the Board of Directors has made Howard president—I'm going to be there every day, looking over his shoulder. And you can be sure that I will be responsive to any problems or questions you men may have, and that I will certainly, on behalf of the Directors, be watching this young man."

After this, the trip became a nightmare for the company and probably for Clark. The strain, according to some, was visible on his face. Reed would crook his finger at Clark and issue some kind of command—impossible to follow, impossible to ignore, impossible to contradict without making an ugly scene. In London, Reed gave another demonstration of how he saw his new role. On discovering that the London office had hired a man without his approval, Reed ordered the employee dismissed. When this news was passed on to Clark, Clark knew he had to stop Reed. Back in New York, the two men met. The exchange was brief, and Clark has always been circumspect on what was said, but when Reed left, even he seemed to appreciate that his era was over. Soon after, the board rescinded Reed's right to travel to offices abroad in an official capacity. Reed moved down to the eleventh floor, where he recreated his old office but without the lines of men waiting to see him, without the signs of power. *

Most of the executives around Clark resented Reed's lack of generosity, his unwillingness to do what was right for the company. When circumstances called for magnanimity, he turned petty. Indeed, Reed's maniacal refusal to leave office created such a lasting negative impression among young executives that the event overshadowed in their minds any of his accomplishments. Throughout the 1950s, revenues and profits climbed steadily. In 1959, revenues stood at $69.6 million.

---

*In 1965, the board of directors forced Reed into retirement; he died three years later.

Net income reached $8.4 million and had risen every year since 1948, an enviable record. Assets topped $732 million, TC sales exceeded $1 billion every year, and the company had 383 offices around the world, more than seven times the number it had during the war years. And of course Reed made two of the most crucial decisions in the company's history: the bank and the card.

There were negatives too, of course, and these negatives were very much tied up with Reed's personality. The organization he insisted upon was so archaic that the company had reached the limits of its capacity to grow. But then, perhaps Ralph T. Reed was the kind of man who was likely to leave big problems behind him: he always seemed larger than life, a Grand Pooh-Bah, more controlling, more egotistical, more domineering, more softhearted than any ordinary man.

"INTO
THE TWENTIETH
CENTURY"

10

Howard Clark took office as chief executive of American Express in April 1960.* Less than four years later, the company blundered into the worst scandal in its history, a scandal that threatened the company's existence. As it turned out, Amexco was extremely fortunate that the board had chosen Clark as CEO. The legal and financial ramifications of the scandal required the knowledge of a lawyer and the skill of an accountant to understand them. Clark, who had trained and worked as both, was the only person in the company who could have handled all the mind-numbing details; even his opponents agreed that he was the best man for the job. He took charge of the affair and guided the company out of the disaster.

---

*Clark was the first person in the company's history to have the formal title of chief executive officer.

Clark proved himself to be a decisive leader during the scandal, but at other times, he seemed a man who could not make up his mind. He would hesitate for months over important decisions, and in the end would do nothing, or put his foot down in what seemed the wrong direction. His supporters claimed he vacillated because he could see all sides of an issue; his detractors called him a "Hamlet." His tendency to delay became more pronounced as the years went by and especially marked decisions over the long-term strategic direction of the company. In fact, he never developed a clear strategy, in large part because he would not decide on the very identity of the company he ran. His failure to define American Express would ultimately prove a major problem for his successor.

At the same time, Clark left his successor a company with enormous wealth. Although Clark hesitated over large issues such as strategy and identity, he came into office with an agenda to replace Reed's personal, eccentric management system with a modern organization capable of growth. He implemented his agenda, and his decisions altered the structure and the character of American Express. Before long, Amexco was making more money each year than it had in the first sixty years of this century combined, and it had changed from a modest travel company with a familylike management into a vast institution. Under Clark, Amexco became one of the richest corporations in America and the world.

When Clark took office, he set out to make basic changes at American Express, to introduce what the business world considered normal managerial practices. As one executive told the press, Clark was going to pull the company "resisting and screaming into the twentieth century."

Clark planned to bring Amexco into the modern world gradually. In his first few months, the biggest change at Amexco was one of style rather than substance. Unlike Ralph Reed, Clark did not care for the limelight or his place on the social register and was a private individual who rarely showed his feelings. He seemed the epitome of the postwar executive: unflamboyant, a gray-flannel type with a near-professional-caliber golf game. He possessed, too, a model executive's outlook on the value of technology and the importance of modern business analysis. But Clark proceeded with caution. "I didn't want to upset the organization by making sixty-five changes the first week," he said later.

Clark took pains to maintain a sense of continuity. Pictures from 1960 show him surrounded by top managers from the Reed era: Page, Bradford, Ravndal, and Mathews. At the same time, Clark slowly began boosting the younger men: James Henderson, Hasbrouck B. Miller, Richard F. Blanchard, and others. The process of replacing Reed's men with his own took several years to accomplish, but by the mid-1960s the average age of executives had dropped from over fifty to forty-six.

Although he instituted most changes slowly, Clark began an immediate overhaul of the branch-office system. The creation of the Overseas Banking Division had stripped the branch offices of authority over one business activity, but otherwise the system (called unworkable back in 1919) remained in place. When Clark Winter proposed a reorganization of the office network to Reed in the 1950s, he observed that managers still had to run several business lines at once and could not do it effectively. Howard Clark agreed that if the businesses themselves were going to grow significantly, they were going to have to be managed separately. He authorized the reorganization of offices along product lines, a plan given the bureaucratic label "functionalization." Instead of one manager for all businesses in a geographic area, he designated a manager for travel, a manager for travelers cheques, one for money orders, and so on.

Howard Clark assigned Clark Winter the task of functionalizing the office system, but as part of the CEO's gradual approach, Winter changed the U.S. network only. The foreign branches posed a more difficult problem because managers abroad enjoyed status and perquisites far in excess of their actual authority. In the countries where they were stationed, they received honors from foreign governments, went to embassy parties, rode in chauffeur-driven limousines, and saw to the needs of prominent people. For them, functionalization was another word for demotion; whatever their new titles would be, such as manager of freight forwarding, they would lose a great deal of status in the process. Any attempt to introduce functionalization was likely to meet opposition, even open hostility, and perhaps inflict an organizational trauma, which Howard Clark feared. Clark intended to reorganize the foreign network eventually, but the U.S. offices posed fewer dilemmas. Domestic office managers did not enjoy much social status, and so did not have the same automatic resistance to change.* As a result, the reorganization went forward with a minimum of discord; Winter completed the task in about a year and a half.

Howard Clark made other changes to bring the company into the twentieth century: he altered compensation plans, introduced computers and high-tech telecommunications systems, and created both a planning department and a marketing department. † But during Clark's early years, the most visible changes at Amexco occurred in the company's advertising. Initially, Clark did not place a high priority on advertising, but eventually mass-market advertising became a symbol of his era. He personally made a decision to adopt a new logo, a simple blue strip—later a blue box—with the American Express name, and in 1962, he changed advertising agencies from Benton & Bowles to Ogilvy, Benson & Mather. Ogilvy was astounded to see how underpromoted the company had been all through the years; in 1960, its ad budget was only about $1 million. But Clark boosted advertising expenditures every year thereafter, and Ogilvy made the most of Amexco's money. The agency developed for Clark a campaign based on the slogan, "The company for people who travel," the first slick, modern ad campaign in the company's history.

---

*Winter sought to provide office managers with jobs suitable to their interests. In some cases, he let them pick their assignments and even the territory they preferred.

†Clark also gave autonomy and responsibility to those who ran the company's divisions. The people appointed to run travel, the TC, and so on were given more authority over budgeting, advertising, and accounting. Previously staff offices handled those functions for the entire company. Under Reed, accounting, especially, was centralized in the comptroller's office.

297

The public soon began to identify the company with its advertising, a process that grew more pronounced in the years that followed. Indeed, Amexco developed a reputation as one of the most persistent and aggressive advertisers in America.

Although Amexco successfully advertised itself as a company for travelers, Clark actually broadened its image. While Small and Reed had tried to convince the world that Amexco was just the world's biggest travel agent, Clark acknowledged that it was a financial company as well. He did not actually *define* it as a financial company, but from the time he took office, he displayed far more candor about Amexco than his two predecessors. In a *Business Week* profile in 1960, written with the company's cooperation, Amexco was described as a "unique type of financial hybrid," which made most of its money from investments. The article emphasized the financial side as well by featuring the company's money managers, Charles A. Cuccinello and Robert Stillson, and the head of the banking division, Robert Townsend. Of course, the magazine referred to travel along with the company's other "non-financial activities," such as freight, warehousing, and Hertz–American Express International. But through this story, readers could finally understand that the float on the TC paid the bills at American Express.

This relative candor with the outside world was matched by an internal candor. Through an accounting system that lumped all business results together, Reed had obscured what made money and what did not. Clark altered the accounting system, and in the process, he made possible an honest assessment of each of Amexco's businesses. From this point on, managers were going to have to set profit objectives and try to meet them—a standard managerial practice unheard of to this point at American Express. In most cases, Clark demanded at least 10 percent growth a year, and those businesses that did not perform might be eliminated, period. "We intend," he warned European managers in 1960, "to re-examine certain services. There is the possibility of instituting or increasing changes, or of discontinuing categories of business that cannot be made profitable."

There was now an honest admission that travel was a loser; Clark even confessed this fact to the press, although he exempted travel from possible elimination because of its tie to the TC. Since sales of the TC now topped $2 billion annually, Clark could not consider anything that might undercut it. But instead of ignoring or denying the losses in travel as Reed had done, he began an intensive effort to reverse them. For his entire term in office, he and senior staff would puzzle over ideas to make travel profitable. None would ever work.

Other units had no such exemption, and Clark's decree endangered several businesses, especially the American Express Card. Though Clark told *Business Week* that the company was "in the credit card business to stay—and at a profit," he was not convinced that Amexco could ever achieve that goal. Less than a year after he came into office, Clark and other officials decided the time had come to think about getting out of the card business.

In 1960, the card looked like a horrible mistake. Losses had continued to grow. No one knew exactly how much the company had lost because Reed's system of centralized accounting disguised the results. But senior executives estimated that the losses had reached at least $10 million by this time, with no end in sight to the red ink. Michael Lively, the head of the card operation, believed better times lay ahead. But in the meantime, Clark, the young chief executive, had the unenviable task of going before the board of directors month after month to explain that the losses continued.

Clark began to consider the possibility of selling the card altogether. For the better part of a year, he discussed it with his staff. In the fall of 1961, Clark finally made up his mind: he would get rid of the card.

Clark pursued an old plan, a merger with Diners' Club.* The deal, supported by Robert Townsend, would have given Amexco a minority

---

*Diners' Club, too, had a lot to gain from a merger. Though still the preeminent card, it had lowered its discount rate and its credit standards to compete with the American Express Card and Hilton Hotels' Carte Blanche card, and its profit margins had fallen considerably.

role in a combined operation.* Though such a move would have been one of the greatest blunders in business history, it made considerable sense at the time. The American Express Card operation did not work; Diners' Club, though hardly a model organization, did. Through a deal with Diners' Club, Amexco could get out of a losing business and start to make some money. Clark decided to try to make a deal.

The two companies engaged in preliminary talks early in 1961. But initial discussions broke off largely because of continued uncertainty among Amexco officials. Without a merger, however, Clark still faced the problem of a division that was seriously draining the company's treasury, and in the spring of 1961, he decided to find a new person to run the card division. He lacked any candidates inside the company, so he looked outside and picked George W. Waters, forty-five, formerly the chief operating officer of a retail and grocery chain. Waters, who had lost his job as a result of a merger, was by his own reckoning "the most disqualified person you could ever have to fill the job of general manager of the card division. I was not in the credit business, I was not in the travel business, I was not in the financial business." But actually, Waters did bring some important qualifications to the position. He had extensive managerial experience, and experience in marketing and data processing, both of which were crucial to the card business. Waters also possessed a large ego and a strong will. He was the kind of individual who would institute change immediately and demand high performance from his staff, a manager who would either save the card or kill it quickly. At this point, a quick death probably seemed a better alternative to the slow hemorrhage the card was undergoing.

While Waters was considering the job, Clark told him next to nothing about the state of the card operation. To get some idea of the

---

*Amexco has portrayed Townsend as the force pushing Clark to make this horrible mistake. Townsend was for a merger, but apparently so was Clark. It is also unclear whether Townsend had very much influence with Clark. The two men did not agree on many things, including the pace of change, and Townsend soon left Amexco to head Avis, the number-two car-rental company.

business, Waters studied the publicly available reports on credit cards generally. He noted two points in particular. One was the phenomenal growth rate of the American Express Card, on the order of 25 percent compounded per year. ("I never heard of such a thing," he said.) Also, based on results from Diners' Club, he estimated Amexco's card division should be producing profits of about $5 million per year. Waters went back to see Clark for a final interview. He told Amexco's CEO that he welcomed the opportunity to run the card division, but he insisted on three conditions. He wanted assurance that Amexco was committed to staying in the business; Clark said yes. He needed a pledge, too, that Amexco was committed to providing money and other resources for the business; Clark once more agreed. And third, Waters insisted that he have full authority and responsibility for the division; if he could not do the job, he would get out, but he had to try it his way. When Clark accepted that condition as well, Waters signed on as the new manager of the card division. It was only then that he learned the truth about the American Express Card: that his job was to rescue a troubled operation.

He had barely settled into his office, however, when Amexco once again began to think of ways to separate itself from the credit-card business. This time the third major card company, Hilton Hotels, which had launched its Carte Blanche card soon after Amexco had launched its card, brought a proposal to Clark. Hilton, like Amexco, had tried earlier in the year to negotiate a deal with Diners' Club. When those talks fell through, it approached American Express. Carte Blanche officials suggested the two companies, Hilton and American Express, spin off their card divisions into one separate company. This way they could join the strengths of the two operations and benefit from economies of scale.

Clark told Waters to study the proposal, and Waters concluded it was a terrible idea. "They were in worse shape than we were," he recalled. He called the two operations "two indigestions, two negatives," and he noted to Clark that the "only place where two negatives make a positive is algebra and this is not algebra, this is business." He told Clark, however, that a merger with Diners' Club might make sense because that organization was profitable.

Clark took his advice, broke off talks with Carte Blanche, and resumed them with Diners' Club. In the fall of 1961, senior executives of the two companies met and made a serious effort to reach an agreement. They exchanged confidential information, worked on the outlines of a merger pact, and were not far from closing a deal. Amexco's board approved a merger in principle, with three members voting against: Reed, Clarkson and N. F. Page.

Though Waters had to some extent rekindled the idea of an Amexco–Diners' Club merger, he was dismayed when he heard the news. He pronounced himself completely opposed to an agreement. But Waters had just arrived, and how could Clark go by the opinion of a man who did not really *know* how much trouble the card had been for four years? Waters tried enlisting supporters among Amexco executives to head off the merger, but that did not help. Clark had decided to make the deal; the board had agreed; most senior managers agreed. There were only the details to work out.

But then, abruptly, Clark was forced to reverse himself. Amexco had consulted with leading antitrust attorneys, and they said emphatically that the merger could not take place. Amexco and Diners' Club could have merged in 1956 or 1957; Amexco had no card then. Now a merger between the two would create an overwhelmingly dominant company in what had become a highly competitive industry. Amexco decided not to test that opinion. On November 22, 1961, the *Wall Street Journal* reported that talks between American Express and Diners' Club had broken off; they would not be resumed.

No one was happier than George Waters. He had already started to attack the problems in the division. He overhauled the accounting system, tried to bring the correspondence up to date, and instituted tough credit policies. He gave orders that when a payment was thirty days overdue, the company would dun a cardholder. (Previously Amexco waited ninety days before it began to press for payment.) Waters quickly took chronic late-payers off the membership rolls and made it tougher for people to qualify for the card. To generate more revenue, he raised the card fee from $6 to $8, and soon after that to $10. But so valued had Amexco's card become that the number of cardholders continued to rise even as the number of bad debts fell dramatically. Waters also managed to raise the discount rate with a minimum of protest from service establishments. Employing marketing concepts he had learned in the retail business, he instituted a cooperative advertising program, taking a percentage of his advertising budget to help plug those companies that accepted the card. The number of service establishments rose steadily, reaching 82,000 in 1962.

Waters's efforts produced results in a year. Clark happily reported at the end of that year that the card had made a small profit, its first profit ever. Charge volume rose 24 percent over the previous year, and the number of cardholders reached 900,000. Because of the turnaround in the card (because it was now adding a small amount instead of significantly draining the company's resources), Amexco recorded profits overall of more than $10 million for the first time in decades.* By 1967, card volume reached $1.1 billion, the number of cardholders more than 2 million, and profits from the card alone $6.5 million. By then, the American Express Card had attained importance equal to that of the American Express TC.† Indeed, it would supplant travel in the public mind as Amexco's single most identifiable product.

Once he had addressed the problems of the card, Clark focused his attention on some of the company's other marginal or losing operations, and he began a process of fiddling with the products and services of the company that was to last to the end of his tenure as CEO. For more than fifteen years, he added, subtracted, and altered businesses,

---

*Waters made an important breakthrough when he signed up the airlines to take the card. He negotiated unsuccessfully with TWA for a time, but had better luck with American Airlines. After he made the deal, he recalled, "we had a problem holding the others off."

†Waters also gave the card a new image, changing its color from purple to green.

seeking operations that could both meet his profit and growth goals, and that also, in some undefined way, *fit* with the rest of the company. It was a process that never had a clear focus and led mostly to dead ends.

Initially, he reviewed four company operations which were marginally profitable: first, an industrial-financing company in Europe, an operation started in 1960 and owned jointly with CIT Financial Corp.; second, Wells Fargo armored cars, in which Amexco had a stake of a little more than 60 percent; third, the European car-rental operation, Hertz–American Express International (HAEI); and finally, field warehousing. Clark decided to get out of the joint venture with CIT, to acquire all or most of the shares of the armored-car service, and he weighed the options of either getting out of the car-rental operation or buying all of the Hertz Corporation. The joint company, HAEI, was profitable and growing, but the arrangement was unsatisfactory to Amexco. It owned 49 percent, Hertz 51 percent; that meant American Express had a large stake, but little authority. In 1962, Clark investigated the option of selling Amexco's stake in HAEI. He asked Lehman Brothers about a possible public offering of HAEI stock, but even though the investment bankers thought the offering would go well, the idea died.

By early 1963, he contemplated an entirely different course—what Townsend had proposed in 1957. Lehman Brothers prepared a memo for both Clark and Hertz CEO Leon Greenebaum for "a possible merger" of Hertz into Amexco. Lehman Brothers thought it would be a terrific combination and pushed it strongly. Clark asked Ogilvy, Benson & Mather for its views, and Amexco's advertising agency gave "an enthusiastic 'yes' " to the idea. By the time Clark submitted a proposal to the executive committee of American Express, he was largely in favor of a deal as well. He noted the strong marketing fit between the companies for "people who travel." Yet Clark displayed one sign of uncertainty: he would only pursue the deal, he said, if he had the board's approval. "I hesitate to start [the process toward a merger]," he wrote, "if there is opposition on the part of the Directors." At the EC meeting and after, Clark found that there was indeed opposition. Members of the committee expressed concern about the deal and about Hertz itself. Some felt that Hertz had not grown very much, a charge Clark tried to dispute. But within a week, he seemed ready to shelve the plan and suggested an alternative: to buy out Hertz–American Express International. But that idea also went nowhere, and by the middle of 1963, Clark had not come to any final decision on HAEI.*

Meanwhile, he had turned to the last of the four marginal operations: field warehousing. But Clark took it in hand too late to prevent a major scandal in the field warehousing subsidiary, which exploded before the end of 1963. The scandal would bring Amexco to the brink of insolvency; it was completely unexpected, unforeseen, and in many ways unbelievable. It seemed impossible to executives of the company and the financial world as a whole that a business which added next to nothing to the company's profits could nearly topple a 113-year-old institution. But it was possible, paradoxically, *because* the operation was insignificant to the company's profits. The subsidiary was not carefully supervised; it was in fact practically ignored by the parent. Nevertheless, if the operation was to remain a part of the company, the executives who ran and sponsored warehousing needed to prove that they could create a profitable enterprise and contribute to Amexco as a whole. They fell victim to fraud or, more accurately, to the illusion of their own success. The men who allowed the scandal to blow up destroyed their careers. But while the scandal threatened to destroy Amexco as well, it had a perverse effect on the company: in the end, it actually strengthened American Express.

Despite Reed's boundless enthusiasm and optimism, field warehousing had never been anything more (or less) than a nuisance. Hasbrouck B. Miller, Reed's assistant, later company secretary and

---

*That summer relations between the partners hit a new low after Hertz founder Walter Jacobs was quoted in the press as saying he regretted the partnership with Amexco. Clark wrote him a testy letter: "I was sorry to note . . . that you had reservations about the value to Hertz of American Express' interest in our joint company. Naturally, we feel that without the contributions we have made including financial assistance, the venture would not be so far along today as it is. Hopefully, you will reconsider sometime."

executive VP under Clark, once referred to this subsidiary as a "net distraction without a future." From 1944 through 1962, the American Express Field Warehousing Corporation (AEFW) lost money in nine years and made money in ten, but still showed a cumulative net loss. The numbers were always very small; neither profits nor losses in any one year ever exceeded $101,000. In 1952, the ledger showed the subsidiary $106 in the red; five years later, it posted a grand $343 profit. Even though Amexco was then hardly the giant it later became, these were meaningless sums.

On top of this, a number of senior executives disliked the business. Even after his retirement, Howard Smith would disparage the warehousing business over lunch with his friend N. F. Page—nominally the head of AEFW as well as a senior VP of the parent company. Clarkson never cared for the warehousing business either, nor did Howard Clark. Even Page, himself, at times doubted the subsidiary could ever be profitable. AEFW had only two strong boosters: Donald Miller (no relation to H. B. Miller), a lawyer who became the operating head of AEFW in the 1950s; and Ralph Reed. Miller reported to Page who reported to Reed. After a while, no one else even knew what was going on in AEFW. Miller promised Reed he could make AEFW profitable, and Reed backed him. Reed would never consider getting rid of warehousing. As Miller acknowledged, "If it had not been for Reed, Warehousing would have been sold long ago."*

After 1960, of course, Clark had the opportunity to get rid of the subsidiary, if he wanted to, but he ignored it during his first couple of years. It was, after all, just a minor nuisance; there were more important matters to worry about, such as the card. Indeed, AEFW was, as Donald Miller promised, making some money. In 1959, it posted its best year ever: a net of $98,871. Though profits slipped in 1960 to only $30,000, it still produced enough black ink so that Clark had no reason to act quickly.

---

*Amexco had offers to sell AEFW at least as early as 1949, but Reed had rejected them.

But, in this case, appearances deceived everyone, including Clark and other senior executives. From 1960 on, there were warnings of trouble, but no one quite believed them. Amexco's management instead preferred to accept the statements of net income, the assurances of Donald Miller, and the theory that, even if something were wrong at AEFW, it could not be very bad because this business was so insignificant. But the profits were illusory.

AEFW had about 500 accounts by the late 1950s, but all the profit came from two—Freezer House Corp. and Allied Crude Vegetable Oil Refining Corporation, most especially the latter. Both companies were controlled by the same man: Anthony "Tino" DeAngelis. The story of DeAngelis was described in full by journalist Norman C. Miller (no relation to either H.B. or Donald Miller) in a book he wrote in 1965. The man Miller called "tubby little Tino" had an ego and ambition that matched his girth. A poor boy, Tino had worked his way up the ladder from butcher to head of several companies, the most important of which was Allied Crude, a major firm in the vegetable-oil business. DeAngelis had even higher hopes for himself. He wanted to be the biggest man in the business, the "salad oil king." To get there, he had to have financing, but there he had a problem. Along the way to the top, he had experienced a few bumps: a bankruptcy, trouble with the IRS, the kinds of problems that made lenders wary, the kinds of problems that required the help of a field-warehousing organization.

In 1957, less than a year after Allied came into being, Tino's cousin, Michael DeAngelis (one of seven relatives on Tino's payroll), called Donald Miller. Miller was taken on a tour of Allied's tank farm, a forest of old oil storage tanks in Bayonne, New Jersey. Miller seemed to like what he saw, but before he took the account, he inquired about Tino's credit history with Dun & Bradstreet. He heard then about the bankruptcy and the tax problems, but Miller also learned that leading exporters had put their credit on the line for Allied. If Allied was good enough for them, he reasoned, it was good enough for AEFW. (Later, everyone else assumed that if Allied was good enough for Amexco, it had to be all right.) By July 1957, Miller informed the board of AEFW that he was taking on the Allied account, which he predicted, "may assume major proportions in time to come."

Though Miller initially reported inventory worth about $100,000, he knew DeAngelis had plans to use AEFW inventory receipts to borrow far more than that from the banks and leading commodity-trading companies. Miller set a credit limit of $900,000. If he had picked $1 million, he would have needed approval from AEFW's board, but this way, Miller avoided any debate.*

The warehouse account was set up in the usual way. Amexco warehousing officials went down to the Bayonne facility and segregated a certain amount of inventory, which became the "AEFW Warehouse." Then they hired some Allied men to act as custodians, subject to supervision and periodic visits from AEFW officials. This was all standard operating procedure, but this was not the standard company. DeAngelis was, to use Norman Miller's characterization, more a "padrone" to his people than a mere employer; they, more loyal retainers than employees. Tino treated them well. Thomas F. Clarkin, for example, was one of the custodians hired by Amexco. AEFW paid him $500 per month, but Tino paid him $400 per *week* as a messenger. This was not a case of divided loyalties. Loyalties were clear; they belonged to Tino.

Amexco could see nothing amiss, and officials were delighted with the account. Page wrote in 1959, "The crude oil account turned in $12,000 in February with damn little expense. That's what we need more of." In fact, this account was not simply profitable. Because of it alone, AEFW could report positive results. "You can easily see," Page added, "where we could be if something happened to the account." Miller, whose job depended ultimately on his ability to make AEFW successful, agreed on the importance of the Allied account. From the outset, he and his men wanted to please Tino DeAngelis lest he take his business elsewhere.

---

*AEFW was an incorporated subsidiary of Amexco with its own board of directors, including Clarkson, who opposed the field-warehousing operation.

This was backwards of course; Tino needed American Express more than American Express needed Tino, and a few people at 65 Broadway noted that fact. Michael W. Casserly, an assistant secretary of AEFW, wrote in 1958, "Without us they have nothing." Casserly also spotted dangers connected to the Allied account. No one at Amexco, he realized, knew enough about vegetable oils to assess the value of the inventory accurately. He called for testing of the oils by qualified chemists and urged that an independent custodian—not an Allied employee—be placed permanently on the scene.

Casserly also pointed out a means of fraud at the Bayonne tank farm. He had discovered that there was a network of underground pipes connecting the tanks. To confound the inspectors, oil could be piped secretly from one tank to the other. This did not seem likely since the pipes appeared to be closed, but as Casserly noted, "It would take a qualified engineer to determine whether one lock on each tank is sufficient to actually lock up a tank because of the underground system." Donald Miller took no action. Already, Tino had become a big account; by the end of 1958, AEFW had given him receipts on which he could borrow of $3.7 million, and he was paying Amexco $150,000 a year in storage fees.

The account grew nicely. In early 1960, at the time Reed finally stepped down, Miller told the AEFW board that the warehousing unit had 65 million pounds of oil in its care at Allied, worth about $6.5 million. (The price of soybean oil—most of the inventory—fluctuated, but averaged about 10 cents a pound.) In some months, however, turnover had a value as high as $17 million. The size of the account began to make some of the bankers who had loaned money on Amexco's receipts nervous. A banker from Continental Illinois Bank & Trust called on AEFW officials one day and asked, given the size of the Allied account, might it not be a good idea to have an independent AEFW custodian at the scene? Thomas J. McLarney, the AEFW inspector who had charge of the Bayonne tank farm, thanked the banker for his visit but politely said no.

Two months later, though, Amexco received an ominous and mysterious telephone call. The caller, who identified himself only as "Taylor," told Miller that Tino was conducting a massive fraud. "Taylor" claimed he worked the night shift at the Bayonne tank farm, and he was willing to give details of the scam but wanted a $5,000 payoff. Although Amexco refused to give "Taylor" the money, he revealed a number of details anyway. He said that Tino had rigged the tanks by putting tubes inside them directly underneath openings; the tubes contained oil, but the rest of the tanks were filled with water. "Taylor" even gave Miller the number of one of the tanks, 6006; this tank was supposed to hold millions of pounds of oil, but "Taylor" said it held mostly water.

Miller discussed "Taylor's" charges with top officials of AEFW, including Page; David H. Coffman, number-two man in operations; Fred H. Turner, Jr., supervising inspector; and Thomas McLarney. Miller thought that "Taylor" was probably a "nut," but he expressed alarm and so did Page. A cautious New Englander, Page called for a new inspection, even though one had taken place a little more than a week before, and he suggested it was time for an independent custodian at Bayonne. Turner, however, defended Tino. The oil business was "tough and not always scrupulous," he said, and he thought therefore that "Taylor" was a competitor trying to ruin DeAngelis.*

Still, AEFW people led by Page were concerned enough to spring an unannounced inspection on Allied. On June 4, 1960, Turner, McLarney, and two others descended on Bayonne and announced that an inspection was about to begin. Allied may have gotten advance word; McLarney was reputed to be a "chatterer," who was friendly with Allied people, and he could have tipped them off inadvertently. Nevertheless, the inspectors found cause for alarm. Several of the tanks contained too much water. In one twenty-four-foot tank, there was eight feet of water. The water limit was supposed to be six *inches*.

---

*Turner's line of argument was one promoted by Tino and clearly AEFW officials accepted it. In fact, they once asked Tino if they could see his balance sheet, but he refused and persuaded them that it was a closely guarded competitive secret. Amexco did not press him.

The water concerned officials because, as McLarney wrote, if there was so much water "it had to have been put in the tank by someone." But as the inspection progressed over the next week, inspectors' fears were allayed. Yes, there was too much water, but the inspection of the tanks showed that there was still enough oil to cover outstanding receipts, with a good margin to spare. Or so it seemed. But in fact, Amexco handled the inspection poorly; AEFW officials even allowed Tino's men to provide some of the tank readings.

Meanwhile, Tino reacted to the inspection with indignation. On June 7, he had cousin Michael deliver a letter to Miller. Tino was upset, Michael reported orally, and had decided to terminate his warehousing contract with American Express. It was Miller's turn to be upset. Though he didn't apologize, he told Michael, "Well, this is something we had to do and that's why we did it. We are not anxious to terminate the relationship with you." Tino pretended to be consoled by this expression of goodwill, and he agreed to let AEFW continue helping him borrow money. He even made a concession: Amexco could station one of its own employees at Bayonne as an independent custodian. Thomas McLarney was given the job.

Tino had, however, begun what "Taylor" had alleged: a massive fraud. In 1960, DeAngelis had tried and failed to win a major contract with the Spanish government, and that attempt cost him over $2 million in out-of-pocket expenses. It was a loss that left him in need of money, and he decided he could get it by duping AEFW.

In November, Amexco received a new set of mystery calls. A man who called himself an "associate of Taylor's" phoned Howard Clark. The call was routed, however, to Hasbrouck B. Miller, who was at the time Clark's assistant. When the caller heard the last name, he demanded first to know if H.B. was related to Donald and spoke only when he was assured H.B. was not. "Taylor's associate" then explained why he would not talk to Donald or his kin: D. Miller had blown the June inspection. The inspection was considered a "joke" in the whole industry, "Taylor's associate" said. He charged that DeAngelis knew the "time, place and nature of the inspection" and had fooled the AEFW men completely. To expose the fraud, "Taylor's associate" recommended six steps, including hiring a team of outside surveyors "who cannot be compromised" to go over the Bayonne tank farm from one end to the other.

H. B. Miller decided that the caller was rational and knew "exactly what he was talking about." He contacted Page and they discussed whether the company should conduct an investigation without Donald Miller's knowledge. But they concluded that Donald Miller was the only person in the company who knew how to set up such an investigation.* As a result, H. B. Miller called Donald and told him about "Taylor's associate." Donald was concerned—concerned about keeping Allied's business. He warned that "if DeAngelis were upset again, the account might be lost." So far from launching an investigation, D. Miller told DeAngelis about the latest calls, compromising even the possibility of a new investigation.

The charges of fraud at the Bayonne tank farm to date were unproven, but D. Miller (H.B. had no further involvement with the warehousing issue after this) made no real effort to learn the facts after June 1960. He and other AEFW officials had developed tunnel vision that got more and more focused on the black ink on the bottom line. This was not greed; the amounts were too small. But as long as the operation appeared profitable, AEFW had some justification for being—all the more important in the era of a new chief executive who made profitability the main criterion for existence.

McLarney was now out in Bayonne keeping an eye on things, and he reported good news back to 65 Broadway. Inventory kept rising, and since storage fees were based on the value of inventory, so was Amexco's income. The account so pleased company officials that they offered to help Tino's business, arranging, for example, for DeAngelis to meet

---

*H. B. Miller and Page consulted Amexco's inspectors office, the unit F. P. Small had created to stop TC counterfeits and fraud. The inspectors agreed that among company officials only Donald Miller knew how to conduct a warehousing investigation.

officials of Container Corp. and Continental Baking Corp. McLarney undertook periodic inspections and filed reports back to New York. But it was later shown that his inspections were entirely predictable and easy for Allied to fix. Above all, McLarney continued to assign Tino's men the job of reading the tank levels. As one admitted later, they would drop a weighted tape into a tank with a loud splash and then they would call out a totally fictitious figure. "[AEFW's inspectors would] never check on any one of us."

At the same time, McLarney was growing closer and closer to the people in Tino's circle. He had regular Friday lunches with Allied officials and made social calls at the home of Tino's brother-in-law, Leo Bracconeri. Also, he participated in investment pools with Allied employees, one of which bought stock in a company controlled by Tino. Miller and Turner knew about the stock purchase; on McLarney's advice, they had bought it, too.

At the tank farm, inventories rose at a spectacular rate—from 165 million pounds in March 1962, to over 300 million pounds by July, to nearly a half-billion pounds in September. By November, AEFW had issued receipts on more than 400 million pounds, $40 million of borrowing power. Through those receipts Tino had acquired money from the leading banks in the country: Bank of America, Bankers Trust, Chase Manhattan, Chemical Bank, Continental Illinois, Irving Trust, First National City Bank of New York, and many others.

The pace of inventory growth showed just how little Tino feared from his AEFW overseers. In one period in September, McLarney recorded inventory changes of more than 100 million pounds a week. Experts later said that it would have been impossible for such large quantities to have been moved in and out of the tank farm so quickly. As court papers would point out, "Perhaps weekly inventory fluctuation of over 100 million pounds were of such magnitude as to raise a duty of inquiry." None was raised. The high levels of inventory did cause some concern at AEFW. Officials worried what might happen in the event of a precipitous drop in oil prices. In that event, Allied could go bankrupt, and the value of oil in the tanks could drop below that of the outstanding warehouse receipts. Given the reported size of the inventory, each drop of one cent a pound meant a loss to Allied of four or five million dollars. If the price of oil fell a few cents, Allied might be forced out of business, and Amexco could be facing a horde of angry creditors. AEFW decided to increase its insurance.

Early in 1963, Howard Clark finally turned his attention to the warehousing subsidiary and reviewed its performance over the years. He concluded that on the whole it was not worth keeping. The company had over 400 accounts, and most of them produced a net loss each year. Also, the business was a nuisance; Amexco had become involved in many small lawsuits over the valuation and handling of inventories. So, when the Lawrence Warehousing Company offered to buy AEFW, one Amexco official noted, "Pass before they change their mind."

Clark agreed to sell all of AEFW for $1.1 million—all except for two accounts: Tino DeAngelis's Freezer House and Allied Crude. Clark was not convinced that hanging on to any part of AEFW was a good idea, but he was persuaded for the time being to retain a warehousing operation. Donald Miller argued that American Express could make $250,000 a year without much effort, and he added, "We have never had a shortage at this account [Allied]. The account has never falsely represented any fact or circumstances to us." Miller won the argument, and in May 1963, Amexco incorporated a new field-warehousing company to handle Tino's business only: American Express Warehousing Limited (just called "Limited"), with initial capital of $100,000 and Donald Miller, president.

A month before this, however, inventories of soybean oil at Bayonne topped 850 million pounds, and AEFW had verified and issued receipts for 804 million. Had anyone taken the trouble to look, he would have discovered that this amount of soybean oil exceeded the quantity the U.S. Census Bureau said existed in the entire country! In other words, the new warehouse subsidiary had assumed responsibility for oil that could not possibly have existed, oil worth many times Limited's capital. As the courts would point out later, the new warehouse sub-

314

sidiary was "hopelessly insolvent from the moment of its creation."

Though Clark had agreed to create Limited, he had not come to a final decision about field-warehousing operations, and he puzzled over what to do next. He asked two of his top aides, VPs Richard Blanchard and George T. Pfifer, for their views on the future of Limited. Blanchard had questions about the Allied account, but he said only that the matter should be decided finally "on a business basis, that is return vs. risk." But Pfifer estimated the company's exposure to be $60 million at Allied and concluded, "I do not believe that a risk this size is justified by the earning potential of approximately $100,000 per year after taxes on income." Others offered a different counsel. N. F. Page argued that so far from having a huge risk, Amexco had virtually none. "Our only risk is that of dishonest operations we failed to detect and it is inconceivable that this could reach proportions greater than our insurance coverage."

Clark still did not make a decision, and over the next few months, he continued to weigh his options. In the summer, he met with Blanchard and Page and proposed a review of the accounts and a visit to Tino's operations in New Jersey. This was arranged, and on a hot day in July (while Donald Miller was in Europe), Clark, Page, Pfifer, Turner, and Amexco assistant secretary Richard J. Waag crossed the Hudson River and paid calls on Freezer House and the Bayonne tank farm. Waag reported later that "it was quite impressive." Clark had a chat with Tino and even scrambled up on one of the tanks. When he left, he told DeAngelis (as Waag put it), "If there was anything that we could do for him to please let us know."

But at the same time, he remained concerned about the possible risks and worried about the adequacy of audit procedures. He ordered a review of the "internal controls and systems" of the warehouse division both by Amexco staff and by Haskin & Sells. The giant accounting firm found deficiencies but concluded that on the whole those controls were "satisfactory." Again, Clark appeared satisfied and content to hang on to field warehousing.

Yet a month later, Clark made up his mind finally to get out of warehousing, a decision he reached more on moral than business grounds.* What changed his mind was his belief that senior warehousing officials had been compromised. In September, Clark learned that Miller owned shares in one of Tino's companies; that news decided the matter for Clark. At a subsequent officers' conference, according to Miller's account, Clark lectured officials for half an hour about the "perils" of such stock ownership, and later, privately, he asked Waag if the stock might have been a bribe. Miller felt aggrieved by it all. He defended himself first by saying he had not hidden anything, that he had reported his ownership of the stock, and he presented proof that he had indeed bought the stock. But then he told Waag, "If Clark thinks I am dishonest, he can have my resignation immediately." Five days later, Miller learned that his resignation had been accepted. McLarney and Turner, who also had stock in Tino's company, were sacked, and Amexco's last warehousing accounts were sold to Lawrence, effective December 1963.† Amexco informed Tino that, because it was leaving the business, it could no longer issue warehouse receipts. Amexco would honor the old receipts of course, but until Lawrence filled the gap about two months later, he would have to make do.

Tino appeared gracious about it, but the news came at a rough time. DeAngelis's dreams had grown more grandiose than ever, and he had decided to use his easy warehouse receipt money to corner the futures markets in both soy and cottonseed oils. He bought thousands of bean-oil contracts and had established huge accounts at major commodity brokerage firms using American Express warehouse receipts, putting several of the firms at risk of insolvency in the process. But

---

*Reportedly Clark also had become alarmed at the size of the Allied account. The account that Pfifer called an unacceptable risk at $60 million had swelled to more than $80 million by September.

†The board meeting to authorize the sale did not go smoothly. Reed and Clarkson supported Miller; Reed claimed that Miller had reported his stock purchase, and therefore said Clark was making a mistake. Clark was not present at the meeting, but the directors finally supported him.

Tino had his own worries. The contracts he had already bought meant that he had a continuing need of cash since any drop in oil prices would mean millions of dollars in margin calls that had to be answered within twenty-four hours. Indeed, the only way he could keep prices up was to keep buying contracts, which also meant more money. His plan was irrational; the exchanges would never have allowed a corner. But his immediate concern was cash.* Ever resourceful, Tino decided that if American Express would not give him receipts, he would get them another way. He took a pad of receipts from the desk of the Amexco custodian and filled them in himself.

On November 15, a joint inspection by American Express and Lawrence indicated no problems at the tank farm. In fact, American Express remained ignorant of Tino's fraud until the week of November 18. Tino had come to the limit of his resources, and even through fraud, he could no longer acquire enough cash. He filed for bankruptcy. For his part in the scheme, DeAngelis headed for jail; he was sentenced to twenty years and served seven; he became a bit of a media folk hero for having swindled so many big people. In the process, he destroyed or crippled three brokerage firms, caused several bankruptcies besides his own, and pushed Amexco into its worst crisis in 113 years.

American Express officials learned of the bankruptcy on Tuesday, November 19. They were concerned but not alarmed. As long as enough oil existed to cover the receipts, Amexco had discharged its responsibility. But when Richard Waag went out to the tank farm, he realized that "there was a lot of oil missing."

How much? He could not say, nor could anyone else. At first, the shortages seemed improbable. After all, the inspection the week before found 900 million pounds of oil at the tank farm, or so everyone

---

*Tino had found two other sources of cash: a second warehousing company, Harbor Tank Storage, and a check kiting scheme. Combined, these gave him a few million, but that was not enough money to keep his swindle going.

thought. At Amexco, the shortages made officials uneasy but as Clark told the press, "If . . . there were some errors, we would be covered by insurance." Indeed, the company had $30 million in coverage, enough to make up for 300 million pounds of missing oil.

But as the days passed, Amexco gradually woke up to a nightmare. The enormity of the affair—called "Salad Oil" in the press, "Soybean" at Amexco—became apparent by the end of the first week. On Thursday, the Bunge Corporation, a leading export firm that did a lot of business with Tino, filed suit against American Express for $15 million. On Saturday, lawyers for the brokerage firm of Ira Haupt talked their way into the Bayonne tank farm; they spoke to the Amexco men on the scene and demanded payment on the receipts held by Haupt. Unless they received payment, the attorneys explained, the brokerage firm would go bankrupt. The Amexco officials examined the receipts, $18 million of them, and told the lawyers that all of the receipts were forgeries.

At American Express there was shock—a feeling made all the more acute by the assassination of President John Kennedy on the Friday after Tino filed for bankruptcy. And the news for the company continued to worsen. Over the weekend, independent surveys showed that *most* of the oil was missing. The following Tuesday, a New Jersey judge ordered Amexco to find 160 million pounds; it was not there. Only about 80 million pounds of oil existed at the tank farm. On the other hand, receipts, counting the forged ones, attested to more than 1.4 *billion* pounds. Amexco's potential liability? As much as $150 million. As Clark said privately, it was as if a bomb had exploded at 65 Broadway.

The liabilities of the affair were enormous, but who was responsible for them? No one knew. Tino was not a factor; he had nothing left. Was Amexco then responsible? Or the banks that held the loans? Or the insurance companies? Someone else? No one? From the outset, liability was the fundamental question, and there was no clear-cut answer. But whether or not liability really belonged to Amexco, the creditors went after it alone. They focused on Amexco for two reasons:

first, it had failed to detect the fraud; and second, it was one of the few parties to this affair that still had any money left. But if American Express did have to pay off all liabilities, it had a problem—it had some money, but not $150 million.

Actually, Amexco's assets were huge: at the end of 1963, over $1 billion. But much of those assets was needed to cover existing liabilities, mainly outstanding TCs and customer deposits for the bank. The company had only about $70 million that it could pay out, less than half what it might need. If Amexco were forced to cover all the outstanding receipts in full, it would have to liquidate.

Amexco would disappear as a company, but it would not go bankrupt in the conventional sense. It still was not a corporation. As it happened, that very year, Howard Clark had begun to work on a proposal for the New York State legislature that would have allowed American Express to incorporate, but the proposal had not been passed yet. As things stood, Amexco remained the joint-stock association set up by Wells, Fargo, and Butterfield in 1850, and if the company could not pay its bills, creditors could go directly to the stockholders and claim their money from them. The shareholders, whose ranks included large insurance companies, were rich enough to pay every penny of the warehousing subsidiary's debts.* Not surprisingly, many shareholders dumped their stock; even Ralph Reed reportedly sold shares. The price of Amexco's stock fell nearly 50 percent in a matter of weeks.†

The question of liability could have been figured several different ways, and Clark faced a difficult decision about how to address it. He could have denied liability completely. AEFW (and its successor Lim-

---

*Whether they recognized their potential liability before they bought Amexco's stock is unclear. But had anyone investigated Amexco's history, he would have had little cause for alarm; the company had not even threatened a shareholder assessment in almost a hundred years.

†Some mutual funds also sold Amexco shares, but others, notably Dreyfus, bought the stock. One of the financial community's canniest investors, Warren Buffett, decided to buy as well.

ited) was an *incorporated* subsidiary. AEFW had liability for the debts, not necessarily Amexco. Liability of any corporation was limited to the amount of its capital and the value of its assets, in this instance, $1 million maximum. If debts surpassed that sum, the subsidiary could declare itself bankrupt and leave the creditors to fight over the $1 million. As for the American Express Company itself, it was in theory a different entity, not liable for anything.

The ability to drop the "corporate veil" like this might, or might not, have worked legally; some directors apparently considered it a lifesaver. But that tactic posed another sort of complication: the banks held the loans and would probably have had to absorb most of the losses. But the banks had a powerful weapon to use against Amexco; they could refuse to accept the TC. If they chose that tactic, they would kill American Express far more definitively than soybean liabilities. Given all the business Amexco brought the banks—about a quarter of a billion dollars in deposits and a few million dollars in TC commissions—they had a vested interest in keeping Amexco afloat. But if the bankers were faced with the choice of absorbing $100 million of losses, or forcing Amexco to liquidate, they might well have picked the latter.

To add yet another complication, Clark knew that an effort to mollify the bankers by paying off the debts would surely anger shareholders. Empty the company's coffers and destroy shareholder equity, for what? To pay off debts of questionable legality? In choosing this option, Clark risked shareholder lawsuits against himself, and the rest of the officials and directors of the company.

Clark had an enormously difficult decision on his hands, but he made up his mind in only a few days. He wanted to reassure everyone: stockholders, customers, and bankers. To the extent that he had to choose between the banks and the stockholders, however, he picked the banks. He and other Amexco officials met with bankers on the first Saturday after the scandal broke to reassure them that Amexco had the financial capability and above all the "moral responsibility" to stand up to its obligations.

Also, Clark wanted to maintain the confidence of the public. Amexco depended on the public's belief that it would pay off its obligations, particularly on the TC, and so Clark wanted to state for the record what he had told the bankers. Before he could make such a statement, however, Clark needed permission of the board. It convened twice: on Monday, November 25, and again on Wednesday. When the directors heard the whole story, they were horrified. As board chairman Ralph "Peck" Owen recalled, they all thought they had gotten rid of the subsidiary already and had no obligation at all. Now Clark was saying that he did not know for sure whether the company had a legal obligation, but he wanted to assume a moral one. Not all the directors agreed with this approach, and some thought the "corporate veil" tactic might work.* But General Lucius Clay agreed with Clark, and the general's fervor on the subject swayed the board.

On November 27, Clark issued this statement to the press: "If our subsidiary should be held liable for amounts in excess of its insurance coverage and other assets, American Express Company feels morally bound to do everything it can, consistent with its overall responsibilities, to see that such excess liabilities are satisfied." Creditors would ask on many occasions just how many dollars this moral obligation added up to, and the answer would hang for months. But in the meantime, the statement added up to good public relations. Most bankers were satisfied with the statement for a start, but they pressed Amexco to do more. The Bank of England, especially, indicated that Amexco had to make a sizable settlement offer soon, or face a boycott of the TC. For the time being, though, there would be no retribution from the banks. December TC sales were up 28 percent over the same month in 1962.

As a first step to settling the claims and arriving at the dollar value

---

*Clarkson pushed this argument. In February, he met with Amexco's attorneys and told them he had discussed the issue with other directors and with lawyers, and he believed that the company should drop the corporate veil, although even the suggestion of such a course risked retaliation from creditors. One of Amexco's lawyers wrote after the meeting with Clarkson, "The old saw about saving us from our friends comes to mind."

321

the banks demanded, Clark, along with Amexco's attorneys at Carter, Ledyard & Milburn, decided they had to try to consolidate the legal actions against the company. If all the creditors sued separately, Amexco could be tied up in court and its financial position left uncertain for decades. Amexco, on the advice of its attorneys, hired an outsider, Peter Kaminer, Jr., of Winthrop, Stimson, Putnam & Roberts, to handle all of the litigation. In the beginning of December, Kaminer faced off against the legion of creditors and their lawyers and began a process of negotiations that would take all of his time and energy for months to come.

On Wednesday, December 11, Kaminer brought most of the creditors and their lawyers together in the board room on the thirteenth floor of 65 Broadway.* Nearly 150 people crowded into the room, and most of them were very angry. Kaminer made a statement calling for "common procedures in the collection of evidence" and indicated his desire to have the creditors form "a small group who might act as representatives of all the receipt holders." When he finished, Kaminer fielded some questions and then left the meeting to let creditors organize themselves. When he returned, he found that they had not organized and were demanding answers to questions they termed "urgencies," answers he could not provide. The creditors did, however, agree to meet with Kaminer again the following Monday.

That meeting was no less hostile, but it did produce results. The creditors formed an informal creditors committee—which later became the Official Creditors Committee—of six top Wall Street attorneys led by David Hartfield, Jr., of White & Case, who represented Continental Illinois. (The Chicago bank had loaned more than $13 million against AEFW receipts.) From Amexco's standpoint, the committee represented a good start to the litigation process, but the company did not know whether it would lead to consolidation of suits or an acceptable resolution. Lawyers for the creditors and their clients re-

---

*Creditors had begun to meet among themselves as early as November 27 to work out "a common approach."

mained in poor humor, and while Hartfield said the committee would ask individuals to hold off bringing Amexco to court, he warned that "any receipt holder could 'kick over the traces' " and file a separate suit. Hartfield also made it clear that the committee was going to look solely to American Express for satisfaction. If the company failed to provide it, Hartfield and other committee attorneys indicated the "financial community" might react angrily and "ruin [Amexco's] business." (These words Carter, Ledyard attorney Richard J. McClung described as "genteel blackmail.") The committee warned of trouble even if American Express just gave the appearance of trying to slip out of its responsibilities. For instance, committee members told Amexco not to file for bankruptcy for Limited without their prior approval.

Throughout the first month after the scandal broke, discussions between Amexco and the creditors remained tense. When Kaminer asked for agreement on investigative procedures, the committee responded with thirteen demands. It claimed the right to decide what evidence was and was not relevant, and it wanted to deny Amexco the normal right of cross-examination of witnesses. Kaminer was also given an ultimatum to respond positively in a week. He could not accept all of the terms, but he tried to be conciliatory and managed to keep talks going.

At American Express, officials remained nervous, but the atmosphere became less gloomy, largely because the disaster had brought out a remarkable esprit de corps among employees. Although the company's survival appeared uncertain, executives did not fear for their jobs but asked what they could do to help. The best thing they could do, Clark told them, was to take on more responsibility in the running of the company. According to one executive, "Clark said in effect, 'I'm going to be working on [the scandal] with Kaminer and the other lawyers. Your help is needed in the conduct of your businesses, so run your businesses and don't come knocking on my door for a lot of counsel and involvement for the next several weeks until we've put this matter to rest.' " Though Clark did not divorce himself entirely from the operating details of the company, he followed that plan, immersing himself in the issues of Soybean. Executives followed the script as well, assuming a level of administrative authority no manager had exercised since the Glass Eye Era. In effect, Amexco's management underwent decentralization of authority by necessity, and in every respect the results were positive. Profits rose and at the same time executives gained faith in their own abilities.* Though the company was still in the midst of scandal, executive morale was soon at its highest level in decades.

Clark's decision to assume all the responsibility for Soybean helped boost morale. The scandal, though in the back of people's minds, never became a burden to the organization as a whole. By isolating himself with the scandal, Clark freed the company from the ups and downs of the negotiations and the implications of events that he alone as a lawyer and accountant fully understood. The scandal became a burden to no one at Amexco but himself. Actually, Clark was suited to the burden of Soybean, not only by training, but also by temperament. Although the effort brought him near exhaustion and kept him off the golf course for months, he never let the often tense negotiations destroy his emotional equilibrium. He displayed extraordinary patience throughout. He was, said an aide, "very determined but not so combative as to become frustrated enough to . . . retaliate," even against those parties he felt were acting unreasonably.

Throughout the early days of the scandal, Clark also had to keep lines open to the press, but he faced a delicate problem: Amexco had to seem forthcoming to maintain customer confidence, and at the same time, the company could not say anything that might jeopardize an agreement. Amexco handled the problem skillfully, maintaining the basic pose Clark had struck at the onset of the affair: that the company would live up to its moral and financial obligations. In

---

*For the most part, Amexco made no changes in the conduct of its business. However, the scandal did lead to a change in Amexco's investment strategy. The company's money managers made Amexco's portfolio more liquid, and they sold municipals and bought higher-yielding corporate paper in anticipation of a change in the company's tax position.

continuing to buy Amexco's products and services, customers demonstrated they had bought the message and still had confidence in American Express.

In the early weeks of the scandal, however, Clark and the lawyers did not entirely share that confidence. They were still unsure whether Amexco would have enough money to cover the lawsuits.* The issue remained in doubt because the company did not know exactly who was going to sue or for how much. To bring all the demands of claimants out into the open, at the end of December, Amexco risked the wrath of the creditors committee and filed for protection for the warehouse subsidiary under Chapter XI of the bankruptcy code. The step did not bring the retaliation creditors had threatened, but initially, what emerged in court confirmed Clark's worst fears: Amexco faced claims of $210 million. On closer inspection, the situation looked a little less threatening. There were duplications of claims; Tino had, for example, given receipts to grain companies, which had used them in turn to get money from banks, and now in court both the grain companies and the banks were demanding repayment of the same receipts. When all duplications were accounted for, the real figure came to $137.3 million, still daunting if Amexco had to pay it all. But of course, the company did not intend to pay 100 percent of the claims, and in fact, it disclaimed liability for $39.4 million of forged receipts. That left $98 million; with insurance, Amexco could probably have paid it all, but it had no intention of offering that much. Attorneys estimated the company could achieve a compromise settlement of about $50 million, and at that price, Amexco would easily survive.

However, the creditors had not received a compromise offer, much less accepted one. Hartfield and the other attorneys on the committee continually warned Amexco not to dawdle in proposing a settlement.

---

*Clark did realize, however, that the company had more than $70 million. Amexco had the opportunity to sell its operations to raise more cash. For example, investment bankers at Lehman Brothers estimated the value of Amexco's share of Hertz–American Express International at $7 million. Freight forwarding, Wells Fargo armored cars, and the card would have brought several million more.

They took the position, according to Hartfield, that "unless the American Express Company came up with a treaty of peace, the official creditors committee would recommend a general warfare, and by that I meant lawsuits wherever possible, and in any jurisdiction most favorable to the individual plaintiff's position." Despite the threats, Amexco appeared to be stalling; Norman Miller called this the company's "strategy." It made sense: the longer Amexco took to pay, the more money it would make in the interim, the more resources it would have to effect a settlement. But finally, the committee put a stop to any stalling tactic and delivered another ultimatum: it gave Amexco thirty to forty-five days to make a proposal. The company asked for an extension to sixty days so that the company's board could meet and approve a pact. The next board meeting was scheduled for April 9, and Kaminer promised there would be a concrete offer on the table shortly thereafter; the creditors agreed to wait until then.

Clark and Kaminer, along with a committee of three Amexco directors, created a proposal and presented it to creditors on April 12. The twenty-five-page document was couched in such legalistic, obscure language that most of the people who read it did not understand it. (The next day, news reports noted different amounts for the proposed settlement.) But behind the tortured sentences, Amexco had offered to pay off all "valid" claims with an initial payment of $35 million, another $10 million in installments, and a guarantee of at least $10 million from insurance. It also would pay out the proceeds from the sale of the oil actually in the tanks at Bayonne, worth about $5 million. In other words, the company was offering around $45 million, and held out the hope of as much as $15 million more if Amexco could collect all of its insurance. After tax credits were figured in, the actual cost to Amexco would have been about $25 million.

Clark called the package fair and essentially "not negotiable," a full discharge of the company's moral responsibility, and he along with Amexco's lawyers gave the creditors until July to decide whether or not they would accept the offer. The reaction to the proposal was mixed. Bankers seemed pleased, and since they were the most important creditors, the company regarded the proposal as a success. Said Harold Helm, chairman of Chemical Bank & Trust, "We feel the directors of American Express should be congratulated on the splendid settlement offer they have proposed." But others were not so delighted. "I am amazed," one creditor told the press, "that American Express has taken all this time to come up with a plan that doesn't nearly cover the claims." Amexco had decreed that its proposal needed acceptance by 90 percent of the creditors to become effective; it was soon evident that the proposal would not gain that approval.

The offer had critics among stockholders as well. At an April 29 shareholders' meeting, Clark came under attack for having let such a disaster happen, and a stockholder group went to court to block a settlement. But despite the new threat from shareholders and the negative reaction from some creditors, Amexco officials became more confident than ever that the danger to the company had ended. The stockholders' suit was real enough, but company lawyers expressed the view it would not prevent a settlement. Creditors continued to attack Amexco in the press, but the offer had been substantial enough so that no one left the negotiating table. The creditors wanted to settle quickly. A few of them, especially the smaller commodity-trading companies, would face insolvency if the legal battle dragged on. As a result, Amexco officials believed they would arrive at a settlement within the company's means. In July, the creditors, still working together, offered a counterproposal and the negotiations resumed. It was not until 1967 that the major claims were finally settled;* Amexco paid out $60 million, absorbing an after-tax cost of only $31.6 million. The company's profits from the day the scandal broke until the settlement was concluded exceeded that amount.

Although the negotiations over the settlement persisted, Amexco officials put the scandal behind them by the fall of 1964. And when

---

*There were several suits outside the action settled in 1967. Lawrence Warehousing, for example, eventually sued American Express. Some of these subsidiary actions were not settled until the 1970s.

executives had a chance to reflect on the events of Soybean, they were amazed at the outcome. They realized that the scandal had actually benefited the company enormously, a result no one could have dreamed possible at the time it broke. Soybean was, Ralph Owen said later, the greatest public-relations event the company ever had. On the whole the company received extremely favorable press for its efforts; it looked a little foolish for having gotten into the mess in the first place but appeared honorable in getting out of it. The public saw the company, as Clark had hoped, as an institution that stood behind its obligations, even ones it did not necessarily have to assume. The most evident sign of public confidence was simply the fact that the scandal never hurt business; in 1964, TC sales rose 11.7 percent. Before the end of the year, the company even began to win back investors; stock analysts were recommending purchase of the stock.

Internally, perceptions had changed. Executives noted that the company was still thriving. They discussed among themselves with some amazement how Amexco had continued to grow despite the diversion of an enormous amount of management time, especially that of the CEO. Only a few years before, every decision had passed through the chief executive. Now, quite by chance, the company had demonstrated that it had a management team capable of exercising authority.* Executives felt a new self-confidence; they had a feeling of pride, too, that the company had stood behind a moral obligation. In fact, so much was gained that someone asked Howard Clark if a Soybean was not a good idea every few years. But he replied, "I don't think I have enough years of my life left to give away for another scandal."

Clark's handling of the crisis increased his own prestige enormously within the ranks of American Express. One branch manager even referred to him as "a demigod." And his new stature made it easier for

---

*After Soybean, the company recentralized to an extent, but it did not return to the structure that prevailed in 1963. The scandal, in the estimate of most executives, changed the company fundamentally.

him, once Soybean was passed, to finish the task he had started in 1960: changing the organization and structure of the company. At the top of his agenda he placed the reorganization of the foreign branch offices along product lines, a step he took in 1965. Predictably, the announcement hurt some feelings and deflated a few egos, but there was no rebellion in the ranks. Within a matter of months, Amexco had completely altered a system that had been entrenched for decades.

After Soybean, Amexco also changed its form of organization and incorporated in 1965, and it kept getting richer and stronger. Thanks to growth in the card and continued growth in TC volume, profits hit $15.6 million in 1965 and $19.2 million a year later. Indeed, operating earnings had risen every year of Clark's term in office. And because of the card, especially, Amexco had the prospect of continued growth ahead, a prospect reflected in the high price-earnings multiple of its stock.* But the high multiple represented another opportunity: Amexco could acquire other companies with stock and grow larger even faster. This strategy made a good deal of sense both to officials inside the company and to people in the investment community.

Clark endorsed the idea of growth through acquisition. From 1964 on, he talked about acquisitions and contemplated various possibilities. But when it came to actually making deals, Clark continually waffled. He wanted to create an acquisition program, but he left out a step. In order to decide what to acquire, the company had to identify what it was and plan what it should become. But Clark never defined American Express, never developed a strategic plan, and in the end, never launched a major takeover. Instead, he delayed and hesitated over acquisition plans and seemed a man who could not make up his mind. He did buy a few small companies, most of which Amexco subsequently unloaded. And finally he did make a very large acquisi-

---

*The multiple is simply the ratio of the price of a share to the per-share earnings of the company. A high multiple—a high share price in relation to earnings—means that the market anticipates good future earnings and builds that expectation into the share price. Obviously, a company with a high relative share price has an advantage in the takeover arena; it can buy more for fewer shares of its own stock.

tion of the Fireman's Fund Insurance Company. But it turned out to be a company he did not seek, and many people in and out of the company thought it a very bad idea.

After Soybean, Clark created a professional planning office at Amexco to develop a long-term vision for the company. In 1965, he brought in Thomas H. Barton, a vice president of Barrington & Co., a management-consulting firm, and made him VP for planning and corporate development. Barton conducted numerous studies and looked into many acquisition ideas. Yet even after Barton's arrival, Amexco did not have a strategic plan or make a real effort to acquire any company of size. Every purchase remained small-scale, and Clark continued to shuffle the marginal businesses as he had done in the early sixties; for example, in 1965 he sold the company's stake in Hertz–American Express International (after again considering an acquisition of Hertz). He made a few new additions: because American Express bought so many municipal bonds, he spent $6 million to acquire the bond-underwriting and investment-banking firm W. H. Morton & Co. (which Amexco later dismantled); and he took over a company called Uni-Serv which offered a revolving charge card for retail stores, called the Uni-card. But this business never produced satisfactory results, and Clark got rid of it a few years later.

So far from clearly defining Amexco, Clark actually seemed to promote two separate definitions. On the one hand, the acquisitions of Morton and Uni-Serv suggested that Clark had decided to define American Express as a financial-services organization. He added to that impression when he talked about other possible targets. In 1964, for instance, he told *Fortune* that Amexco was looking for a big acquisition among insurance companies and mutual-fund groups.* But his interest in large financial companies did not lead to a takeover, nor did it mean that Amexco had settled on a definition. Indeed, at the same time Clark was pushing the idea of Amexco as a financial-

---

*Amexco did have discussions with the Putnam family of mutual funds, and it bought a block of Presidential Insurance, but it never made a public offer for either.

services organization, Amexco was defining itself to the public in a different way, as "The company for people who travel." Some executives in the company saw this not simply as an ad campaign but as the basic identity of American Express, and Clark himself appeared to endorse this view when he called "tourism the glue that holds our company together." (Some executives worried that if Amexco were known as a financial company, it might lose travel and TC business.) Even while Clark talked insurance, he was also considering the purchase of hotel chains, travel companies, and Club Méditerranée.

The question of definition had become so confused that the planning office appeared to promote a third concept as well. Barton's group contemplated making Amexco a conglomerate. In the mid-1960s, the planning office compiled a preliminary list of takeover candidates, which included Bell & Howell, TRW, CBS, Pitney-Bowes, Montgomery Ward, Singer, Thomas Cook & Son (an idea proposed for the fourth or fifth time in the company's history) and Booz, Allen, Hamilton, the consulting firm.

Conglomerate building was of course the fad of the 1960s. Management theorists wrote solemn works on the need for "diversification," and companies like Ling-Temco-Vought, ITT, Gulf & Western, and others built empires of disparate companies. But whatever Clark wanted Amexco to be, he did not ever display an interest in following the conglomerate fad. He always wanted something that "fit" into American Express, though exactly what that was no one could say. It was, however, a measure of the confusion over the company's long-term strategy that Barton's group was thinking conglomerate at all.

Actually, to the extent most company officials thought about conglomerates, it was to worry that Amexco might become part of one. They believed that Amexco would become especially vulnerable to a takeover in the event of Peck Owen's death. If his estate chose to sell his stock (about 11 percent of Amexco), it would give a conglomerate builder an important block with which to launch a takeover bid. If a takeover materialized, Amexco executives were betting the raider would be Transamerica Corp., which already owned a block of Amexco's stock and had spoken to Owen about acquiring his stake. As a result, the *fear* of a takeover became an important strategic concept at American Express; many officials thought the company needed to make a major acquisition in order to become too big for a conglomerate to swallow.

While Amexco pondered strategies and self-definition, the conglomerate fad was making another CEO nervous, and unlike Clark, he planned to do something about it. In fact, his fear would lead to the biggest acquisition in *Amexco's* history to date. Out in San Francisco, Fred Merrill, chairman of the Fund America Group, which included the venerable Fireman's Fund Insurance Company (as well as four mutual funds), worried that his company was a target. The question seemed to be not whether Fireman's Fund would be taken over, but by whom. Insurance-company stocks, particularly the property and casualty (P&C) insurers such as Fireman's Fund, had lost a good deal of market value. The inner-city riots of the 1960s made investors fear a huge increase in claims and a drop in P&C profits. As a result, insurance-company stocks were selling below their liquidating values, making them tempting targets for raiders. By 1967, Merrill learned that at least two conglomerates—Teledyne and ITT—wanted his company. That summer Merrill went to his board and told the directors the company had three options. It could liquidate; he guessed the breakup value at about $50 a share, versus a market price of $28 or so. It could do nothing and wait for a raider to make an offer. Or it could find a suitable partner; his board told him to make a good marriage.

Merrill had already chosen a partner. He settled on Amexco because he believed in the concept of diversified financial-services organizations. In Merrill's view, Fireman's Fund would function best in an organization that offered products and services complementary to P&C insurance and mutual funds. On the basis of what Amexco's CEO had told the press about mutual funds and insurance, Merrill believed that Clark was thinking along the same lines. Both Amexco and Fireman's Fund would be strengthened by adding insurance to the card, the investment banking company, the TC, and the overseas bank, Merrill reasoned. He believed both already had the same basic product: money.

Merrill planned to persuade Amexco to acquire his company. Although Fireman's Fund was three times as large as Amexco, Merrill never doubted that Amexco should emerge as the surviving company. Its stock was at a much higher multiple, and so Fireman's Fund shareholders would benefit far more by exchanging their shares for shares in Amexco than the other way around. Also, the name recognition of American Express was so much greater than Fireman's Fund that it would add to the insurance company, while the reverse would not be true.

To put his plan into motion, he called a friend of his, Amexco board member Joe King, and asked for some help in implementing his plan. King liked the idea and went to William Morton, now Amexco's vice chairman. Coincidentally, Morton felt that Amexco should acquire a P&C insurance company, and while his first choices were Hartford Fire and the Insurance Company of North America, he quickly adopted Merrill's plan. Merrill, King, and Morton had only one crucial task left: to convince Howard Clark to accept the idea.

In September 1967, Merrill stopped in New York en route to Europe, and through King, he met with Howard Clark in one of the upstairs bedrooms of the Links Club. Clark was briefed before the meeting and was not surprised when Merrill proposed a merger, but neither was he convinced that it was a good idea. The meeting, however, set off a decision-making process at Amexco that would drag on for eight months. That process would lead to the conclusion that the acquisition was a terrible idea; the arguments against an acquisition would appear far stronger and more numerous than those for it. But in the end, Clark would choose to make the deal anyway.

Merrill led the drive to sell Howard Clark. Merrill was a great salesman, affable and persistent, and although he had never sold anything quite this big before, he was nonetheless the man to do it. By December, after his trip abroad, he was in regular contact with Clark, and already, he was writing "Dear Howard" letters and signing them "Fred, Chairman." Clark remained the uncertain buyer, who had not said yes but also had not said no. And until he did, Merrill, like any good salesman, kept making his pitch.

In this case, though, others were pitching from the opposite side. By December, Clark and his senior staff engaged in a debate over what to do about Fireman's Fund, sometimes called "Project F" at 65 Broadway. Clark quickly discovered that several of his senior managers strongly opposed the idea, and for very good reasons. They told him first that the P&C business had not been especially good for a decade and was always cyclical, with very good years followed by very bad ones. As for Fireman's Fund itself, according to securities analysts, it was not even the best company in the industry. Also, an acquisition might have a negative impact on Amexco's stock. Fireman's multiple was low, below ten, while Amexco's was nearly thirty; even Merrill acknowledged that Amexco's multiple would fall to around twenty.*

Essentially, the debate raged over whether or not Amexco should pay hundreds of millions of dollars to acquire a company that everyone thought was at best mediocre. But there were supporters of the takeover at Amexco, and they had several reasons for wanting the deal. In late 1967, when Barton drafted a paper summing up the discussions to date, he cited five reasons why American Express should make the acquisition: the company would be larger; it was an opportune time for an acquisition because of the high multiple; the acquisition would be a step in diversification; it would broaden stock ownership; and it would be a defense against a takeover. In fact, all but two of the advantages were connected to a takeover defense; in other words, the main reason for an acquisition was fear.

Besides a takeover, Amexco had a second fear: it had become a competitor with the banks. The banks were issuing their own cards, Master Charge and Bankamericard. These cards differed from the American Express Card since they permitted installment-credit pur-

---

*Owen was especially concerned with the drop in the multiple—which was understandable since he owned 11 percent of Amexco's stock. He consistently argued against the acquisition and did not attend the board meeting that approved it.

chases, but they also offered the same conveniences as Amexco's card: single billing and blank-check borrowing. Although Clark and his managers did not know the upshot of the competition, it posed two dangers: first, the loss of card market share; and second, with the banks now competitors, the possible loss of sales outlets for the TC. As a result, some officials at Amexco believed the company needed to protect itself by acquiring a new source of income.

But was that fear (or the fear of a takeover) a good rationale to buy Fireman's Fund? Richard Blanchard argued no. "Are we motivated by fear rather than trying to achieve a definite pre-set objective?" he wrote. "It seems to me that we should see this posssibility in perspective against other possible acquisitions. We should take the initiative rather than look only at opportunities that are brought to us."

There was, in fact, only one clear business fit between Fireman's Fund and Amexco. Insurance, like the TC, was a float business. Insurers acquired money through premium payments and paid out claims, but they always carried an average positive balance, an average net amount of money to invest. Insurance, then, seemed a business Amexco could acquire and, on one level, understand. Amexco officials, however, did not understand the P&C business and never really would.

From the outset, the problems of Fireman's Fund clearly outweighed the advantages. Against five advantages, Barton listed seven "problems," which went to the heart of the P&C business and to the performance of Fireman's Fund as a company. Barton noted, for instance, the insurer's "poor historical growth record" and its "massive dividend requirements," which in some years Fireman's Fund could not meet out of its earnings.

Barton also saw another problem, which demonstrated Amexco's difficulties with its own strategic goals. He worried that the takeover of Fireman's Fund would destroy Amexco's image because such an acquisition would define the company as a diversified financial-services company. Such a step, he warned, would be a "shift from the present travel concept. . . ." That this was raised as a problem in 1968 showed

335

the extent of the company's own confusion. After all, Clark had talked about insurance in 1964; four years later, the company's strategic planner still could not decide if an insurance business fit into American Express.

Officials continued the discussions of Project F for weeks, going over and over the problems and advantages. One senior officer became so enthusiastic that he expressed the belief that American Express might "revolutionize the fire-casualty business," but it was not a hope others took very seriously. Finally, the debate came down to a simple question: was American Express going to spend a lot of money to increase its size and scope, or was it *not* going to spend the money because Fireman's Fund was a weak company not worth buying?

Clark pondered this without arriving at an answer, and he finally sought outside advice. First, he called in Mc Kinsey & Co., and the consultant's report was not encouraging. "Our overall assessment is that the candidate's image among leading agents and brokers can be characterized as bland—neither strongly positive nor strongly negative. Thus it would seem unlikely that this candidate could achieve an above-average rate of growth in commercial lines in the near future." This appraisal did not sway Clark, and he asked for another outside opinion.

With Merrill's consent, Clark turned to the corporate-research division of the Morgan Guaranty Trust. Clark picked Morgan in part to get the view of an institutional shareholder, and he asked the bank's analysts specifically what they thought of the price Amexco was planning to pay. Amexco and Fireman's Fund had talked of various prices, but both sides agreed that the cost would eventually be in the area of 0.75 Amexco shares for each share of Fireman's Fund. The Morgan analysts effectively criticized both the basic idea of a merger and the specific plan. The acquisition, they said, "would come as a shock to A's shareholders," and because the market saw the outlook for the P&C business as "bleak," the acquisition would mean a "sharp decline" in Amexco's multiple. As for the deal, the analysts regarded a price of anything over 0.4 Amexco shares as a bad one.

Initially, the report disheartened Merrill and his men; Merrill said that if Clark accepted the report, the merger talks would end. However, when Clark indicated that he had not entirely agreed with the analysts' conclusion, Merrill went on the attack. One of his aides wrote a lengthy rebuttal to the Morgan report, calling it "devoid of significant research and lacking in imagination." He said that even at 0.9 Amexco shares for each Fireman's share, Amexco would be doing well. Merrill came back to New York, and he and Clark resumed discussions in the old price range, around 0.75.

That Clark was haggling over the price indicated that he had probably come to the decision to make the acquisition. Merrill believed that Clark had done so after the shareholders meeting in late April. At the time, Clark again spoke of acquisitions, including mutual funds and insurance, but for all the talk he had not made an acquisition. Now he had the chance to buy a company that offered *both* insurance and mutual funds. In Merrill's opinion, Clark had backed himself into a corner and had no choice but to acquire Fireman's Fund. If Clark had decided to buy the insurance company, though, he had not told his staff. As late as May 22, Barton advised him that "the Morgan memorandum and the F/A reply further reinforce the view that if we are interested in insurance, it should be in a company no more than one-fourth the size of F/A. . . ."

Clark made up his mind no later than the following week. The board of directors of Amexco met and, following Clark's recommendation, approved the acquisition. The agreement called for the exchange of Fireman's shares for one of two issues of new convertible preferred, one convertible to 0.7 of an Amexco share, the other to 0.8 (the former carried a higher yield). Because shareholders were given the option of picking one or the other, the cost of the acquisition was put at somewhere between $485 million and $555 million. Typically, the stock market defied expectations; Amexco's stock went up, not down, shortly after the deal. But, in time, the analysts proved correct; because Amexco carried the burden of the P&C cycle in its earnings, its price-earnings multiple would fall dramatically by the mid-1970s.

For its half billion dollars in stock, American Express acquired three separate operations: an insurance company with $2 billion in assets and equity of more than $350 million; a family of mutual funds; and a stake in a computer-leasing organization. Clark reorganized American Express as a holding company to accommodate Fireman's Fund: he became chairman and chief executive; Morton became president, and Merrill, chairman of the executive committee. It was unquestionably the most significant acquisition in the company's history, one that transformed the scope and size of the company; and, at the time, it made American Express too big for a raider to swallow.

In the first year of the acquisition, Clark could point with pride to the fact that Amexco earned over $60 million with almost half of that amount coming from insurance. Profits for the year equaled what total *revenues* had been when Clark took over. Revenues had soared to a billion dollars, three quarters of that from insurance. Yet Amexco executives could never fully integrate Fireman's Fund. Although Amexco executives shuttled back and forth across the country, Fireman's Fund always seemed to them an alien organization, engaged in an alien business. Even the earnings from the insurance subsidiary, though impressive at times, were almost untouchable by the parent company. Amexco could report the profits, could use some of it for dividends, but it could not capture the profits for most other uses. Insurance regulators would not have allowed Amexco to take its subsidiary's earnings for itself.

Clark would later term 1968 "the most impressive year of change and achievement in the 118-year history of American Express." He was speaking not only of Fireman's Fund, but of other developments as well. Amexco bought Ralph Owen's Equitable Securities and combined it with W. H. Morton & Co. This put American Express briefly in all areas of retail and institutional brokerage and investment banking, but within a matter of months, Clark decided to concentrate on investment banking and institutional business and phase out retail operations. This expanded the company's financial services for a time, but before long Equitable/Morton became a virtually inactive operation. In 1968 also, the company acquired a magazine called *U.S.*

Camera.* Later renamed *Travel & Leisure* and made part of the travel department, it would prove a profitable and enduring enterprise.

More significantly, that year Clark made a deeper commitment to develop the bank. Chemical Bank and a leading Canadian bank had both expressed an interest in buying Amexco's overseas banking operations. But Clark rejected the sale and chose instead to expand the bank and make it a more professional organization than it had already become. It took four more years before Clark actually put a banker in charge of the bank (which had been renamed the American Express International Banking Corporation, AEIBC). Richard Blanchard, by training a securities analyst, remained head of the bank until 1970 and was replaced by an investment banker from White, Weld & Co., James D. Robinson III. Robinson had come to Amexco not to run the bank, but rather as a possible successor to Howard Clark. As part of his training to become CEO, he ran the bank for two years and then moved on to head the division created in 1971 that encompassed the card, TC, and travel, the Travel-Related Services (TRS) group. Only then did Clark turn the AEIBC over to a real banker, Richard Bliss from Bankers Trust. Bliss embarked on a program to expand assets and make the bank competitive in all phases of business with such giant international banks as Citicorp and Deutsche Bank. Assets indeed grew rapidly, doubling in Bliss's first four years at AEIBC to $4 billion.

In the 1970s, Clark talked of making more acquisitions, of adding a fourth major income stream to TRS, the insurance company, and the bank—what he referred to as "the fourth leg" of American Express. In the early seventies, Amexco's profits remained strong, its price-earnings multiple stayed high, and the investment community continued to believe that Amexco should use the opportunity to acquire for growth. Both in the company and on Wall Street, people feared that the TC had reached maturity, that card growth would slow, that insurance would face years of poor earnings. A fourth leg appeared the solution.

---

*Amexco made an offer for *Holiday Magazine* earlier that year, but the offer was rebuffed. When the publisher of *U.S. Camera* heard Amexco was looking for a travel magazine, he wrote to Howard Clark and offered his.

Clark talked again of acquiring businesses that in some way fit into American Express: real estate, mortgage banking, finance companies, resort development, and information-processing companies.*

Clark made no major takeover bids until March 1974, when he announced a $150 million offer for Avis, the second largest car-rental company.† The deal seemed designed to bolster the company's travel image, even though not long before, Clark had told the press that Amexco's travel identity was outmoded. Then a month later, Amexco announced that it was not acquiring Avis after all. The company refused comment on why it had dropped its offer. Reportedly, Amexco had decided, somewhat late in the game, to take another look at Avis's books. On closer inspection, the deal was not as attractive as it had first appeared. Some Wall Street analysts, however, believed Clark had changed his mind when he saw the price of Amexco's stock go down by over 10 percent. He had correctly interpreted the price drop as a sign of investor disapproval. This one offer proved a failure on all counts. Amexco managed to muddy the sense of its identity and direction, and Clark made himself look like a corporate Hamlet, vacillating and indecisive. He never again pursued a major takeover.

Meanwhile, Clark continued to fiddle with the marginal products, more small additions and subtractions. He commissioned a consultant to report on the prospects in freight forwarding, and the consultant said it could be a growth area. But Clark quietly sold the freight-forwarding division to the Pacific Intermountain Express Co., removing Amexco from its original business. Freight had become so insignificant a part of Amexco that the sale was, according to company executives, a

*Between 1968 and 1972, Amexco made public that it was considering two major takeovers: California–Western States Life Insurance Co., and, once again, Thomas Cook & Son. In both instances, Amexco decided not to make a formal bid.

†Though Amexco officials had discussed the takeover of a car-rental company for seventeen years, the Avis bid was not the result of deliberate planning and analysis. It came about when ITT put its 52-percent stake on the market, and Amexco bid for it along with the remaining 48 percent. A decade later one senior company official admitted it would have been an absurd acquisition. The company would have become a competitor with other car rental companies, which by 1974 already provided millions of dollars each year in card charges.

"nonevent." Clark also sold off Wells Fargo armored cars, sold off the mutual funds acquired in the Fireman's Fund deal, and added a language school and a computerized-reservation service for hotels and car-rental agencies. He pushed Amexco's board to agree to let him buy a 25 percent stake in the investment-banking and institutional-brokerage firm of Donaldson, Lufkin, Jenrette. He abandoned the purchase three years later at a considerable loss.

The little acquisitions failed to amount to much, and Clark, though he spoke about a fourth leg, ultimately left his successors the challenge of finding it. His unwillingness to make another major acquisition also gave Amexco a very particular and not very flattering reputation in the investment community: Wall Street considered American Express a rich, venerable company of great integrity that "hadn't done a damn thing for a decade."

If Clark failed to develop a strategic vision, he succeeded greatly in the development of short-term operating plans. The main divisions continued to grow rapidly. By 1973, the average outstandings of TCs, still a company mainstay, surpassed the billion mark, and the card grew at a spectacular rate. Cardholders reached nearly 5 million by 1972 and then 8 million in 1977, and charge volume tripled every five years: from $1.1 billion in 1967, to $3.6 billion in 1972, to over $10 billion by 1977. Profits overall continued to rise at a phenomenal pace in the 1970s. They topped $100 million (in 1971), then $150 million (1973), then nearly $200 million (1976), and then in 1977, in the year Clark left office, more than a quarter of a billion dollars.

Profits rose every single year—or at least they seemed to rise every year. Clark placed a high priority on maintaining a record of continuous earnings growth that had begun in the late 1940s.* Through the 1970s, in the first or second paragraph of each annual report, Clark highlighted the continuing saga of "the long earnings record" of American Express.

---

*Clark took the losses from the Soybean scandal as an "extraordinary charge," preserving the Record of operating income growth.

341

But he kept the Record alive at times by what others considered tricks, maintaining the *appearance* of earnings growth, instead of the reality. In 1974, the P&C underwriting cycle hit bottom, and as many had predicted in 1968, earnings from Fireman's Fund fell. But Amexco managed to preserve the Record—barely. Fireman's Fund made an abrupt change in its accounting practices—a move which opened eyes and provoked an official inquiry. Fireman's Fund had what was called a "catastrophe reserve," a pool of funds set aside to cover a jump in claims from an unexpected disaster. Before 1974, Amexco's Fireman's Fund subsidiary had put into the catastrophe reserve 1.25 percent of premiums from certain categories of disaster insurance. But in April of that year, Fireman's Fund decided to lower its contribution to 0.9 percent a year and amortize the payments over time. The timing of the change startled observers. It came in a month when tornado and storm damage had led to a jump in claims. One analyst called the change "inappropriate," and the SEC launched an investigation. It concluded that Amexco had done nothing illegal, but market analysts regarded the accounting change as little more than a tactic to "present a picture of stable earnings growth." Amexco did produce another "record year" in 1974, but earnings overall rose less than $6 million and the company's tinkering with the catastrophe reserve had added an estimated $9 million.

In 1975, Clark's tactics raised even more questions. Fireman's Fund again posted poor earnings, and this time Amexco used two maneuvers that appeared designed to keep the Record alive. That year the Financial Accounting Standards Board decided that insurance companies should abolish catastrophe reserves altogether because they were misleading. Most insurance companies took out the money from their catastrophe reserves and reported it as "extraordinary" gains. Fireman's Fund used the cash in its reserve to boost income by several million. * The same year, Clark also avoided taking a big loss on the company's

---

*Amexco's annual report noted that the change in accounting added $4.6 million to net income. An article in *Fortune* claimed that the change boosted income by $8 million.

investment in the firm of Donaldson, Lufkin, Jenrette. Rather than sell the stock, he distributed it to Amexco's shareholders. In distributing the shares, he kept a loss of around $25 million off the books. But he cost the company some $6 million, money it would have recouped if it had sold the stock and taken the tax losses. Some on Wall Street believed that preservation of the Record was the only reason for the maneuver. Amexco reported a net gain in 1975 of only $8 million.

The company did have a business rationale for maintaining the appearance of steady growth. Some executives believed that the investment community looked for an upward earnings path, and that the appearance of continuous earnings would protect the stock price and its price/earnings multiple. In the mid-1970s, the multiple fell anyway, and indeed Wall Street became distrustful of Amexco's earnings reports. Market analysts thought Clark was merely trying to make Amexco seem invincible, as one put it, "to make it seem like the company could defy gravity." But the policy took on a life of its own. The company had always been concerned with appearances and now became even more so.

Of course, a good deal of Amexco's growth *was* real, and an extremely visible advertising effort helped create it. In Clark's last few years, Amexco launched one of the great advertising campaigns of all time, a campaign that centered on a slogan: "Don't leave home without it." The line became a cliché of modern life, and the television ads created specifically for the card turned into advertising classics.

The campaign started after Amexco grew dissatisfied with its ad agency, Ogilvy & Mather. Amexco VP George Waters went to James Robinson, then the head of TRS, and suggested that Amexco put the account out for bid by all advertising agencies. But Robinson decided to give Ogilvy one more chance. He and Waters called in Ogilvy chairman Andrew Kershaw and demanded a new campaign. What they wanted, especially, they told Kershaw, was a campaign that had what Waters called "a synergy tag line." Ogilvy's first campaign had been a success, Waters thought, because its tag line, the "company for people who travel," effectively united the marketing efforts of travel, the TC, and the card. When Kershaw suggested that Amexco create its own line, Waters delivered an ultimatum: "You will come up with [a line] or you won't have the account." Faced with the threat of a lost account, Ogilvy produced the lines, "Don't leave home without it," for the card; "Don't leave home without them," for the TC; and "Don't leave home without us," for travel.

The most notable use of the tag line was in TV commercials for the card. In the early 1970s, Ogilvy's creative staff had tried a series of spots using "ordinary people," but by 1974, they realized that approach was not working. They looked for new ideas, ways to use the new line. Under the direction of William B. Taylor, Ogilvy shot three different ads for the card. One was a song, which Kershaw vetoed: "We do not *sing* about American Express." The second was so unremarkable that a few years later even Taylor could not remember what it was. But the third was an idea that bloomed into a long-running series of commercials known primarily by their first line: "Do you know me?"

The idea Taylor pursued was intended to create a sense of mystery and surprise. He put a semifamous person, whose face or name might be familiar but not both, in front of the camera, and the semicelebrity asked television viewers, "Do you know me?" Taylor started with actors who played supporting roles, Norman Fell and John McGiver.* Then he moved on to an astronaut, a former Miss America, and the voice behind Bugs Bunny. The ad series became a major hit only after an Ogilvy writer suggested William Miller, onetime candidate for vice president of the United States, for the series. Taylor credited this one spot with turning the series into a fixture; the concept still aired more than a decade later. †

By the 1970s, Amexco had become a radically different company from the one Clark had taken over. Amexco was no longer a family,

---

*Fell never said the line "Do you know me?" The first to use it was McGiver.

†Both "Don't leave home without it," and "Do you know me?" have become formal company trademarks that the company zealously guards.

but rather a huge, impersonal corporation. The change left Clark with a problem of staffing. He felt he needed to find a new generation of young leaders able to work in a more aggressive, competitive environment. In the seventies, the turnover of executive personnel increased as Clark brought in bright young men with MBAs and the latest ideas in management technique. In addition to James Robinson and Richard Bliss (at the bank), he hired Roger Morley, an accounting "whiz" and strategic planner from Gould Corporation. By 1975, Robinson had demonstrated to Clark and the board that he was capable of taking over as CEO. Clark named the young man as his successor and made plans to step aside.

Two years later, Clark, age sixty-one, left office. He stayed on as chairman of the executive committee and chief counselor, but he made it clear he was handing over the reins for good. He left his successors with several related problems: a policy of continuous earnings growth; the need for a fourth leg to maintain that policy; and the need to define the company to figure out what the fourth leg should be. But at the same time, Clark also left Robinson and Morley with resources to do just about any deal they wanted.

There were two symbolic changes made in the last couple of years of Clark's era. American Express left 65 Broadway for a new glass-and-steel tower at the tip of Manhattan, an address to be known as American Express Plaza. Then in 1977, American Express was once again listed on the New York Stock Exchange, ticker symbol AXP. Both changes seemed fitting. When Clark took over, Amexco was a rather small, old-fashioned, unincorporated association; by the time he stepped down, Amexco had changed fundamentally. It had become a modern corporate giant.

FIREMAN'S FUND AND THE FUTURE

11

James D. Robinson III finally achieved what Clark had only talked about; through the acquisition of Shearson Loeb Rhoades in 1981, he added the fourth leg of American Express, and subsequent acquisitions enhanced both the banking and investment operations of the company. In the process of making these acquisitions, Robinson established Amexco's identity and definition as one of the leading financial services companies in the country. Profits continued to grow rapidly, more than doubling between 1977 and 1982.

But in 1983, after thirty-five years, American Express lost its earnings record. The end came when Fireman's Fund, the company Amexco never quite wanted, suffered a major reversal of fortune. The analysts who had predicted that the property and casualty underwriting cycle would inevitably trip Amexco were proven correct. An unusually long down cycle combined with management mistakes wiped out the earnings of Amexco's insurance subsidiary.

However, this was not another Soybean scandal. While the company lost its earnings record, it had grown so vast and rich and complex that it still made a profit of half a billion dollars in 1983. Amexco suffered mainly a public relations problem. Press reports were widespread and sounded dire. Of course, no one at Amexco had ever taken PR setbacks lightly, and under Robinson, the task of keeping up appearances remained a major preoccupation. Maintaining the earnings record was only one part of the story. The problems at Fireman's Fund were magnified when it tried to maintain the appearance of continuous growth in a cyclical business. But most of all, Fireman's Fund made the company look bad at controlling its operations.

The insurer did have real problems. In the two years prior to its fall, Amexco's insurance subsidiary had gone to great lengths to avoid posting an earnings decline. Following the policy James D. Robinson III had established after he took charge of Amexco, Fireman's Fund stayed out of a price war that engulfed the P&C insurance business. Showing great restraint, Fireman's Fund refused to write below-cost policies simply to retain market share and adopted Amexco's own approach to business, offering prestige and high-quality service for a premium price.

In the late 1970s and early 1980s, Fireman's Fund maintained this policy and still managed to show earnings that rose continuously each year, as the parent company demanded. In 1981, Fireman's chairman, Myron DuBain, was able to say with satisfaction: "I believe we have demonstrated that restraint and realistic pricing are not out of fashion." In fact, Fireman's Fund had not simply managed a good performance, it had produced an extraordinary one. No other P&C insurer generated earnings that rose continuously year after year. Robinson and Amexco's president Sanford I. Weill were impressed with the results and expressed confidence in Fireman's management.

But Fireman's Fund had managed such a remarkable performance because, to an extent, those results were not real. Starting in 1980, income from insurance premiums and investments had actually started to fall off, and officials of Fireman's Fund sought ways to maintain the appearance that profits were pointing steadily upward. Although all of its tactics were legal, they had the effect of obscuring the reality of the subsidiary's performance rather than enhancing it.

One way Fireman's Fund kept up appearances was through changes in its "loss reserves," the money set aside to cover claims in the future. Although insurance regulators have strict rules about the amount and character of such reserves, Fireman's Fund nonetheless played with reserve figures. The insurer managed this through what was called the loss reserve "margin." Because the *exact* amount of insurance liabilities can never be known in advance, companies must estimate reserve requirements, and often they add extra reserves in order to protect themselves from a sudden increase in claims. They call the amount above the estimate the "margin." Fireman's Fund seemed to be putting money into the margin when profits exceeded expectations and taking money out when they fell short. So, in 1977, Fireman's Fund maintained a margin of only $2 million on total reserves of $1.7 billion. But 1978 was a great year for the P&C business; Fireman's Fund actually made $240 million but took $78 million of that amount, added it to the margin, and reported profits of $163 million. That figure corresponded with the amount Fireman's officials had promised Robinson for the year and was consistent with the policy of slow, steady growth in income. In other years, however, Fireman's Fund took money out of the margin and reported it as profit. In fact, it raised and lowered the margin each year. Fireman's Fund did not admit that this was in any way a bookkeeping procedure to manage earnings, and indeed some leading accountants saw no misdeeds in the insurer's handling of its margin. But others regarded the changes simply as an earnings-management technique, one designed to keep the appearance of a smooth, upward curve intact.

In the early 1980s, however, because of falling insurance profits, changing the margin could not alone prevent the subsidiary from showing an earnings decline. Still, Fireman's Fund managed to keep up appearances by finding "special items" to boost income. It particularly used reinsurance deals. Reinsurance is an obscure business, described in *Fortune* magazine "as a mystery not worth solving." But it proved, temporarily, to be worth a great deal to Fireman's Fund. In a series of deals with Insurance Company of North America (INA), the two companies together added profits totaling about $150 million, and all they really did was swap nearly identical liabilities. But the rules for accounting reinsurance deals differ from those for many other kinds of insurance. In some cases, reinsurance requires lower reserves than insurance of the same policy. As a result, the two companies swapped liabilities, refigured reserves, and drew the difference out as profit. Over eighteen months, Fireman's Fund took out $66 million; such was the magic of reinsurance.

Through 1982, various earnings-management tactics allowed Fireman's Fund to report gains continuously year after year. But since insurance earnings actually *fell* continuously, each year Fireman's Fund needed more and more maneuvers like the INA deal to keep profits pointing up. In 1982, such tactics produced over $60 million (about one quarter) of Fireman's net income.

That year, the head of Fireman's Fund, Myron DuBain, left the company and was replaced by one of his senior officers, Edwin F. Cutler. Cutler, along with Fireman's new president James J. Meenaghan, continued to promise Robinson and Weill that the insurance subsidiary would maintain earnings growth. For 1983, they projected income of $266 million, up 10 percent over the previous year. Combining this projection with those of Shearson, the bank, and Travel-Related Services (TRS), Robinson and his men estimated net income for Amexco as a whole at around $700 million, the thirty-sixth straight year of record results.

Cutler and Meenaghan expected to make $266 million with the help of another $120 million in "special items." But they also had come to believe that the industry was ending its price war, and so Fireman's Fund could recoup profitably some of the market share it had lost. Meenaghan, in particular, thought that the price war was over and changed the policy that Robinson had decreed six years earlier. When Meenaghan met with his staff, he urged expansion of market share and de-emphasized prudent pricing. According to the company's house organ, *The Visiting Fireman*, Meenaghan called for a doubling of market share by 1987. Suddenly, Fireman's Fund became more aggressive in selling policies. In the first nine months of 1983, the company wrote so many new policies that premium volume increased 13 percent over the previous year, a gain far above the industry average. But the price war had not ceased, and Fireman's Fund had written many of these policies below cost. Meanwhile, policy reserves—estimates of the money needed to cover future claims—rose more slowly than premium volume, leaving the insurer profitable, but suddenly vulnerable to a rise in claims.

Robinson and Weill noted the rise in premiums and asked some questions, but they indicated later that they were misled; the insurer's management had assured Amexco officials that the policy of prestige and quality service was winning customers. Since Fireman's Fund still reported growth in income, no one at corporate headquarters saw any reason to inquire further.

By August, with the industry price war still raging, Cutler became alarmed, and he wrote a memo to Robinson warning of lower profits. * Cutler indicated that it would be difficult to come up with the kind of "special items" like the INA reinsurance deal, and without something like it or a sudden and dramatic improvement in the P&C business itself, he might be forced to report earnings far below those of the previous year. He estimated that the P&C business would bring in only $146 million.

Robinson did not appear to do anything in response to this memo, and Cutler said later that he wrote it primarily to impress *Meenaghan* of the problems the company was experiencing. (As *Fortune* noted: "Business sometimes proceeds in convoluted ways.") But whether or

---

*The memo was sent anonymously to *Fortune* magazine, apparently by a Fireman's Fund employee who implied that the insurance company was engaged in widespread manipulation of its earnings.

not the memo impressed Meenaghan, the plight of Fireman's Fund only worsened. The P&C business did not improve; the price war did not end; and Cutler could not find enough special items to make up the shortfall. By autumn, American Express revised its earnings expectations downward; it saw Fireman's Fund providing only $215 million, $51 million less than forecast, a substantial drop, though not enough to undercut the Record. However, the bad news from Fireman's Fund continued. Soon after Amexco offered its new projection, the insurance subsidiary faced a sudden jump in claims. The combination of rising claims and underpriced policies sabotaged even the revised earnings forecast.

Despite Cutler's memo in August, Robinson and Weill maintained that they did not fully realize how bad the situation at Fireman's Fund had become until October, when they met with actuaries from the insurer. Amexco's top officials were appalled. They suddenly faced not just an immediate earnings problem, but the possibility of a significant earnings drain for several years. By the time the board of directors of Amexco met in Europe in November, Robinson and Weill felt they would have to take drastic action.

In December, Amexco announced it was adding $230 million to the insurer's reserves.* After tax credits were figured in, Fireman's Fund produced a net loss in the fourth quarter of 1983 of $141 million; for the year, the insurance subsidiary's profits totaled only $30 million. Earnings for American Express overall fell 11 percent to a level slightly under results for 1981, the first official decline in earnings since 1947. The news sparked a wild selling spree of Amexco's stock. In one day, over 3.7 million shares were traded, and the price of the stock fell almost 10 percent. The drop represented a loss in market value of close to $700 million.

The collapse of earnings at Fireman's Fund provoked recriminations and finger pointing. Some Wall Street observers placed responsibility

---

*Some Wall Street observers wondered if $230 million was too much, but it proved inadequate, and eventually Amexco added some $200 million more.

351

on Robinson's shoulders for demanding continuously increasing profits from a business that could not produce them. "Robinson's the guy to blame," one insurance analyst told the press. There was no doubt some truth in it; Weill later agreed that part of the problem at Fireman's Fund was pressure on the insurer's management to produce yearly increases in earnings. Even Robinson acknowledged that as CEO he bore some responsibility, and he demanded that the board cut his overall compensation for the year. But Cutler and Meenaghan paid the highest price. Both men were demoted* and replaced by William McCormick, head of international operations for TRS, and at the board's insistence, Sanford Weill himself. Weill became the new chairman of Fireman's Fund, while remaining president of the parent company.

Amexco's leaders felt deep disappointment and chagrin. The feelings arose not so much over the loss of the thirty-five-year earnings record, but rather over the way they lost it. Although the company had promoted the Record for more than a decade, executives had begun to place less emphasis on it after the Shearson takeover. In buying a brokerage company, Amexco had acquired another cyclical business, and there seemed a tacit acknowledgment among officials that industry cycles would one day put an end to the Record. But executives expected the drop to come from outside forces, such as a falling market, a weak economy, or exchange controls. The Fireman's Fund losses stemmed partly from the insurance cycle, but failures of management strategy and control magnified the problems. While the failure belonged mainly to the Fireman's Fund management, it also extended all the way to American Express Plaza in New York to those with ultimate responsibility for the company.

From a business standpoint, the problems of Fireman's Fund caused only a dip in earnings. The vastly wealthy American Express Company of the 1980s continued earning millions of dollars, and for all the embarrassment felt at company headquarters over the Fireman's Fund

---

*Soon after, both Cutler and Meenaghan left the company altogether.

affair, it had no impact at all on the performance of Amexco's other divisions. Nevertheless, this was a major public relations setback, the first for Amexco since the disastrous takeover attempt of McGraw-Hill in 1979. Prior to the problems at Fireman's Fund, Amexco had been rolling on a long string of PR successes. The press depicted it as a model organization; *Dun's Business Month* had pronounced Amexco one of the five "best managed" companies in America, and Robinson's own image had evolved from that of a green, even inept, executive to one of the best managers in corporate America.*

In the aftermath of the insurance losses, however, opinion shifted. Amexco and Robinson faced rising criticism from the press and the financial community. Suddenly financial writers and Wall Street analysts wondered whether Robinson had lost control of his company. After having celebrated Robinson's strategy that led to the acquisition of Shearson, IDS (Investors Diversified Services), the Trade Development Bank, and several smaller companies in a period of a little more than two years, Wall Street began second-guessing it. Had Amexco grown too fast?

By August 1984, the *Wall Street Journal* suggested that the answer to that question was yes. The article spoke of "rivalries" among executives and an "overextended management." It reported discontent throughout the organization: IDS officials worried their division would become little more than a training ground for Shearson; staff members from Lehman Brothers, the newest acquisition, were being humiliated by Shearson's leaders; Weill's personal style was said to be rankling the feelings of Fireman's Fund employees; Peter A. Cohen, the head of Shearson, was reported feuding with Weill; Louis V. Gerstner, Jr., the head of TRS, was reported unhappy at his lack of recognition. At the same time, other reports said Edmond Safra, head of American Express International Bank Corp., was unhappy as well.

The press noted, too, that the company was having trouble getting its parts to mesh. During Amexco's merger binge, Weill made a state-

---

*In March 1983, *Financial World* magazine named Robinson a "CEO of the year."

ment that became a company rallying cry: all the subsidiaries would work toward what Weill termed "One Enterprise" to create a company of interlocking products and services. Back in 1980, Amexco officials actually had considered the idea of interlocking services as a major reason for them to make the Shearson acquisition. As Gerstner explained, company executives noted that Amexco card holders were also stockholders. That presented the opportunity for what he called "cross selling." Amexco could sell Shearson's financial products to cardholders, and the card and other TRS products to Shearson's clients.

But "One Enterprise" did not develop as officials had hoped. Shearson, for example, could not entice card members to change stockbrokers. "One Enterprise [was] a broad concept or goal, but consumers don't buy goals," Gerstner admitted. Amexco officials realized they would not be able to achieve their goal easily. If the divisions of the company were going to cross sell, executives acknowledged, they would have to start slowly, with a lot of planning and preparation, and even then some of the projects might not work. Although Robinson demanded top officials submit plans for "One Enterprise" ideas every year, few actual operations had developed by 1984, and some outside analysts wondered if the concept was a terminal flop.

The bad publicity, the second-guessing in the media, had an effect on Robinson. The press claimed he had become more "tight-lipped," and certainly he became more defensive. "They say [the Fireman's Fund problem] shows we're spread too thin and we can't manage a big shop like this," Robinson told trainees in September 1984. "Well maybe we can't . . . but we can do it as well or better than anyone else around."

The financial community and the press promoted the idea of turmoil at Amexco throughout 1984. In October, the company announced that after less than two years on the job, the legendary banker Edmond Safra was leaving, and observers speculated that he might take his old bank, Trade Development Bank (TDB), with him. When Amexco turned down his offer to buy back TDB, the financial community wondered if his departure would destroy Amexco's bank, if the bank without Safra would lose its clients and employees.

Amexco tried its best to salvage the public-relations situation, and company officials, together with Safra, marked his departure with an exchange of statements so polite they almost obscured that he was leaving. Safra called his experience at Amexco "exceedingly satisfying." Robinson said that the arrangement had been worth a try, and he claimed that Amexco got "value" out of twenty-two months exposure to Safra. But the surface diplomacy failed to mask the intense clash of style and personality between Safra and Amexco. Safra's friends maintained that the banker had been treated badly and that company officials never took his advice. Reportedly, he did not get along with Weill in particular, and coming from a tradition where business was handled personally, directly, and unbureaucratically, Safra found it impossible to function as head of the subsidiary of a large organization.

But Amexco felt aggrieved as well. Company officials noted that Safra refused to base himself in America where the bank has its headquarters, and tried to conduct most of his business by phone from Europe, a nearly impossible task. And they scorned the way he ran the joint AEIBC-TDB operation. As his successor as bank chairman, Robert F. Smith, would say some months later, "[Safra] was running a ma and pa shop instead of an institution."*

Despite friendly public statements, the press called Safra's departure another "crack" in the organization Robinson had built, and the rumors persisted on Wall Street and even around American Express Plaza that more cracks would appear in the near future. The rumors centered on Weill. He was dissatisfied with being number two, people were saying; and, since he had no hope of becoming CEO, he would soon leave. The rumors proved correct. In the spring of 1985, Weill resigned. Gerstner, the head of TRS, was named to replace him, becoming the company's fourth president in six years.

After all these reversals, Robinson decided it was time to take a careful look at the state of the company. He and his senior executives

---

*Most senior Amexco officials have not spoken openly about their relationship with Safra. When asked why Safra left, Sanford Weill smiled and said, "I'll tell you in twenty years."

began with what he called a "tough minded strategic reassessment" of American Express, an assessment that led to major changes in the company and its direction. Essentially, as Gerstner later explained, Amexco had been using the same assumptions and pursuing the same plan since Robinson and his first president, Roger Morley, took over in 1977: growth primarily through acquisition. Now Robinson felt it was time to adopt a new strategy, one that focused on the organization as it existed in 1985. He and the eight senior executives who comprised what was now called Amexco's "Planning Committee" agreed that it was time to halt the acquisition program and to build from within; Robinson described it as "fine-tuning."

In fact, so far from embarking on new acquisitions,* Robinson and his men decided to unload parts of the company that either did not work or that in their view no longer fit. They made two key decisions. First, they agreed to sell the company's 50 percent stake in the Warner-Amex cable-television operation. It had never been profitable. Construction costs exceeded expectations; the return failed to meet them. Also, Warner-Amex had never offered, as Amexco had hoped, a significant opportunity for direct sales of financial and retail products through the video screen. By the fall, Amexco concluded an agreement to sell the cable system to its partner Warner Communications for $450 million; after years of losses, the sale gave Amexco a substantial capital gain.

But a far more dramatic decision revolved around Fireman's Fund. Robinson made up his mind to take Amexco out of the P&C business after seventeen years. Fireman's Fund had never fully rebounded after 1983; in 1984, the P&C business produced a net loss of $7 million.

---

*Actually Amexco did expand in some areas. The company opened two limited service "nonbank" banks, which offered consumers mortgage loans and certificates of deposit. Wall Street has often speculated that if the Glass Steagall Act, which prohibits a company from owning a domestic commercial bank and an investment bank, were repealed, Amexco would buy a major banking company in the U.S. Robinson answers such questions by noting simply that Amexco *cannot* own a commercial bank. The company also is careful to reiterate that it does not want to compete with the banks that sell billions in TCs each year.

But the most basic question for Robinson and his planning committee was this: what did a P&C business really add to American Express? Robinson's answer: nothing. Not all of his men agreed with him. Weill argued against a sale, and when it became clear that Robinson intended to dump the insurer anyway, Weill offered to buy Fireman's Fund himself.* But in the hope of an upturn in the P&C business, Robinson and the board decided to retain a portion of the insurance company as an investment. The directors rejected Weill's proposal, and he resigned.

Robinson and the planning committee actually made two decisions on Fireman's Fund. Amexco would buy the insurance company's life division for about $300 million; the life-insurance operation had grown slowly over the years and now was substantial and had potential ties to various parts of Amexco—for example, life insurance for travelers. At the same time, Amexco would sell off over 50 percent of the P&C operation to the public in what was then the largest initial public offering in history. Although the Fireman's Fund had gone through troubled times, the offering, managed by Shearson Lehman, was a success and brought Amexco over $900 million.† Amexco still remained the largest shareholder in the Fireman's Fund and so stood to benefit if profitability returned to the P&C business. But Amexco had relegated Fireman's Fund to its stock portfolio, and the insurer could no longer damage profits as it had done in 1983.

Robinson, who had been hailed by Wall Street for adding businesses, was celebrated again, this time for subtracting them. Once again the press and Wall Street portrayed Robinson as a decisive corporate leader. "He's really come into his own," one member of the

---

*Some analysts agreed with Weill that Amexco either should not have sold Fireman's Fund or at least should have waited. The company sold the stock at the bottom of the cycle, and the value of Fireman's Fund shares rose more than 50 percent within a year after the offering.

†After the initial offering, Amexco sold another large block of Fireman's Fund stock. As of the summer of 1986, it still owned 27 percent of the insurance company.

financial community told *Business Week*. The talk of turmoil at Amexco faded as well, and both Wall Street and the press singled the company out again for its achievements; one banker called it "one of the great success stories of the last twenty years." By the end of 1985, with its public-relations image enhanced, Amexco seemed a company restored and, shorn of its P&C insurance unit, transformed as well. Fittingly, Amexco ended the year by moving from the headquarters it had occupied for a decade to a new fifty-one-story granite tower in a development known as the World Financial Center, near the World Trade Center in New York.

Wall Street's renewed approval of Amexco owed much to the fact that the company enjoyed what analysts considered outstanding performances in 1985 and in 1986. With the aid of a surging stock market and a boom in the financial services business, American Express completed a record year in 1985. Net income reached another all-time high, $810 million, up 33 percent over 1984, and up almost a hundredfold over the previous twenty-five years. Profits at every one of the remaining subsidiaries rose over those of 1984. The bank's improvement appeared only modest—profits up 5 percent—but it actually did better than the numbers indicated since it used income to strengthen its balance sheet and increase loan-loss reserves. At the same time, it also managed a return on assets of 1.12 percent, well above the industry average. The loss of Edmond Safra did not appear to have any negative effect on business.

At the other subsidiaries, income rose as well: IDS, up 23 percent; Shearson, 95 percent; TRS, 19 percent. TRS sold a record $16.1 billion of its ninety-four-year mainstay, the TC, and average outstandings of the long-term float reached $2.9 billion; card volume soared to $55.4 billion, and the number of cardholders to 22 million. Even travel was profitable, primarily through a "travel management" program for corporations. Altogether, TRS had revenues of $4.22 billion and profits of $461 million.

In 1986 profits continued on a steep upward path. Net income reached $1.11 billion, topping the billion-dollar mark for the first time. Again, revenues and profits rose in every division. Card volume soared to $63.6 billion as the number of cards worldwide neared 24 million. That included 6.6 million cards outside the U.S., an increase of 11.9 percent over the previous year, and Amexco officials hoped that card growth in countries such as Japan and Germany would keep charge volume expanding at its historically rapid rate. All of this good news helped the stock price, of course. By early 1987, Amexco's market value had reached $14 billion.*

American Express, by the mid-1980's, had in many ways become the realization of a dream. Not of Robinson or Gerstner or Weill or Clark or Reed, but of Howard K. Brooks. In 1919, Brooks had asked his trainees to dream along with him, and he projected for them a company of the size, scope, and direction that Amexco became sixty-six years later. Brooks, of course, had been off on his timetable, never foresaw the detours along the way, and imagined great things in the transportation end of the export-import business that never materialized. But more than anyone else, Howard Brooks had actually thought of what the company could become; it took American Express more than half a century to prove him correct.

Company officials exude optimism and confidence for the future as well. They seem sure of themselves and of their company. Of course, since all of their businesses run on confidence, they have learned an

---

*There were signs in 1986 that Amexco was once again seeking big acquisitions. Late in the year, the press reported extensively on an offer by Shearson Lehman to buy the brokerage firm of E.F. Hutton. The bid was rebuffed. When asked if this bid represented a new strategic direction, an Amexco spokesman said no, although he recalled that Robinson had often said that the company would "always be opportunistic" about acquisitions. However, the Hutton offer did not appear to be an example of mere opportunism. Instead, it appeared a calculated decision to add to Shearson's retail brokerage operations. But Hutton was not for sale at a low price (as Lehman had been, for example); Shearson's offer, reportedly over $50 per share, was considered high by some analysts. Indeed, the offer surprised one leading expert who regarded it as an uncharacteristic move by Shearson, which usually bought companies at distress-sale prices. This analyst felt, however, that in the event of a market decline, Shearson might try again to buy Hutton or another brokerage house at a bargain.

optimistic message, which they communicate skillfully. They also promote themselves as paradigms of modern managers: flexible entrepreneurs, up-to-date in the latest in management theory, but also rigorous and hard-nosed, able to exercise control over the vast operations of American Express. Because they are entrepreneurs, they suggest, they will push for change and innovation; because they are rigorous, they will face up to problems and find answers.

Whether they can do either remains to be seen. Although observers hailed their performance in 1985 and 1986, those two years represent a small span of time in the company's own history. Such a short period provided no way of knowing how successful Robinson's strategy would be even one more year into the future.

In fact, in 1986, it was easy to see problems in the future of American Express. A downturn in the stock market could hurt profits at Shearson and IDS. The card could finally reach maturity, slowing earnings growth significantly. A few Wall Street analysts saw the card's maturity as the company's most important problem.

In 1986, the greatest short-term threat to the bottom line, however, was the prospect of loan defaults by the less-developed countries (LDCs). Amexco's bank (renamed the American Express Bank Ltd., or AEB) had, according to its chairman, Robert Smith, "more than our fair share" of LDC loans, altogether $2.3 billion. Most were to Mexico, Brazil, and Argentina. Repayment of all of these loans, and especially the ones to Brazil, remained uncertain at best. Though Amexco would survive even if all the LDCs defaulted, the event would, Smith admitted, "put a hell of a dent in our equity," and damage profits more dramatically than Fireman's Fund did.

Smith, however, maintains the message of confidence—confidence that the company will not experience a grave crisis over LDC debt. Smith has tried to develop strategies to cope with the debt problem; he has taken the bank effectively out of the LDC government loan business and had the AEB set up a unit to work out swaps of existing debt for equity. The bank hopes to convert a "substantial portion" of its debt into local currencies for local investment opportunities. By late 1986, the AEB had completed one swap in Chile and was concluding deals in two other countries. "You'll see more of this," Smith maintains. Whether or not Smith's plans work, he at least has the support of the company in his efforts. For the first time ever, there is no talk at American Express of getting rid of its bank.

The bank also seems to be in the forefront of the "One Enterprise" effort. In 1985, the AEB participated in and promoted significant interdivisional activities. Most notably, the merchant-banking operation of the AEB joined Shearson Lehman in twelve major financing transactions, including a $700 million underwriting for the World Bank. At the same time, the AEB's private-banking operation has provided its clients with investment opportunities from Shearson, IDS, and the real-estate packager Balcor, and has even tied in to activities of TRS—for instance, the bank has offered customers what it calls Premier Services, which include a multilingual, twenty-four-hour TRS hotline for travel arrangements. *

But while Amexco executives project confidence, they are in risk businesses and competitive businesses, and in businesses that depend heavily on image and customer trust. Polls show that the company retains that trust, has in fact for decades. No one can say how that might be lost, but no corporation's trust is unshakable. Although Amexco has endured scandals, such as Soybean, and embarrassments, such as McGraw-Hill and Fireman's Fund, what will happen in the next unforeseen scandal, the next sudden blunder? Over time, that is the real test for management—the unexpected disaster rather than the ones it can foresee. How quick and flexible will Amexco be; how adaptable will it be the next time?

Robinson and Gerstner maintain that they not only can adapt to change, they push it as part of their professed entrepreneurial ethos. In

---

*By 1986, Amexco could report one other notable One Enterprise success. The company was selling life insurance policies to customers throughout the organization. Robinson, meanwhile, continued to push for more such programs and rewarded managers for developing One Enterprise projects. Smith for his efforts in 1986 received a bonus of $80,000.

recent years, the company changed dramatically: it gained new businesses, gave up on old ones, changed strategy, changed character, even gained a new definition. But in the history of Amexco, other leaders engineered change at one point and mounted resistance to it soon after. What Amexco's current group of leaders has done provides no assurances of what it will do.

Gerstner says that American Express is a company that does not look back, that is "present and future oriented." That perspective has left Amexco ignorant of its history. In fact, some company executives believe that their own history does not apply to the present, because they are the first forward-thinking, entrepreneurial managers ever to head the 136-year-old company, and so of what relevance is the past? Even the 1970s are part of a distant era that only a handful of managers can, or want to, remember. Indeed, few can recall it. So many people have come and gone since then; of the top twenty senior executives in 1980, only four, including Robinson, remained with the company five years later. But, of course, Amexco has gone through many stages, some more forward-thinking than today's executives think. And whether American Express solves its problems in the future will likely depend on the same things that got them through before: individual insight, opportunity, and the luck of the draw.*

*   *   *

The history of American Express has not ended; its story continues and changes. However, it is worth noting that as this book was going to press in March 1987, Amexco announced plans for a dramatic move: it decided to sell 13 percent of Shearson Lehman Brothers to a huge Japanese life insurance company for $538 million and offer

---

*How long Robinson will remain at Amexco is an open question. As of 1986, he had made no plans for a successor and did not appear ready to leave office soon. Some Wall Street observers speculated that he might resign one day to run for public office or take up an appointed position in Washington. However, he has made no public statements of such ambitions.

another 18 percent of the brokerage unit to the public. Why would American Express entertain giving up any of its highly profitable brokerage subsidiary? The financial community suggested many reasons, from conflict between Shearson executives and their Amexco bosses to a desire for image-conscious Amexco to separate itself from the brokerage business, which in early 1987 was plagued by insider-trading scandals.*

Actually, the sale seemed to have little to do with public relations. Amexco appeared to have three principal goals: boost its stock price, add more capital to Shearson so it could better compete in global capital markets, and further an important strategic aim. Despite record earnings in both 1985 and 1986, Amexco never regained the favor it once enjoyed in the investment community; its price-earnings multiple, which was around thirty in the early 1970s, stood at fourteen in early 1987, below the average of the stock market generally. At a meeting with market analysts in February 1987, Robinson himself expressed his displeasure with Amexco's low share price. According to analysts, Amexco's stock was suffering because the market was expecting a cyclical downturn in brokerage earnings. But by selling 40 percent of Shearson (another 9 percent was earmarked for Shearson employees), Amexco reduced the impact of brokerage industry cycles on its earnings. Also, by boosting Shearson's capital, Amexco's subsidiary would be a more valuable asset. Wall Street greeted the news enthusiastically. In fact, even the rumor that such a move was pending boosted American Express stock from under $70 to nearly $80 in only a couple of weeks.

---

*In late March 1987, Amexco and Shearson Lehman were subpoenaed by the SEC in connection with alleged market manipulation in the stock of Fireman's Fund Insurance. Reportedly, on May 8, 1986, Robinson's long-time friend, Salim B. (Sandy) Lewis, and the firm of Jefferies & Company traded the stock heavily, boosting the price one day before Amexco sold $300 million in Fireman's Fund shares and warrants to the public. Amexco pledged complete cooperation with the SEC probe and maintained that an internal investigation showed no wrongdoing at either Amexco or Shearson.

The sale of 13 percent to Nippon Life, meanwhile, appeared to have its own separate strategic rationale. Through the giant insurer, Amexco hoped to gain greater access to Japanese markets, many analysts feel. For some time, officials had felt that Japan offered tremendous untapped opportunities not only for Shearson but for Amexco generally. Months before the sale, Gerstner argued that the company had barely touched the potential for the card in Japan; he believed the number of Japanese cardholders could grow tenfold in the next few years. Significantly, at the time of the sale to Nippon Life, Amexco announced that it and Shearson would "explore mutually advantageous, nonexclusive business and investment opportunities" with the $90 billion Japanese insurance firm. Later, the *New York Times* reported that the companies were already developing a joint Shearson Lehman–Nippon Life operation in London as well as ventures relating to the card and to life insurance.

Some observers wondered if Nippon Life and Amexco really complemented each other, and asked whether the insurance firm would provide the kind of access to Japanese business—both in the home market and abroad—that Amexco wanted. Still, the planned sale demonstrated one thing: despite its success, Amexco has not grown complacent. Amexco's leaders have acted boldly; time will reveal if they have also acted wisely.

MANAGEMENT THEORY VS. AMERICAN EXPRESS

12

How did American Express survive for 136 years and grow into the giant it is today? How did it manage to change and make decisions for change? Does Amexco's story provide a formula for corporate success?

The questions seem particularly relevant in this age of business scholarship and management theory. Theorists have concentrated their analyses on successful companies, attempting to draw systematic lessons from them for others to emulate. Analysts have tried to develop blueprints for company organization and have identified concepts and philosophies of management designed to provide keys to success. Often they use as exemplars companies with a record of success less than a decade old. What about a company that has endured as long as Amexco? Does its story offer a system for success?

In many ways, Amexco's story seems to contradict contemporary management theory. Though theorists have an interest in pointing out that companies guide their own destiny, no business is entirely self-directive. Corporations, even the largest, cannot create a world of their own making and so are inevitably reactive organizations. What they must react to are unpredictable forces such as war, politics, economic conditions, and social and technological change. All of these have had an impact on American Express. The Civil War, for example, made it a rich company; the political climate of the late nineteenth century let it prosper; the Depression saved it from dissolution. Indeed, Amexco's history is replete with examples of fortuitous circumstance and historical accident.

At the same time, companies are partly self-directive. Amexco had to make decisions and choices, take steps, and adopt policies affecting its destiny. Indeed, Amexco had to do more things right than wrong; it had to make enough correct decisions over 136 years to survive. And because of those decisions, Amexco has evolved into the company it is today—an organization that is by any measure, time or profit, successful.

But, at first glance, it appears impossible to make generalizations about Amexco's success. The company has had so many different systems and been guided by so many different approaches. Consider some of the concepts of modern theory: for example, entrepreneurial (or intrapreneurial) management has been one of the most widely touted ideas of the 1980s, an idea, in fact, that Robinson and Gerstner note in almost every interview they give. But Amexco has had a number of different management systems. It has been run by a contentious directorate, autocratic rulers, and for two distinct periods, systems that encouraged internal entrepreneurship. Other theorists have focused on different keys to business success. A popular notion is that companies need to build a strong, identifiable "corporate culture." But Amexco has had several different cultures. In only the last twenty-five years, it went from the company-as-family, where no one was ever fired, to a modern, aggressive institution, where turnover was so rapid that employees seemed to face a new boss every month. Amexco today actually operates with separate cultures, which Robinson has pushed to compete with one another. But even this is not really new: in other eras, the company has had different cultures going on in different places at the same time. Still other theorists point to strategic planning as a major key to success, and again Amexco's history shows many approaches. It has planned rigorously in some periods, sporadically in others, and at times not at all.

And what were the results of these phases? Some of the best decisions were made under what are today considered most unfashionable systems. Both the TC and the card were adopted by autocrats. The period of openness and entrepreneurship in the 1910s led to a burst of ideas and development, but it ended in the Glass Eye Era. The company has in other ways followed contemporary theory and arrived at the opposite of what might be expected. F. P. Small required that Amexco "stick to [its] knitting" almost sixty years before business consultants Thomas J. Peters and Robert H. Waterman, Jr., made the slogan almost a moral imperative. But the result of Small's policy was to drive the company into its shell and miss substantial opportunities for growth. Howard Clark did not have, to note another Peters and Waterman concept, "a bias for action," especially where big, strategic decisions were concerned. He agonized and analyzed, and sometimes did nothing, but the company's profits expanded geometrically nevertheless because he happened to have products people wanted, and he sold them well.

As for strategic planning, the TC and the card, Amexco's two greatest products, did not stem from any systematic plan. Indeed, both appeared somewhat counterintuitive and perhaps dangerous. When Reed asked consultants what to do about the card, they told him to forget it and protect the TC instead. One can only imagine what planners would have told J. C. Fargo in 1891 about the TC. It was a product in search of a market that carried an enormous risk of fraud and counterfeit. Yet J.C.'s *feelings* in that instant proved a better guide than business logic. Contrast that with the scientific way Howard Brooks went about creating a trade office—careful, strategic thinking

367

and a market survey. Yet the TC became a multibillion-dollar business, and Amexco's trade department died after a few years.

But the history of American Express does not stand the world upside down either. It does not prove that the contemporary view of good management is all wrong and that bad really equals good. The quirky, idiosyncratic management systems of American Express produced mixed results. Although Reed created the card, his personal management system led to the loss of millions in its operation, and his fierce devotion to corporate pride contributed to the mess of Soybean. J. C. Fargo's emotions and prejudices led to quick, brilliant steps like the TC, but he also pursued rigid policies in the express business that helped destroy it.

While it is impossible to systematize Amexco's success, it is nevertheless possible to make one generalization about the decision-making process throughout its history: ultimately, every decision came partly from the program and choice of an individual (or a few individuals) and was an expression of an individual will. The men in charge, the chief executives, did not alone make the choices or force the decisions; lower-ranking executives like Berry, Dalliba, Brooks, and Townsend imposed their ideas on American Express. And it did not matter in the end which management system Amexco had adopted. These men found ways through or around whatever structure existed to impose their views of what the company should do and what it should be. This is not a "great man" theory of corporate history. At times, these same men failed to effect their ideas; at other times, they succeeded, but their ideas were flawed, their reasoning inaccurate, or the management of their decisions, botched. Yet they did succeed in influencing or forcing decisions for change, and in the process affected the makeup and the destiny of American Express. To a large extent, Amexco became the sum of their individual visions, the effort of their individual wills; that above all is the story of American Express.

Such historical understanding does not provide a predictive tool for other companies. Unlike management theory or economic analysis, the study of history cannot foretell how decisions will be made or should be made in the future. It can even be argued that the deeper one goes into the anatomy of a single decision, the more specific the issues become, the less applicable the decision becomes to other cases. Yet the American Express story is applicable to other businesses in this sense: in the end, decisions are a matter of vision and choice. Other businesses may face issues different from those of Amexco; they may have a less quirky history, undergo a more gradual evolution. But every company faces decisions that have no clear answer. No system provides those answers; no philosophy guarantees a right choice; no code offers a foolproof key to success.

When a former senior executive of American Express heard the theme of this book, he laughed and said to me, "Aren't you ashamed of yourself? Disillusioning young business students by telling them how business decisions are really made: that there is no system, that decision making follows no rational plan, and that people make decisions sometimes for the worst of reasons?"

I see no reason for disillusion in the history of American Express, however. While some of its good fortune has been pure luck, that is part of any success. At the same time, Amexco's story speaks of the value of the individual in corporate life. Its executives were not anonymous functionaries in a management system, reduced to performing jobs according to the latest buzzwords and slogans. Instead, they exercised their intuition and their insights, and demonstrated their willingness to face risk and uncertainty. They were wrong and they were right. But the story of American Express is of how much the company was dependent not on structure or theory but on its people.

SOURCES AND NOTES

NOTE ON SOURCES

Primary Sources

The archives of the American Express Company (AE Archives) provided the principal source material for this book. The archives contain thousands of documents: letters, memoranda, circulars, notices, reports, financial statements, deeds, contracts, company publications, advertising materials, articles, books, manuscripts of unpublished histories, reminiscences, and the minutes of the board of directors meetings and the meetings of the executive committee of the board from the period 1850–1970. The most important source material—letters and memoranda—were once part of "The President's File." The file included at least some of the papers of company chief executives over the years.

The archives also contained a series of more than thirty interviews conducted in 1974–75 as a special 125th anniversary archival project. Among the key figures interviewed were former chairman of the board Ralph Owen and vice president and board member Frank Groves.

Also of considerable importance for this book were the Alden Hatch Papers (Hatch Papers) in the manuscript collection at the University of Florida. Hatch compiled several hundred pages of notes, mostly based on interviews, for his one hundredth anniversary book in 1950. They included interviews with F. P. Small, Robert Livingston Clarkson, Lynde Selden, Theodore Happ (an assistant VP who began working at the company in 1899), Howard Smith, Ralph Towle, S. Douglas Malcolm, C. R. "Dick" Merrill, Edwin deT. Bechtel, R. E. Bergeron, and Gerald Berkey.

I conducted more than two dozen interviews, most of them with current and past officials of the company. Among those who spoke on the record were James D. Robinson III, Sanford I. Weill, Louis V. Gerstner, Jr., Howard L. Clark, Jr., Gary A. Beller, Peter A. Cohen, Robert F. Smith, Harry L. Freeman, George W. Waters, and Norman F. Page. I also interviewed many Wall Street analysts and observers.

Secondary Sources

American Express has commissioned two histories. The first, *American Express: A Century of Service* (Garden City, N.Y.: Doubleday, 1950), was written by the late Alden Hatch, in his day a well-known writer of popular nonfiction. Hatch was given less than a year to research and write the book and was told explicitly to make the work a paean to the president of the company, Ralph Reed. His manuscript was taken from him and heavily edited by the company's attorney Edwin deT. Bechtel and one company official. They sanitized and altered the book, creating a work filled with errors and misrepresentations. However, it has some enjoyable anecdotes and was not wholly valueless as a source.

The second company history, *Promises to Pay*, was written in 1975 for Howard L. Clark. This book, too, was taken from its author and edited at the company's behest. As a result, the author removed his name from any association with the book. The book was so laudatory of Clark, it proved embarrassing to him, and he had it printed privately. This book has many errors and omissions, but it proved valuable because it apparently reflected Clark's own view of events for the period from the late 1950s through the early 1970s and contained the views of several other officials who were not available for this book.

Sources and Notes

1: The Fourth Leg

Interviews: Robinson, Weill, Clark, Waters, Beller, Smith, Cohen, Freeman, Gerstner, Wall Street analysts, others; stock market analyst reports; Amexco annual reports; press features.

Early acquisition efforts and the company's problems: interviews; press accounts, especially—
"American Express: Why Everyone Wants a Piece of Its Business," *Business Week* 12/19/77.
Ehrber, A. F., "Hazards Down the Track for American Express," *Fortune* 11/6/78.

McGraw-Hill takeover effort:
Phalon, Richard, *The Takeover Barons of Wall Street*, New York: Putnam, 1981.
Interviews; press reports, notably features in the *New York Times*, the *Wall Street Journal*, and *Fortune*.

Planning effort: interviews; Financial Services Industry Study, November 1979 (company document).

Shearson, Weill, and the Shearson-Amexco merger:
Brooks, John, *The Go-Go Years*, New York: Weybright and Talley, 1973.
Carrington, Tim, *The Year They Sold Wall Street*, Boston: Houghton Mifflin, 1985.
Welles, Chris, *The Last Days of the Club*, New York: Dutton, 1975.
Interviews; press reports; especially—

Feinberg, Phyllis, "What Makes Sandy Run," *Institutional Investor* May 1980.

O'Donnell, Thomas, "The Tube, the Ticker and Jim Robinson," *Forbes* 5/25/81.

Company's image after Shearson and other mergers:

Carrington, *The Year They Sold Wall Street*.

Auletta, Ken, *Greed and Glory on Wall Street: The Fall of the House of Lehman*, New York: Random House, 1986.

Interviews; press reports, especially—

Heinemann, H. Erich, "American Express: Symbol of Change," the *New York Times* 7/13/83.

Rehfeld, Barry, "Deal Maker," *Esquire*, Nov. 1983.

Loomis, Carole J., "Fire In the Belly at American Express," *Fortune* 11/28/83.

"The Golden Plan at American Express," *Business Week* 4/30/84.

Amexco's name recognition and use reported in *American Banker* 10/24/84.

2: *The Treaty of Buffalo*

The best material for this chapter was contained in the collection of papers of E. B. Morgan and Henry Wells, Wells College, Aurora, N.Y. The archives contain letters to and from both men, as well as letters from Johnston Livingston, W. G. Fargo, John Butterfield, D. H. Barney, and many others. It has illuminating material on Faxton's challenge, the creation of D. H. Barney's U.S. Express, intraboard conflict, the wealth of the expresses during the Civil War, the challenge from National Bankers Express, the Merchants Union Express struggle, and the succession of W. G. Fargo (Morgan/Wells).

A selection of the letters from Wells to Morgan were published in *The Letters of Henry Wells*, Aurora, N.Y.: Wells College Press, 1944–45; also, AE Archives, particularly the minutes of the meetings of the board of directors, 1850–68.

Express history and personalities:

Conkling, Roscoe P., and Conkling, Margaret B., *The Butterfield Overland Mail*, Glendale, Calif.: A. H. Clark, 1947–48, two volumes.

Giblin, John J., *Record of the Fargo Family*, Los Angeles: Philatelic Research Center, 1968.

Harlow, Alvin, *Old Waybills: The Romance of the Express*, Boston: Appleton, 1937.

——, *The Road of the Century: The Story of the New York Central*, New York: Creative Age Press, 1947.

Hungerford, Edward, *Pathway to Empire*, New York: McBride, 1935.

——, *Men and Iron: The History of the New York Central*, New York: Thomas Y. Crowell, 1938.

Neu, Irene D., *Erastus Corning: Man and Financier*, Ithaca, N.Y.: Cornell University Press, 1960.

Stimson, Alexander L., *History of the Express Business*, New York: Baker & Godwin, 1881.

Other publications:

"An American Enterprise," *Harper's New Monthly* no. 303 (August 1875).

Teiser, Ruth, and Harroun, Catherine, "Origin of Wells, Fargo & Co." *Bulletin of the Business Historical Society* June 1948;

Recollections of W. G. Fargo's term as mayor of Buffalo, *Sunday Times of Buffalo* September 7 and 14, 1919.

The express industry trade publication, *The Express Gazette*, also contained reminiscences of the origin and early years of the business. Also, AE Archives; Morgan/Wells Archives.

Merchants Union Express struggle: *New York Tribune*; AE Archives; Morgan/Wells.

Criticism of the expresses:

Adams, Charles Francis, Jr., "Railway Problems in 1869," *North American Review* 110, January 1870.

3: *J.C., TC, M.F., and MO*

AE Archives.

Personalities: Hatch Papers (notably interviews with Theodore Happ and F. P. Small); among the AE Archives materials of special importance were a series of anecdotes and reminiscences of S. Douglas Malcolm.

MO: Berry's lobbying efforts for the MO were recalled by Howard Brooks in a reminiscence in the AE Archives. Berry's comments about the problems of the postal money order appeared in the *Express Gazette*. The fight with the Post Office was recorded in the AE Archives.

TC: Various versions of the story of J. C. Fargo's trip to Europe are recorded in the company archives. Ralph Reed noted J.C.'s "slow boil" in a speech. Berry's struggle to create the TC, its birth and establishment are all recorded in the AE Archives.

4: *Chicago and Paris*

AE Archives. J. C. Fargo accorded William Swift Dalliba a measure of autonomy in the conduct of affairs abroad. However, he insisted Dalliba keep him informed. As a result, the AE Archives contain many letters from Dalliba to Fargo and other New York officials.

Dalliba's background: Family records of William Swift Dalliba, Jr.

Anecdotal material: Hatch Papers.

World War I: The favorable letters and press were reprinted in booklet form by Amexco, called *A Record of Efficiency*; all other, AE Archives.

5: *The Decline and Fall of the Express*

AE Archives.
Harlow, *Old Waybills*.
Atwood, Albert W., "The Great Express Monopoly," *The American Magazine* February–May 1911.

T. C. Platt and his challenge: Gosnell, Harold Foote, *Boss Platt and His New York Machine*, Chicago: University of Chicago Press, 1924. *Express Gazette*; AE Archives.

Progressive and Populist movements:
Hays, Samuel P., *The Response to Industrialism: 1885–1914*, Chicago: University of Chicago Press, 1957.
Hofstadter, Richard, *The Age of Reform*, New York: Vintage, 1955.

Court cases: *Fargo v. Hart*, 1902, U.S. Circuit Court, Indiana District, No. 9620 Chancery.

Ledyard deposition on the Boston & Maine (in connection with *Fargo v. Hart*) Report of Examiner Vol. II.
Spraker v. *T. C. Platt et al.*, 143 New York Supplemental.
Dudley v. *Platt*, 118 New York Supreme Court 1058.

Press attacks: Most notably—
Dixon, Frank Haigh, "Publicity for the Express Companies," *The Atlantic Monthly* July 1905.
The New Republic, 81, no. 2089 (1905); Editorial, *The Independent* October 28, 1909.

Strike of 1910: *New York Times*; Atwood; other contemporary accounts.

ICC: Bringing the expresses under ICC jurisdiction, press reports; ICC hearings 1909–12, press reports, especially the *New York Times*; Atwood; *Express Gazette*. Lane's report, *In the Matter of Express Rates, Practices, Accounts and Revenues*, Interstate Commerce Commission Reports, March 1912.

G. C. Taylor personality: Hatch Papers; Obituaries November 1923; AE Archives.

Small waybill story: Hatch Papers; AE Archives, especially Douglas Malcolm anecdotes.

Forced consolidation of the express: Hatch Papers (Bechtel recounted the near fistfight between Taylor and Caldwell); papers of William Gibbs McAdoo, Library of Congress (includes a long memo from ICC Director Prouty on the alternatives for the expresses); accounts in the *Express Gazette* and major New York newspapers. The feeling about the loss of the express business is from an interview with N. F. Page.

6: *The Age of Entrepreneurs*

AE Archives; Hatch Papers (includes remembrances about Brooks, Frothingham, Johnson, Gee, Brooks's friendship with Taylor).

Foreign exchange: AE Archives.
Brooks, Howard K., *Foreign Exchange*, Chicago: H. K. Brooks, 1906. Brooks also published a series of articles on foreign exchange in the

Express Gazette in 1902; his example of the grain dealer is from that series.

Miller, Hugh F. R., *The Foreign Exchange Market*, London: Arnold, 1925.

Expansion: AE Archives; *New York Times*.

Howard Brooks's "daydream" of the future was part of a speech he gave to trainees, text in the AE Archives.

7: A Different Vision

AE Archives; Hatch Papers (especially Small interview); N. F. Page interview.

Amexco as travel company: AE Archives; press accounts; company publications; Hatch Papers.

Banking: AE Archives, including Frank Groves interview; material on the Guaranty Trust from reports published in the *New York Times*.

8: Saved by the Depression

AE Archives; papers of Winthrop W. Aldrich, Baker Library, Harvard University School of Business Administration; N. F. Page interview.

Wiggin personality and career:
Pecora, Ferdinand, *Wall Street Under Oath*, New York: Simon & Schuster, 1939
Prescott, Marjorie (Wiggin), *New England Son* (memoir about her father), New York: Dodd Mead, 1949.
Williams, Frank J., "Rise of New York's Great Investment Houses," *New York Evening Post* November 1, 1926; also, Obituaries May 21, 1951.

Chase takeover: Material on the strategy sessions comes primarily from the testimony of Medley G. B. Welpley in connection with the suit *Bookbinder et al.* v. *Chase National Bank*, action commenced October 1933. AE Archives; newspaper accounts, notably B. C. Forbes's column in the *New York American*; Hatch Papers.

Chase absorption plans: Aldrich Papers; AE Archives.

Banking crisis:

Johnson, Arthur M., *Winthrop W. Aldrich*, Boston: Division of Research, Graduate School of Business Administration, Harvard University, 1968.

Pecora, *Wall Street Under Oath*.

Perrett, Geoffrey, *America in the Twenties*, New York: Simon & Schuster, 1982.

Separation of Chase and Amexco: Aldrich Papers; press accounts; AE Archives.

Clarkson and the era before World War II; Hatch Papers; Page, other interviews (Ralph Towle reported that Clarkson had turned Reed into a "gladhander"); Amerex's "wang doodling" note to Aldrich, Aldrich Papers; AE Archives.

9: *The Pooh-Bah and the Card*

Interviews; AE Archives; annual reports.

Reed's succession and character: All of the interviewees in the AE Archives collection had stories about Ralph Reed, as did most of the former officials interviewed specifically for this book; "Broom in Cairo" from the interview with Ralph Owen; N. F. Page, Livingston's aide, recounted the surprise at the succession, a report confirmed by other interviewees; anecdotes also from the company history, *Promises to Pay*; Reed's quote on creating leaders from Hatch's book, *American Express*; also, AE Archives.

Field warehousing: Field warehousing information is contained in a separate file that had been compiled by Carter, Ledyard & Milburn in connection with the actions stemming from the salad-oil scandal of 1963, now contained in the AE Archives. The principal document is a digest, *A Report of the Creditors Committee*. U.S. District Court, July 1964.

Post war travel: AE Archives; press accounts, notably Harris, Eleanor, "Travelling Companion," *Colliers* July 17, 1948; Reed's own article, "Now We Can Go Places," *The American Magazine* January 1947; the "Grand Pooh-Bah" reference was in *Time* April 9, 1956. Also, Hatch Papers; the company publication *Going Places*; *Promises to Pay*; interviews.

American Express Card creation: The AE Archives contains an enormous record of all proceedings, including summary transcripts of several key meetings; interviews; creation of Diners' Club, *Wall Street Journal*; the card phenomenon of the 1950s was extensively reported in such publications as *The Reporter, Business Week, Barron's,* and *Life.*

Start-up of the card: Interviews; *Promises to Pay*, which includes recollections of Michael Lively.

Reed's last years: Interviews; the story of the last tour is in *Promises to Pay*, corroborated and expanded by interviews.

10: "Into the Twentieth Century"

AE Archives through 1970; Interviews; press accounts; annual reports.

Changes after Reed: Interviews; press accounts.

Selling and saving the card: Interviews, especially George W. Waters; *Wall Street Journal*; AE Archives.

Soybean: Carter, Ledyard file in the AE Archives;
Miller, Norman C., *The Great Salad Oil Swindle,* New York: Coward McCann, 1965.
There was enormous coverage of the swindle in the press, especially in the *Wall Street Journal,* the *New York Times,* the *Newark Star-Ledger,* and the *New York Journal American.*

Strategic planning: AE Archives; press accounts, especially Faltermayer, Edmund K., "The Future of American Express," *Fortune* April 1964; interviews.

Fireman's Fund takeover: AE Archives, including reports from Mc Kinsey & Co. and Morgan Guaranty Trust in the AE Archives; interviews; press reports of the actual merger.

Post Fireman's Fund growth and planning: Interviews; press accounts; annual reports.

Ad campaign: Waters interview; recollection of William B. Taylor of Ogilvy & Mather, *Advertising Age* August 27, 1984.

11: Fireman's Fund & the Future

Interviews with senior AE officials and Wall Street analysts; press accounts; annual reports; company press releases and publications; Robinson speech to trainees.

Fireman's Fund: Interviews; press accounts, particularly articles in *Fortune* by Carol J. Loomis, November 28, 1983; January 9, 1984; June 25, 1984; Fireman's Fund releases and publications.

Departure of Safra and Weill and criticism: Interviews; press accounts, especially—
Hilder, David B., and Metz, Tim, "A Spate of Acquisitions Puts American Express in a Management Bind," *Wall Street Journal* August 15, 1984.

Changes of strategy and prospects: Interviews, particularly Robinson, Gerstner and Smith; press accounts, especially—
Bianco, Anthony, "American Express: The Financial Supermarket That Works," *Business Week* June 2, 1986.

12: Management Theory vs. American Express

Peters, Thomas J., and Waterman, Robert H., *In Search of Excellence*, New York: Harper & Row, 1982.
Rowan, Roy, *The Intuitive Manager*, Boston: Little Brown, 1986.

Articles on current trends in management theory in *Business Week, Management, Across the Board, Management Review*, and others.

INDEX